ENDING THE SILENCE
The Origins and Treatment of Male Violence against Women

Police statistics, government studies, and media reports all indicate that male violence against women is escalating. But very little has been done to understand the deep roots of the phenomenon. Until that happens, no means to eradicate male violence will be effective.

To this end Ron Thorne-Finch offers an incisive analysis of the causes of male violence against women, and places the issue in a political context. He argues that men's emotional, physical, and sexual violence are all inextricably linked: to end the violence we must address the effects of academia, the family, the media, the military, the peer group, pornography, and sport in creating violent men.

The women's movement has played a pivotal role in breaking the silence about male violence and providing the political pressure to compel state funding for victim and offender programs. But Thorne-Finch argues that changes in the current state response are unlikely to occur unless more men take individual and collective reponsibility for male violence. He provides a detailed examination of the responses among North American men in encouraging and resisting male violence against women.

Male violence must not remain 'just' a women's issue. Thorne-Finch calls upon men to become more active in the struggle to end it. In a skilful balance between clinical intervention, social analysis, and political action he offers both the professional and the layperson a way to proceed in the struggle to end violence against women.

RON THORNE-FINCH is a therapist at Klinic, Inc, a community health centre in Winnipeg. He is the author of *Exporting Danger: A History of the Canadian Nuclear Energy Export Programme.*

RON THORNE-FINCH

Ending the Silence

The Origins and Treatment of
Male Violence against Women

UNIVERSITY OF TORONTO PRESS
Toronto Buffalo London

© University of Toronto Press 1992
Toronto Buffalo London
Printed in Canada
Reprinted 1993

ISBN 0-8020-5989-9 (cloth)
ISBN 0-8020-6923-1 (paper)

∞

Printed on acid-free paper

Canadian Cataloguing in Publication Data

Thorne-Finch, Ron
Ending the silence: the origins and treatment of male violence against
women

ISBN 0-8020-5989-9 (bound) ISBN 0-8020-6923-1 (pbk.)

1. Abusive men.   2. Abused women.   3. Sex role.
I. Title.

HV6626.T56 1992   364.3'73   092-093220-7

Cover photograph by Gabriel Guillen
Design by Elaine Cohen

This book has been published with assistance from the Canada Council and
the Ontario Arts Council under their block grant programs.

This work is dedicated to my father, Al Finch,
for letting me know very early in my life that
I did not have to be violent to be a man, and to
my four-year-old son, Jesse Thorne-Finch, in the
hope that the men of his generation will be less
violent toward women than the men of mine.

Contents

Figures

Acknowledgments

The support, criticism, ideas, and good humour of many people facilitated the writing of this study. Among others, I wish to thank David Adams, Laura Anderson, Morgan Arnold, Dano Demaré, Beth Dudenhoffer, Erin Dudenhoffer, Lawrence Ellerby, Ken Fisher, Shirley Galloway, Karen Greenberg, Brenda Gutkin, Dave Inkster, Tom Kaczmarz, Roy Klymchuk, Traci Libitka, Robbie Mahood, Eric Malmsten, Anne Merrett, Lorraine Parrington, Dan Politi, Donna Reid, Chyrisse Regehr, David Rice-Lampert, Maureen Rice-Lampert, Debbie Schwartz, Ron Schwartz, Jean-Pierre Simoneau, Rick Stordeur, Cheryl White, Rudy Wierckx, the Thorne, Finch, and Kazmir families, and the volunteers, staff, and management of Klinic Community Health Centre, Winnipeg.

Several people in particular have made this project possible. The encouragement, critical questioning, and essential editorial assistance of Shirley Grosser, Lorna Sandler, Tom Vadney, and particularly Neil Tudiver were indispensable and very much appreciated. Virgil Duff, the Managing Editor at the University of Toronto Press, enthusiastically supported this book and was instrumental in getting it to press. Magda Kryt, my editor, brought her writing skills and awareness about the subject-matter, both of which were highly valued. Most important, Nancy Thorne-Finch's energy, humour, and clarity about what is important in life and love have helped me through several crucial portions of this project, and of my life.

While I acknowledge the help and support of colleagues, friends, and family, I alone am responsible for any errors or omissions.

Introduction

For centuries men have exercised control over women. Emotionally, physically, and sexually, violent males have made women serve their needs and succeeded in maintaining a powerful patriarchy. While some contemporary men have adopted a feminist perspective,[1] the majority have not, and the threat of violence always lurks not far beneath the surface of gender relations. The history of this violence is not well enough known.

Even people sensitive to the situation of women sometimes conclude that the relations between the sexes have stabilized and genders are now reasonably equal; they credit the women's movement of the 1970s with having rectified any earlier injustices. Indeed, often the effect is to suggest that the feminists have succeeded and should now quietly disappear. After all, we need to move on to more compelling crises – for example, child abuse or teen suicide.

The pages which follow explore the fallacies behind such complacency. While many of the practices and laws restricting women have changed, very often they have only been modified or updated. There may be an improvement in the opportunities available to many women in the Western world, especially among the middle and upper classes, but the gains have not been such as to offset the overall, global, inequality of power between men and women.

Change, of course, is always threatening. Rather than restructuring the foundations of our social system to create a new one based on equality for all, regardless of sex, age, colour, religion, sexual preference, or social class, we have deluded ourselves if we believe that the power of men over women is decreasing.

Even if the power imbalance between men and women is changing, any progress made to date has failed to alter the reality that women as a group are subjected to ongoing emotional, physical, and sexual abuse by men. To verify this fact, the first chapter will examine the pervasiveness of male violence against women, and review what we know so far – many gaps still exist in the literature – about the sexual, physical, and emotional abuse of women by men. A theoretical framework that integrates the seemingly different forms of male abuse of women will be proposed as well.

With the parameters of the problem thus delineated, chapter 2 will enumerate the numerous short- and long-term emotional and physical effects of male violence. For far too long, our society has ignored, trivialized, or simply denied the horrific and diverse effects of men's abuse of women.

The third chapter will review theories of what motivates men to commit violent acts, and why they have allowed violence by other men against women to continue unchecked and failed to take collective responsibility for their behaviour. After examining the answers proposed by various physiological and intrapsychic theorists, the discussion will proceed to a scrutiny of many key components of contemporary culture – the family, the media, pornography, schools, sport, and the state – and the extent to which they generate and perpetuate male violence against women. Recognizing the function of each will make it clear that the concept of masculinity and its corollary, violence against women, are primarily cultural constructs.

The next two chapters will examine what is being done to stop male violence against women. In chapter 4, the discussion will begin with a critique of the traditional treatments of violent men, then move to study the feminist movement as a force in making male violence a public issue and pressuring the state for the social and political changes necessary to eradicate it. The responses of the state to this pressure will be evaluated in chapter 5; it will be evident that despite various measures, government has, as yet, failed to address the problem in all of its magnitude and pervasiveness, and left intact the social factors and institutions which create violent men.

The feminist demands for an end to male violence have generated a response from men as a group as well as from the state. How men have reacted to these demands will be the focus of chapter 6. One attempt at reform can be seen in the gathering of men in groups to examine and redefine their image of what constitutes healthy masculinity. This relatively new phenomenon will no doubt be helpful in the expansion of our limited knowledge about men intervening to stop male violence against women. There may be great untapped potential in this third force, which makes it worth researching carefully. The rising consciousness among some men in our society is indeed a positive sign. At the same time, an atrocity like the December 1989 massacre of fourteen women in Montreal by an enraged male shouting 'You're all a bunch of feminists!' attests to society's deep-seated misogyny and the strength of its resistance to change.

Whatever gains have been made in eradicating male violence against women, a tremendous amount of work remains. In evaluating our society's response to male violence, the first six chapters will have identified the issues and social institutions that require significant change if we are to put an end to this odious tradition. Chapter 7 will provide an outline of how concerned individuals, working together, can pool existing resources to do so.

Before proceeding to the first chapter, it is necessary to explain two important parameters of this study. The first relates to the decision to focus only on the abuse perpetrated on adult victims. While there are similarities between the issues faced by abused children and adults, there are some factors which are unique to children, and it seems best for such issues to be dealt with at another time and in another forum. One might hope that someone will do this in a context which examines the anti-child aspects of much of contemporary Western culture.

A second limitation concerns the specific focus on abuse perpetrated by men against women. The rationale for this is based on several points. First, when one reviews the possible permutations of abuse among humans, namely, female-female abuse, female-male abuse, male-male abuse, and male-female abuse, the last is numerically the most significant of the four. Second, while male-male abuse may also be frequent, it occurs less often between acquaintances than does male-female violence. A third consideration is that until recently male violence against women received very little public attention. While we have studied at length the violence men have inflicted on other men in the streets or on the battlefield – the latter often with the intent of documenting 'heroism' rather than questioning the violence – insufficient attention has been focused on men's abuse of women. For a long time it was simply not seen as an important issue. The present study is an attempt to redress this omission. It is hoped that the issues examined here may be of use to researchers examining other violent dyads.

It also should be noted for whom this study was undertaken. At one level it is for all those involved in the issue of male violence against women. Thus, women who have experienced some or all of the various types of male violence, or counsellors working with the female victims and male offenders, will find it helpful. But the real target population for this work is a much larger and more general audience: all men. Whether they are perpetrators of violence, counsellors working with offenders, or simply average males attempting to comprehend what it means to 'be a man,' in the pages which follow they may find help in recognizing in what manner they themselves have abused women and, more importantly, how to end the violence. Men can no longer excuse themselves and pretend it does not happen. They are all responsible in some way – even if only indirectly. Distancing themselves from this issue will not accomplish anything; only active involvement will bring about the needed changes. The time has come. The longer men procrastinate, the more they jeopardize the emotional and physical well-being of millions of women.

ENDING THE SILENCE

1 / How Bad Is the Problem?

The majority of men do not recognize the fear that grips the lives of most women. Typically, men are oblivious to their responsibility in creating and maintaining a large portion of that fear. Even if they are not able to fully comprehend the depth of the feeling, they can no longer ignore what they are doing to the other half of the human race.

As a society, we need to start asking questions, some of them painful. We need to know: What are the numerous ways in which men abuse women? What are the short- and long-term effects on women who, as a group, are relentlessly subjected to emotional, sexual, and physical attacks by both strangers and loved ones? How do women endure this virtual reign of terror? To deal with these questions and more, this chapter is divided into two sections. The first will provide a theoretical framework for connecting the diverse ways in which men sexually, emotionally, and physically abuse women. The second, by reviewing the contemporary literature, will establish the frequency of the major manifestations of male violence against women. Chapter 2 will highlight the short- and long-term effects of abuse.

While we do not yet possess all the pieces of the abuse puzzle, there is an abundance of available information on the extent and effects of the problem which enables us to develop a fairly clear picture. The picture is indeed a grim one.

A Theoretical Framework

For far too long our society has managed to bury the issues of sexual, emotional, and physical abuse. This is hardly surprising, as we have not always had adequate information to recognize the connections among them. Traditionally, victims[1] did not feel safe enough to talk publicly; if they chose to speak to trusted family members or friends, the secret commonly remained closely guarded. Perpetrators, meanwhile, were usually content to remain silent or pretend that nothing was happening. If they did discuss their abusive habits, generally the intent would be to joke about how badly the woman wanted or deserved the treatment she had received. While tales of some incidents did make it to the community grapevine, often they remained things about which people would only whisper. Such secrecy artificially reduced the perceived frequency with which crimes against women occurred, and served to further victimize the few unfortunate women whose stories did become the talk of the town.

Scenarios like this still exist in most parts of the world. But important changes are under way. The major catalyst was the feminist movement of the early 1970s, which established a milieu in which millions of previously silent women could talk about the pain inflicted upon them throughout their lives.[2] As the numbers of women speaking out continued to increase, it became evident that men do abuse women – sexually, emotionally, and physically. Though often there are important issues that distinguish the victims, common themes emerge. When male offenders are asked to convey their reasons for abusing women, typically the answers include a desire to degrade, discredit, embarrass, hurt, use, abuse, or isolate them.[3] The similarity in the motives and effects helps us recognize that the various methods of abuse are all variations on a larger theme – male violence against women.

In attempts to understand this pernicious phenomenon, there exists a popular perception that the three major varieties constitute a continuum, with emotional and sexual abuse at the low and high ends respectively, and physical abuse in between. This model is an important break from the tradition of ignoring crimes against women; it succeeds in linking together the many varieties of male violence. Yet the continuum concept also contains certain theoretical and practical flaws.[4] One of the most important is that it can trivialize some very destructive behaviours, and create arbitrary divisions between victims and among offenders. What we are learning from the painful stories told by abuse victims is that physical abuse, for example, is not necessarily more destructive than emotional abuse, nor is it always less painful than sexual abuse.

In an attempt to integrate this reality into a working theory, it would be advantageous to utilize a circular perspective (Figure 1.1), which

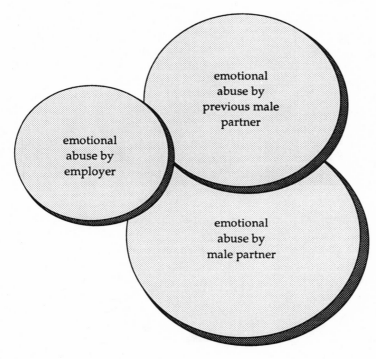

Figure 1.1
Representation of a woman's experience that has involved only emotional abuse

highlights rather than ignores the links between the various forms of male violence against women, and in which no one form of violence is prioritized before another along a linear continuum.[5] The major advantage of such a model is that it is easier for each individual victim to clearly articulate her experience, since she is not struggling to fit it to a theoretical perspective.

Clients and clinicians need to be creative in adapting this model to best illustrate each individual's history of violence. Clients might use several circles, each representing a form of emotional, physical, or sexual abuse they have experienced in their lives. How a woman places each circle in relation to the others will match her experience. If she perceives a significant overlap in the effects of certain abuses, for example, she can move the circles accordingly. She may choose to

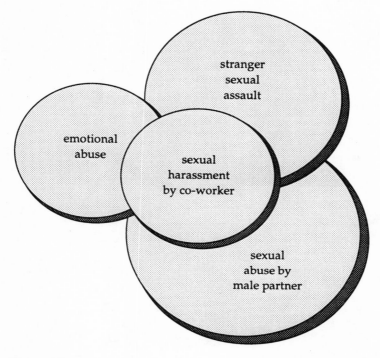

Figure 1.2
Representation of a woman's experience that has involved emotional, and significant sexual, abuse

depict the various ways in which she was abused by one offender, or her collage of circles might depict the abuse she has suffered from several men. A woman may also work according to themes. Three different drawings could represent how she feels she was abused by relatives, acquaintances, and strangers. Or, the woman could use drawings to represent phases of her life, or to depict the major issues she is addressing during different phases of therapy. The results of each collage will be unique to each woman, and the completed image may be very powerful. By identifying and classifying their various encounters with male violence in this manner, women can begin to notice the connections between the assaults and their effects (see Figures 1.2 and 1.3).

The circle model's integrative approach not only helps victims clear-

Figure 1.3
Representation of a woman's experience that has involved significant levels of emotional, physical, and sexual abuse

ly chart their experience; it can also go a long way towards reformulating the popular and professional perceptions of the various forms of male violence against women as relatively distinct entities. In recognizing the links between the various types of male violence against women we can better expose, and then change, that which contributes to our culture's vast array of misogynist behaviours.

Types and Frequency of Abuse

To substantiate the theoretical proposal established above, this section will examine numerous variations of male violence against women. They will be reviewed alphabetically; to do otherwise might give emphasis to certain forms of male violence, and minimize others that

have traditionally been viewed erroneously in our society as less
harmful.

BATTERING

As with all forms of abuse against women, the statistics on battering
are incomplete. The reasons for this are clear enough. While reports
can be found in police files, numerous abused women do not feel safe
to call the police. Even if they or a neighbour should call, often victims,
once the police arrive, will deny that anything was seriously wrong,
for fear of exposing the family secret or, more immediately, of infuriat-
ing the abuser and facing even greater violence after the police have
left. And unless there are obvious physical signs of abuse, many investigating police officers will simply report the incident as a lovers' quar-
rel or family dispute and leave it at that. Even among police officers
sympathetic to the plight of the female victim, there is a reluctance to
become involved in domestic disputes; they know that of all police
calls, 'domestics' are the ones most likely to end with an officer killed
or wounded.[6] Hospital files are as unreliable as police reports for battering statistics. Many women in serious and immediate need of medical attention nevertheless avoid health care institutions. They know
the social stigma against battered women and they fear discovery. One
wonders how many broken bones mend improperly at home because
women are too afraid to go to a hospital.

Their incompleteness notwithstanding, the statistics on battering
allow us to know that the lives of many women are filled with terror
and a frequent and frightening series of violent episodes.

• In Canada it is estimated that 800,000 women are beaten in their
  homes each year.[7] This represents approximately one in ten women
  in a marriage or marital-type relationship.
• An October 1988 Gallup poll found that 23 per cent of Canadians
  personally know a woman who has been assaulted by her spouse.[8]
• A U.S. study by Murray Straus revealed that 1.8 million women each
  year are beaten by men with whom they are in a marital or common-
  law relationship. Straus notes that this figure, while sizeable, does
  not include the increasing number of women in dating relationships
  who are also susceptible to abuse. Straus's figure also masks the frequency of abuse: how many of these women were struck once only,
  and how many were hit repeatedly?[9]
• U.S. FBI statistics indicate that a married woman is beaten every 30

seconds in the United States. This translates into 2,880 women beaten every day, or 1,051,200 every year. The researchers note this is a conservative figure, and estimate that 28 per cent of all couples experience violence in their relationship.[10]

- Lenore Walker estimates that in the United States, there is a 50 per cent likelihood that any woman has been battered.[11]
- A rising number of women who are dating or in the early stages of a relationship are being physically abused by their male partners.[12] Like many of their married counterparts, these women hope that the violence will end and often ignore the fact that both the frequency and severity of the attacks generally increase over time.[13]
- Not surprisingly, men – even when asked directly – underreport their levels and frequency of violence.[14]
- Abusive men show a marked tendency to attribute their violence to external factors. While their partners may be aware that the anger originated internally, the men were more likely to believe it was provoked by their situation or something or someone in their environment.[15]
- Men who are violent toward their female partners frequently abuse alcohol or drugs. One study by Frances Fitch and Andre Papantonio found alcohol and drug abuse rates of 59 per cent and 18 per cent respectively.[16] Another, by Patricia Eberle, found that only 16 per cent of the batterers used alcohol excessively during the test period and that 65 per cent showed an inconsistent pattern of use, no use, or some use.[17] Kenneth Leonard et al. found, among a community-based sample of blue-collar workers, a higher percentage of battering among those with alcohol problems than among those without.[18] These variations in the literature are changing the previous belief that violence is a result of excessive alcohol consumption. Alcohol, while often involved in violent incidents, does not on its own cause male violence.[19]
- Domestic violence is not restricted to the poorer classes. One study revealed that at least 10 per cent of professional men beat their wives. The exact numbers are unknown, since with financial status, one can keep out of the statistics: instead of going for help to places such as state-funded shelters and counselling centres, where researchers often collect data, one stays in hotels and seeks private therapy.[20]
- The major sources of conflict between men and women are three issues – possessiveness and jealousy, money, and domestic labour.[21]
- Police response affects offender recidivism. One study conducted by the Minneapolis Police Department found that of the batterers who received only counselling from the police, 35 per cent reoffended

within six months. Among the batterers that were arrested, however, only 19 per cent beat their partners again within six months.[22] A Canadian study revealed slightly less favourable results: from 75 to 100 per cent of violent men are non-abusive while in treatment, but in four months, the rate drops to between 50 and 60 per cent.[23]

- While one 1985 U.S. nation-wide study[24] found that men and women attack each other in roughly equivalent numbers, and it is not uncommon for men to talk about being abused by their wives, such findings and statements need to be placed in a social context. Without minimizing violence by women against men, one should remain critical of offenders' self-reports for several reasons. First, while there may be similarities in the numbers of attacks, between 75 and 98 per cent of the attacks by women against men are retaliatory – they are trying to fight back or defend themselves against their partners.[25] Second, a woman who has been repeatedly abused by her male partner, and knows that he is heading toward a violent episode, may try to precipitate the violence, rather than continue waiting for it. Third, women generally are smaller than men and therefore tend to inflict less physical harm. Fourth, even if the man and woman are of similar physical stature, generally the woman is not as practised in using her physical strength to fight; thus, she may overestimate her potential. It is also the case that when a man is abused, statistically he is less likely to be financially dependent.[26]

- Many male batterers suffer from serious self-esteem problems. Regrettably, rather than dealing with their issues, they take it out on their female partners.[27] A study by Diane Goldstein and Alan Rosenbaum supported the association between low self-esteem and battering, and demonstrated that abusive husbands were more likely to perceive their wives' actions as threatening to their self-concept.[28]

- Batterers tend to be less expressive than their female partners. While most men are socialized not to convey a very wide range of emotions, a batterer's communication skills – and his willingness to use them – appear more restricted than is the norm. Most batterers report difficulty in identifying their emotions when they do occur. At the same time, they are well aware of how effective emotional inexpressiveness can be in maintaining power within the family: it compels other family members to keep guessing what the man wants or needs and attempting to provide it in the (usually) vain hope that a violent incident may be avoided.[29]

- Many people are very quick to blame the victim of an assault.

Gertrude Summers and Nina Feldman found that bystanders, upon viewing various violent encounters, blamed the women directly in relation to the supposed intimacy of the relationship: the more intimate the relationship, the more the woman was held responsible for the violence.[30]

- While battering levels tend to be higher in second marriages than in first, this is not simply a function of the increased complexity often associated with second marriages. It is the experiences and coping mechanisms of the individuals before the marriage that influence the levels of violence.[31]

- The length of time one has been in a relationship does not guarantee that one will not be physically abused by one's partner. Some women experience their first physically violent incident after years of physical non-violence; others are battered shortly after meeting the individual, while some women are battered on their wedding night. The research, while displaying a wide range, does indicate that most violence appears within the first five years of a relationship.[32]

- The evidence on the typical age of the abuser is conflicting. Straus et al. and the U.S. National Crime Survey found the rates highest among offenders under 30. Gelles found the most violence among men between 41 and 50 years, while O'Brien obtained 64 per cent of his reports of abuse in couples who had been together for 13 to 37 years.[33] Thus, there does not seem to be any period when a man will not be violent if he is physically capable.

- Physical size of the abuser is not a factor determining whether abuse may occur. Abusers seldom look 'the type' – that is, muscular, brawny, young, and working-class. Batterers can be paunchy, balding business executives in three-piece suits. The traditional stereotype serves to mask violent middle- and upper-class men. A second stereotype that batterers are alien or demented in their physical appearance only serves to further negate the possibility that the guy next door beats his wife.

- There are certain situations, locations, or times of the day when a man is statistically more likely to become physically violent to his female partner. Richard Gelles notes the following:

  1. The typical location of marital violence is the kitchen. The bedroom and living room are the next most likely scenes of violence.
  2. The bedroom is the most likely place for a female to be killed. Here conflicts often occur at night, when there is no place to go.

3. The bathroom is the most frequently occupied room during an assaultive incident. This is typically the room in the house that always has a lock and is often used as a refuge.
4. Marital couples most often engage in physical conflict between 8:00 p.m. and 11:30 p.m.
5. Marital violence is more frequent when neither spouse works outside of the home, or when they work on alternating shifts.
6. Dinner time is a particularly dangerous time of the day because of the accumulation of frustration by the end of the day.
7. Weekends are more conducive to domestic violence than weekdays.
8. Holidays, such as Christmas or New Year's Eve, are notable 'trouble times.'[34]

The work of Gelles and others shatters the notion that the home is a safe place – at least for women. For men, meanwhile, it appears that the home is where they are relatively free to rule as they please. And judging from the statistics reviewed above, for an alarming number of men this involves the use of physical violence. Yet seldom do they restrict themselves to just one form of violence. They may also practise emotional abuse.

EMOTIONAL ABUSE

How many generations of children have grown up chanting the schoolyard rhyme 'Sticks and stones may break my bones, but names will never hurt me'? One still hears it today. As children, we hoped that it would ward off the bullies who hurled names at us. The names did, in fact, hurt, but adults told us to ignore the pain and pretend otherwise. Generally, we were not given permission or support to assert ourselves. Then, somewhere along the way, as we were growing up, this generic message was turned into two very different ones. Little boys increasingly were encouraged to stand up and say no to insults, even if that meant being emotionally abusive in return. While physical fighting may have been frowned upon in some families or social classes, often it was at least tolerated, if not encouraged. After all, 'boys will be boys.' For girls, however, there was a powerful cultural impediment that restricted their freedom to speak. Girls had to be 'nice.' Many words that were quite acceptable coming out of a boy's mouth were forbidden for a girl. Physical contact also was unthinkable – one would not want the young lady to mess her dainty clothes or reputation. What is worse, this double standard was maintained and strengthened as the young girl matured. If she wanted to be a good wife, for example, she was expected again to avoid confrontation and defer to her husband on most issues.

This dichotomous socialization process is not limited to the distant past. Emotionally abusive behaviours are an integral part of contemporary culture. Slowly we are recognizing that emotional abuse is not accidental, and that one of its primary functions is to keep a specific group – in this instance, women – stereotyped and subservient. Interestingly, relative to physical and sexual abuse, it is the negative effects of emotional abuse which our society trivializes most often. This may explain why it appears to be the most acceptable form of male violence against women and the variety with which men appear to be the least discriminating. While statistically men are more likely to sexually assault an acquaintance, or physically abuse only their relationship partners, the same limits do not exist when it comes to emotional abuse. All women are targets: wives, dates, friends, co-workers, even anonymous women on the street.

While some might argue that too little research has been done on the effects of emotional violence, we must not allow this deficiency to be used to delay changes in our society until a sufficient number of studies have been completed. If we listen to women talking about their past experiences, we learn that emotional abuse can be extremely traumatic. For many, it may be virtually unbearable, and even more devastating than other forms of abuse. Lenore Walker, in her interviews with battered women, found that abuse through attacks on self-esteem had the most hurtful and debilitating effects.[35]

It may be fairly easy to define emotional abuse as 'behaviour sufficiently threatening to the woman so that she believes her capacity to work, to interact in the family or society, or to enjoy good physical or mental health, has been or might be threatened.'[36] Yet, in many day-to-day situations, it is difficult to know when one is emotionally abused. Even if a person's perceptive skills have been expanded through counselling or education, emotional abuse can remain intangible. Commonly, we are unarmed against, and vulnerable to, the damaging words or actions of others. The subtlety with which emotional abuse can be delivered encourages people to minimize the potentially long-lasting and devastating effects. This contrasts sharply with sexual assault and battering, for example, where an attack is generally hard to mistake. Emotional abusers can be covert; the criticized person often feels that the insults or allusions are too subtle or insignificant to quibble over, but they are offensive enough to hurt, and the cumulative effects can be serious.

The insidious nature of emotional abuse is not the only reason it can be so devastating. Even in cases where the abuse is blatant, there are women who will not protest. If she grew up in a familial or social context where women accepted such treatment, it is less likely that an individual will openly question the status quo and confront the abuser. The scope of this problem extends beyond the family setting, since emotional abuse is practised not only by individuals but also by various large institutions. A prime example is the pornography industry (discussed at length in chapter 3). The massive increase in the availability of pornographic material is a horrifying trend.[37] It is equivalent to having hate literature available at your corner store. Women are portrayed in the most limited of roles – always as objects wanting sex and often enjoying violence. Among the very negative repercussions of depicting women in this manner is the limitation of a woman's belief that she can validly be other than the seductress of the porno fantasy.

Emotional abuse may take numerous other forms. One example is the husband who makes a habit of putting down his wife in public. When the couple socializes, the woman will be the brunt of supposedly humorous jokes or teasing, or may have to listen while her husband regales the assembled acquaintances with the five most recent pieces of evidence proving she is stupid, fat, unattractive, or not interested in sex. Though the content may differ each time they go out, for that woman the process and effects remain much the same. Over time, if she does not assert herself and initiate a revision of the dynamics of their relationship, it is likely that she will suffer a reduction in her self-esteem and assertiveness, and she may become quite out of touch with what it is she needs for herself to feel positive, happy, and self-satisfied.

An insidious yet often-ignored variety of emotional abuse occurs when a woman goes to perform a task and a man quickly rushes to do it for her. While his motives may be well-intentioned, he needs to recognize that by not letting her do things for herself, he implies that she is incompetent, and reduces her sense of autonomy and independence. If this happens repeatedly – as it often does for women in our society who want to open a door, hammer a nail, change a flat tire, or adjust the idle on their carburettor – a sense of helplessness can be induced,[38] so that, with time, the individual will begin to believe that she is incapable of accomplishing these and other tasks.[39] This male attitude of superior capability affects women not only personally but also professionally; it is a major stumbling-block for women seeking to enter traditionally male professions.

There are numerous other ways in which men can be emotionally abusive. They may refuse to express their feelings, ignore their partner when she speaks or cut her off in mid-sentence, sulk, refuse to talk, withdraw affection or sex in order to punish, threaten to end the relationship, tell other people untrue or secret things about their partner, insist she is demented, evil, or crazy, create physical exhaustion or dependency, enforce trivial demands, control by a system of rewards for obedience, block any desire or attempts to work or study outside the home, enforce social isolation, or embarrass or proposition their partner's friends.[40] An episode of emotional abuse can result in the woman hiding for several hours, trying to avoid her partner; in relationships where physical violence is practised, many women even ask to be beaten 'to end the unbearable tension and uncertainty.'[41] They are in such extreme mental agony that the experience of physical pain seems desirable in comparison.

Numerous women are repeatedly threatened with weapons. When the threats are made regularly, whether or not physical abuse takes place in fact makes little difference in the effect on the victim. Straus et al. have found that at least 190,000 American men each year menace their female partners with a gun or knife, and that 144,000 of these males shoot at or stab their female partners, on average, over five times each.[42]

Pat Hoffman,[43] in one of the few studies to date, interviewed twenty-five self-identified psychological abuse victims of husbands or live-in partners. She discovered something particularly noteworthy: nineteen of the men criticized their partner's point of strength. If a woman excelled at cooking, she was told her food was terrible. If she was creative in her decorating, she was told things looked awful and did not match. Hoffman recognizes the devastating effects of such derision. It creates more dissonance. Even when we know our weaknesses and expect some criticism about them, we do not enjoy it. It is much more traumatic, then, when something in which we take particular pride is ridiculed.

Seldom were the women affected by the insults immediately; most could not pinpoint when they began adopting the abuser's perceptions of their abilities. All stated that the longer the abuse continued, the more they were likely to believe what they heard. Similarly, the women were repeatedly told that the relationship they were in was the best they would ever get. Seventeen of the women in the study left the relationship when the situation became unbearable. Significantly, however, women only left the situation once they were concerned about the mental health of their children, or had established important supports through friends. This evidence reinforces the need for social and community supports if women are going to be able to end abusive relationships.

Eight of the women in Hoffman's study suffered extreme physical effects from the abuse. In three of these cases the women suspected they had a brain tumour, and five were suffering extreme gastrointestinal difficulties. Four of the eight women had seen a neurologist who had been unable to find anything physiologically wrong, suspected psychological abuse, and referred them for an appropriate counselling follow-up.

Hoffman makes reference to the similarities in responses between the women in her studies and the subjects examined by Jenkins[43a] (1981) and by Hatcher[43b] (1981). The women Hoffman studied wanted to speak out, but were afraid to tell their stories. Often it was too painful or they were afraid nobody would listen. This was understandable. All of the women had seen a physician or psychologist for symptoms related to the abuse. The women seeing the former were given antidepressants for their nervous condition. None of the psychologists the women saw had informed them that they could be suffering from psychological abuse, nor did any pursue the nature of the relationship with the abusive man. Psychiatrists and physicians who push pills are often just taking the 'easy' way out of addressing women's problems; ironically, this in itself is a type of abuse of women.

At the time Hoffman's article went to press, two of the women were continuing to have severe anxiety attacks, despite being in new relationships. Responses included hyperventilating, extreme depression, fear, and dissociative disorders. Flashbacks often impaired a woman's ability to distinguish her new from her old relationships. For many women the longer-term effects made it difficult to choose appropriate actions in their day-to-day functioning.

Seven women had chosen to stay in their relationships at the time of the article. Hoffman expressed concern for their emotional and physical well-being. Not surprisingly, the women who remained in abusive relationships did not report any improvement in their emotional state, while all women who left reported a significant improvement. Hoffman also found that a woman's positive rating increased in proportion to the length of time she had been away.[44]

FEMICIDE

In reports about homicide in various countries, the statistics are often not broken down according to the sex of the victim, and are without any facts outlining the context in which the murders occurred. This is another example of how abuse toward women may be obscured, ignored, or trivialized, and how women are omitted from human history. While it is important to know that the homicide rate has increased by a certain percentage over a specified time period, such information by itself is not very helpful. If we are to identify and implement social policy changes to reduce the number of dead, we need to know who is being killed, why, and in what context. Increasing numbers of researchers are arguing for a revision in our mode of data collection in order to make women's experiences visible in the statistics.[45]

Whatever the need for improvements in our information-gathering systems, the available figures are already disconcerting:

• In 52 per cent of spousal murders, women are the victims.[46] Husbands are six to seven times more likely than their wives to have initiated the violence in the setting that eventually led to the woman's death. Another study found that approximately 9 per cent of wives murdered were killed after they had initiated violence, compared to 60 per cent of the husbands killed in such 'victim-precipitated' murders.[47]

• The Canadian Centre for Justice Statistics indicates that of the 210 solved domestic homicides in 1987, more than one-third involved the murder of a woman by her husband. They also note that of the 16 per cent of cases where the husband was killed, many of the wives were acting in self-defence.[48]

• Specific structural appeasers of male violence also need to be exposed. One American study found that in 85 per cent of domestic homicide cases, the police had been called for help at least once, and in 50 per cent of such cases, the authorities had been called at least five times prior to the murder.

• The list of serial killers is noticeably devoid of female offenders; women form the majority of the victims. From Jack the Ripper to the Yorkshire Ripper or Ted Bundy, these killers compulsively and systematically prey on women. Deborah Cameron and Elizabeth Frazer argue that to study serial murderers without also examining gender issues is to miss one of the central problems – it is men who are more likely to kill.[49] Elizabeth Stanko notes the significant degree to which

such murders remind all women of their vulnerability to attack and the limited effectiveness of the state in protecting them.[50]
• The lives of many Third World women are at risk because of various misogynistic cultural traditions. *Suttee* – though outlawed in 1829 – remains one of the most difficult to eradicate. This is a Hindu ritual in which a widow is burned alive on her husband's funeral pyre. Since 1947, twenty-two cases have been reported, with the incidence increasing in the more recent period.[51]
• A newer variety of femicide recently has been made possible because of advances in medical technology. Amniocentesis, a procedure usually used for determining if a fetus has genetic defects, reveals the sex of the fetus. Many Indian medical clinics have run ads saying, 'Boy or girl, know the sex of your unborn child.' The result has been the large-scale abortion of baby girls, considered a severe liability in India – women who deliver girls lose social status and the parents later will have to pay substantial dowries to marry them off. One study in Bombay of 8,000 abortions following amniocentesis in 1986 revealed that all but one were performed on female fetuses.[52] The practice of aborting female fetuses is motivated by, among other things, dowry-burning, another illegal misogynist custom. The groom and his family often threaten the bride's family with the death of the daughter unless they pay handsomely. Typically the threat is repeated and the ransom raised each time. When the money, jewels, appliances, and sometimes cars are not forthcoming, the woman often ends up burned alive. The official statistics are that five Indian women are murdered each day in this fashion; activists' groups contend that there may be ten unreported cases for every reported murder.[53]
• Third World countries do not by any means have a monopoly on femicide. In the First World, newspapers provide a continuous supply of death reports. Often recited without much of an accompanying story, the facts of lives snuffed out are a painful, but daily, fare. Here are some examples from the San Francisco Bay area:

Janet Ann Taylor (age 21): Strangled and dumped by the side of the road in San Mateo County.
Mariko Sato (age 25): Stabbed, hacked and shot. Her body was stripped from the waist down, wrapped in a blanket and stuffed in a trunk in a San Francisco apartment.
Darlene Maxwell (age 28): Tied at the neck, wrists, and ankles with a rope.

Gagged with her own underwear, strangled and left in an industrial area of San Francisco. Her body was not identified for 2 days after being found.

Betty Jean Keith (age 25–30): Stabbed in the throat and left in the water off Richmond sometime between midnight and 5 a.m. Her body was found the same day, but not identified for three days.

Mary E. Robinson (age 23): Stabbed eighteen times by her boyfriend. 'She called me a coward,' he said. 'She said I was afraid to fight for my rights.'

Lucy Ann Gilbride (age 52): Slashed and clubbed to death in her home in San Rafael.

Diane David (age 36): Beaten, tied, gagged, and stabbed, and left in her apartment in San Francisco.

Arlis Perry (age 19): Stabbed, strangled. Raped with altar candles in a church on the Stanford campus. She had been stripped from the waist down.[54]

One need not live in the San Francisco area to be exposed to such horrors; they are a common part of our society. The murderers who commit these acts are rarely as abnormal as we might like to think, nor is the occurrence of these crimes as rare as we might hope. And even if it were, the fear of being a victim is an important element of social control which severely restricts a woman's sense of freedom in her society.[55] That men are not taking to the streets to end these crimes against women, or thoroughly understanding and respecting women's legitimate fears, implicates even those who have not committed femicide, and never will.[56] But as women know, femicide, albeit probably the worst, is not the only form of male violence they need to fear.

SEXUAL ASSAULT

For the purposes of the present study, the following definition of sexual assault is used: 'Unconsented use or attempted use of a woman's body (kissing, fondling, or sexual intercourse) due to her being forced, emotionally or physically threatened, drugged, unconscious, or in some way made physically helpless.'[57]

Who Are the Victims?

To be a victim of sexual assault one does not need to be either particularly young or particularly old. Victims reported to police have ranged in age from children several days old to seniors well into their nineties. Victims need not be stereotypically attractive; they can be blond-haired or brown, tall or short, thin or fat, dressed as a stripper or a nun. They may or may not possess faculties of sight, speech, or hearing; they need not be able to walk, run, or even crawl. They can be walking down the street, or locked within the house. If a woman is attacked on the street, she will likely need to actively prompt bystander assistance. If she is fortunate, they may call the police, but bystanders seldom physically intervene.[58]

Many people think women should be afraid of strangers; yet the fact is that sexual assaults are committed by acquaintances more frequently than by strangers. It is a woman's co-worker, boss, neighbour, lawyer, doctor, classmate, plumber, priest, and emotional partner whom she most needs to fear. Women who have been sexually assaulted by an acquaintance are less likely to seek counselling, get medical attention, or report to the police. Victims of the 'classic' sexual assault, i.e., involving a violent attack by a stranger, are most likely to report to the police, as they see themselves as true crime victims. Women who feel the criminal justice system is not very effective or likely to take their report very seriously are less likely to report. From this one can anticipate that native Indian, black, Hispanic, Asian, and other North American minorities – particularly if they are in the working class – are less likely to report or get help. In summary, a person need not possess any trait in particular – not even female gender, though that does increase the probability of being assaulted. Just being near men statistically increases the likelihood of a person being sexually assaulted. Even the dead are sexually assaulted.[59]

Types of Sexual Assault

It is a myth that there is only one type of sexual assault – that is, the stranger jumping out of the bushes at night and assaulting a randomly chosen woman.[60] While this still happens, in the vast majority of cases offenders are known to the victim. Chances are high the offender is even someone the woman is dating or is married to.

Date Rape. This is one of the emerging subcategories of sexual assault. During the 1970s, as more women talked about their sexual assaults, it became clear that large numbers of sexual assaults were occurring in various dating situations. The significance of this originally was minimized, largely because people still wanted to believe that most sexual assaults involved strangers. But as the numbers of reported cases continued to rise, writers such as Karen Barrett began to question whether, in fact, there was an epidemic.[61] As women continued to come forward with their stories, the answer clearly was yes.

The results of a three-year study conducted by Mary P. Koss, a Kent State University psychologist, published in *Ms.* magazine in September 1982, for example, are rather startling. The survey included more than 7,000 students at thirty-five American college campuses. Of the women surveyed, 52 per cent had experienced some form of sexual victimization and, according to a standard legal definition of sexual assault, one in eight women were victims. One in every twelve men admitted to having fulfilled the prevailing definition of sexual assault, 'yet virtually none of those men identified themselves as rapists.' The study also revealed that of the women who were sexually assaulted, almost three-quarters did not identify the experience as a sexual assault. This says something about what appears to constitute 'normal' male heterosexuality, and also about the willingness of women to speak up. The *Ms.* study also found that 47 per cent of the sexual assaults were by first or casual dates, with eighteen being the woman's average age. The location of the assaults also was of interest. While 80 per cent occurred off-campus, more than 50 per cent occurred 'on the man's turf: home, car, or other.' Despite the frequency with which the offence occurred, more than a third of the women surveyed did not discuss the offence with anyone, and over 90 per cent did not report the offence to the police.[62]

The secrecy of this sampled population does not differ greatly from that of other groups. Repeatedly we are learning that the more a woman knows the rapist, the less likely she is to identify the event as a sexual assault and to report incidents to anyone – let alone the police.[63] Thus, it is not surprising that traditionally there has not been much publicity afforded to date rape.[64]

The scenarios for various dating assaults do vary. In some, the two people may have just met and are on a first date; in others, they have been in a relationship for a long time. R. Lance Shotland refers to 'early date rape' and 'relational date rape,' respectively.[65] While Shotland's categories may be helpful, the most important point from the current evidence is that the assault can occur at any time within a dating relationship.

Marital Rape. This is one of the least-discussed forms of woman abuse.[66] A major reason is that in many jurisdictions, marital rape remains a legal impossibility. The historic origins of this situation are in the seventeenth century, when British jurist Matthew Hale proclaimed that women were, in essence, the chattels of their male owners. Hale's oft-quoted phrase is as follows: 'The husband cannot be guilty of a rape committed upon his lawful wife, for by their mutual matrimonial consent and contract the wife hath given up herself in this kind unto her husband which she cannot retract.'[67] Despite the significant changes that have occurred during the last 300 years regarding the property, franchise, and legal rights of women, the Hale doctrine is frequently cited to prevent the charging of husbands with sexual assault of their wives. Up until 1983, when the Canadian sexual assault laws were changed, it was not possible for a man to be charged with marital rape.[68] In 1986, a similar situation existed in twenty-seven American states.[69] While many courts continue to argue whether marital rape is possible, for thousands of women throughout the world there is no doubt. Increasing numbers of those women have begun talking to various interested researchers; the evidence accumulating is sobering.

One estimate is that marital rape affects at least one in eight wives.[70] To make matters worse, most marital rape victims are being victimized in other ways. The man who sexually assaults his wife is also likely to be abusing her physically and emotionally as well.[71] Estimates as to the number of battered women sexually assaulted by their husbands range from 18 per cent[72] to 41 per cent.[73] Daniel Sonkin, Del Martin, and Lenore Walker found that 59 per cent of the battered women in their sample were coerced into having sex with their partners. Forty-nine per cent stated that this had occurred more than once. Approximately 41 per cent of the women sampled also acknowledged involvement in various sexual acts after being threatened with firearms, physically battered, tied up, or intimidated.[74]

Many batterers explain their behaviour by saying that after they have physically abused their wives they feel very guilty about what they have done and want to make up with their partners. That is why, instead of leaving their partners alone, they force them into sexual intercourse, which of course only adds to the existing physical and emotional abuse. Such a rationalization for violence should be seen for what it truly is. Marital rape, like other forms of abuse against women, is, in reality, an attempt by the man to assert power or control over his partner. The often brutal nature of this power struggle is becoming clearer as each victim speaks out.

Lee Bowker collected information from 146 in-depth interviews with women who had experienced marital violence, but had been free of violence for at least one year prior to the interview. She found that thirty-three (or 23 per cent) of the relationships covered by the interviews involved marital rape. Bowker notes that because of the voluntary nature of the sample recruitment, the results of the study do not represent all marital rape victims. She refers to her findings as 'exploratory results.' Although the results cannot be generalized to the larger population, they are of interest.

Bowker found that the families in which marital rape occurred were not any more socially isolated than families in which the violence was restricted to non-sexual forms. The relationships where marital rape occurred were also characterized by low relationship satisfaction and an increased degree of continuous disagreement over finances, friends, drug/alcohol use/abuse,[75] and marital violence. In these marriages, the number of violent incidents was greater than in physically violent relationships where rape did not occur. If the women sought help, most did not identify themselves as having been sexually assaulted, and the sexual violence often remained undiscovered and undiscussed.

While reminding the reader of the non-representative nature of the sample, Bowker concludes the following: counsellors should as a matter of course anticipate the presence of marital rape and not wait until the woman offers the information, women in raping relationships will likely need supplementary services to deal with the additional degradation associated with sexual assault, and marital rape is likely to damage a relationship to the extent that workers in the field may be best advised to help the couple learn how to live their lives apart.[76]

Another survey of 323 women directed by David Finkelhor and Kersti Yllo in the spring of 1981 does not have the same sampling problems as the Bowker study. Finkelhor and Yllo were conducting a larger study on the issue of child sexual abuse and recognized that since they already had a cadre of well-trained interviewers asking individuals about sexual victimization, it would be opportune to adapt the survey and add questions about marital rape. It was fortuitous that they were able to piggyback the two surveys and obtain the additional information. But like most studies, this one too has some limitations. While the results are representative of the city of Boston, Massachusetts, they are representative only of those women who had a child between the ages of six and fourteen living with them. Thus, the survey does not include women who were married but childless or women who were married but whose children were old enough to have left home, and includes very few women who were married less than six years. Regardless of these limitations, the results were startling.

The question 'Has your spouse ever used physical force or threat to try to have sex with you?' resulted in the following picture:

- 10 per cent of the married or previously married women's partners had 'used physical force or threat to try to have sex with them.'
- Of this 10 per cent ($N = 50$), 59 per cent either had some college courses or a college degree. Most of the women were married to their abuser (76 per cent), with the remainder cohabiting.
- While there was a variation in the length of relationship from less than 1 year to more than 15 years, the mean length was 6 years. At the time of survey, 52 per cent had divorced, 24 per cent separated, 18 per cent did not specify, and 6 per cent were still living together.
- The major reported areas of conflict were housework (5 per cent), jobs (17 per cent), jealousy (27 per cent), children (27 per cent), drinking (27 per cent), money (29 per cent), and, not surprisingly, sex (49 per cent). While 28 per cent of the victims had had forced sex once only, 50 per cent of the women had endured it more than twenty times.
- The men raped their partners at the beginning (31 per cent), or in the middle (40 per cent), of a relationship, but the frequency clearly increased near the end of the relationship (69 per cent) with rapes also occurring after separation or divorce (24 per cent).
- The characteristics of the marital rape experience included forced sex after a beating (40 per cent), forced vaginal intercourse (94 per cent), forced anal intercourse (32 per cent), forced oral-genital sex (20 per cent), and forced sex in the presence of others (24 per cent).
- The majority of the assaults occurred in the couple's bedroom (74 per cent), with the husband drinking during at least one episode (70 per cent), and the woman being unable to successfully resist the forced sex (73 per cent).
- While 72 per cent of the women called it rape, 40 per cent did not tell anyone.[77]

Assessing the Frequency of Sexual Assault

Another major myth about sexual assault is that it does not happen very frequently. But the enormous, and still growing, body of statistical and anecdotal information about sexual assault attests to the inaccuracy of this myth. A.G. Johnson, for example, has estimated that 'the average American woman is just as likely to suffer sexual attack as she is to be diagnosed as having cancer, or to experience divorce.'[78] And Johnson's calculations excluded married women and females under twelve years of age.

One of the most statistically reliable studies[79] to date is the Diana Russell survey.[80] Russell's major goal 'was to obtain a more accurate estimate of the incidence and prevalence of rape and other forms of sexual abuse (i.e., the sexual abuse of children) among the general population of women.' To achieve this goal, carefully trained interviewers, during the summer of 1978, met with 930 randomly selected adult women residents of San Francisco. Whenever possible, the race and ethnicity of interviewer was matched. Each participant was paid $10.00 for her participation. By establishing a good rapport with the subjects, Russell's interviewers worked to minimize underdisclosure.[81]

The results are startling. Of the 930 women interviewed, 41 per cent had been a victim of sexual assault or attempted sexual assault at some time in their lives, and 3 per cent had been sexually assaulted by their husbands. Of the women who had been victims of sexual assault or attempted sexual assault, 50 per cent reported more than one such experience. Russell estimates that a woman in San Francisco has a 46 per cent probability of becoming the target of sexual assault or attempted sexual assault at some point in her life.

Russell's results shatter the myth that sexual assault rarely occurs in our society, and reveal the weakness of other surveys. Russell's estimated incidence of sexual assault and attempted sexual assault in 1978 (35 per 1,000 women over seventeen years of age) was just over seven times higher than that reported by the National Crime Survey for San Francisco (1978), and more than thirteen times greater than for the Uniform Crime Reports (1978) – although the latter included women of all ages. Such differences should prompt other researchers of sexual assault to utilize similar information-gathering techniques; a man in a business suit standing on a woman's doorstep or in the hallway of her apartment asking questions about her sexual assault history is not likely to obtain a high incidence rate.

The Russell survey's statistics on reporting and conviction are equally unsettling. Only 9 per cent of the non-marital sexual assaults and attempted sexual assaults experienced by the women surveyed were reported in police files; 2 per cent resulted in arrests; and 1 per cent resulted in conviction. Russell's survey found that there was a sizeable

difference between reported and unreported cases. The reported cases
were more likely to involve a stranger (30 per cent) than a date (1 per
cent). Thus, it is erroneous to generalize conclusions based on reported
sexual assaults to unreported sexual assaults. Yet many earlier studies
involved clinicians interviewing the first fifteen sexual assault victims
who came into an emergency ward.[82] Similarly, given the very low conviction rate for sexual assault, studies based on incarcerated sexual
offenders are an unreliable source of information on rapists in general.

Another issue the Russell study illuminated is sexual assault by an
acquaintance; it emerges as the most prevalent type when sexual
assault and attempted sexual assault are combined. The breakdown of
victims is as follows: 14 per cent by acquaintances,[83] 12 per cent by
dates, 11 per cent by strangers, 8 per cent by husbands or ex-husbands,
6 per cent by lovers or ex-lovers, 6 per cent by authority figures, 6 per
cent by friends of the respondent, 3 per cent by boyfriends, 3 per cent
by relatives other than husband, 2 per cent by friends of the family.[84]
When the category of sexual assault/attempted sexual assault by an
acquaintance is expanded to include rape by the respondent's friends,
friends of the family, dates, boyfriends, lovers, ex-lovers, and authority
figures as well as acquaintances, then 35 per cent of the women in Russell's survey were sexually assaulted at least once by an acquaintance
as compared to 11 per cent by strangers and 3 per cent by relatives
(other than the husbands or ex-husbands).[85]

SEXUAL HARASSMENT

Of the various types of abuse against women, this is one of the most
elusive. The major problem here is in attempting to define what, indeed, constitutes sexual harassment. Kamini Maraj Grahame, a feminist researcher of sexual harassment, has examined several of the existing definitions and created one that is most inclusive. She states that:
'sexual harassment can be defined as persistent or abusive unwanted
sexual attention made by a person who knows or ought reasonably to
know that such attention is unwanted. Sexual harassment includes all
sexually oriented practices and actions which may create a negative
psychological or emotional environment for work, study, or the buying
or selling of services. It may include an implicit or explicit promise or
reward for compliance or an implicit or explicit threat for noncompli-
ance. Threats may take the form of actual reprisals or denial of opportunity for work, study, or the purchase or sale of services.'[86]

Very often women do not identify specific actions by men as being sexually assaultive, particularly if they have been socialized to accept responsibility for having invited the unwanted and harassing male advance. Yet, even if they cannot put a proper label on the action, those same women usually recognize the knot of fear, anger, and shame in their stomach. They have felt this before.

Women have grown up in a society which both overtly and covertly tells them that at any moment any male may choose to perceive them not as an equal human being but as a sexual object – to be leered at, fondled, promised job advances if they are compliant, or threatened with reprisals if they are not. All this often is communicated through a nebulous code of innuendo, fleeting glances, or obscure body language. How many women working in offices have wondered, 'What did he mean when he said I was the best office manager he had ever employed and why did he have that look in his eye?' Often the response for the woman is a sense that something is wrong, clouded by doubt, thanks to the socialized cognitive process that encourages her to dismiss her own intuition and senses and assume that the man in question is trustworthy.

At other times the harassment is overt. A female employee is called into her male boss's office, supposedly to discuss a recent corporate opening with increased pay and fringe benefits. While asking for more details of the position the woman notices that her boss is massaging his genitals through his suit and leering at her while he licks his lips. She realizes what is going on – this is not the first time this has happened to her, and it is unlikely to be the last.

Numerous studies and surveys attest to the frequency of sexual harassment. In 1980 the Thunder Bay Committee on Sexual Harassment asked women if they felt sexual harassment to be a serious problem – 83 per cent said yes and forty of the respondents admitted already having suffered serious repercussions from sexual harassment. Among the respondents to a 1981 Women in Trades questionnaire, 92 per cent felt they had been sexually harassed.[87] The Women's Rights Committee of the British Columbia Federation of Labour and the Women's Research Centre questioned unionized women in British Columbia about their sexual harassment histories. Surveys were sent to those women that requested them. Of those who completed forms, admittedly a skewed sample, 90 per cent had experienced sexual harassment.

American statistics similarly indicate a serious problem. Percentages of women reporting that they have experienced sexual harassment on the job range from 40 to 88 per cent depending upon the study.[88] One of the most extensive studies to date was done for the U.S. Merit System's Protection Board (MSPB). In 1981 the board asked 23,000 American federal employees about their sexual harassment histories. They found that 42 per cent of the respondents had experienced sexual harassment within the two years prior to the study. Of the 42 per cent, 12 per cent had experienced what was termed 'less severe' sexual harassment. This included a variety of unwanted behaviours – sexual teasing, jokes, remarks, or pressure for dates. The 29 per cent who experienced 'severe sexual harassment' received unwanted letters, phone calls, or materials of a sexual nature, were touched or pinched, or pressured for sexual favours. One per cent of the respondents experienced actual or attempted sexual assault.

Elizabeth Stanko reviewed the highlights from the MSPB study in *Intimate Intrusions: Women's Experience of Male Violence*. She notes that age and marital status varied among the women who reported sexual harassment. Younger single women seem more likely to report being sexually harassed: 67 per cent of women age 16 to 19 reported being sexually harassed as compared to 33 per cent of women ages 45 to 54; 53 per cent and 37 per cent of the women that reported having been sexually harassed within the last two years were single and married, respectively.[89]

Stanko also examined several British studies and found that the results were comparable. In one survey of the Liverpool City Treasurer's Department, by TV Eye and NALGO, the union of local civil servants, 36 per cent of the respondents reported experiencing sexual harassment. One 1982 study of 799 managers and employees from Alfred Marks Bureau Ltd. branches throughout the United Kingdom found that 66 per cent of the employees and 86 per cent of the management were aware of some form of sexual harassment in their office. Furthermore, 51 per cent of the females reported having been sexually harassed in their working lives. Stanko states that a study in the United States by the *Harvard Business Review* found that approximately 42 per cent of women experienced sexual harassment at work. When Carey Cooper and Marilyn Davidson took the same approach in the United Kingdom, they found that 52 per cent of the women managers had experienced sexual harassment.[90]

The research to date indicates two main findings. First, sexual harassment is obviously a serious problem. Second, the current statistics underestimate the actual level in our society. Gillian Walker,

Lynda Erikson, and Lorette Woolsey, in a study of sexual harassment in academic settings, indicate that the recognition and identification of an act as sexually harassing depends to a large degree on the perceptions of the viewer.[91] Different women may view the same action by a man in different ways. It follows that women possessing more traditional sex-role beliefs are less likely to identify an incident as sexually harassing,[92] which attests to the need for more education and awareness about the issue.

Another point worth making concerns the myth within many middle-class circles that distasteful things such as sexual harassment are more of a working-class phenomenon. The presumption is that middle-class women are not harassed as frequently and that middle-class men are not as likely as their working-class counterparts to be perpetrators. The evidence to date, however, indicates that sexual harassment, like all other forms of violence against women, readily crosses class lines. Each appears to have less to do with the class of the offender or victim than with the perceived power level of one person relative to the other. Thus, a wealthy woman may be abused by a poor, unemployed man in any situation where the man holds a power advantage. He will probably not be inclined to sexually harass the woman while applying to her for a job, but in another context – for example, were he to meet her on the street – her power advantage may well be non-existent.

The street, while clearly one area where men's power remains largely unchallenged, is not an isolated example. A second is the family home, the primary setting for most physical, and a considerable amount of sexual violence. Sexual harassment of female family members remains fairly common – though probably it is less willingly tolerated than ever before. The opposition to male sexual abuse from within the family has developed largely as a result of increasing public awareness and exposure of this crime. Either intuitively or from their past experience, they recognize that sexual harassment may result in, or may be an indication of, other forms of sexual abuse.

The workplace, however, remains the main context in which women have been asserting themselves against sexual harassment. This is where most of the public opposition, resistance, and legal challenges to sexual harassment have been generated. While women may feel relatively isolated when demanding changes on the street or in the family, in offices and factories, they have a strength in numbers, which they are using to their advantage. The workplace is also a more public institution, so women can more easily draw upon civil liberty legislation to protect themselves. Unfortunately, it is somewhat more difficult to get the state involved in protecting women's rights within the family. Yet even there, major victories have been won. While the power struggle is far from over, there is hope for those opposed to sexual harassment. Slowly, more people are recognizing that the main purpose behind the sexual harassment of women is not just to have some harmless fun but to exert male power over women.[93]

There is mounting evidence from around the world to verify that the lives of millions of women are traumatized by many additional, less well known kinds of abuse. These include: female castration,[94] compulsory sterilization,[95] surgical mutilation,[96] persecution of lesbians,[97] forced prostitution,[98] mandatory motherhood[99] or abortion,[100] psychological and institutional brutality,[101] and other atrocities. While some differences or variations in the way men abuse women exist between First World and Third World countries, the abuse of females is by no means limited to the Western hemisphere.

Summary

There appear to be no limits beyond which men will go in order to abuse women. Our society is one in which women are devalued, derided, manipulated, beaten, kicked, raped, mutilated, maimed, violated, and murdered on a daily basis. When one studies the behaviour of men towards women, what emerges is a common element of violence; the choice of a particular act is secondary to the fact of violence. This is particularly evident in chapter 2, which examines the effects that male violence has on women.

2 / The Effects of Male Violence

Identifying the ways in which men are violent toward women is an important first step toward comprehending, and then changing, how men relate to women; the next step entails understanding the pervasive effects of this violence. Without such knowledge it is easy to allow the trivialization of male violence as being inconsequential to women's lives to continue. In an attempt to rectify the problem, this chapter will review the various emotional and physical effects of male violence.

Admittedly, the effects can be mediated by numerous factors. These include: the woman's previous value system, her history of abuse, the nature of the violence, whether the assailant was known to the victim, the woman's age, how soon she sought help after the violence, and how effective that help was.[1] The one thing we have learned from twenty years of women telling their stories is that vast differences exist in how individual women respond to male violence. There is no one appropriate or typical reaction. Thus, the following catalogue of the effects of male violence against women will proceed alphabetically; any other method might prioritize certain effects as either more or less significant.

It is also worth acknowledging that not all victims of male violence suffer all of the effects listed. Victims of emotional abuse, for example, will not necessarily experience the physical effects endured by victims of sexual or of physical violence. Traditionally, such differences were used to justify keeping separate any examinations of the three different main areas of male violence against women. There is emerging, however, a consensus that the similarities among the effects in these three areas far outnumber the differences. From the victim's perspective, often it does not matter how many effects of male violence she may be suffering; all are significant and can make her life difficult to bear, even to the point of suicide.

Emotional Responses

ANGER

Considering the statistics reviewed in chapter 1, it is understandable that many women are extremely angry with the way things are in our society. Yet our society generally deems any anger exhibited by women as unacceptable or invalid. What contains the incredible levels of anger experienced by victims of sexual harassment,[2] battering,[3] and marital, acquaintance, and stranger rape,[4] for example, are the numerous individual and social mores which tell a woman that she has no right to be angry at men, and that if anyone is to be blamed, it is herself. The result of internalizing anger for many women is that they learn to divorce themselves from their feelings – the only way to cope with the rage within is to ignore it. This, however, compels them to spend inordinate amounts of time and energy trying to keep a lid on the seething kettle of their anger, all the while questioning what is wrong with them, either that they have these feelings or that they experience difficulty feeling any feelings. Our society's tradition of blaming female victims for male violence perpetuates the silence of women because it restricts their ease of connecting with, and their willingness to externalize, the anger that is a normal and healthy response to having been violated and victimized.[5] This constraint can rob the individual of much of the pleasure in life, as well as limiting the potential contributions to our society of the millions of women who often are destined to remain forever silent and angry. This internalized anger is frequently the basis of other responses to male violence.

DEPRESSION

Many women present themselves at various social service agencies stating that they are feeling depressed. While differences may exist between the popular and clinical uses of the term, the typical symptoms associated with depression include lowered affect, decreased physical or emotional movement, and changes in sleep and eating patterns. It is common for women, particularly those who have lengthy abuse histories, to not connect their negative feelings with having been abused. Whether or not they connect cause and effect, many women suffer short- or long-term depressive episodes. This occurs among women that have been victims of sexual,[6] physical,[7] or emotional[8] violence. Unfortunately for many women, depression often is treated as the problem, rather than as the symptom of some other issue. Many women have been needlessly doctored with antidepressants and psychosurgery because their would-be helper failed to discover that the client had been beaten or raped at home.[9]

DISINTEREST IN/OR FEAR OF INTERPERSONAL, EMOTIONAL, OR SEXUAL CONTACT

Violence encourages isolation. Many women separate themselves from potential supports because they are embarrassed or afraid of being close to others. Proverbs such as 'Once burned, twice shy' have their roots in a social context.

Many men will not let a woman isolate herself from them. A woman who is uninterested in or fearful of emotional or sexual contact is a surprise to many men. They are socialized to believe that all women are always anxious to copulate with the ever-virile male and that 'making love' is the best way to start, or to repair, a relationship. While a woman may want sexual contact in order to be cuddled, supported, and caressed, this is not likely to happen if she is partnered with a traditional goal-oriented male, who views a successful sexual encounter as a conquest that ends in ejaculation during penile-vaginal intercourse.[10] Many sexual assaults are committed under the rubric of trying to move a relationship along its course or as attempts at reconciliation after an argument.

Not surprisingly, such attacks often only further isolate the woman. The violence can affect a woman's general view toward all men. Diana Russell's study of rape in marriage found that 37 per cent of the wives reported 'increased negative feelings/attitudes/beliefs/behaviour about (toward) men in general.'[11]

Another study, by Judith Becker et al., of 367 female sexual assault survivors (aged eighteen to sixty-seven), revealed significant fears about sex, and that arousal dysfunctions were common. These effects are relatively long-lived; 60 per cent of the subjects reporting assault-related sexual problems had been assaulted more than three years prior to their assessment for the study.[12] It also is not uncommon for women who feel they have resolved the abuse as best they could to be overwhelmed years later with a series of immobilizing flashbacks, triggered simply by the slightest move or gesture by their current sexual partner.[13]

These studies do not stand alone. Repeated references verify the above effects among victims of marital rape,[14] sexual assault,[15] sexual harassment,[16] and acquaintance rape;[17] all can significantly affect existing and future relationships.[18] Not surprisingly, as more counsellors have begun approaching their work with a feminist awareness, they have learned that the vast majority of women involved with sexual dysfunction clinics have been victims of some form of male violence.[19]

INCREASED FEAR AND ANXIETY

Abuse survivors are less likely than other people to view the world as a safe place. Their fears often are directly related to their experience. For example, if a dog was used in the assault or if the rapist wore a heavy gold chain, the victim may well have phobic responses to these stimuli. Very often the memories, long locked away, can arise unexpectedly. The victim may have forgotten about the gold chain (to use that example); several years later at a job interview, when her prospective employer wears one, the woman panics, without necessarily knowing why.[20]

One study, by José Santiago et al., revealed the predictable: when women who had been sexually assaulted were compared to non-assaulted controls, they were found to be significantly more depressed, generally anxious, and fearful. Those who had suffered repeated assaults had higher degrees of depression and anxiety.[21] High levels of abuse in our society also induce several fears among women in general. Typically, women are afraid to walk the streets at night, feeling that the streets are ruled by men; women know they are walking targets for sexual harassment.[22] Such a simple pleasure as spontaneously strolling down a tree-lined street on a hot summer evening is denied. Other women, doing shift work in order to feed their families and needing to use public transport, know their safety is in question every working day. Yet it is not darkness necessarily that is the problem; many women feel, and are, just as vulnerable to attack in bright daylight. Nor are strangers the only ones to avoid: female victims of acquaintance rape also experience high levels of fear.[23] Not surprisingly, after being sexually assaulted, many women change their perceptions of the safety of their world in radical ways.[24] Those who have been repeatedly abused can have near-phobic fear levels.[25]

Most men, however, either are oblivious to, or deliberately prey on, the fear that grips women. Such men need to consider what it must be like for a woman living in an abusive relationship. Men need to try to comprehend the level of fear that can overcome a woman when she realizes that her male partner is beginning to escalate toward violence; she knows what lies ahead for her. Women deal with this situation in different ways. Some actually wish their partner would hit them; having to endure the wait can, in fact, feel more abusive, to the point where some women will even strike the first blow in order to start the process.[26] It is these incidents, often taken out of context, that distort the nature of female violence against men. In reality, most battered women are not physically violent. Instead, they usually cower in constant fear of future reprisals.[27] This possibility makes many abused women too afraid to betray the family secret; therefore, they endure the abuse in silence.[28]

A recent trend has been for women to train themselves to fight back, either as individuals or in groups.[29] At one level, this is very practical. Knowing how to gouge a man's eyes out with your car keys, or kick him in the groin at the first opportunity, may be helpful in preventing an assault. But there is no guarantee that it will not provoke even greater rage and violence from the attacker. The real point is that once again women are having to adapt their lifestyles in attempts to protect themselves that are often futile. It is not women who should be doing the work here. If the violence really is to end, it is men who need to change.

MEMORY LOSS, NUMBNESS, OR DISASSOCIATIVE BEHAVIOURS

Abuse very often renders the victim emotionally and physically numb. This may be the only way to cope with the trauma of male violence. Some women may block out certain physical sensations, even to the extent of having no sensation, for example, from the waist down. Others will block their emotions about specific incidents. If a woman feels she must keep the abuse a secret, she may have to shut down her natural responses and to carry on her life in a robot-like fashion. Still other women are compelled to block not just their feelings, but their entire memory of the violent event, or they may choose to 'space out' or withdraw – even to the point of creating alternate personalities to deal with the abuse.[30]

Memory loss is particularly frequent among sexual assault victims.[31] Unfortunately, this is not yet common knowledge. Many victims are doubted by friends, family, police, lawyers, and judges, who wonder why a person could not remember what happened. And since victims cannot often remember large portions of the assault, many people – professional and otherwise – conclude it is an invention. Memory loss also creates considerable doubt for victims themselves. Did it really occur? And if so, what actually happened? Memory loss makes it extremely hard for a victim to proceed to court after charging an individual. Even if she does charge an offender, her credibility is shaken when she suddenly remembers new or different evidence than what was recorded in her police statement immediately after the assault. This variability of recall, while increasingly understood in some courtrooms, still significantly reduces the likelihood of convicting a higher percentage of offenders, since it places the focus of the trial on the credibility of the key witness, the female victim, rather than on the guilt of the offender, the man.[32]

Memory loss may also be suffered by survivors of physical abuse. They may receive severe cranial injuries, which can impair their cognitive capacities. Victims of emotional and physical violence also may experience the loss of selected memories from conscious recall. In order to protect themselves from the horrors of their present existence, they may need to ignore earlier, good memories of a time in their life, prior to the abuse, when they experienced relative freedom and independence. The contrast between the two periods may be too painful. Physical abuse victims may also selectively forget the numerous beatings they have endured; to remember them could be too traumatic – particularly if, as most women do, the individual woman blames herself. If, for whatever reason, a woman feels she cannot leave an abusive relationship, she may rework her memories to include only her abusive partner's promises to change, and ignore the number of times he has put her in the emergency ward.

Realizing that one is not remembering small or large chunks of time, not feeling parts of one's body, or experiencing one's full range of emotions can be very frightening. Women in such situations need to be reassured that their responses are normal, that they may last for a varying length of time and need not be permanent. The goal is to help the individual realize that she did what she needed to do in order to survive and should be proud of her ability to do so. In time, the individual may be able to move on to other coping mechanisms.[33]

DIMINISHED SELF-ESTEEM AND SELF-CONFIDENCE, AND INCREASED SELF-BLAME AND DEFERENCE

Having been sexually harassed,[34] attacked, and assaulted by her husband,[35] a stranger,[36] or an acquaintance,[37] or repeatedly beaten[38] or ridiculed by her partner is likely to reduce a woman's self-esteem and self-confidence, while increasing her self-blame and deference to men. Told often enough that one is worthless, one will begin to believe it. We know this from research on concentration camp survivors,[39] child abuse cases,[40] and from basic learning theory.[41] Subsequent acts of abuse only aggravate the damage to a victim by reaffirming the message given by earlier perpetrators.

The loss of self-esteem – if unresolved – can weaken one's sense of being a healthy, normal person deserving of love and appreciation, capable of intelligent, independent thought and creativity. Like internalized anger, low self-esteem contributes to women's silence. Women who do not feel equal to their male counterparts may not even try for things they really want to obtain. After all, if one's past record reflects failure, why set oneself up for another fall? Deference to men reinforces a woman's low self-image. Examples of this abound. One that commonly occurs in public and private forums happens when two people are starting to respond to an earlier speaker. Rarely does a woman not defer to a man. Once one is aware of this dynamic, it is frightening to witness how frequently this transpires. This is a sad statement on female and male socialization processes. Our society overtly and covertly conditions women to remain silent until the nearest man has finished speaking, regardless of the quality of his content. This can have disastrous implications in a woman's personal and professional life.[42]

Deference is encouraged even without overt violence, though many men do use violence to punish women who step out of line. The result is that numerous women, particularly those who have already been battered, are continually varying their behaviour in a desperate attempt to figure out how not to provoke the violence for which they have come to believe they are responsible.[43] Violence or the threat of violence robs these women of their freedom; most live in constant fear.[44] For many victims of abuse, a large portion of their recovery time is spent rebuilding self-esteem.

SUICIDAL OR HOMICIDAL THOUGHTS AND ACTIONS

Suicide is one of the coping mechanisms chosen by many abuse victims. Homicide – the desire to kill others – is another consequence of male violence, though statistically less frequent than suicide. Many people, trivializing the effects of male violence, will question what could have been so bad that the victims should have wanted to kill themselves or their abusers. Clearly we need to raise some awareness here and recognize the incredible trauma that male violence can inflict if women are willing to go so far as to kill in order to escape the pain. Undoubtedly, it is not always just the acts of violence by individual men that may compel individual women to feel that suicide or homicide is the only answer. The shameful manner in which our society ignores male violence against women, or revictimizes them within the social service and legal systems, also plays a significant role.

The existing literature – which in fact may underrepresent the real extent of the problem – already indicates significantly high levels of suicidal and homicidal thoughts among abused women.[45] While it may be expected that such feelings would occur in the short term, in Diana Russell's survey of marital rape victims, for example, 13 per cent said that in the long term they experienced an increase in their 'general anger, vengeance, desire to hurt.'[46] Other studies report similarly high levels.[47]

Increased suicidal and homicidal ideation is not limited to victims of marital rape. One study examined the victimization experience and mental health of a representative sample of 2,004 women aged eighteen and older. After classification of the women into victimization groups, the occurrence of three mental health problems was compared across type of crime. Rates of suicide attempts, suicidal ideation, and 'nervous breakdown' were significantly higher among crime victims than among non-victims. Women who had been victims of attempted rape, completed rape, and attempted sexual molestation had mental health problems more frequently than did victims of attempted robbery, completed robbery, or aggravated assault. Approximately one rape victim in five (19.2 per cent) had attempted suicide, whereas only 2.2 per cent of non-victims had done so. Problems were not mediated by income and were affected only marginally by age and race.[48] Most of the emotional difficulties experienced by sexual assault victims occur after their victimization.[49]

Battering is responsible for many homicides: one-fifth of all those in Canada. The statistics reveal two trends. First, the vast majority of the victims are women; and, second, the woman who kills her husband is usually a battering victim acting in self-defence. Canadian murder data from 1961 to 1974 show that 60 per cent of all female homicide victims were killed within a family context.[50]

The phenomenon of women acting in self-defence and murdering their male attackers was making media headlines in the late 1980s. The issue was discussed on television talk shows and was the subject of made-for-television movies.[51] The legal and moral questions that captivated audiences were twofold: should a woman who murdered in self-defence be charged, and if so, how does the defence prove its case if the woman was the only witness? While this consideration of the issue was interesting and important, the focus was misguided. The media afforded significant attention to the death of relatively few men, when the hourly abuse of women was disproportionately ignored.[52]

DAMAGED OR DESTROYED TRUST

Trust should be a sacred entity. Once it has been damaged it is particularly difficult to repair. Despite this, numerous social traditions work against our ability to trust others. For example, we tell children to fear sexual abuse by unknown men. The stranger with a trench coat and a bag of candy loitering near the school playground has always been the one to fear. The reality, though, is different: for most children, the abuse is inflicted by heterosexual men whom they know.[53] We tell our children to trust the adults in their lives, without also warning them that statistically it is those loved and trusted adults who are the individuals most likely to abuse them. While we have started a healthier trend of encouraging children to listen to their intuitive instincts as to whether or not they feel safe with specific individuals, our task is not complete. If Susie does not like Uncle Harry because he gives her a 'yucky feeling,' we need to respect the child's perceptions, not invalidate or deny them – for example, by telling her what a good fellow Uncle Harry is, and inviting him, in spite of her desperate protests, to come and babysit on Saturday night. To do so is both to betray Susie's trust in our integrity as parents, and to damage her trust in her own feelings. If we do not listen to our children, how can we ask them later, when they finally divulge sexual abuse by a family member or friend, 'why didn't you tell us?'

Violated trust is a central issue for most adult victims of emotional, physical, and sexual violence as well. Women who have been sexually assaulted, for example, have a particularly difficult time rebuilding trust in men.[54] After an assault, a woman will encounter the attitude from numerous (most?) men that when a woman says 'no' to sexual intercourse she actually means 'yes.' Many men think they have failed sexually if they do not 'score' on a date. Thus they may rape the woman. The second assault only compounds the painfulness of her recovery, and may well shatter any progress she has made in sorting out her experience. It is bad enough when strangers cannot be trusted, but after a marital or acquaintance rape, many women ask themselves if, in fact, they can trust any man at all.[55]

A woman in a physically abusive relationship is in a similar situation. For example, she has recently been beaten by her husband of many years. While the sutured wound near her eye is still draining fluid, the house has filled up with flowers and chocolates as he apologizes profusely and promises never to hit her again. But she has heard this many times before. After each of the last three beatings he also promised to quit drinking, but he has not done so. Intellectually, she knows she should leave – and everyone else around her is telling her to do so – but she still wants to believe him. If, as is often the case, she does not have the financial or emotional resources necessary for independent living, she is likely to try and convince herself that her only option is to trust him.[56]

One other alternative is to utilize the existing social service system for legal, financial, or clinical assistance. The evidence, however, reveals a dismal state of affairs for victims of all types of male violence. It suggests that victims typically are revictimized by current social, medical, and legal processes. Anticipating systemic ineffectiveness and failure significantly reduces the probability of an abused woman reporting the crime, receiving medical attention, or even telling significant friends or family members. Ironically, the initial assault is compounded by the very system established presumably to provide assistance.

Other researchers have shown that, more than the type of crime, the characteristics of the victim significantly affect how the criminal justice system responds. Susan Chandler and Martha Torney, for example, studied a total of 408 women – all the sexual assault victims served by the sex abuse treatment centre of a large urban hospital between October 1976 and September 1978. The cases most likely to successfully move through the justice system were those where the rapist was a stranger, a non-Caucasian, or armed. The victim's behaviour and lifestyle were of crucial importance. In a court of law, certain factors which are not legally relevant will make victims appear more credible. Caucasian women who have not consumed alcohol, do not know the offender, and have suffered significant physical injuries are more likely to have their cases successfully moved through the criminal justice system. In most sexual assault cases, it is the victim, rather than the offender, who is on trial.[57] Chandler and Torney's evidence supports the many critics who state that the existing system often is better at protecting the assailant than the victim, in cases of both sexual and non-sexual assault.[58] The untrustworthiness of the system is a major reason why physically or sexually assaulted women do not report. Yet many people will ask, usually incredulously, why battered women, for example, stay in their abusive relationships.

Physical Responses

INCREASED DRUG/ALCOHOL USE AND ABUSE

Abused women often resort to drugs and alcohol as a means of numbing the pain of their experiences; victims of male violence fill North America's drug and alcohol treatment centres. Whether they have been assaulted sexually[59] or battered,[60] the reason for women victims turning to drugs and alcohol is often the same – it is an attempt to live with a problem they do not know how to solve.[61] Yet this is not always recognized. Too often, drug dependencies are treated as being the problem itself, rather than a symptom of the true problem – male violence. Abused women may be further victimized by a society that has little tolerance, and many judgments, of alcoholics and drug addicts/ abusers.

EATING DISORDERS

Abused women frequently experience significant changes in their eating habits.[62] For many victims, these changes, which are likely to be relatively short in duration, are concurrent with the violence. Other victims, particularly if they have an incest history,[63] may develop chronic eating disorders.

Regulating her caloric intake may be the one area where an abused woman feels she can exert influence in a world that otherwise appears completely beyond her control. That legions of women would stuff themselves with thousands of calories and then purge themselves through induced vomiting or mass consumption of laxatives (bulimia), or starve themselves to emaciation over a long period of time (anorexia nervosa), is a serious indication of the degree to which women are suffering. A February 1989 poll of 33,000 women by *Glamour* magazine discovered the following: 50 per cent of respondents used diet pills, 27 per cent used liquid formula diets, 18 per cent used diuretics, 18 per cent 'sometimes' or 'often' used laxatives for purposes of weight loss, 45 per cent had tried fasting or starving, and 15 per cent had practised self-induced vomiting.[64]

Eating disorders often go undetected, because of the great value our contemporary society places on thinness in women. Thus women who may actually be starving themselves to death often are never questioned or challenged about their extreme weight loss. Similarly, a heavy woman who is purging herself with laxatives might be ignored; many would likely assume she is – commendably enough – trying to lose weight.[65]

GASTRO-INTESTINAL IRRITABILITY

Many assaulted women complain of stomach pain and significant changes in appetite. Very often, simply recalling the violent incident can induce nausea. While actual vomiting tends to be limited to sexual assault victims, emotional and physical abuse sufferers may experience severe gastro-intestinal difficulties. For the latter group the problem may be less acute but more chronic in nature. Knowing that one's partner is about to be physically violent, or having flashbacks to a sexual assault, can induce numerous physiological responses. That women in our society traditionally are not encouraged to talk about what has been done to them only aggravates the problem.[66]

GENITO-URINARY DISTURBANCES

Women who have been abusively penetrated frequently experience vaginal discharges, itching, chronic yeast infections, burning sensations when urinating, and general genital discomfort. Vaginal and anal bleeding are not uncommon. Internal and external suturing is often required.[67]

PHYSICAL TRAUMA

Physical trauma can include: general soreness in various parts of the body, broken and fractured bones, missing teeth, torn ligaments, chunks of hair and scalp removed, irritation or trauma to penetrated body parts, temporary or permanent spinal damage, irreparably damaged eyes, and bruised, cut, or burned flesh. Whether the woman has been battered[68] or sexually assaulted,[69] the resulting physical trauma can leave permanent physical and emotional scars.

Many workers at abuse shelters and hospitals have made the important observation that large numbers of batterers hit only in areas of the body that normally are not exposed in public. Thus, rather than bruise their partner's face, many men will kick and punch her abdomen or upper legs. The use of such a strategy seems to confirm that violence is not a spontaneous and uncontrollable reaction, but rather a deliberate choice.

UNWANTED OR TRAUMATIZED PREGNANCIES

Countless women throughout history have borne children simply because their male partners, their family, society, or all of the above maintained that to do so is to fulfil one of the major requirements of the female role. No doubt this is one reason why some married women who have become pregnant against their will during a sexual assault by their husbands will nonetheless carry on with the pregnancy. Another reason is that they are too afraid to report the assault; women who report at a hospital after a sexual assault are, of course, routinely treated to induce menstruation and prevent pregnancy.[70] There doubtless also exist women who, after being sexually assaulted by an acquaintance or a stranger, carried a pregnancy to term and raised the child simply because they were too afraid to tell anyone of the assault, or did not have access to safe, affordable abortion services.

For other women, however, the difficulty may not be one of unwanted motherhood. Frequently, women wanting to proceed with a pregnancy find that they have to contend with increased violence from their male partner. Many men will question the child's paternity – and thus the woman's fidelity – or pressure their female partner to have an abortion. Other men pursue extramarital affairs when their partner's interest in sexual intercourse diminishes later in the pregnancy. The beginning of pregnancy is also known to be a common time for men to begin or increase physically violent behaviour.[71]

SEXUALLY TRANSMITTED DISEASES (STDS)

Victims of sexual assault are at substantial risk of acquiring a sexually transmitted disease. One recent study found that up to 20 per cent of the reported sexual assaults resulted in STDs.[72] These can include

chlamydia, gonorrhea, syphilis, trichomoniasis, or AIDS. Most STDs can
be dealt with immediately at the hospital and eventually cured. Others
– such as AIDS – can only be treated to a limited extent. Many women
receive medical care from their family physician only once an ailment
has developed; large numbers do not obtain preventive medical attention. Numerous victims report that having to undergo an internal
examination would feel as humiliating as a second assault.[73] While not
all sexually assaulted women contract an STD, many live in fear that
one will soon develop. The fear or reality of receiving a STD only adds
to their already overwhelming resentment and sense of having been
soiled.[74]

STDs are not restricted to victims of sexual assault; they can also be
found among those who are abused emotionally. For example, a couple has made a commitment to monogamy and the man engages in
unsafe sex practices with another person; this could end in the transmission of a disease to the original partner. Commonly, it is when STDs
are transferred to the other partner that it becomes difficult to ignore
that someone has been engaging in extramarital sex. However, many
people – victims as well as offenders – will continue denying the truth,
notwithstanding the incriminating medical evidence. The implication
of such activities in the AIDS era could be death.

Aside from the direct acquisition of a sexually transmitted disease,
male violence can disrupt a victim's emotional and physical homeosta-
sis, so that she can be at a significantly increased risk for other diseases
in the period immediately following the violent assault, or during the
often lengthy recovery period.[75]

SKELETAL MUSCLE TENSION AND SLEEP DISORDERS

Tension headaches, fatigue, and physical and emotional tenseness are
common. Many women report becoming edgy and jumpy over minor
incidents. Such somatic responses often contribute to the development
or advancement of sleep disorders. These may range from wanting to
sleep excessively, to sleeping badly, to not sleeping throughout the
night, to not being able to sleep at all. Nightmares, unsettling dreams,
sudden awakenings, and night sweats are also frequent. Many victims
frequently wake up screaming or scream during their sleep.[76]

All of the above symptoms, while most commonly found among victims of the various types of sexual assault,[77] occur among others as
well. Sleep difficulties may occur, for example, if the abuse was in

some way associated with the victim's regular sleep time or location. Did her husband beat her in the bedroom? Was it late in the evening when her partner was most often emotionally violent toward her? Did her husband have a habit of being violent if he was out late drinking with 'the boys' on a certain night of the week? Whatever the scenario, the reality is that untold numbers of women suffer silently each night. A common result is that many women turn to increased use of prescription and over-the-counter sleeping medications, which can create a particularly dangerous situation if the individual is suicidal.

Summary

With a horrifying frequency, men continue to endanger the emotional, physical, and sexual well-being of women. The effects of this attack by one-half of humanity against the other often are brutal and typically do not disappear within a short period of time. While bruises may fade, other effects – for example, a shattered self-esteem – can be of extended duration, or even permanent. Some women will go into a state of crisis shortly after the violence, proceed through a difficult period, and then more or less recover.[78] Others may struggle with the effects of the violence for the rest of their lives.[79]

Male violence against women takes a tremendous toll on individuals, society, and the next generation.[80] The obvious next question is: *why* are men violent? This will be the focus of the following chapter.

3 / Why Are Men Violent?

Explanations of male violence against women up until now have been based on three main theories: physiological, intrapsychic, and social constructionist. Physiological theorists focus on genetic and biological factors. Advocates of intrapsychic theory rely on characteristics of individual personality. Social constructionists emphasize social and psychological agents. By reviewing these three approaches, the present chapter will establish a theoretical foundation for the review of existing treatment approaches in chapters 4 and 5.

Physiological Theories

There are two main approaches to examining genetic and physiological factors. Sociobiologists focus exclusively on biological factors, while biosocial researchers examine the influence of biology in the context of social and environmental factors.

SOCIOBIOLOGY

Sociobiologists are concerned with determining how specific social behaviours – such as violence or nurturing – are the product of evolution.[1] Sociobiological theory has its roots in Darwin's nineteenth-century Theory of Evolution, and continues to be propounded by contemporary advocates.[2] David Barash states that 'sociobiology is the application of evolutionary theory to understanding the social behaviour of animals, including humans.'[3] Barash and colleague E.O. Wilson argue that numerous forms of human behaviour, including violence, militarism, and sexual assault, are genetically coded to promote the adaptive capacity of individuals to spread their genes, and thus to ensure the longevity of their specific gene pool.[4]

For sociobiologists, society is 'a very thin veneer over a basic "core" of human nature, which is grounded in evolutionary theory.'[5] The core of human nature relates male and female reproductive strategies to the different social roles for men and women. Sociobiologists argue that genetic composition determines reproductive fitness, which is 'the relative number of genes an animal contributes to the next generation.'[6] Traditional gender roles are seen as a function of the different genetic reproductive capabilities of men and women.

Since one man is capable of producing millions of genetically coded sperm each day, it is in his genetic interest, sociobiologically speaking, to fertilize as many females as possible and to play only a limited role in child-rearing. Spending time raising children will reduce the time available for seeking out more partners for impregnation, thus threatening the perpetuation of his genetic code. According to sociobiological theory, men who focus attention on child-rearing are genetically less fit. Through a process of natural selection over the span of years, their genetic material will decline in comparison with that of the more 'fit' males who have focused primarily on reproduction.

Conversely, women produce no more than about 400 ova in a lifetime, and can actually carry to birth only a limited number of pregnancies, owing to the length of gestation and lactation, and a relatively shorter reproductive life cycle.[7] Thus, the more genetically fit female would need to expend considerable time and energy to nurture and protect her offspring in order to ensure the perpetuation of her gene pool. She would also be required to be more selective about her breeding partner. As Wilson states: 'It pays males to be aggressive, hasty, fickle, and undiscriminating. In theory it is more profitable for females to be coy, to hold back until they can identify males with the best genes ... Human beings obey this biological principle faithfully.'[8]

Sociobiological theorists offer these genetic reasons as explanations for social differences between men and women. Thus, at least until the relatively recent advent of effective contraception, virginity and chastity have been culturally important for women. Meanwhile, men, in order to ensure the future of their genetic material, must often fight, both among themselves and against women. Territorial wars and sexual assaults are explained as functional requirements of ensuring the genetic material of specific males. Sociobiologists view such actions not as crimes of violence but as biological imperatives.[9]

Sociobiology fuelled the historic – and often heated – nature/nurture debate by providing credibility to individuals wanting to ignore the role of social forces in human behaviour. A sociobiological perspective leaves us with no control over our social environment. It implies that we cannot change the relations that exist between men and women, and that we remain forever enslaved by the dictates of our genetic material.

Critique of Sociobiology. Critics of sociobiology were quick to point out its numerous fundamental flaws. First, sociobiology is based on a collection of unsubstantiated, ethnocentric generalizations; advocates often describe as universal perceptions which stem solely from their own white, Western, and industrial cultures. As Ruth Bleier, a critic of sociobiology, states, 'sociobiologists make unwarranted generalizations about characteristic human behaviors, such as that ... women are coy and marry for upward social mobility.'[10] Obviously, the limited number of wealthy, powerful men in the world would make it difficult to support such an assumption.[11]

A second flaw emerges from the failure to precisely identify how genes are coded with complex human behaviour and how the codes are translated into behaviour. No such genetic coding has ever been scientifically discovered or demonstrated.[12]

Sociobiologists also do not account for the ahistorical nature of their analysis. Our genetic compositions have been evolving for hundreds of thousands of years, while our current mode of human interaction is related to a specific historic period and can change within relatively short periods of time. Sociobiologists assume that existing gender divisions are permanent, when, in fact, evidence to verify this is lacking.[13]

The major failing of sociobiologists is their total disregard of the interaction between biological and social factors in creating human behaviour. Sociobiologists trivialize cognitive capabilities. Ruth Bleier emphasizes that 'what has evolved in response to environmental challenge is the brain and its capabilities for learning and culture, not behaviors themselves. Behaviors are products of the brain's functioning in interaction with the external world, and the innumerable patterns of social behaviors, relationships, and organizations that characterize human societies have evolved through cultural transmission within specific historical contexts.'[14]

By ignoring the significant role played by the human mind in acquiring social values and using them in interpreting the external world, sociobiologists have reduced the complexity of relationships between humans to sheer genetic necessity. While the evidence does not support sociobiological suppositions, sociobiology does provide encouragement for those wanting to 'rationalize and perpetuate the subordination of women.'[15] Such opportunists also have gathered evidence from bio-social researchers.

BIOSOCIAL RESEARCH

Biosocial researchers have attempted to determine the interrelationship between human physiology and environmental factors. In relation to male violence against women, the factors of human brain structures and hormonal variations have received the most attention.

Brain Structures. Frederic R. Stearns, D.D. Thiessen, James R. Averill, Frank Elliot, and John Lion are some of the researchers examining the role of basic brain structures in contributing to violence.[16] Elliot's work is of particular interest, as he highlights the phylogenetically ancient limbic system of the brain which includes the hippocampus, the amygdala, and the septum. The limbic system is associated with, among other things, certain aspects of emotion and behaviour, and thus is involved in the progression toward violence.

Another researcher, S. Grossman, found that stimulation of the amygdala and septum resulted in defensive and attack behaviours, respectively; lesions in this area have produced a calming effect. Grossman also noted that the septum appears connected with feelings of pleasure, often with sexual overtones.[17] Moyer reviewed the animal studies in which the relationship between the amygdala and aggression was examined. He found that different parts of the amygdala seem to control different types of aggression, though he also found there was considerable overlap. While evidence is amassing about the role of the limbic system in behaviour, much remains to be learned. From the available material, it would seem that the limbic system may be 'important in the instigation and organization of aggressive behaviors that are elicited by a variety of environmental conditions.'[18] What has not yet become apparent in the research, however, is why men are disproportionately more violent than women. One possible explanation involves men's testosterone levels.

Hormonal Factors. Testosterone, a hormone fundamental to male/female differentiation, is most frequently cited as a significant contributor to male violence. Yet the evidence does not consistently support the claim. One study of eighteen young men indicated a significant correlation between testosterone levels and measures of hostility and aggression.[19] Another study, of ten prisoners with a history of violent and aggressive crimes during adolescence, revealed significantly higher testosterone levels than in a comparable group of eleven prisoners without such a history.[20]

Other evidence, however, indicates that the links between testosterone and violence are not so clear.[21] Two factors weaken the argument that increased testosterone causes male violence. First, we are not always certain whether the increased testosterone reported in many studies was a cause or an effect of the violent behaviour. Second, the effects of testosterone on humans are not as direct as with other animals. It appears that while testosterone may be associated with increased violence, the extent of its effect is not really known, and its function is influenced by a multitude of external social factors.[22]

SUMMARY OF THE PHYSIOLOGICAL FACTORS IN MALE VIOLENCE

Physiological factors – though not to the degree advocated by the sociobiologists – do affect human behaviour. Various components of the brain are involved in acts of aggression. There is some evidence that higher testosterone levels may lead to increased levels of violence. But the essential point – ignored by the sociobiologists and inadequately emphasized by many biosocial researchers – is that environmental factors play a crucial mediating role. Activated brain systems and increased testosterone, of themselves, do not cause male violence; however, they appear to increase the likelihood of an individual being violent, if the environmental factors are conducive to such a response.[23]

The role of external factors should not be underplayed. If activated brain centres and increased testosterone levels caused male violence, offenders would be indiscriminately violent. Yet most offenders are not violent at random. They are far less likely to hit their boss than assault their wives. Furthermore, most sexual assaults occur between acquaintances.[24] If offenders had no control, it seems unlikely that they would be so selective. Similarly, many batterers consciously choose to hit their female partner on the legs or back instead of the face, where the wounds would be obvious, and friends and family likely to realize what is going on.[25] Despite this evidence, there remains the popular perception that men periodically 'blow their cool' and that they have little or no control over such events.

Popular explanations for what are perceived as sudden outbursts often emphasize the various physiological explanations.[26] Yet humans cannot instantaneously move from a complete resting state to one of being physically or sexually violent. While escalation times vary, all of us need some time to psychologically and physiologically prepare ourselves for violence. In the process of moving toward violence, numerous physiological responses – as distinct from causes – will ensue, and can facilitate the progression toward a violent incident. It is true that numerous social mores and institutions (many of which will be examined later in this chapter) foster male violence – particularly against women. Ultimately, however, men select the actions they implement. While a sexual offender may be in a state of sexual arousal, he makes the choice to attack; he is not a slave of his physiology. Nor is the batterer. He may be very angry at his female partner, but non-violent response options also exist: he can choose to walk out the door.

As of yet, the nature of the relationship between male physiology and social factors is not common knowledge. There continue to thrive numerous myths about male violence that are based upon inaccurate interpretations of physiological theories – for example, women should not sexually overstimulate, or anger a man, as he may lose control. At one level, such myths indicate a basic ignorance of human physiology. At another, they serve an important political purpose by absolving men of responsibility for their violence.

Additional research is needed to more accurately delineate the role played by physiological factors in the progression toward violence. Yet this research should be placed in the proper context, to ensure that the numerous social factors are not ignored or minimized. Equally important is the need to increase the popular awareness of the issue and the existing evidence on the importance of social factors in encouraging male violence against women.

Physiological researchers are not alone in having often understated the social origins of male violence. This process has been aided for nearly a century by various intrapsychic theorists.

Intrapsychic Explanations

Early in the twentieth century, researchers, particularly within the fields of psychiatry, psychology, and sociology, began to examine individual personalities for explanations of human behaviour. They argued that we should not simply explore physiological interpretations, but should also investigate the potential individual psychopathology in men, women, or both.[27] This shift away from physiological explanations resulted in a wide variety of potential intrapsychic explanations. Building upon the work of Freud and others, some clinicians believed they had found the root of male violence in various psychological problems. Among others, these researchers identified the following: 'immature personalities, personality disorders, poor impulse control, low frustration tolerance, dependency, depression, developmental trauma leading to misogyny or other ego functioning problems, fear of intimacy or abandonment, jealousy, addiction, and other psychiatric illnesses.'[28] Male offenders often were portrayed as 'sadistic or psychopathic, pathologically passive and dependent or potentially brain-damaged.'[29] Alcohol frequently was cited as a causal factor for most male violence.[30] In other studies researchers offered a slightly different version of the dominant myth about offenders being suddenly overwhelmed by uncontrollable surges of aggression or sexual desire.[31] While not relying on physiological explanations, they argued that offenders often were provoked by victims and that abusers were 'psychologically sick men or part of a criminal subculture.'[32]

The evidence suggests that violent men have not been common in the case-loads of intrapsychic therapists, either as self-referrals – these have always been rare, since offenders usually deny what they are doing – or as court referrals, because convictions continue to be uncommon and those who are convicted are still frequently treated as criminals and incarcerated.[33]

Larger case-loads would not have been the solution. For several reasons, intrapsychic explanations were not favourable to the development of a better understanding or treatment of male violence against women.[34] Donald Dutton cites the following problems: '(1) a tendency to generalize from psychiatric or prison populations to the population in general, (2) a failure to use large samples of wife batterers systematically, (3) the tendency to rely on data provided by the victim, and (4) failure to account for acute situational pressures in the battering relationship.'[35] There is also considerable evidence that few offenders suffer from psychopathology[36] and that those who do fail to display a consistent pattern for batterers.[37] Furthermore, recent evidence indicates that alcohol appears to facilitate, but not to cause, male violence.[38]

The major problem with the intrapsychic approach is that it fails to consider the social context in which the violence occurs, or to seriously acknowledge the role of society in encouraging and legitimizing male violence against women.[39] While focusing on the individual man's intrapsychic pathology, little attention is afforded to the origin of his values. Nicholas Groth, a clinician working with sexual offenders, argues that when we examine male violence against women, 'we are obviously talking about an issue that is much broader than simply a clinical or psychological issue. It is a cultural, legal, a political, an economic, an educational, a medical, spiritual issue. And if we are going to be effective in combatting this problem, it really means approaching it from all of these perspectives.'[40]

Largely because of the failings of intrapsychic explanations to address the root causes of male violence, they typically are not used by current group programs.[41] Increasing numbers of therapists have turned toward examining the role played by society in creating violent men.

The Social Construction of Male Violence

The third major explanation for male violence is that it is a learned behaviour. To understand why men and not women typically learn violence, we need to place male actions within a social context. We live in a culture that is predicated upon the subjugation of women by men. While the exact historical origins of the patriarchy are open to debate, there is a general consensus that it has thrived for at least several millennia. Often, its sheer longevity is used by some observers to support their physiological assumptions. But however unsure we may be as to the precise conditions and events that led to the establishment of the patriarchy, we can certainly draw conclusions as to how it has replicated itself since its inception.[42]

One explanation is that through the creation and perpetuation of a complex system of ideas, values, customs, and institutions, men have been able to obtain and maintain power over women.[43] While accurate to an extent, this version of feminist theory is also greatly condensed, and does not sufficiently explain our social reality. We need to recognize that our society is divided by other issues as well as that of gender; these include class, race, age, sexual preference, and able-bodiedness. A perspective that does not connect these seemingly divergent issues can impair our ability to understand people's actions when they are united or divided around these issues.[44]

While the majority of contemporary researchers accept that our society creates violent men, there is considerable disagreement as to which social forces are most influential in the development of male violence.

Many researchers either fail or refuse to acknowledge the function of specific social structures, beliefs, and traditions as catalysts for male violence.[45] The political and clinical implications of a restricted social constructionist perspective on the treatment of violent men will be outlined in detail in chapter 5. For the purpose of the present chapter, it will suffice to acknowledge that such ideological differences should not come as a surprise. Many people prefer to leave certain sacred cows undisturbed. This is convenient avoidance of an issue which can no longer be ignored. Undoubtedly most agents of male socialization have positive features that contribute to the development of non-violent men – one's family and peer group, for example, can be essential sources of support, encouragement, and love – and these facts are not being questioned. However, attention needs to be drawn to the dysfunctional aspects of these agents. Like the child who recognized the emperor wore no clothes, this chapter will expose the unquestioned components of the major agents of male socialization that elicit, encourage, and legitimize the creation of violent men.

As was done in chapters 1 and 2 in identifying the various types and effects of male violence, the discussion will proceed alphabetically. There are three reasons for this. First, to do otherwise could prioritize, and thus inherently assign either more or less value to specific agents involved in the social construction of violent men. Second, not enough is known about each agent for it to be rank-ordered. And third, at an individual level, some agents have been more significant for certain men. Many of the differences among men are likely to have resulted because of variations in social class, regional and ethnic cultures, or specific familial traditions. Whatever differences exist in the relative importance of one agent over another between particular men or within groups of men, the common message imparted by the following agents of male socialization is that it is acceptable to be violent toward women.

THE IDEOLOGY OF TWENTIETH-CENTURY ACADEMIA

Social scientists involved in the creation of the male sex role identity (MSRI) theory have inadvertently encouraged and perpetuated male violence. By giving intellectual respectability to the restricted qualities valued in men by our society, they have legitimized violence as normal male behaviour and obfuscated or ignored the fact that men enjoy greater social, political, and economic power than do women in our society.

The century-old[46] male sex-role identity theory has been the dominant tool used by post-1945 Western psychologists to explain male behaviour. Proponents contend that for people to become psychologically mature members of their sex, they must adopt either a male or a female sex-role identity, which includes various traits, values, and actions that are deemed appropriate to their biological sex. According to MSRI theory, there is no guarantee that this process will be completed. For men, absent or ineffective male role models are two factors that may impair an individual's acquisition of sex-role identity. If this occurs, the potential outcomes for males include effeminacy or homosexuality (too little masculinity), and hypermasculinity (too much masculinity).[47]

Male sex-role identity theory has been the intellectual construct used in thousands of experiments to try to determine the masculinity, femininity, or androgyny of individuals and groups. While some researchers have struggled to assess the degree of sex-role identity acquisition within specific populations, others have tried to create generalizable assessment tools that could be used with a variety of divergent populations to determine to what extent they adhered to expected sex-role behaviours. Despite the failure in creating a cross-cultural analysis, rarely has it been questioned whether such a goal was even possible. Only recently is the validity of MSRI theory being seriously scrutinized.[48]

With a critical examination of the emergence of sex-role identity theory, one point becomes clear: the very theory used to test our socially constructed values is a product of the culture from which it emerged. Specific historical realities created and sustained the enthusiasm for MSRI theory. Its popularity has increased whenever there has been a significant concern about the 'manliness' of adult males. In the late nineteenth century, for example, there was a growing consensus among European and North American elites that increased urbanization and industrialization were placing undue limits on the presumed needs of men to be adventurous pioneers. Many feared that men were – in the vernacular of the time – being 'feminized.'[49] This concern was a major catalyst for the resurrection of the Olympic Games in 1895,[50] and the establishment of the International Boy Scouts in 1907–8.[51] The intent was to strengthen the national stock of men through sport, physical exertion, and other traditionally male activities. Despite these efforts, there was a sense that it might be too little, too late. This belief was reinforced in the United States, for example, when almost half of their

First World War recruits were deemed physically or mentally unfit for military service.[52]

Many of those concerned about the feminization of Western males were relieved by what they viewed as the positive opportunities of the First World War. Although millions were dying, men were once again on their own, away from women, fighting for their lives. Traditional acts of soldierly heroism, such as charging enemy lines, or braving the privations of trench warfare, were glorified; conscientious objectors and post-traumatic shock victims, meanwhile, were ridiculed and offered as proof of the deterioration of masculinity. A real man relished battle – or so went the mythology.[53]

Panic struck again when the war ended and millions of soldiers returned from the battlefields only to be thrown back into the factories – those who were lucky enough to get a job, that is, for unemployment was rampant. While the mid-1920s seemed to bring some stability, the Great Depression of the 1930s was viewed as yet another threat to the bread-winning virility of men in industrial societies. There was a real concern that, even if the economy could be revived, male workers would have lost, through idleness, many of their skills and their commitment to hard work. The fear was that the economy might never again be as productive.

It was in this milieu that Lewis Terman and Catherine Miles wrote *Sex and Personality*. Its publication in 1934 gave popular perceptions about men's and women's roles intellectual credibility. Terman and Miles were very clear in their approach: men and women were normal to the extent that they possessed specific sex-appropriate characteristics, and abnormal to the extent that they did not. Their work rapidly gained in popularity and was expanded upon by an army of theorists, particularly in the post-1945 period, when there was a quick shift from examining masculinity and femininity to focusing primarily on males. There was growing concern, once again, about the feminization of men.[54]

With the Cold War escalating between the United States and the USSR, American leaders in particular became obsessed with prioritizing traditionally masculine characteristics and qualities. MSRI theory was a favourite tool, used, for example, to prove that homosexuality was the antithesis of traditional heterosexual masculinity. Homosexuality and communism were seized upon as the two main threats to American society, and often portrayed as two sides of the same coin. With Senator Joseph McCarthy's House Committee on Un-American Activities in full swing – and ruining the lives and careers of many innocent individuals caught in the political maelstrom – it was a dangerous time for men to exhibit any characteristics other than those narrowly defined as traditional. To be free of suspicion one had to walk, talk, sit, act, and be sexual in very specific, prescribed patterns.[55]

Male sex-role identity theory was often used to verify what was appropriately masculine – as opposed to homosexual – behaviour. Yet the presumption that homosexuality could not be a masculine characteristic points to one of the five major failures of sex-role theory. First, masculinity is not a historic constant but, instead, a socially produced, fluid concept, constantly in the process of creation and evolution. Those qualities highly valued in men during the 1980s were likely less important during the late 1940s or, for that matter, the fifteenth century. As one critic has stated, sex roles, sex-role stereotyping, and sex-role socialization are 'often written and talked about as if they exist concretely rather than being analytic constructs.'[56] A second failing of MSRI theory is that the male's most valued traits vary not only historically, but also among specific groups. Characteristics expected in men in an immigrant Italian-American community will differ considerably from those desired in an Inuit community in the Canadian Arctic. Third, even within a designated community, and during a specific time period, there will be variations among individuals as to what is most valued in a male.

Fourth, sex-role theorists fail to recognize that the very process of identifying specific traits as either more or less masculine (and thus more, or less, valued) played a big role in legitimizing and solidifying the very thing they were testing. Masculinity is not a single concept. Not all men are goal-focused, divorced from their feelings, disposed to be violent, and heterosexual. The fact is there exists a multitude of masculinities. The MSRI theorists of the 1950s and 1960s disallowed or altogether ignored this rich diversity of masculinities, favouring instead a specific hegemonic variety.[57]

Thus, MSRI theory really only compares the individual against the currently dominant, socially constructed cluster of traits most valued by the influential in our society – primarily those qualities found among men who are young, white, middle- and upper-class, English-speaking, heterosexual, and able-bodied.[58] To obtain a highly masculine score when tested, one should be rational, virile, low in affect, interested in physical activities, hard-working, willing to fight for a principle, usually under control, sometimes short-tempered, and always ready for sex.

By the very act of prioritizing certain values, traits, and goals, MSRI theorists reinforce the value or importance of those specific qualities. If a majority of men exhibit a certain trait, it should not automatically follow that the trait is masculine – and thus of intrinsic value. All it really means is that a majority of men tested exhibited that trait. It should not follow, as is often the case, that low-scoring individuals should be pathologized for being out of step with the majority of their sex. MSRI theory, with its incumbent notion of hegemonic masculinity, creates and helps reinforce the prevalent social myths of what it means to be a 'real man'; it can also make individuals feel very inadequate or guilty for not being more stereotypically male. It implies that the individual should be concerned if he is not like most other men, and that he should try to rectify his shortcomings. That is why MSRI theory comes to the fore whenever there is anxiety about the feminization of men – as happened in most industrial countries before the First World War, then during the 1930s, and again in the United States in the immediate post-1945 period – the real concern was over popularization of specific varieties of masculinity that are not in the best interests of business and government.[59]

The fifth failure of sex-role theory, which, in fact, strengthened and ensured its popularity, is that power and class differences among individuals are masked. Robert Connell notes the potential affinity for role theory and social conservatism. He states that role theory 'offers no resistance to a dominated image of people and a consensual theory of society; most role theorists talk as if these *were* correct, and most role applications argue as if they *ought to be correct*. Role Theory plainly appeals to those who like to think that the social order works by mutual agreement; that people ought to do what they are told, and that there is something wrong with those who don't; that force, oppression, and exploitation aren't very important in the everyday working of society; and that the constraints that do operate on people reflect some kind of wisdom, whether of the older generation (socialization) or of the society as a whole (function).'[60]

It is in this sense that MSRI theory legitimizes and obfuscates the issue of male violence against women. It establishes violence as masculine, and thus, in our social context, an acceptable characteristic.

Both Pleck and Connell, among others, call for an end to the sex-role theory, although they differ in estimating the ease of accomplishing this process. Pleck appears somewhat optimistic about the decline of sex-role theory as a dominant paradigm; Connell, however, seems to recognize that we still have a distance to travel before sex-role theory is no longer taken very seriously.[61] As an indication that things have not changed dramatically, Figures 3.1[62] and 3.2[63] reveal that sex-role theory reached new levels of popularity during the 1970s. It seems more than coincidental that concomitant with the rise of feminism and the inability of the American military to win a decisive victory in Indo-China, many individuals turned to sex-role theory to try and conceptualize the changes that were happening to modern men. Once again, twentieth-century social sciences were on hand to perpetuate a corrupt system.

THE CONTEMPORARY FAMILY

Social learning theorists commonly acknowledge that the family is one of the most important contexts in which many males learn that violence against women is acceptable.[64] Richard Gelles's research is frequently cited in this context. Gelles found that a person abused at home as a child is 'as much as 1,000 times more likely than a child raised in a nonviolent home' subsequently to be violent toward a spouse or child.[65] Despite the consensus that the family can be crucial as a place where we learn to be violent, several problems exist with the literature.

Significant Methodological Weaknesses

A typical example is Maria Roy's survey of 150 women sampled at random from 1,000 callers on a crisis line. She found that 33.3 and 81.1 per cent of the women and men (or victims and perpetrators), respectively, came from homes where they were beaten or had witnessed their fathers physically abuse their mothers. Unfortunately, when gathering this information, Roy did not speak to the men. She obtained the information only from the female respondents, who were relaying what had been told to them by their partners and in-laws.[66]

Roy herself acknowledged the difficulty in making generalizations from such studies. The use of inferential information garnered from second-hand subjects from one crisis centre does not allow one to transfer, with any confidence or accuracy, these results to other populations. Although the information is interesting, it is virtually anecdotal, and does not give one an accurate impression of what is occurring, or why.

Straus, Gelles, and Steinmetz present some methodologically

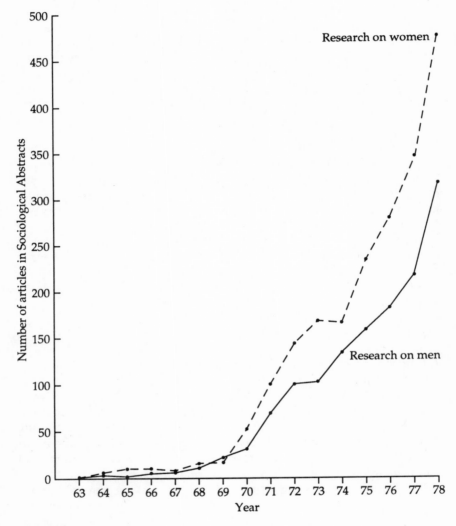

Figure 3.1
The growth of sex-role research (from Carrigan, Connell, and Lee, 'Toward a New Sociology of Masculinity'; reprinted from *The Making of Masculinities*, edited by Harry Brod, by permission of the publisher Routledge, Chapman and Hall, Inc.)

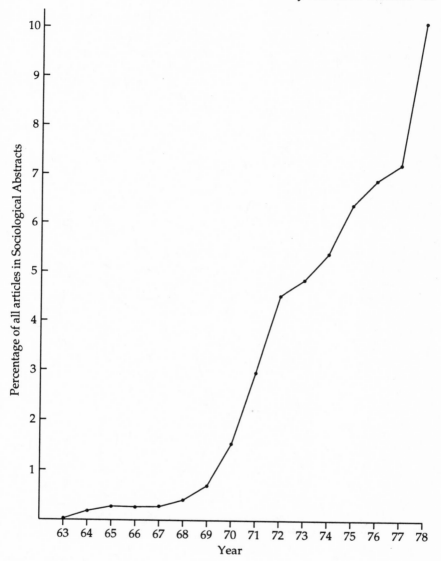

Figure 3.2
How sex-role research claimed a growing share of research interests (from
Carrigan, Connell, and Lee, 'Toward a New Sociology of Masculinity'; reprinted from *The Making of Masculinities*, edited by Harry Brod, by permission of
the publisher Routledge, Chapman and Hall, Inc.)

stronger studies. They found that having witnessed parents attack each other resulted in a tripled rate of conjugal violence for both men and women. Thirty-five per cent of the men who witnessed domestic violence repeated the cycle. This is significantly different from the 10.7 per cent of offending partners who never witnessed violence between their parents.[67]

Thus, while more reliable evidence does exist, it is what we do with the results that is politically important. The problem is less that people underestimate the role of the family in facilitating the generation and transmission of violence than that they minimize and ignore other, extra-familial, factors.

Varying Value Placed on Extra-Familial Issues

Significant differences exist among various researchers and clinicians as to the relative weight they afford extra-familial factors in male socialization as encouraging violence. There exists a common tendency to emphasize the role of the family and to ignore or minimize factors such as the ideological, economic, and political structures within our society that promulgate beliefs that women are inferior to men and are acceptable targets for their violence. Such authors typically will acknowledge and summarize the importance of extra-familial factors in several paragraphs, while spending entire chapters examining intra-familial causes.

Labelling the Family as Dysfunctional

All too frequently, when attempting to explain why violence occurs in a specific family, theorists label the family 'dysfunctional.' Yet, it is the violent male, not the family, who is malfunctioning. To deny his sole responsibility for his violence works to implicate the other family members – the victims of the violence – as causes of the dysfunction. Certainly, the man may be very stressed and angry about some important, painful circumstance or event in his life, to which other family members may have contributed, but he is able to choose when, where, and how – and if – he will be violent. He does have other options. If he needs help in being made aware of them, the necessary counselling services and support are available, but the other family members must not be implicated as co-conspirators to the violence.[68]

Relative Silence on the Role of the Family in
Encouraging Sexual Violence

While the family is often implicated as a milieu where males learn to
be physically and emotionally violent toward women, there is a considerable gap in the literature when one attempts to discover how men
become sexual offenders. Did they learn within their family of origin to
be sexually violent? While some males have witnessed sexual violence
against their mothers, for example, this is not the case for most sexual
offenders.

At one level, it may be that the family teaches individual men specific acts of violence. A boy sees his father hit his mother and learns that
it is acceptable to hit his own wife when he is an adult. Yet we do not
know how precisely sons replicate the patterns of violence demonstrated by their fathers. Thus the intergenerational transmission of violence may also be occurring at a second level. Children may learn not
only that specific acts of violence (punching one's female partner, for
example) are permissible, but also that violence against women, in
general, is permissible.

If indeed young males learn in their family of origin that specific acts
and/or violence in general are acceptable, this dualistic principle can
help explain the vast differences which exist between male offenders.
At any given point, each offender has an approximate level of violence
beyond which he will not pass, at least for the time being. Thus, some
men may slap and punch but will not rape their female partners. Other
men will sexually offend, but will not maim and mutilate. But over
time, the severity and frequency of the violence often increases.[69]

It appears that a similar dualistic principle operates independently
of, though interacting with, what was learned in the family. Our society teaches men that specific acts of violence against women, and/or
any violence against women, regardless of the manner in which it is
enacted, are acceptable, or, at least, tolerable. It is these extra-familial
agents of male socialization that must now be examined.

IMAGES FROM THE POPULAR MEDIA

Among the factors outside of the family that are central in perpetuating hegemonic masculinity and its incumbent acceptance of male violence against women, the popular media play a large role. While it is

the effects of television which have been most thoroughly researched in this regard, the following patterns are evident in most media.[70]

Limited Male Roles

From Rocky and Rambo and Dirty Harry to Magnum, P.I., numerous movie and television plots revolve around young, physically fit, muscular, able-bodied, often wealthy males who are independent and capable of solving any problems. Of course, to do so, such a hero, or someone in his pay, may need to blow up a few bridges, beat up, shoot, or otherwise 'waste' several people, engage in car chases, and so forth. But he always emerges either unscathed or indifferent to his wounds – real men never cry – to walk off the set with the ever-grateful buxom blonde, who fawns over his rippling biceps or bulging bank account as the credits roll and the theme music ends the show. While there are some exceptions to the rule, too frequently we witness the same theme with only slight variations.

Such stereotypes are presented throughout the day and the week, and are perhaps most evident on the Saturday morning television cartoons. A limited variety of masculinities and femininities are packaged and sold to a young and impressionable audience. While the programs intended for girls involve cleaning, vanity, helplessness (or at best, resourcefulness until a male should appear), and caring for others, the boys are provided with violent images: creatures running with guns and shooting people, in order to protect or rescue the town, city, or planet. During the commercials, the girls pretend to bake and clean, while the boys play at shooting and slaughtering.[71]

Adoption of Modelled Roles

The limited male roles contribute to the belief that males are supposed to behave in certain prescribed ways. Admittedly, many researchers will not state that television, for example, directly creates traditional sex-role stereotypes in children. There is, however, a growing consensus among those examining the issue that media images can strongly reinforce existing values.[72]

Nancy Cobb, Judith Stevens-Long, and Steven Goldstein indicate that advertisers who want to target their product to a specific gender need only advertise the product accordingly. They found that the children in their study, aged four to six, after watching videotapes in which a fantasy character assigned masculinity, femininity, or sex-role neutrality to a standard set of sex-neutral toys, overwhelmingly preferred to play with the sex-appropriate toy. In a separate test, they found that when the same toys were identified as inappropriate for their sex, the children preferred to play with another set of less desirable comparison toys.[73] This result is encouraging as it indicates that it may be possible, at a young age, to teach children alternative sex roles. However, most toy manufacturers are not interested in social change. If they want to sell an all-new plastic sub-machine-gun, they will show several young boys having tremendous fun shooting each other.

Some research indicates that if parents watch television with their children and later discuss the content of the specific shows or commercials, they can significantly counter the effects of the media in promoting consumerism and sex-role stereotypes.[74] This is good news for parents who are inclined and able to do so. But the reality appears not very promising for a positive shift in the current generation's sex-role perspectives. Most children spend many hours soaking up media images. One estimate is that the typical five- or six-year-old watches about two and a half hours of television per day, with an increase in viewing until it peaks in early adolescence at approximately four hours per day. Thus, 'the average child born today will by the age of fifteen have spent more time watching television than going to school.'[75] And by the time they are twenty years old, most young people will have viewed approximately 800,000 values-laden commercials.[76] Of the extensive hours spent watching television, the vast majority are unsupervised, and even if the parents are in attendance, their presence does not guarantee any discussion following a show – least of all one that may be critical of the sex roles portrayed in the show. If the child's parents maintain traditional views on sex-role socialization, the post-show discussion – if it happens at all – may only reinforce the status quo. So while changes are possible, we still have a long way to go if we are to break old patterns.[77]

Linking Men and Violence

The research on the issue of violence and the media has been thoroughly investigated – one estimate is that since 1950 there have been over 2,500 studies.[78] While considerable evidence points to the negative effects of viewing television,[79] a significant lobby – typically with vested interests in the media or corporate communities – continues to fund the production of an equally substantial body of literature refuting the claims of the media critics. This defence of the neutrality of television originated in the late 1950s and early 1960s, a period of rapid expansion in the television industry. Advocates argued that watching violent television is cathartic; the vicarious experience of violence would reduce general aggression as it purges the viewer of such feelings. A 1961 study by S. Feshbach, for example, would appear to furnish proof of this. College students showed decreased hostility after viewing a violent film – even though they had been goaded by an experimenter's assistant before the experiment to increase their anger.[80]

Critics of Feshbach's study argued that the decrease in aggression probably was a result of a temporary increase in internal restraints against aggressive acts. To test this hypothesis, Berkowitz and Rawlings, in a 1963 study, once again provoked college students before they viewed a filmed boxing match in which one of the fighters is savagely beaten. The variation on Feshbach's study involved informing half of the subjects that the violence they were going to witness could be interpreted as 'brutality that was unjustified by the victim's prior behavior,' and the other half that it was 'justified punishment for an unrepentant villain.' If the catharsis theory were accurate, the aggression levels would be reduced in both situations. However, as hypothesized by Berkowitz and Rawlings, the subjects who received the 'justified punishment' description exhibited more hostility toward the experimenter who had initially provoked them. In believing the retribution in the film to be justified, they showed fewer inhibitions about behaving in an aggressive manner.[81]

Discrediting the catharsis theory in an experiment is one thing; changing the popular opinions of millions of people is quite another. Throughout the 1960s, many efforts were made to further study and reduce the levels of televised violence. In 1970, for example, after three years of study, the influential United States surgeon general's scientific advisory committee concluded that there existed a 'causal relationship' between televised violence and viewer aggression. No previous conclusion of causality had ever been reached by a scientific group.[82]

Yet, even the surgeon general's report could not redirect television programming. Clearly, opponents of the catharsis theory were up against not only popular beliefs but also the large corporate entities backing television programs – the advertisers. If car chases and shootings obtain high ratings, which in turn mean big advertising dollars, it is unlikely that the studios will choose to reduce their violent content;

only federal legislation or significant public opposition will be effective here. Since the state has shown little interest in enacting laws to restrict television programming, and public opposition has been sporadic and lacking funding, the violence has not been reduced. In fact, in the two decades since the release of the surgeon general's report, there appears to have been an *increase* in television violence, particularly in the 1980s with the arrival of music videos. This escalation has highlighted yet another negative value conveyed in much of the contemporary media.

Violence against Women

On 1 August 1981, Warner Amex Satellite Company launched Music Television (MTV). While originally in only two million homes, by 1984 MTV was in more than twenty-two million, produced a profit of more than $60 million in that year alone, and had permanently changed the television and recording business. MTV's success motivated a number of channels and programs to copy the MTV format in the hope of cashing in on a trend.

Not only did music videos provide a new forum for creative visual and audio expression, simultaneously reviving declining record sales, they also compelled television advertisers to revise the format for most commercials. After witnessing the slick, capital- and technology-intensive music videos, viewers were not as likely to be impressed by standard commercials with pedestrian scripts and thin soundtracks. Pizazz was essential. This, coupled with the proliferation of remote-control devices for televisions and VCRs, which made switching channels easier than ever before, taught advertisers that if they did not captivate the audience within the first five seconds of a commercial, the channel might be changed, and some other product with a flashier commercial might entice the viewer. The result of this technological change has been a rapid acceleration in the speed at which images are transmitted.

One study by Richard Baxter and associates revealed the frequency with which violent images are conveyed. With the participation of undergraduate student coders, a random sample of sixty-two MTV music videos were rated for content. Visual abstractions occurred in 90.3 per cent of the videos. Second-highest was sex or the portrayal of sexual feelings or impulses, at 59.7 per cent. Third was dancing, at 56.5 per cent. Fourth was violence and/or crime, at 53.2 per cent. The breakdown for this category was as follows: physical aggression against people, 26 per cent; physical aggression against objects, 16 per cent; dance movements imitating violence, 15 per cent; destructiveness, 15 per cent; use of weapons, 11 per cent; physical aggression against self, 8 per cent; chase, 7 per cent; murder, 3 per cent; and victimless crime, 2 per cent.[83]

A larger study by Barry Sherman and Joseph Dominick illuminated the gender, class, and racial content of music videos. Between 6 April and 18 May 1984, all videos appearing on MTV, NBC's 'Friday Night Videos,' and WTBS's 'Night Tracks' between 12:30 and 2:30 a.m. (considered video prime time) were recorded. This totalled forty-two hours, or 366 videos, an average of 8.7 per hour. The researchers were not interested in performance videos, which totalled 200, so they subtracted them, leaving 166 concept videos (approximately 45 per cent of the total), which were the main focus of the study. Their results are not surprising.

The music video world appeared as predominantly male (men outnumbered women by two to one – the same as in conventional television) and white (there were four times as many whites as non-whites). Most of the people were between eighteen and thirty-four years of age; few teens were seen, and seniors and children were rare. Raters found that violence occurred in 56.6 per cent of the sampled concept videos (in the study cited above, Baxter and associates found 53.2). The average number of separate aggressive acts was 2.86, with some videos containing ten or more. Men were the aggressors in almost 75 per cent of the cases and an even larger number of times they were the victims. Older adults were twice as likely to be the aggressors as victims; children were twice as likely to be the recipients of the violence. The unanticipated occurred when the researchers combined the demographic variables. Forty per cent of the women were upper-class while only 30 per cent of the men were rated as such. More than 90 per cent of the teens were portrayed as lower-class while less than 40 per cent of adults fit in this category. Similarly, non-whites were portrayed as younger and lower in status. Men were hurt or killed three times more frequently than women, but violence against men was presented more realistically. When the violence was against women, only one woman in ten appeared visibly affected. Sherman and Dominick noted that all too often the effects of violence against women were glossed over. Similarly, the researchers found that half of the women were provocatively dressed and tended to be portrayed as upper-class. Most of the teens in the videos were male, non-white, and lower-class. And non-whites were more likely to use weapons and have them used against them than whites. Thus the women were portrayed as 'upper-class objects for lower-class males with visions of sexual conquest' and weapons were often used to coerce non-white females.[84]

Based on the causal relationship found in the surgeon general's report and the evidence in the Berkowitz and Rawlings study, where subjects were more aggressive when told that the punishment was justified if the victim was unrepentant, one can recognize the deleterious implications of a highly violent, sexist, and racist media content.

In an attempt to quell middle-class fears that television is encouraging new levels of violence in children, corporate officials often refer to studies indicating the benefits of parents selecting the shows for children, viewing them with the children, and then facilitating a discussion after the show. Such a process can help children separate myth and image from reality and thus potentially reduce the negative effects of television consumption. Aside from implicitly blaming the victim by shifting responsibility for safe television from the producer to the consumer, the corporate giants artfully ignore the fact that most television viewing by children is not followed up by such 'deprogramming.' Most rock videos, for example, are viewed in the company of a peer group rather than in a family or individual setting.[85] While adolescents clearly are capable of reasoned thought, like all humans, they are extremely susceptible to peer pressure. Whether with friends or family, if the viewing environment is such that the adolescent does not feel safe to be critical of the values on the tube, he or she is unlikely to speak out. This reticence can reinforce the violence.[86]

Summary of the Effects of the Popular Media

Many of our contemporary media convey the idea that it is acceptable for males to be violent to other humans. While this violence may more often be directed toward other men, it still reinforces the belief that men should use violence to deal with their problems. This, in turn, strengthens the other powerful media message that minimizes, tolerates, and condones violence toward women. The media, however, are by no means the only social forces which promote this idea.

THE MILITARY

One may question how an institution like the military can significantly affect the behaviour of individuals who, by the time they are recruited, have had at least eighteen years of socialization as civilians. This section will review several of the strategies utilized by the military to more than compensate for this disadvantage.

Effects on the Individual

Military recruiters are not subtle about their desire to ensure that male recruits are properly programmed.[87] They waste no time in breaking down the individual they have obtained. If the young man has not done so already, armed services personnel work to ensure that he adopts the rigidly hierarchical, hostile-to-compromise, unfeeling, and violent values of the military.[88] Every new recruit is thrown into basic training, the military's expression for the process of turning civilians into soldiers, in order to be developed into a human fighting machine; this is where, as the saying goes, boys are turned into men.[89] Gwynne Dyer, a critic of international military systems, states that 'the secret of basic training is that it is not really teaching people things at all. It is about changing people so that they can do things they would not have dreamt of otherwise. If you want to change people, quickly and radically, what you do is put them in a place where the only right way to think and to behave is the way you want them to. You isolate them. And you apply enormous physical and mental pressure.'[90] Dyer notes that basic training has not significantly changed over the centuries, simply because the raw material recruited into the military is essentially unchanged. Our society produces young men who have a fair degree of aggression, a strong tendency to hang around in groups, and an absolutely desperate desire to fit in. The military uses these traits to develop millions of killers who will operate automatically against the enemy – whoever that may be at the time.[91]

The military skilfully exerts constant pressure to mould the men they want. New recruits are coerced into accepting a variety of masculinity that is held out as the only real option for a soldier. In the military mindset, if one is not a 'real man,' one has three other options: boy, homosexual, or woman.

Being Labelled as a Boy. This makes one somewhat redeemable, but change had better occur quickly as this status is not long tolerated. To become a man, one must endure gruelling physical endurance tests. One also must silently tolerate various psychological abuses, such as derogatory name-calling during seemingly endless hours of marching drills, or possibly suffer the indignity of not being allowed a bowel movement during the entire first week of basic training.[92]

To become the type of man highly valued in the military, one cannot merely pretend to have adopted the values of the military. To succeed, one must thoroughly integrate the military's hybrid value system, which combines heterosexuality with violence. The following example offers an insight into this connection: the recruit grips his rifle with one hand and his crotch with the other and shouts 'Sir: This is my rifle / This is my gun / This is for pleasure / This is for fun!'[93]

Being Viewed as a Homosexual. This is the second option, if one is not viewed as a man. In the military, calling someone a homosexual is about the worst – and certainly the most frequently used – insult. Most military establishments have a nearly hysterical fear of homosexuality. They know it has the potential to be a major threat. After all, if the army is trying to break any connection individuals may have with their emotions, the last thing it needs is men becoming intimate with each other. Homosexuals, both real and imagined, have repeatedly been attacked by the military.[94] In many countries, the accusation of being a homosexual is adequate reason for a dishonourable discharge. Thus the threat of an accusation helps keep the recruits in line; they will work particularly hard to prove they are the type of man desired by the military.[95]

This system becomes self-reinforcing. While it may have started with the commanding officers accusing the recruits of being so-called faggots, the recruits themselves quickly pick up the practice, taunting their fellows about being gay if their behaviour is not hypermasculine (as if hypermasculinity precluded a man from being gay). While gay-bashing is not limited to the military, being identified as a faggot by one's fellow recruits can be a very frightening experience because of potentially life-threatening consequences.[96] It is not uncommon for an individual to respond to such a situation by acting particularly violent towards either someone or something, in an attempt to forever remove the label.

Being Viewed as a Woman. Reflecting our society's misogyny, it is also very insulting in the army to call a recruit a woman, simply because women often are seen as a devalued, though threatening, entity. This combination of females as something to be both feared and conquered endangers women's safety. Basic training reinforces this perspective.

For example, recruits are shown films warning them of the evils of venereal disease. While it is admirable that the military is concerned with restricting the spread of sexually transmitted diseases, the women in the films typically are portrayed as evil disease-carrying sluts. Creating such distrust later legitimizes conquering females; there is little official recognition or respect for mutually enjoyable sex. The military does not want a bunch of sissies; during a sexual encounter, as in any situation, men are supposed to be in control and call the shots. Women are the 'receptacle for ... sex drives too long held in check.' Locker- or bar-room bragging is right at home in the military. As one person stated: 'in basic training ... people talked about fucking sheep and cows and women with about the same respect for them all.'[97] The use and abuse of women is sanctioned as a way of enabling individual men to affirm their chosen brand of masculinity. Donna Warnock, an American writer, quotes veteran Richard Hale telling troops on the way to Vietnam: 'There's lots of loose ass over there, men, and they just love G.I. dick and best of all they are only gooks so if you get tired of them, you can cram a grenade up their cunt and waste them.'[98]

Effects on the Peer Group

The military endeavours to make individual men subject to the will and orders of their commanding officers. In addition, and because officers cannot be in attendance in all situations, the military fosters the peer group as a maintainer of the value system. One means to this end is the 'buddy system.' Upon arrival at basic training, each new recruit is paired with another new recruit. The buddy system helps ensure that individuals are not left alone to think and thus possibly question the military establishment. The buddy system was not created for the encouragement of intimacy. Indeed, any hint of this happening is dealt with brutally: 'When a recruit mentioned that he and a friend had been separated in violation of the "buddy system" under which they joined, the drill instructor is reported to have asked, "Do you like Private R?" The next question was, "Do you want to fuck him?"'[99] The group can assist the officials in controlling and influencing the individual so as to maintain intact the military hierarchy. While an individual soldier may want to question authority in general, or the rationale behind specific orders, he may not do so for fear of reprisal from the group. Thus, the peer group can play a large role in facilitating the implementation of military-inspired violence.

Effects on the Family

The official word has remained that the military does not have a significant negative effect on the family.[100] This seems strange. Clearly the training requires that the men kill the sensitive, caring, nurturing – the feeling – parts within themselves. They live in an environment that sanctions violence against women, particularly if they are in combat. They are to be tough and brutal, and their problem-solving skills are based on violence. All day they practise how to punch, shoot, maim, and kill. Even if a man has not done a tour of combat duty, it seems unlikely that when he goes home to his family in the evening he will always be inclined to settle disagreements through peaceful discussion.

The veil shrouding the issue of violence within military families needs to be lifted.[101] While the frighteningly high levels of child, woman, and drug abuse have become something of an open secret among those connected with the military, officially they have been minimized. Most of the rank and file are afraid to say anything. When administrators have acknowledged the problem, there remains a preference to deal with things internally; they do not like admitting the military has negative repercussions on the host society. In their view, if there has been a problem with violence directed either toward the self or others, military counsellors are available. However, as everything is placed on the soldier's medical record, relatively few people will risk reaching out for help. Any sign of reduced mental health – whether it be to question why he and his peers are being trained to kill or to admit that he beats his wife – could impair the individual's upward mobility in the military. Unless an abuser really goes out of control and flagrantly violates the laws of civil society, the abuse often is allowed to continue. People pretend that everything is all right, including the abuse victim, who feels that to disclose the abuse might very well threaten the military career – upon which typically she is dependent – of her father, husband, or friend.

Traditionally, the military has viewed families as liabilities. Their concern has been that the new recruit will not adapt as easily to the military value system if the family continues to exert a significant control over him. Thus, a central part of basic training is to break the bonds between the recruit and his family. Except for attendance at the birth of a child or the death of an immediate family member, personal contact is prevented. While recruits may be permitted to accept the occasional letter or phone call, both are easily restricted. The ideal woman, in the military's view, is a stoic martyr, enduring the worst, knowing that her partner or son is doing what is best for her, for their children, and for the country.

Maintaining silence on the issue of military violence against women is aided by the extreme isolation most military wives endure. As their husbands receive various postings, they are expected to move around the planet on a fairly regular basis, thus distancing themselves from family structures and established friendships. Living on a military base or in compound housing further isolates military wives from civilian peers (or 'civies,' as they are pejoratively referred to). Even when contact is desired, differences in linguistic or cultural backgrounds, frequent relocations, and the knowledge that certain activities (such as staying out late, or having specific political affiliations) will raise the eyebrows and suspicions of the military brass only further isolate these women. At best, military wives associate with other military people. Their world is extremely closed, isolated, and often reduced to being the support crew for the man in uniform. Such isolation does not guarantee abuse, but significantly raises the ease with which it can occur and remain undetected.

Effects on Society

We live in a global military order that demands tremendous social, political, economic, and ecological contributions.[102] Growing numbers of people are recognizing that even if we avoid global nuclear annihilation – which many would argue is unlikely without a major shift in our priorities – we will succeed in destroying the values and societies we are so desperately trying to defend. Criticizing the existing military structure is not, as its many defenders would argue, equivalent to advocating that the entire structure be abolished.[103] However desirable that might be for some, the reality is that we would still need individuals trained to defend territories from invasion.

Existing military establishments excel at making the domestic population feel militarily insecure whenever support seems shaky.[104] This is done in a typically masculine manner. Their bragging of who has the biggest and best missiles is strikingly reminiscent of little boys comparing the length of their penises.[105] This blatant self-promotion occurs despite an abundance of evidence indicating that, thanks to exaggerated military spending, most industrial, socialist, and Third World economies on this planet are fiscally overextended. This exacerbates both monetary and political dilemmas. High inflation is fuelled by massive deficits; capital investment for civilian necessities (houses, social services, or factories producing consumer goods) is reduced. Numerous governments, faced with a disgruntled population that witnesses their unwillingness to democratically provide the basics of civil society while giving the military all that it desires, will restrict, silence, or slaughter their own citizens in order to maintain control. The following statistics (1986) illustrate the global emphasis on military spending.

- The two superpowers, the United States and the USSR, have less than 11 per cent of the world's population, but 97 per cent of all nuclear warheads and bombs.
- In the United States, 170 times as much public research money goes for transport into space as for mass transit on earth.
- Three governments in five spend more to guard their citizens against military attack than to protect them from all the enemies of good health.
- Military-controlled governments are more than twice as likely as other Third World governments to make frequent use of torture and other violent forms of repression against the populace.
- At the cost of less than half an hour's world military outlay, the United Nation's FAO (Food and Agriculture Organization) destroyed a plague of locusts in Africa, saving enough grain to feed 1.2 million people for a full year.
- Weapons of mass destruction, on hair-trigger alert, now effectively hold all of humanity hostage. Enough nuclear weapons are scattered over the globe to kill everyone on earth at least twelve times over.
- At present levels of world arms spending by governments, the average individual can expect to give up three to four years of his or her working life to help foot the bill.
- Arms imports of developing countries between 1975 and 1985 amounted to 40 per cent of the increase in their foreign debt in that period.
- Every three days 120,000 children die unnecessarily – the same toll of casualties following the atomic bombing of Hiroshima. Indeed it may be said that the children of the world already are living in the rubble of World War III.[106]

Other heavy human prices are paid that are harder to quantify in monetary units. One example relates to the training of millions of men around the world to kill. In the United States, for example, the military still has to recruit an estimated 1 out of every 4.6 eighteen-year-old males.[107] Similarly, most European countries have a mandatory two-year military tour of duty. Facilitated by our glorification of the military hero,[108] which is buttressed, in part, by a multi-billion-dollar war-toy industry,[109] and high unemployment in the civilian economy, there are an estimated eighteen million full-time soldiers on this planet[110] who continue to be inculcated with violent values. Each one of those men brings back to civil society a high degree of what he has learned in the military. Repeated exposure to injunctions such as 'you can cram a grenade up their cunt and waste them' is bound to have some long-term effects.[111] We need to recognize the contribution of the military to the currently existing variety of hegemonic masculinity and its acceptance of violence against women. It seems more than just a coincidence that the variety of masculinity most preferred in civilian society is not appreciably different from that prized by the military.

Not surprisingly, many of the arguments used to justify male violence against women and war are identical. One popular notion is that war is part of the human condition. Yet just because a behaviour may be widespread does not mean that it is part of our biological nature. While the majority of civilizations may have produced pottery, it does not mean that there is a human gene for throwing clay. A second belief is that aggression and war are universal. The existence of peaceful tribal cultures refutes this contention. Similarly, if it were universal and part of our natural heritage, one would assume, from an evolutionary standpoint, that the more primitive the society, the higher its level of violence. Yet as Erich Fromm has stated, 'the most primitive men are the least warlike ... warlikeness grows in proportion to civilization. If destructiveness were innate in man, the trend would be the opposite.' Thus, war, like male violence against women, is socially constructed. In diverting ever-increasing amounts of time, resources, money, and people to the military we are making individuals within our societies less and less able to peaceably resolve conflict, and more and more disposed to be violent.[112]

While the military cannot be held responsible for all of the indirectly sanctioned violence perpetrated by the men within its ranks, it is no longer acceptable for it to ignore its responsibility for encouraging violence among these men, within its ranks, and fostering a global milieu in which conflict must be resolved through violence. The military's pretense that it does not contribute to both individual and international violence is a strategy that is wearing thin. If we choose to continue training millions of killers every year, we must recognize that there will be some spillover effects. Besides, we squander precious human and natural resources that could be turned to human development rather than destruction. An equally important question is whether we can successfully reintegrate these trained killers to become productive, responsible, and non-violent members of society. It is unlikely that all of them will abandon their military values when they hang up their machine-guns and battle fatigues. As Gwynne Dyer notes: 'there is aggression in all of us – men, women, children, and babies. Armies don't have to create it and they can't even increase it. But most of us learn to put limits on our aggression, especially physical aggression, as we grow up. A crucial part of turning people into soldiers is teaching them to ignore these limits so that in the right circumstances, against the enemy, they'll go all the way and kill.'[113] This is particularly frightening when one recognizes that the pornography industry – one of the Western world's largest and most profitable – bases its success on portraying women as the enemy. This component will be examined later in this chapter. But even before most males are exposed to pornography, they have already endured the pressures of one or more peer groups that encourage them to be violent.

PEER GROUP

As much as we may not want to admit that our parents were right, who we hang around with can have a tremendous impact on what we think, say, and do. While the effect that others may have on us will vary at different times in our lives and among individuals, it is undeniable that we are influenced by others. Despite the rhetoric of masculine independence, research indicates that men are not significantly less influenced by peer pressure than women.[114] That men are influenced by others is not of itself problematic. Groups of people can influence individuals toward impressive achievements. What is troubling is that, for many men, the peer group is an important conduit of social learning through which they absorb both the acceptability and the methods of male violence against women.

There are two main types of peer groups influencing men – the immediate and the mythical. Both exert a strong influence on the individual. The immediate peer group is the one whose existence is generally recognized by the individual. It may be composed of friends, acquaintances, schoolmates, or co-workers. For the individual man, the number, size, and influence of such a group will vary significantly throughout his life. Stereotypically for men, the peer group is most influential during childhood and adolescence. During their twenties, most men move away from their support networks. If they remain connected, they typically characterize these friends as helpful and important, but not as individuals with whom they could easily talk about crucial personal matters. Since most men at this point in their lives are working to shift their focus from the peer group to an individual, female significant other, and are extremely homophobic, it follows that their friendships suffer.[115]

The second, the mythical peer group, is considerably different in form, but very similar in effect. This group is composed of all the other men in the life of an individual man – all the nameless males that he furtively glances at and quickly compares himself with so as to reassure, or to castigate, himself for making, or not making, the grade. The mythical peer group plays a big role in the development and socialization of an individual male. It is not concrete, like the immediate peer group, which has real names to go with real faces. It is based on experience – for instance, a man's memories of his father ridiculing him for the way in which he threw a football – and perceived values – such as his interpretation of a glance he received from an unknown male on the street for wearing a specific article of clothing. The mythical peer group plays a crucial role in encouraging men to thoroughly adopt a hegemonic masculinity, and its incumbent acceptance of violence against women. The mythical peer group is a compilation of images, values, and restrictions that men accumulate and carry with them, throughout their lives. Whether or not a man has an immediate peer group in his life at a specific point in time is not important, for he always has a mythical peer group which affects his actions and choices as a man. It is the mythical peer group which, when the typical male's immediate peer groups are dissolved in early adulthood, continues to significantly influence his behaviour.

What are the values transmitted through the peer group? While individual differences do exist among them, some generalizations can be made about the following late-twentieth-century examples of important male peer groups.

Boys' Clubs (Scouts, Cubs, Beavers, Rovers, etc.)

All of these groups aim to transmit certain values to the current generation of males. Boys learn how to tie knots; light fires; be independent, thrifty, physically active, and resourceful; how to set and meet goals. Each group tries to ensure that young males learn skills deemed essential for all boys when the Boy Scouts was first formed, early in the twentieth century.[116] While current scouting organizations may try to distance themselves from their early roots (they have toned down the rhetoric about making boys into men), their goals, activities, and structures have not substantially changed. These groups were formed in an effort to compensate for a perceived feminization of men by industrial society. Scouting was presented as an institution to boost a flagging masculine vitality. It also provided an opportunity for many adult male group leaders, frequently men restricted in their careers to dull factory occupations, to fulfil their notions of traditional masculinity.[117]

The result is that young boys are removed from female contact and overtly informed that the only valued variety of masculinity depends upon their following certain guidelines. The successful Scout is eager to acquire all his badges for civic duty, construction, cleanliness, and more. He is also deferential to authority; a good Scout respects his elders. Scouting reinforces the mentality of the gang or, in scouting terms, the 'wolf-pack.' A good scout is tough, active, and can handle himself in any situation. Reliance on others and cooperation have not traditionally been scouting values. An early-twentieth-century quotation is indicative of the scouting ideal: 'The *real* Boy Scout is not a "sissy." He is not a hothouse plant, like little Lord Fauntleroy. There is nothing "milk and water" about him; he is not afraid of the dark ... Instead of being a puny, dull, or bookish lad, who dreams and does nothing, he is full of life, energy, enthusiasm, bubbling over with fun, full of ideas as to what he wants to do and knows how he wants to do it. He has many ideals and many heroes. He is not hitched to his mother's apron strings. While he adores his mother, and would do anything to save her from suffering or discomfort, he is self-reliant, sturdy and full of vim.'[118]

While scouting does not directly teach boys to be violent toward women, it does introduce and reinforce two important notions that are common to other male peer groups and to society at large. The first is a mistrust of women and all things feminine. The message is clear: beware of women, for excessive association with them will make you less of a man. The second is that the important values in one's life are to be found among men, particularly among those within the wolf-pack – or at least among those who endorse a similar, generally a hegemonic, notion of masculinity. Scouting's promotion of these two principles forms a foundation upon which increasingly misogynist values of other male peer groups are laid.

Competitive Sports

While the role of sport in encouraging male violence against women will be examined in greater detail at the end of this chapter, it is important to first point out the role it plays for many adolescent males. It is through school or community sports that many youths try to validate their masculinity or assess the extent to which they fall short of their peers. Their degree of success in this area can significantly alter their status within the peer group and, in turn, affect the degree to which they are able to influence the peer group. Once again, conformity to hegemonic masculinity is rewarded. Use of the body for goal completion, physical coordination, and fitness are rewarded.

It is in the sporting arena that many young boys first have the experience of not measuring up against their peers. Early failure can influence future actions: many of these boys grow into men who will spend the rest of their lives trying to avoid the ridicule they experienced when they were young. This results in many men who are extremely competitive, focused on physical exertion while ignoring physical feelings, and intent on winning.

School

The great length of time we spend in school during our formative years makes school peer groups particularly important. Young boys entering school quickly learn how their older peers will maintain the pecking order; too often it involves emotional intimidation and physical force. Fighting between young boys on school playgrounds is an important activity, both for those involved in the fight and for the spectators: it demonstrates clearly that physical force is a fundamental component of male power, and legitimizes its use. If males rely on physical strength to solve their problems it seems less likely that they will develop and perfect skills in resolving conflict without violence. Indeed, in many circles, a man who advocates the inclusion of conflict resolution skills in a school curriculum may find people either overtly or covertly questioning his masculinity and sexual preference.

The school or adolescent peer group is also an area where most males acquire large portions of their ideas about human sexuality.

Early on, they are exposed to, and absorb, a significant number of myths about male sexuality. These include:

1. Men shouldn't express certain feelings.
2. Sex is a performance.
3. A man must orchestrate sex.
4. A man always wants and is always ready to have sex.
5. All physical contact must lead to sex.
6. Sex equals intercourse.
7. Sex requires an erection.
8. Good sex is increasing excitement terminated only by orgasm.
9. Sex should be natural and spontaneous.[119]

Nowhere is it allowed that young men will not know how to be sexual or will be clumsy. A real man just knows how to fuck and there is nothing he needs to learn. The message imparted is that men always are, or at least ought to be, in control; women are physical commodities available for a male's sexual pleasure. Young boys start to view women for the parts of their body, as rated against the current (mythical) feminine ideal. The competition between males for females increases as rape myths are adopted, and young males know that to brag of real or fictitious conquests among many male peer groups can score them significant ranking points. In a context where, for example, 'No always means Yes,' a male regaling his friends with a story of how he ripped off the shirt of a female friend before she succumbed to his evidently sexual advances is not likely to be accused of acquaintance rape by his peers. His actions, in fact, may prompt his peers to follow suit; many adult sexual offenders begin offending in this way during adolescence.[120] Within numerous male peer groups, any means, after all, can be justified by the end of 'getting laid.'[121]

Common Threads throughout Hegemonic Male Peer Groups

Boys are exposed to at least four common themes in most hegemonic male peer groups. Each one, in and of itself, is problematic. The compounding factor is that the way in which they often act in concert increases the likelihood of violence against women. They are as follows.

Don't Admit Your True Feelings. This results in males ignoring their spontaneous emotional responses to situations and reacting instead as they think others expect them to. Such is particularly dangerous over time. If a male continually ignores his authentic emotional responses to life's multitude of experiences and situations, he may impair his capability to ever connect with those feelings. Not that the feelings are forever lost; however, the work involved in reconnecting with them will be substantially more difficult.

Edward Gondolf, among others, has written about the effects on men of funnelling their emotions, and particularly on how the process can be a significant contributor to male violence against women.[122] He argues that a number of factors come together to restrict men from displaying their full range of emotions (see Figure 3.3).[123] What happens over time for many men in our culture is that they eventually come to believe that the only acceptable male emotion is anger. What, in fact, has occurred is that they have ignored or denied the full range of their emotional experience – which includes feeling vulnerable, scared, or intimidated, emotions that are not generally acceptable within a hegemonic masculine framework.

The implications of this process are quite evident. A man who cannot connect with or identify his own emotional responses in various situations will possess only a limited ability to communicate honestly and effectively with others. He runs the risk of never becoming really close to other people, simply because he is too afraid or lacks the capacity to let them know he cares.[124] More obviously dangerous is the scenario of a man who, accustomed to ignoring his emotional responses rather than dealing with them as they happen, funnels his feelings; this man may escalate to violence against the women in his personal life. Attacking a wife or partner is not likely to cause many significant repercussions; men know that while their boss or teacher may make them extremely angry, they are unacceptable targets for violence.[125]

Be Aggressive. Building on the pressure for young males not to express a full range of emotions are the rewards and encouragement provided for aggressive behaviour. This process starts very early – and seldom ends. Many parents promote the hegemonic brand of masculinity to ensure their sons fit in with their peers and get ahead in life. Some parents overtly encourage aggressive behaviour in sons, who, in the parents' view, are not acting tough enough to become 'real men.' Among others, the process is much more subtle, though less effective. Just as girls are socialized into specific roles – for example, by being dressed in frilly clothes that are impractical for children's play – so too are boys. The examples are numerous:

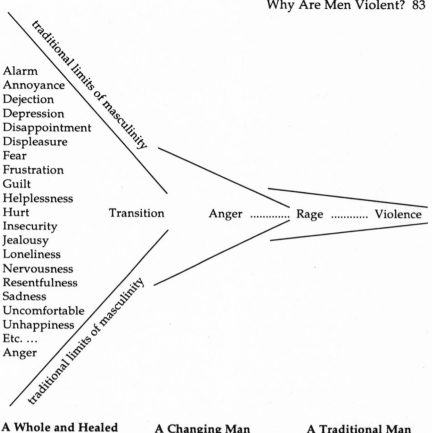

A Whole and Healed Person feels accepting of conflict, and more easily identifies feelings.

A Changing Man understands that conflict yields choices, and struggles to identify feelings.

A Traditional Man believes that conflict leads to violence, and denies or ignores feelings other than anger.

The task for men who wish to change old violent or abusive behaviors is to move from the traditional model on the right where anger is the primary negative or painful feeling identified, toward the left where anger is but one of many clearly identified negative/difficult feelings. As men, we must reclaim our right to the natural human emotiveness that is denied us by the limits of traditional masculinity.

Figure 3.3
The process of men funnelling their emotions (from Don Long, RAVEN, St Louis, MO, 1991; reprinted with permission)

- Advertisements in baby magazines promote army fatigue camou-
flage sleepers complete with hunting caps, 'for the best buddy you'll
ever have.'[126]
- Studies repeatedly indicate that parents are more physically rough
and less cuddly with young boys than girls.[127]
- As children mature, boys are allowed to run, jump, and use physical
force more than girls, who are likely to be reined in and reprimand-
ed. Boys, after all, will be boys.[128]
- From birth, boys in stereotypical families are more likely to be provided with war toys. Rather than being taught how to cook, clean,
and take care of themselves and others, they are encouraged to shoot
toy Uzi machine-guns and fantasize with G.I. Joe (who made a profitable comeback in the reactionary 1980s) as he plunders villages and
bombs towns. To help develop eye-hand coordination, computer
video games reward players for killing or obliterating their prey. It is
not in the least coincidental that the word 'Atari,' popularly known
worldwide as the name of a top-selling computer video game of the
early 1980s, is also the Korean verb 'to kill.'[129]

Goal Achievement. The encouragement of aggression and violence in
males is compounded by a concomitant emphasis on goal achievement. In all parts of hegemonic male culture, goals are most important.
Whether the target is a high-level corporate job, a wife and two kids in
the suburbs, or a simultaneous orgasm with one's sexual partner, the
process itself is less important than reaching the end. This focus on the
goal obviously precludes evaluating whether, in fact, it is necessary,
and why, or whether the chosen means might be harmful to oneself or
others. In the peer group, goal achievement can be a way of earning
membership in the desired group. Through increasing levels of dares
and taunts, boys can be cajoled or bullied into drinking, drugs, break-
and-enters, and crimes of violence against people in an effort to fit in.[130]
It is not good enough to just be who one is; one has to have accomplished something highly valued by the group. Unfortunately, the
achievable goals frequently involve the degradation of women.

Devaluation of Women. The peer group reinforces for young males many
of the values they have already learned within their family of origin.
The devaluation of women occurs in two ways. The first involves the
multitude of putdowns males hurl at their female peers. While the
focus typically is on the young woman's physical attributes, the jeers
also may include comments about her personality or her social skills.

The second form of devaluation often is not recognized as such: it is the practice of idolizing women and putting them on pedestals. Traditionally this has been considered complimentary, but many women have realized there is not much room to manoeuvre up on a pedestal. In fact, the very situation strengthens a variety of hegemonic femininity that is drastically confining; it allows women only certain actions and beliefs, thus restricting – rather than widening – their options.

Whether men are condemning women or complimenting them ultimately amounts to the same thing: women are objectified. A full human person, complete with a history, emotions, life experiences, potential, and a soul, is transformed into a thing with 'a fat ass' or 'huge tits.' Objectification is an important prerequisite for violence. It is certainly easier to beat and rape an entity which you do not treat as human, something which is perceived as an object; it is considerably more difficult to push Diane or Joanne down the stairs than a 'fucking bitch' or a 'whore.' Meanwhile objectification of women into *Playboy* Bunnies, or *Penthouse* Pets, is no less effective in diminishing their humanity. The end result is a decrease in the inhibiting factor of compassion, which in turn facilitates violence. Objectification of women is discovered repeatedly during interviews with men who have been violent to women.[131]

High Levels of Conformity. Conformity has been defined as 'a change in a person's behaviour or opinions as a result of real or imagined pressure from a person or group of people.'[132] An increasing body of evidence substantiates that the pressure to conform is too often irresistible. Conformity, however, is not a simple *fait accompli*; there are many factors involved that influence when, where, whether, and to what degree we will change our behaviour to fit with others.

One of the earliest studies on conformity was Solomon Asch's work with groups of people evaluating the length of various lines. In one box were three lines of different lengths. In another was one line, identical in length to one of the three in the first box. The differences among the lines were substantial enough to make it fairly easy to determine which of the first three lines the single line equalled. What pressured subjects to conform was the use of experimenter confederates who would respond according to a predetermined plan. By manipulating the situations in which individuals were asked to respond, Asch obtained a number of important results. If the subject was asked first to respond, the answer was likely to be correct. If one other person answered first with an incorrect answer, the subject was not likely to conform. However, when the opposition was increased to two, the outnumbered subject would accept the wrong answer 13.6 per cent of the time. If three opposed, the subject's error was 31.8 per cent. Raising the ratio higher than three to one did not significantly increase the conformity. What did make a big difference was having just one person side with the subject. Subjects were likely to answer incorrectly only 25 per cent as often as under the pressure of a unanimous majority. Asch also verified that having a partner, and then being deserted by him or her, dramatically increased conformity. Other factors included the credibility of the dissenters or the ally to the subject; it is easier to disagree with people with whom one does not want to be associated.[133]

The problem, of course, is that within a peer group, one generally is trying to fit in. Thus the levels of males conforming to other males are high. Elliot Aronson contends that there are at least three responses to social influence. Compliance is the first. The person agrees to behave in a specific manner only as long as there is either promise of a tangible reward or a threat of punishment. Identification is the second. This involves the person trying to be like the influencer. As with compliance, we are only emulating a specific behaviour. Identification, however, involves a degree of believing in the values or opinions we adopt where compliance does not. The third response is internalization. This is the 'most permanent, most deeply rooted response to social influence.' At this point one has completely adopted the values or actions as one's own. Once it reaches this stage, the influencer is of little importance any more. The value has become the individual's and will be extremely resistant to change.[134]

We do not know where all men stand in relation to these three responses to social pressure. It appears that most men have internalized an acceptance of the violence against women. The particular actions, however, will vary among individuals, depending upon what they have internalized about what is acceptable. Yet, at another level, whether or not a man has gone so far as to internalize misogynist values is less important than the fact that all too often, even if it is only at the level of being willing to comply with the prevailing social influence, men will commit acts of emotional, physical, and sexual violence against women.

It is within this context that the destructive effect of men's silence on violence against women must be placed. With Asch's results, one can anticipate what the effect could be of just one male in a peer group speaking out against, for instance, a sexist joke, or arguing that No really does mean No. If he finds just one ally in the group, it increases the likelihood of others not conforming to the group majority. If he remains silent it will increase the social pressure on other group members to conform. While speaking out may not change the views of those who have internalized misogynistic values, those who are just complying or identifying with those values may suddenly be willing to dissent. Most men to date, however, have been content to maintain, rather than to break, the silence that perpetuates male violence against women.

Among the men who are content to be silent, many are willing to move toward violence. Another famous experiment on conformity, conducted by Stanley Milgram, illustrates the degree to which humans will hurt one another in order to 'fit in.' Milgram's classic 1963 study involved naïve subjects agreeing to 'administer increasingly more severe punishments to a victim in the context of a learning experiment.' The subjects utilized a shock generator that had thirty graded switches ranging from 'Slight Shock' to 'Danger: Severe Shock.' Of the forty subjects, twenty-six obeyed the experimenter's commands and administered the highest shock, while fourteen broke off the experiment once the victim protested and refused to continue answering questions. Though Milgram observed expected signs of tension such as sweating and trembling, he also witnessed the 'regular occurrence of nervous laughter, which in some [subjects] developed into uncontrollable seizures.'[135]

Conformity is by no means limited to the male gender – but it is particularly dangerous when one considers that high levels of conformity are occurring within groups of individuals who systematically devalue women.

Conclusions on the Role of the Peer Group

Admittedly, the peer group is not the only context in which men learn, or relearn, violence toward women. For many males it may start in the family or with the media's portrayal of women and men. But the peer group is a fundamental and, for many men, the crucial, learning ground. Peer groups influence many boys into either compliance or identification with, or internalization of, hegemonic masculinity and its myths about male sexuality, and the consequent acceptability of using emotional, physical, or sexual violence against women to achieve a desired goal.

Like the individual male, the peer group as an entity is influenced by many social forces. One of the chief means by which many male peer groups acquire their misogynist values is the consumption of large quantities of pornography. Its role in encouraging male violence against women bears some examination.

PORNOGRAPHY

While pornography appears to have existed at least as far back as ancient Greek times,[136] the current multi-billion-dollar global industry dates primarily from 1945. Several factors explain why a significant, and until then American-led market suddenly expanded worldwide in the middle of the twentieth century.

The United States had recently finished fighting the Second World War and the Korean War. Millions of American servicemen had received extensive military training, if not actual combat experience, and been exposed to wartime propaganda extolling the virtues of a military brand of masculinity. War heroes were tough, fearless, uncompromising, and fiercely independent. As regards the feminine ideal, these men had grown accustomed to the scantily or provocatively clothed 'pin-ups' of the 1940s and 1950s. The Betty Grables and Lana Turners were provided to ensure that the American GI would remember what awaited him back home, and would not waver in his commitment to battle.

When the wars ended, however, and the soldiers returned home, the structure of the domestic economy and of society was not such as to easily allow them to uphold the wartime hegemonic brand of masculinity. Soldiers, while still needed to maintain the global U.S. postwar economy, were much less in demand. This was the grey-flannel-suit era; conformity to a new variety of masculinity was encouraged and, indeed, rampant. As Barbara Ehrenreich argues, the expectation for American men in the immediate postwar period was to obtain a good job, get married, buy a house, have a couple of children, live in the suburbs, and spend summers at the cottage.[137]

The sharp contrast between the varieties of masculinity expected of the heroic soldier and of the grey-suited office worker eventually led to a male rebellion. While many men were happy with the security and lifestyle, the masculinity of the grey flannel suit was too claustrophobic for men raised on images of wartime heroism. They were looking for something more.[138]

It was in this context, with the publication of the first issue of *Playboy* in December 1953, that Hugh Hefner heralded a new era in pornography. As a way of packaging pornography for the masses, *Playboy* advocated a new lifestyle for middle-class heterosexual men who, according to the magazine's editorial position, were overly burdened by family obligations. Hefner secured for himself at least thirty years' worth of prosperity by creating and marketing a fantasy of wealth, no commitments, and fabulously beautiful women ravenous for sex.[139]

Packaging was all-important. Early advertisements informed readers that *Playboy* was a trend-setter; no longer did one need to carry home a 'dirty magazine' in a plain brown wrapper and keep it hidden under the mattress. Consumers were assured that this was a 'men's magazine' they could readily leave on the coffee-table without fear of ridicule.

Although *Playboy* was promoted as a great novelty, in actual fact it was not a quantum leap from the wartime cheesecake photos of Betty Grable straightening the seams in her nylons or Lana Turner stretching the seams of her sweater to the premier issue of *Playboy* – showcasing Marilyn Monroe, at the time one of America's newest starlets, stretched out on the red satin sheets of a large bed, various parts of her body strategically exposed. The real shift precipitated by *Playboy* was not just the increased production of images of naked women. What *Playboy* was selling was a philosophy, a lifestyle, which legitimized the increased consumption of these visual images.

The values associated with the magazine and lifestyle included being uncommitted to a relationship, exuberant heterosexuality, and making lots of money and not having to share it with a wife or children. This lifestyle, though in part a rejection of postwar hegemonic masculinity, actually facilitated the U.S.-dominated economic order through the exploitation of women. Many men were unhappy with having to conform to the pressures of large bureaucratic corporate organizations. They feared that the grey flannel suit was threatening their masculinity. With *Playboy*, however, they could escape to another world that featured frequent, unbridled heterosexual encounters, where they were in control.

The exact number of men who achieved all the components of the *Playboy* lifestyle is not important. *Playboy* was selling *the perception that it was possible*. Suddenly, through the objectification of women, the dull corporate job became less oppressive. Office work could be a means to an end; other options existed, even if only as escape fantasies. The hot sales figures from *Playboy*'s inaugural issue verified it had found a ready market.[140] These figures also announced the arrival of a modern slave trade.

Important similarities and differences exist between this and the last major slave trade, which from the sixteenth to the nineteenth centuries transported primarily black men from Africa to provide a cheap labour resource for the expanding agricultural economies of the New World. While this human commodity exchange was eventually abolished, many would argue that an equally exploitive version has arisen in our time, with women as the major victims.

While the former slave trade used to sell whole humans, the current one sells them both whole and in portions – packaged for various specialty markets. Magazines, movies, and videos offer gigantic breasts, shaved vulvas, whipped buttocks, leather-wrapped torsos, and more. Though only blacks were sold in the past, today's pornographers will trade in any colour of flesh. They know that if a specific race is not popular with the majority of the pornography-consuming public, they can peddle their wares to the specialty market where certain buyers may have a fetish for it. The pornography industry mixes and matches its products to ensure that there is something for every consumer's most bizarre taste.

A woman's earning power within the pornography industry reflects the degree to which she mirrors the current ideal goal for a traditional female: young, slim, and fit. A woman falling short on these criteria, however, is not necessarily discarded by the industry. In the best – or worst – sense of free enterprise, such a woman can make herself marketable if she is willing to provide a unique product. Will she douche with whipping cream, apple pie filling, or chlorine bleach? Perhaps she can copulate with a canine or pose as a schoolgirl in knee-socks, or perform fellatio on an entire football team? Such are the wonders of the current pornography industry that each and every working woman can create a niche for herself and make a career. But she must do it quickly – wrinkles are one thing the industry does not tolerate, and production costs escalate when time is spent airbrushing them out.

Not unexpectedly, proponents of the multi-billion-dollar industry struggle to protect their profits. They defend the magazines, films, videos, and stage shows as legitimate business ventures providing an important form of entertainment for an established market. Despite frequent allegations of substantial links with an underground economy funded by international drug smuggling, many within the business take a very high moral position to defend their product. They allege that women are not forced to enlist and that the effects of the industry are only positive. They say it makes the consumers feel good and employs thousands. Who could complain? Of the ten most profitable magazines in the United States, six are classified as 'men's entertainment' ventures; the top two, *Playboy* and *Penthouse*, combined outsell *Time* and *Newsweek* combined. In the United States, the pornography industry is larger than the film and music industries combined. Pornographic video cassettes outsell non-pornographic cassettes by a ratio of three to one. Pornographers allow that since the 1960s their annual profits have shot from $5 million to $5 billion. This profit level need not be surprising. A well-situated so-called adult bookshop, peep show, and live show can pull in over $10,000 each day. And there is no shortage of adult bookshops: 20,000 across North America, according to one estimate, which would mean that they outnumber McDonald's restaurants by four to one. Pornography is a capitalist success story; it is 'America's most profitable frontier.' For years, pornographers' claims went virtually unchallenged. This is no longer the case, however; the critics have gathered strength.[141]

The original opposition to pornography came from various churches. Their main concern was with the display of flesh and with the verbal and pictorial acknowledgment that people could be sexual and sexually active. It was deemed important to keep a strict rein on parishioners' morality, as many church officials believed it blasphemous to engage in sex for any other purpose than procreation. Extramarital sex, of course, was of increased concern, but even sex with one's marital partner was declared sinful if undertaken for the sake of pleasure alone. For many years, churches were the pornographers' major opponents.

Things changed during the 1960s. The power of most churches eroded and their weekly attendance plummeted. A generation of young people was actively challenging religious doctrine and rejecting many of the remaining repressive remnants of nineteenth-century Victorianism so closely tied with most Western religions. People felt that for too long individuals had been prevented from, or chastised for, enjoying their bodies. We were not to touch ourselves or others in a sexual manner – or at least we were not to admit to it. We were to keep the body covered as much as possible – even when swimming – for naked flesh was sinful. Yet, in rebelling against this claustrophobic, deprived perspective, we ran full speed in the wrong direction. Feminist writer and artist Kate Millett argues that instead of embracing erotica, we were hoodwinked into accepting pornography; the pornography industry burgeoned by manipulating a sincere desire for a less repressive sexuality into legitimization of an exploitive product.[142] By the end of the 1960s, the industry was enjoying its most unfettered period. This tranquillity, however, did not last long.

In the early 1970s, the emerging women's movement began to raise significant opposition to pornography. Feminists had little difficulty with nudity and, in fact, often celebrated it as a welcome move away from the earlier repression of sensuality; obviously, though, pornography is far more than just nudity. Feminists were angered by the flagrant and violent display of power by men over women. Violence was the key factor. The repeated images of women on their knees, or handcuffed, or – in one famous instance in *Hustler* – being put through a meat grinder, or in some other way being violated or degraded, while still voraciously desiring any available man, woman, or, for that matter, animal or broomstick, precipitated many local and national efforts to resist or ban pornography.[143]

The debate over censorship has been difficult. Part of the problem has been the use by pornographers of the Western world's belief in freedom of the press to defend their business ventures.[144] The difficulty for many feminists opposed to pornography has involved establishing a workable definition of what in fact constitutes pornographic material. At a general level, most would concur that pornography involves the visual or auditory display of sexual actions which are demeaning and violent toward women. This definition, however, is too subjective. How do we as a society establish a consensual agreement as to which images are demeaning to women? While most people may agree that chain-saw massacre and violent rape scenes are pornographic, there are many scenes in magazines and movies which fall less definitely into this category. Many people may contend that a picture of a kneeling woman performing fellatio on two standing males portrays a power imbalance between the men and the woman and thus is pornographic. Yet does that picture suddenly become non-pornographic if accompanied by an image portraying the two men performing cunnilingus on the woman? What is one person's pornography may be another's erotica.

Trying to define what pornography is has been complicated by the disparity of the various groups that have coalesced in censorship campaigns. It has been an interesting mix of political philosophies, what with radical feminists frequently joining forces with right-wing conservatives. Their reasons for wanting to limit or ban pornography are generally very different. Pro-censorship feminists want to end the production of material that encourages exploitation of and violence against women. The more right-wing elements of the coalition appear less concerned with violence than with restricting the availability of material which they believe is contributing to the erosion of moral values in our society.[145]

On the other side of the censorship debate are many feminists who, while no less appalled by the misogyny central to pornography, fear the potential outcome of censorship legislation. They know from past examples that the track record has not been promising for exploited social groups.[146] The very laws created to ban pornography could be used to silence birth-control counselling, AIDS prevention programs, art displays, and even free speech. Although initially intended to protect women, such laws could be used by specific powerful groups to fulfil various items on the social conservative agenda. The political goals could be 'anti-sex education, anti-gay rights, anti-pornography, anti-ERA, anti-abortion amendments and anti-evolution.'[147]

The pornography and censorship debate has become something of a stalemate. Pro-censorship activists have continued to try and restrict the sale and distribution of pornography. The major effort by anti-censorship feminists has been to encourage significant changes in social values by asking numerous questions about the consumption of pornography. For example, if a man spends his lunch hour watching a film in which a female office worker, apparently in unbridled lust, suddenly rips off her clothes and those of her male co-workers in order to hold an orgy on the office floor, is this not going to affect how he views the women in his office upon his return from the theatre? Is he going to see them in a different way? Will the women appear less like skilled, knowledgeable professionals and more like sexual commodities? How successfully will he separate the film 'fantasy' from reality? How many men, having viewed the same film, will want to *make* that fantasy their reality? In short, how does pornography affect the way in which men relate to women? This question has motivated a cadre of researchers to look for answers. Their findings, while not yet complete, confirm three major fears of feminists.

Desensitization to Violence against Women

Numerous researchers are showing, through laboratory investigations, that media portrayals of aggression against women generally result in more negative attitudes toward, and increase aggression against, women.[148] Daniel Linz, Edward Donnerstein, and Steven Penrod, for example, have shown that 'men who viewed five movies depicting violence against women came to have fewer negative emotional reactions to the films, to perceive them as significantly less violent, and to consider them significantly less degrading to women.'[149]

Neil Malamuth was one of the first researchers to point to the connection between viewing filmed pornographic violence and increased levels of aggression against women. He had males view either aggressive or non-aggressive pictorials from *Penthouse* magazine that had been judged to be equally sexually arousing. The aggressive stimulus pictures implied that the woman was sexually aroused by rape. The non-aggressive pictures depicted mutually consenting sex. In order to reduce inhibition against aggression, half of the subjects were told that it was acceptable to behave as aggressively as desired. After the stimuli, subjects were insulted by a female confederate and allowed to give her electric shocks if they chose. The males who viewed the violent pornography and received the disinhibitory message delivered significantly more shocks than those who had not.[150]

The work of other researchers has supported these results. Edward Donnerstein, for example, had his male subjects either angered or treated in a neutral manner, then exposed to either a non-aggressive pornographic film, an aggressive pornographic film, or a neutral film. Upon viewing the films, subjects were given the opportunity to aggress against a male confederate of the experimenter; others were paired with a female confederate. The combination of exposure to aggressive pornography, a high level of pre-exposure anger, and pairing with a female confederate led to the highest level of aggression. Also of significance, even non-angered male subjects exposed to violent pornography showed substantially higher levels of aggressive behaviour when paired with a female confederate.[151]

There also is growing research verification for what many have argued for years, namely, that pornography devalues women not only in men's eyes but also in their own. Suzin Mayerson and Dalmas Taylor investigated the effects of reading pornography on women's self-esteem and their attitudes about rape and interpersonal violence and how these effects were mediated by a woman's degree of sex-role stereotyping (SRS). They had ninety-six undergraduate females, rated at various levels of SRS, read one of three sexually explicit stories portraying different combinations of a woman's consent to (or absence of consent to), and arousal by (or absence of arousal by), forceful sexual activity. They found that differences attributable to the consent and arousal manipulations were minimal. Yet, compared to not reading a story, reading it generally led to changes in self-esteem and greater acceptance of rape myths and interpersonal violence. Individuals indicating high SRS generally reported lower self-esteem and more tolerance of rape and other violence.[152] This is particularly disturbing in that we know that women with high SRS or women whose self-esteem is weakened are significantly less likely than other women to report assaults or seek help.

To compound the pornography problem, there has recently emerged the argument that its effects on men may in fact be short-lived. After examining individual subjects' self-reported likelihood to rape (LR), Neil Malamuth and Joseph Ceniti have speculated that, depending on the degree, LR may be an important factor in buffering the effects of pornography. Males who had a high LR score did rate high on their likelihood to act violently against women. But the results did not indicate that repeated exposure to violent or non-violent pornography had a significant effect on laboratory aggression in the longer term. Malamuth and Ceniti's work has important parallels with that of L. Berkowitz on media effects. All three warn that one should not trivialize the significance of an apparently short-lived effect from viewing violence. While short-lived, it is sufficient to stimulate the viewer's existing behavioural tendencies. Berkowitz alleges that there may be 'retrieval cues,' found in our environment, which will reactivate an earlier message portrayed in the media and again strengthen the potential expression of behavioural inclinations. The Malamuth and Ceniti study, likewise, revealed that the effects of pornography may not end completely after a short time, as they may mix with previously held views through the presence of a retrieval cue. The absence of a retrieval cue of some sort may well prevent the violence from being exhibited; once it appears, however, the effects may be displayed.[153]

This idea that violent pornography, though not directly causing men to be violent, may in fact reinforce previously held views is supported by a growing body of researchers. They argue that by the time males encounter pornography, even as adolescents, they have already internalized many of society's negative values about women.[154] Yet even if we were to definitively determine that pornography only reinforces, instead of creating, values dangerous to women, or that its effects may only be short-lived, there is still substantial reason to be concerned.

The extensive availability of pornography and the annual volume of sales make it appear that a large portion of our adult male population are pornography addicts.[155] Because pornography is always available in some form, be it on videotape or on paper, the effects, however short-lived, can be produced frequently and repeatedly. The *cumulative* effects, meanwhile, may be more long-lasting. Furthermore, even if pornography does not create, but only reinforces, negative values, what we reinforce in this generation, we are establishing for the next. Even if pornography reinforces only one man's views against women, that man plays an important role in the creation of his son's and daughter's views about women.

Linking Sex and Violence

Feminists argued that the display of sex in combination with violence, and not sex itself, was the problem. The emerging evidence indicates that their concerns were well-founded. It is the level of violence in a society rather than sexual explicitness that affects women's safety; research indicates that it is erroneous to assume high sexual explicitness ensures high levels of violence.

Ted Palys, a criminologist at Simon Fraser University, wanted to determine if the advent of home video technology was increasing the market and, consequently, the availability of sexual, aggressive, and sexually aggressive material. The experiment involved the selection of 58 videos that were classified in the video outlets as 'Adult' (or single-X) and 92 that were labelled triple-X.[156] While all the videos were gathered from various outlets in and around Vancouver, Canada, 89 per cent of the videos had been produced in the United States, 4 per cent in Canada, and 7 per cent in Europe. As anticipated, the triple-X videos depicted considerably more sexually explicit content than the adult videos. Quite unexpectedly, however, the adult videos 'contained significantly more aggressive and sexually aggressive content, and depicted this violence with significantly greater severity.'[157]

Palys's results also helped dispel a popular notion that videos had become more violent. He found no significant increase in aggressive images between 1979 and 1983 for either the triple-X or adult videos; indeed, he noted that the triple-X videos had become less sexually violent.

This information signals our need to be aware of the effect of images of violence against women in pornography and in the media generally.

It is these images which encourage and reinforce male violence against women, particularly sexual assault. Sexually violent media images typically are versions of rape scenes which are a fusion of violence with sexual content. Many of these images, by portraying women as wanting and enjoying the violence, reflect the third detrimental effect of pornography: it perpetuates various myths that are supportive of sexual assault.

Pornography Creates and Reinforces Several Sexual Assault Myths

Myth 1: Men rape because of uncontrollable sexual urges. This belief portrays male sexuality as an autonomous instinct and, like all the myths, absolves the man of all responsibility for his actions. It implies that the woman is responsible for making sure that she does not precipitate a sexual assault through any actions or dress that could sexually arouse the male. In reality, sex drive is a learned behaviour, part of sexual socialization; in our society, boys learn that to satisfy their sex drive, they have a right to use – or abuse – any woman at any time. Yet, if sex drive is so instinctual, studies would not show that 71 per cent of sexual assaults are planned in advance, or that only 11 per cent are between strangers.[158]

This myth also subtly coerces women into feeling they have to participate in sex when they do not want to, for fear of physical effects (for example, that once a man is sexually aroused it can harm his sexual organs if he does not ejaculate) and/or of emotional consequences (it is better to submit than to get him angry or upset). This situation is often referred to as 'grey rape.'

Myth 2: It is not really possible to rape a non-consenting adult female (i.e., no woman can really be raped against her will). Implicit in this myth is the belief that there is in fact no such thing as sexual assault; a woman must consent to sexual intercourse for it to occur. This ignores the reality that fear physically and psychologically impedes, if not completely paralyses, a woman's ability to resist and thereby prevent assault. Not only do 82 per cent of the sexual assaults in Canada involve verbal threats or threats with a weapon, but also women are in general socialized to be passive and not fight back.[159]

This myth removes the responsibility from the man by implying that if the woman really wants to, she can stop the assault. It is this myth that often impairs a woman's recovery from the post-assault feelings of self-doubt, guilt, shame, and blame. Unless the woman has been severely beaten and bruised, police, hospital workers, clinicians, friends, family, and the victim herself will often believe, at some level, that she did not adequately resist and thus, in effect, consented to the attack. There is a preposterous double standard at work here. If, for example, a person is robbed of a wallet, the violation is validated regardless of whether he or she was physically beaten. (Muggings usually happen without severe visible physical trauma to the victim.) Sexual assaults, however, must result in blood, bruises, and broken bones to be authentic; otherwise there is an assumption that the woman was 'just wanting it.'[160]

Myth 3: 'Nice girls' do not get sexually assaulted. This myth gives the false impression that if a woman conforms to the current, socially prescribed notion of nice-girl behaviour, she will be immune to sexual assault. It is predicated on the assumption that there is an absolute way of judging what is 'nice' and what is 'loose' or 'bad.' Yet even if there were some collectively agreed-upon distinctions, one must ask why 'loose' women should be more deserving of sexual assault than any others. It is a no-win situation for women. Society, on the one hand, says women are supposed to be attractive and alluring, yet, on the other, blames them for their provocative appearance if they are sexually assaulted.

The fact is all women are vulnerable to sexual assault; virtue is no guarantee of freedom from it. And in any case, a woman's consent – not her socially evaluated level of virtue – should be the only criterion for a sexual interaction.[161]

Myth 4: Women ask to be raped ... and probably enjoy it. Once again, the woman is held responsible for behaviour that a man or men may interpret as an invitation for sexual assault. If she does not avoid certain behaviours, she takes the consequences. One problem is that virtually any action by a female could be construed as 'asking for it.' Not surprisingly, many males in our society feel that women who step beyond certain unspoken limits (e.g., by walking alone at night) are subconsciously asking to be sexually assaulted. Belief in this myth undoubtedly puts tremendous constraints on women's activities and behaviour. It is an important form of social control. However, even if our society could codify the unspoken limits, and women did conform to them, they still would not be safe from sexual assault; it happens just as often to women asleep at home or opening their doors to allow in service personnel.[162]

Myth 5: Most rapists are mentally ill. This myth as well removes responsibility for the assault from the man. It says that the man who sexually assaults is mentally disturbed, is not rational, and is therefore not responsible for his actions. Yet numerous studies disprove this, showing that fewer than 5 per cent of all men who sexually assault were psychotic at the time of the assault.[163] So, if indeed the vast majority of sexual assaults are committed by normal males, this myth has two serious effects. First, it wrongly blames a segment of our population that already is largely maligned and ostracized. The myth says that rapists are mentally ill – and therefore, it is assumed, all mentally ill males are rapists. This works to isolate many individuals who, as it is, are struggling for a place in society – to say nothing of dealing with mental illness itself. Second, the 'most rapists are mentally ill' myth encourages women to trust all other 'normal' males. This myth often gets combined with the 'nice girls don't get raped' myth: the woman assaulted by an acquaintance might conclude that by somehow failing to be 'nice' she was responsible – because, after all, he was such a nice 'normal' guy.

How Do These Myths Affect Us?

Sexual assault myths have been defined as false beliefs about sexual assault 'which seek to deny or make light of its effects on the victim, in fact blame the [sexual assault] on the victim.'[164] Sexual assault is a function of a certain kind of society which historically and traditionally defines women as the property and possessions of men, and men as patriarchs, breadwinners, and rulers. People are accorded status, authority, control, and power in part according to their gender.

As with any social or political value system, the ideology it represents becomes entrenched in the day-to-day functioning of the society. With little or no resistance to the ideology, it becomes accepted as reality, as truth. Moreover, it becomes internalized by both women and men and, consequently, shapes their beliefs and attitudes. When those beliefs dictate distorted definitions of and responses to sexual assault, or deny or trivialize its effects on the victim, or work to perpetuate male-oriented conceptions of sexual assault on the victim, they create a mythology of attitudes and beliefs around sexual assault.[165]

The feminist movement has repeatedly argued that male socialization involves learning how to be violent to women.[166] Martha Burt, in an attempt to establish the connection between sexual violence and sociocultural supports for sexual assault, was the first to move from literary critique to operationalizing the concept of sexual assault myths. She empirically linked acceptance of these socially transmitted rape myths to stereotypic sex-role socialization, sexual conservativism, adversarial sexual beliefs (e.g., 'In a dating relationship, a woman is largely out to take advantage of a man'), and acceptance of interpersonal violence against women (e.g., 'Being roughed up is sexually stimulating to most women'). Burt found the myths to be at least partially endorsed by a majority of the university males she sampled.[167]

More recently, Neil Malamuth and colleagues have shown a direct relationship between acceptance of the attitudes described by Burt and self-reported likelihood of raping a woman if given hypothetical freedom from punishment. Briere, Corne, Runtz, and Malamuth reported that, across a variety of samples, approximately 35 per cent of college males admitted to some likelihood of sexually assaulting a woman under such circumstances.[168] Briere and Malamuth found that the level increased to 60 per cent when the men were asked if they would force a woman to engage in (unspecified) sexual behaviour.[169] Briere, Corne, Runtz, and Malamuth found that 75 per cent of their male subjects predicted they would experience at least some arousal while committing a hypothetical sexual assault. The researchers argue that sexual assault behaviour 'arises from the sexualization of aggression, dominance, and misogyny, such that sexual aggressors experience sexual arousal while engaging in violence toward women ... such "compound" arousal reflects the mechanism whereby cultural "needs" to dominate and control women are translated into individual motives for sexual aggression.'[170] It is as yet unclear whether a high self-reporting rate by an individual male given hypothetical freedom from punishment for a sexual assault is the same as that man's probability of actually sexually assaulting a woman. While more research is required, the emerging evidence is that 'normal' male sexuality appears to include aggression, dominance, and perhaps, to some extent, achievement. Thus, it is not necessarily only the poorly socialized male who sexually offends; indeed, it is any man who acts out what is socially conveyed to all contemporary men. Pornography plays a crucial role in the socialization of normally violent men, as it encourages males to perpetuate sexual and non-sexual violence against women, and teaches women to feel responsible for such crimes. The problem is not sexual explicitness; it is pornography's portrayal of violence against women and its fusion with hegemonic male heterosexuality.[171]

SPORT

Sport has many positive aspects. It can be a forum for learning about co-operation and healthy solidarity, setting and pursuing goals, building team spirit, seeking excellence, recognizing the value of losing as well as winning, and establishing a context for the healthy expression of aggression.[172] It can also be a vehicle enabling an individual to take better care of his or her mind and body; when one reviews the statistically average North American's high caloric intake, generally poor cardiovascular health, and propensity to watch rather than to participate in sports, it is clear that more physical activity is needed. The positive effects of sport are commonly acknowledged. What is not as widely recognized, however, is that sport also contributes to the creation of violent men. This section will focus on the manner in which this is accomplished.

Sport has many critics. Some have a strong class bias. The presumption is that it is not so much the team sports per se which cause the violence, as the greater representation of unemployed and working-class individuals within those sports.[173] This notion derives from a physiological myth that the lower classes are more violent than the more refined and wealthy – who are more likely to be involved in individual, rather than team, sports. If there are differences in the class composition of individual and team sports, this is more likely a function of working-class individuals simply not having the resources to engage in the typically more expensive individual sports than of a preference for team sports. Shooting a few baskets into a hoop on a vacant lot is feasible for most inner-city poor; escaping to the mountains for downhill skiing is not. There do not exist any studies indicating that when the wealthy are involved, the levels of violence are significantly less.

Sport both mirrors and perpetuates the class divisions within our society. At one level, there are many noble ideals about sport as a great leveller between the classes. On the playing field all are to be equal. It is the skill of the players that is being tested and nothing else. The reality, however, is different. Children of the wealthy can afford better equipment and coaches. Even when the poor kids win a game at the expense of the wealthy, the victory does not immediately alter the relations between the classes. Mike Messner has said that it is not uncommon for a losing team of rich kids to assuage their sorrow with a team cheer: 'That's all right, that's OK, you'll be working for us someday!'[174]

Other critics of sport, arguing that it is not the class origins of individual players that is of concern, have focused on large team sports as the real culprit in the creation of violent men. They emphasize sport's perpetuation and glorification of male violence through large, organized team competitions such as hockey, football, soccer, baseball, and basketball.[175] Many parents also fear that their community and high-school leagues may contribute to this process. They recognize that, whether at the local or the professional level, sport frequently becomes more valued as a vehicle for earning money, prestige, and power for those involved; winning becomes more important than playing the game.

While these criticisms of team sports are valid, numerous individual sports such as boxing, weight-lifting, fencing, javelin, and shotput also can contribute traits which encourage male violence. It is not simply the type of sport that is the problem, but rather the social context in which it is undertaken. This involves all that is associated with organizing, teaching, practising, evaluating, or advertising the game. Engaging in physical activity – team or individual – can expose an individual to powerful pressure to conform to the currently hegemonic notions of masculinity and femininity. It is in this sense that sport has contributed to some very dangerous traditions.

Sport Encourages a Deference to Authority

The large and necessarily hierarchical structure of team sports can encourage in the individual a greater deference to authority. John Mitzel, in *Sports and the Macho Male*, has provided one of the best critiques of sport's role in creating a hierarchy which encourages deference among individuals. He points to all that is involved in selection of those who get to play the specific sport, in the training needed to regiment them, in the submission to a greater authority as a requirement of a team effort, and in the broader context, in the exploitation of men, women, and children to manipulate them into fans. He recognizes the importance of the team hierarchy to which all adhere: rookies, seasoned players, captains, assistant coaches, head coaches, managers, and owners.[176] The existence of this system, with its rules and regulations, can be very restrictive for the individual player.

Too often the primary overt or covert goal is to create a winning team, and the degree of regimentation needed to achieve this can be very harmful to the development of the individual. Coming late for practice, not working one's hardest (in the estimation of the coach), or merely questioning the content and duration of the exercises can get one thrown out of the organization. If a person does persist, he or she may be subjected to gruelling practices under some less-than-desirable conditions – for instance, very early in the morning or late at night. Children are often tired and tears are not uncommon as the kids agonize over not achieving the perfection desired by their coaches, parents, or team-mates. Already rampant numbers of sports injuries are escalated by the pressure on children to do physical things that are not natural for any human, or that should only be undertaken when the body is more mature. One example is the pressure on boys not to throw a baseball 'like a girl' – which is to say, in more of a shotput style, with the hand and ball starting behind the ear and the elbow leading the way. Drilled into young boys is the fear of derision if they do not throw 'like a man' – pulling the arm straight back as far as it will go and snapping the ball overhand past the ear. This is done despite the evidence that 'throwing like a girl' is actually more anatomically more correct for the human arm, and the fact that many Little League Pitchers seriously damage their shoulders.[177] It is clear that the intent here is not simply to teach a sport, but rather to identify a specific type of activity as masculine and thus afford it significantly more value. Those who achieve this skill can win the rights of privilege; those who fail suffer the scorn of the crowd.

The parallels to military basic training are unmistakable. As in the army, young recruits are moulded through physical and emotional endurance tests to obtain the skills and embrace the values of hegemonic masculinity. Mitzel emphasizes that for men sport is an important training ground for the military life. Physical fitness and a willingness to defer to authority are two attributes needed to advance within the ranks of the army. Mitzel argues that the sport and military hierarchies are very similar, as evidenced particularly by the support afforded each by our society. Robert Kennedy, at one time the U.S. attorney general, recognized the links between sport and the military: 'Except for war, there is nothing in American life – nothing – which trains a boy better for life than football.'[178]

Whether in the military, in sport, or elsewhere, becoming part of a larger whole can be a very positive and rewarding experience. One can feel supported by other individuals while the group cooperates to pursue similar goals. Yet problems can arise in group settings when individuals relinquish some, or all, responsibility for their thoughts, principles, and actions. This may help lead the team to victory. But reducing one's ability to question or dissent from a perceived group consensus can be very dangerous; it can, in some contexts, facilitate male violence.

As was seen in the examination of the peer group, individuals may lose their capacity to disagree with the group's goal. At a larger level, this is part of what occurs every time citizens put their unquestioned faith in their leaders. The phenomenon of Nazi Germany is an extreme example of what can occur when we abandon individual reasoning to defer to a larger authority. Another example – this one more related to the experiences of many women – is the deference to authority that occurs among a group of men when they gang rape a woman. Studies repeatedly indicate that many of the males involved in a gang rape do so more to fit in with a group of males, or out of fear of disagreeing with the perceived group consensus that it is acceptable for men to abuse women, than out of a desire to rape.[179] Yet another example – this one being more common and socially acceptable – is when men in a group chuckle as their peers joke or talk about being violent to the women in their lives.[180] Once again, while their thoughts may differ, they defer to the group, and their responses support the violence. In both examples, whether the men are too afraid to stand on their own, or recognize the potential rewards for being part of the group, or are being goaded by an individual male within the group who is testing the loyalty of the other group members, the violence toward women is condoned. As is too often the case, a woman's body is the testing ground for male rivalry.

Sport Reinforces Hegemonic Masculinity and Its Links with Violence

One of the key components of most sporting activities is competition. It is not an inherently evil quality. Competition can be an incentive to improve one's skill and performance levels.[181] It is something different, though, when winning the game becomes the overriding reason for playing. This reinforces the goal-focused component of hegemonic masculinity. In order to win the game men may refuse to cooperate, be willing to disregard the needs of others, and ultimately use physical force to achieve a goal – and they are generally rewarded by society for having done so.

The social context in which sport occurs too frequently gives positive reinforcement only to hegemonic masculine behaviour – win at all costs, might is right, and cooperate only if it helps you reach your goal. It is from engaging in sports that many adolescent males first learn they are 'not man enough' to compete and endure the derision of their peers and family. A male not interested in being overly competitive or aggressive quickly learns that if he does not want to be excluded from a team or a highly valued peer group, he needs to play the game like the 'big boys.' If he has not already done so, he may bury his sensitivity. He hides his interest in things such as plants, insects, flowers, or the creation of beauty. Instead, he crushes, stomps on, and obliterates anything in his path that may betray his tenderness or vulnerability. One thinks of a twelve-year-old boy playing hockey. He tries his best with a shot on goal, but misses. Instead of commending his effort, the loudest roars from the crowd deride him for his incompetence, or question his sexual preference – as if this were something all twelve-year-olds have even sorted out, or as if being gay precludes the capacity to score a goal.[182] To win the approval of that crowd and of others, weight and barbell sets are purchased, by the parent, the son, or both, so he can bulk up his muscles to look like the stereotypical (super)man.[183]

The Charles Atlas scenario typifies the dreadful alternative if one does not measure up to the physical standards of hegemonic masculinity. If one is a 'ninety-eight-pound weakling,' like the protagonist, not only will one get sand kicked in one's face; there is the also the probability of losing one's girlfriend. Aside from not giving the girlfriend any cognitive capacity to decide with whom she wishes to spend her time, the ad epitomizes the way in which sport is sold as an important vehicle for conformity to hegemonic masculinity.

This form of masculinity also has been important to the nation-state. The connections between masculinity, sport, and the state, in fact, were central to the revival of the Olympic Games, the pinnacle of sporting events, by Baron Pierre de Coubertin in the late nineteenth century. Born in Paris in 1863 to a wealthy French family, de Coubertin witnessed first the humiliating defeat of his country in the Franco-Prussian War of 1870 and then the continued ascension of German and British power over France during the next several decades. He developed a belief that Frenchmen must be toughened up by sport in order to return their nation to its rightful place among world powers. He spent much of his life and his personal wealth in pursuit of this goal. That de Coubertin was able to achieve the re-establishment of the Games attests not just to his determination, but also to the receptiveness of other countries to the venture. This tradition of using the Olympics as a way of proving superiority – either the individual's or the nation's – continues unabated.[184]

For a long time in sport, there have been certain myths cultivated regarding the superiority or inferiority of specific groups of people. While it is not as easily done in the contemporary period, in the past sport was an important means of segregating sexes, races, and classes.[185] People of colour or those of the lower classes (which were often one and the same) at one time were not allowed to partake.[186] This began to change, however, after several important challenges to the colour bar – Satchel Paige struck out top white players in an exhibition game, Jesse Owens captured the gold at the 1936 Olympics in Berlin, and Jackie Robinson broke into the all-white baseball leagues.[187]

While the colour and class barriers have either become more subtle or have disappeared altogether, the division between the sexes continues – not until 1984, for example, were women officially permitted to run in the Olympic marathon. There is evidence that within the next few decades, male and female athletes may compete on an equal basis, thanks to the steadily declining gap in various performance records.[188] Yet many people in our society continue to firmly believe that girls and boys should or should not play various gender-coded sports.

The continuing popularity of such myths has prompted Lois Bryson to critically analyse connections between sport and hegemonic masculinity. Bryson argues that sport 'serves to ritually support an aura of male competence and superiority in publicly acclaimed skills, and a male monopoly of aggression and violence. A corollary of this is an inferiorization of women and their skills, and their isolation from the ultimate basis of social power – physical force.'[189]

Hegemonic men have largely appropriated sport and used it to perpetuate various class and gender inequities. One of the results is the pervasive manner in which sporting metaphors are used to describe actions valued within hegemonic masculinity and certain nation-states. In the discussion of sexual exploits, for example, certain phrases are common: 'Did you get to first base?' 'Did you steal a base?' 'Did you make it all the way to home?' 'Did you score?' (And if so, 'how many times?') When describing military activities, individuals may talk about a nation's 'first-strike' nuclear capacity, or accuse another country of 'not playing by the rules.'[190] Organized sport reinforces a notion central to traditional male culture that all male interaction – whether at the individual or national level – is adversarial and requires competitive skill and cunning to be practised successfully. Whatever the metaphor, the notion regarding women is the same. Like enemy territory during war, they are to be conquered and this is best done by able-bodied athletic hulks. Limp-wristed faggots need not apply.[191]

Summary

While many of the negative hegemonic traits reinforced by sport may be learned elsewhere, when one considers the large amount of time many men spend throughout their lives either participating in or watching sport,[192] this important agent of male socialization needs to be held accountable for its contribution.

THE SOCIAL CONSTRUCTION OF MASCULINITY: A SUMMARY

While each individual is unique as to the exact configuration of crucial influences in his life, a multitude of powerful social forces foster, allow, and legitimize male violence. All the major institutions within our society encourage men to be violent. When we realize that most males go through their lives moving from one agent of male socialization to another, or simultaneously under the influence of several, it becomes clear why most men do not openly reject hegemonic masculinity and its incumbent acceptance of violence against women. With this in mind, the levels of male violence discussed in chapter 1, though never excusable, become more understandable. That many of these agents have been dominating male culture for centuries makes the mentality of violence that much more ingrained.

An overwhelming majority of male spheres of activity do not encourage talking about one's feelings, acknowledging tenderness or vulnerability, or giving up control over people and situations. To open up and admit one's humanness within a traditional male value system is tantamount to admitting failure – not a highly respected quality among many men. But this role-playing is not done without cause. Men restrict the full range of human emotions in order to maintain their power over others or to perpetuate the illusion of being in control of themselves.

While some men have begun to look at the dysfunctional nature of the currently hegemonic male role as a factor in higher stress levels, heart attacks, and early deaths, typically the focus has been only on how it harms the individual male.[193] We must not ignore that it can also be life-threatening to others connected to him, his dependents and/or victims of abuse. The restriction of acceptable masculinities and the glorification of a hegemonic masculinity dangerous to women form a fundamental part of the problem. As long as this remains unchecked, male violence will not significantly decrease.

Yet despite the role our society plays in facilitating and legitimizing male violence, it cannot be held completely responsible. Our society also offers other ways of handling situations. The problem is that such ways often are afforded less respect or status by our society. Ultimately each man is responsible for his own behaviour: he can choose to be violent or not. Whether he learned his violence in his family of origin, through the media, from reading pornography, by hanging out with his friends, attending university, or playing football, he makes choices when he acts. It follows, then, that he can choose to reject violence.

Summary

Psychosocial factors are the main reasons for male violence in our society. Whatever the specific causes, which vary among individuals, our society, through numerous vehicles, generally creates violent men. The next two chapters will examine what has been done to treat male violence.

4 / A Critique of the Traditional Treatments of Male Violence against Women

The traditional response to male violence has been to either pretend it does not exist, or to accept it, or to seek various physiological or psychological explanations. The problem of male violence has been viewed as insignificant, and attributable mainly to individual – and frequently to female – pathology.

During the early 1970s the women's movement exposed numerous long-ignored factors which support male violence. Feminism was a major catalyst for developing social constructionist explanations and treatment.

The present chapter and the two that follow examine the difficulties of making the transition from traditional approaches to social constructionism. There are many clinical and political factors involved in moving toward, or away from, social constructionism. This chapter examines the two chief ones: the failure of the traditional treatments of male violence, and the women's movement as the major force pushing toward social constructionism. Chapter 5 analyses two major stages in the state response to male violence against women: family systems therapy, and a more extended social constructionist approach. Chapter 6 examines recent responses among men to the demands for an end to male violence against women. It will be evident that significant social changes must occur if male violence against women is to end.

Traditional Treatments of Male Violence

Three major realities predate the 1970s revival of feminism. These were: the existence of legislation authorizing male violence, a reliance upon physiological explanations and treatments, and the dismissal of male violence as a function of various intrapsychic disorders.

LEGISLATIVE SANCTIONS

For centuries, male violence against women was viewed as something completely normal, often necessary. While this tradition is beginning to break down, it is still far from extinct. Many men still want to exert physical power over women.

The actions of men were sanctified, while women were blamed for the smallest step beyond the acceptable and narrowly prescribed boundaries. R. Emerson Dobash and Russell Dobash, in *Violence against Wives: A Case against the Patriarchy*, have provided an excellent history of how men have legislated their power and control over women. Dobash and Dobash note that 'history is littered with references to, and formulas for, beating, clubbing, and kicking [women] into submission. Women's place in history often has been at the receiving end of a blow. This history is a long and sad one – sad because of the countless women who have been browbeaten, bruised, bloodied, and broken and sad because the ideologies and institutional practices that made such treatment both possible and justifiable have survived, albeit somewhat altered, from century to century and been woven into the fabric of our culture and are thriving today.'[1]

The following brief list illustrates the range of legislative sanctions throughout history.[2]

- One of the first marriage laws was proclaimed by Romulus, the legendary founder of Rome (753 BC). While outlining that the woman would share in the man's possessions and rites, it also 'obliged the married women, as having no other refuge, to conform themselves entirely to the temper of their husbands and the husbands to rule their wives as necessary and inseparable possessions.'[3]
- 'Roman husbands had the legal right to chastise, divorce, or kill their wives for engaging in behavior that they themselves engaged in daily. But it did not take something as extreme as marital infidelity to rouse the man of the house to raise club and boot – or sandal – to the erring wife. If she were caught tippling in the family wine cellar, attending public games without his permission, or walking outdoors with her face uncovered, she could be beaten.'[4]
- By the time the Punic Wars ended in 202 BC, significant social changes had occurred. Women had assumed many of the responsibilities previously held by men. While the laws restricting women were altered, the improvement was minimal; though there were fewer crimes for which women could be punished publicly, men were still encouraged to abuse their wives at home with whips or rods.[5]

- The rise of Christianity did little to improve the status of women or deal with male violence. Dobash and Dobash note that with regard to 'the relationship between husband and wife, it was not the revolutionary principles of equality but the retrogressive principles of patriarchy that were taken up most enthusiastically and vehemently by later Christians and that have largely prevailed.'[6]
- Throughout the medieval period, women were important commodities in the pursuit of building alliances or buying peace with other large households or political entities. With this shift, the concern over a woman's chastity increased significantly. For women, adultery was viewed as a grave property offence committed against the husband, or owner, and was severely punished. 'For example, in 1240, a Spanish woman who committed adultery could be killed with impunity by a husband or fiancé.'[7] 'The Italian adulteress was "severely flogged through the city streets … and exiled for three years."'[8] 'It was legal for a Frenchman to beat his wife when she wronged him by committing adultery, or by preparing to do so, or by refusing to obey him.'[9] 'The English husband was enjoined not to inflict bodily damage other than that which "pertains to the office of a husband for lawful and reasonable correction."'[10]
- In the city of Siena, Italy, men were cautioned not to beat their wives without good reason. 'You should beat her … only when she commits a serious wrong; for example, if she blasphemes against God or a saint, if she mutters the devil's name, if she likes being at the window and lends ready ear to dishonest young men, or if she has taken to bad habits or bad company, or commits some other wrong that is a mortal sin. Then readily beat her, not in rage but out of charity and concern for her soul, so that the beatings will redound to your merit and good.'[11]
- During the Protestant Reformation, Martin Luther's views on male violence were considered fairly progressive, compared to those of his contemporaries – he did not support public ridicule of women. Yet, even for Martin Luther, women's roles were very circumscribed: 'Men have broad shoulders and narrow hips, and accordingly they possess intelligence. Women have narrow shoulders and broad hips. Women ought to stay at home; the way they were created indicates this, for they have broad hips and a fundament to sit upon, keep house and bear and raise children.'[12]
- A popular sixteenth-century adage from Gloucestershire, England, affirmed that 'a woman, a spaniel and a walnut tree, the more they are beaten, the better they will be.'[13]

- One of the most famous laws allowing violence against women was Britain's 'rule of thumb,' which allowed men to beat their wives with a stick no thicker than their thumb.[14]
- In 1736, Matthew Hale, England's chief justice, proclaimed that 'the husband cannot be guilty of a rape committed by himself upon his lawful wife, for by their mutual consent and contract the wife hath given up herself into this kind unto the husband which she cannot retract.'[15]

In each of the above examples, the woman was judged to have violated a moral or political code; male violence was viewed as a necessary sanction to maintain control over women's behaviour. This attitude, ingrained in many European societies, was perpetuated in North America. The Hale doctrine, for example, was a significant influence. It was instrumental in the creation of many American and Canadian laws authorizing marital rape and impeding the passage of other laws to prevent the crime.[16] Similarly, the British 'rule of thumb' law shaped North American laws on battering.[17]

The long-standing tradition of blaming women and sanctifying male violence was not significantly altered by the late-nineteenth- and twentieth-century practice of seeking physiological explanations for male violence.[18]

PHYSIOLOGICAL TREATMENTS

Most physiological therapists work from a biosocial theoretical perspective (discussed in chapter 3). They argue that it is necessary to examine the role of physiological and social factors in facilitating male violence. In practice, however, the major focus has been on the possible physiological contributions to male violence; social factors have received little attention.[19] The efforts of these practitioners bear further examination. To date, physiological advocates have emphasized two treatments: stereotaxic surgery and testosterone reduction.

Stereotaxic Surgery

This involves identifying and surgically altering the brain structures that are involved in a person's escalation toward violence. Frank Elliot, for example, has emphasized the role of the phylogenetically ancient limbic system, which includes the hippocampus, the amygdala, and the hypothalamus, and is associated with certain aspects of emotion and behaviour.[20]

Surgical proponents often miss many clinical indications that medication or surgery is excessive and unnecessary. Averill highlights this point in a case study about Thomas, a young man, who was often violent toward his wife, and sometimes his children.[21] While Averill states that each 'assault on his wife was typically preceded by an experience of severe abdominal or facial pain,' he missed the significance of these physical symptoms as an opportunity for intervention. He could have helped Thomas learn that humans make choices about when, how, and with whom they will be violent. Thomas might have taken his pains as a cue to alert him that he was escalating toward a violent incident. He could have learned to establish an interval between the physical event of abdominal or facial pain and the violent incident. During this break, Thomas could leave the potentially violent situation. Averill might have helped Thomas identify other physical, emotional, or situational cues to serve as warnings of imminent violence. He might also have explored whether these physiological manifestations were linked to earlier emotional or physical trauma that was inadequately resolved and was contributing to Thomas's violent actions as an adult.

Averill eventually performed stereotaxic surgery on Thomas, after seven years of unsuccessful psychiatric involvement and the use of anti-seizure and other drugs. Bilateral lesions were made in the medial amygdala part of the brain. Averill notes that although the violence stopped, Thomas began suffering from occasional epileptic seizures (previously unmentioned by Averill) and periods of confusion and disordered thinking.[22]

This example is indicative of the problems with stereotaxic surgery: the price of reduced violence may be the infliction of significantly damaging side-effects. This raises numerous ethical issues. Who makes the decision regarding brain surgery? Is it to be a medical or a legal decision? Who decides which patients qualify for the treatment? Are those who authorize the surgery responsible for any potential side-effects? And if authorities are not legally responsible for the side-effects, what is there to prevent inferior or poorly implemented surgical interventions? These and other questions have yet to be answered satisfactorily.

To date, our limited knowledge of surgical interventions has severely restricted the use of stereotaxic surgery. Nevertheless, it still receives important support. A u.s. government task force of the late 1970s, while recommending 'that its use be confined to designated research centers to try and assure proper safeguards,' argued that stereotaxic surgery does hold some therapeutic promise.[23]

Despite such high-level endorsements, the limited use of stereotaxic surgery rules it out as a viable treatment option for most sexual or physical offenders. Consenting patients are extremely rare, and even when they do consent, their families may in fact attempt to block such interventions.[24]

Testosterone Reduction

As noted in chapter 3, many contemporary biosocial advocates believe that elevated testosterone levels, occurring within the appropriate external social context, can facilitate a man's progression toward violence. So far, there have been two ways to eliminate or reduce testosterone production: castration and hormone administration. Castration has long been viewed as a technique for preventing men from being sexually active. Various rulers created eunuchs to care for their many wives and female sexual partners. While the ancient tradition of castration has some contemporary supporters, other biosocial researchers favour the reduction of hormonal production by chemical, rather than surgical, means. Sex offenders in particular have been targeted as candidates for testosterone reduction, in the hope of preventing recidivism.[25]

Underlying much of the research on testosterone reduction are two assumptions: decreased testosterone will lead to reduced sexual activity, and diminished sexual activity will decrease violence against women.

Testosterone and Sexual Activity. The research on castration and hormonal interventions reveals a continuing, because as yet unresolved, debate on the extent to which decreased testosterone reduces sexual activity.

Castration does not, as is commonly believed, guarantee termination of a man's sexual activity.[26] Studies cited by Barbaree and Marshall indicate that young animals, not yet sexually active before castration, were likely to have a reduced level of sexual activity. But animals that had been sexually active prior to castration maintained high levels of copulation for several years after the operation.[27] Thus, even non-human animals appear to be significantly influenced by previous learning.

One of the most important studies of castrates to date is that conducted by Nikolaus Heim. He examined thirty-nine released sex offenders who had agreed voluntarily to surgical castration while imprisoned in West Germany. He discovered that castration does not guarantee an end to male sexual functioning. Thirty-one per cent of the castrates stated they were still able to engage in sexual intercourse. Heim noted that this supports other evidence which indicates that between 30 and 40 per cent of castrates fail to show a reduction in sexual potency after surgery.[28] Heim also found that heterosexual rapists proved most likely to continue sexual activity after surgery. Of the rapists Heim studied, 73 per cent continued to engage in some form of sexual behaviour. Significantly lower rates of sexual activity were found among pedophiles (32 per cent) and homosexuals (17 per cent). And of the castrates who considered their sexual activity to have been reduced, 89 per cent still engaged in at least occasional activity.[29] Heim, however, did find a reduced rate after castration among men between the age of forty-six and fifty-nine years. He contends that 'there seems to be a tendency for castration effects to be stronger the higher the castration age, but only from around the age of 45 on.'[30] Yet, even with an older age group, the offender's self-perceived emotional state remained an important component affecting the frequency of sexual activity. Heim concluded that, in general, the findings do not justify recommending surgical castration as a reliable treatment for incarcerated sex offenders.[31]

Barbaree and Marshall state that Heim's results confirm evidence by Ford and Beach that 'the effects of castration are dependent on the subject's attitudes rather than his changed hormonal state.'[32]

With regard to *hormonal interventions*, D.D. Thiessen has emphasized that 'glandular secretions, especially gonadal steroids, act to organize neural patterns, trigger aggressive acts, stipulate sexual dimorphism, and influence social status.'[33] Thiessen reviewed the influence of various hormones on a variety of creatures, including Red Sea fish, cleaner fish, Medaka Japanese rice fish, rhesus monkeys, mice, and ring-necked pheasants. When Thiessen finally addressed the issue of hormones and human aggression, he cited John Money's work, which was based on a sample of only eight male sex offenders. Money found that within approximately one month, the intramuscular administration, every ten days, of between 300 and 400 mg of an anti-androgenic drug medroxyprogesterone acetate (MPA), or Depo-Provera, radically lowered plasma testosterone levels to those 'typical of the female, or lower. Concurrently, potency and ejaculation are radically reduced, and may become zero. Both of these effects are reversed when the treatment is gradually tapered off and terminated.'[34] Money notes that some men were weaned off the drug in a matter of months, while others required 'booster' injections if their behaviour deteriorated.

Fred Berlin, psychiatrist and co-director of the Biosexual Psycho-Hormonal Clinic at Johns Hopkins Hospital in Baltimore, administered approximately 500 mg of the drug to about eighty sex offenders weekly. The drug was intended to curb sex drives and sexual fantasies by suppressing the production of testosterone.[35] John Bradford contends that MPA and cyproterone acetate (CPA) can effectively suppress the sexual drive. While Bradford admits that the 'exact site of action and mode of action of these drugs is not fully understood,' he argues that few serious side-effects have been documented, and all the studies note the side-effects are essentially reversible.[36]

Despite the possible utility of hormonal interventions, contrary evidence from researchers critical of their use indicates that 'as one moves along the phylogenetic scale from rats, to primates, to humans, the influence on sexual activity of the sex steroids seems to be less and less dramatic.'[37]

Sexual Activity and Violence against Women. Even if an unequivocal link were established between a reduction of testosterone and diminished sexual activity, this would not guarantee a similar reduction in male violence against women. While some researchers have shown significantly lowered recidivism rates among castrates, for example, many of these studies were based upon patients who voluntarily chose castration to avoid a long prison sentence. The possibility that 'the voluntary castrated group contained more patients genuinely motivated to stop offending behavior cannot be entirely excluded.'[38] Thus the offender's motivation, rather than surgical or hormonal interventions, may be more responsible for the reduced rate of recidivism.

We need to recognize that while levels of testosterone, sexual activity, and violence against women may at times coincide, they are relatively separate entities. Testosterone levels, for example, can be expected to fluctuate throughout the day, dropping 25 per cent from morning to early evening. As states Neena Schwartz, professor of neurobiology at Northwestern University, we 'certainly haven't seen any data suggesting that men are more aggressive in the morning than at night.' She rejects the argument that testosterone facilitates violence; 'men who don't mainline steroids can't blame their hormones for a sudden urge to kick the cat or throttle an overbearing boss.' She argues that men and women do not 'think or act entirely with their glands, and the true place of testosterone in the rich mix of male personality defies simplistic explanations.'[39]

While a man's testosterone level may have been reduced through castration or drug therapy, if nothing has been done to alter his acceptance or tolerance of violence against women, he could still be violent. John Bradford comes close to this point but still misses it. He notes that MPA and CPA are 'not ... suitable for the treatment of aggressive behavior per se but possibly reduce aggression that is sex-drive related.'[40] This is important in light of the growing evidence that the violence is not sex-drive related and that sexual offenders typically do not have elevated sex-drive levels.[41] While an assault may involve sexual contact, primarily it is an act of violence.[42] A man does not need an erect penis or an ejaculatory capacity to be sexually violent toward women; this would presuppose that sexual assault consists exclusively of penile-vaginal intercourse.[43] Yet forced oral sex, fondling, and the insertion of various objects (e.g., broomsticks or broken beer bottles) into a victim's orifices are a commonplace, and equally or more injurious, means of sexual assault.[44]

The failure of testosterone reduction to live up to the expectations of its advocates is only one part of the problem. Even if it were effective, relatively few men would willingly consent to castration or hormone treatments. State coercion and enforcement would be necessary. This, in turn, would raise many of the same ethical questions associated with stereotaxic surgery: Who decides which men would be castrated, and which crimes are to be treated by castration, which by hormonal interventions? Who is responsible for the potential short- and long-term effects of drug therapy? What would prevent these treatments from being used in situations that are non-voluntary, unmonitored, and indiscriminately punitive, rather than remedial. Recognizing the potential political problems with testosterone reduction, most state officials have shied away. Even where convicted offenders have agreed to castration – for example, in lieu of a prison sentence – few state officials appear interested in such a proposal.[45]

Conclusions

The vast majority of people working with violent men do not apply physiological treatments. One 1986 U.S. survey found that only 14 per cent of the 297 identified services for male juvenile and adult sex offenders used Depo-Provera, and 52 per cent of those using this drug were concentrated in five states (California, Maryland, Oregon, Texas, and Washington).[46] The limited use of physiological treatments is due to three main factors. First, their effectiveness in reducing violence against women is questionable. Second, there are numerous ethical concerns. A third factor is the growing clients' rights movement. Fewer individuals are willing to undergo procedures that have a dubious performance record. Suppressing information critical of physiological approaches is one option in dealing with this reluctance, but not one likely to be politically popular.

We need to question why, despite theoretical weaknesses and debatable clinical effectiveness, there remains an enduring professional and popular interest in physiological contributions to male violence. Part of the problem, no doubt, is simply that until relatively recently the physiological approach was the one adopted by the majority of professionals. And to a certain degree, the retention of outdated beliefs in the public's mind could be explained by lack of awareness of the most recent literature on the subject. This answer, however, seems insufficient.

Physiological approaches remain popular because they concentrate on individual pathology and disregard the societal factors which create violent men; they focus on changing individuals, and leave intact the society that teaches violence. While research into the physiological contributions to male violence may be important – some even argue it should be accelerated[47] – it is incumbent upon physiological investigators to recognize the social context into which they release their findings. Researchers need to take some responsibility for ensuring their findings are considered in context, and challenging their peers who assign too much weight to physiological influences. Without adequately placing their work within the proper context of an examination of the numerous social factors encouraging male violence, physiological researchers can help perpetuate the many physiologically based fallacies about male violence (such as: male hormones make men sexually uncontrollable, men can get so angry they lose control of themselves, or men have always been violent and thus are more likely to act first and talk later).

While human physiology is an element in male violence, we must avoid exaggerating its responsibility for it. By disregarding the enormous influence of the media, the military, pornography, the peer group, and other social forces in encouraging or legitimizing male violence, physiological treatments provide no threat or challenge to the existing social order. In fact, they may even aid in its replication.

INTRAPSYCHIC TREATMENTS

Proponents of intrapsychic therapies have argued that it is psychological abnormalities in individual men which cause them to be violent toward women (chapter 3). Attention has been focused on the role of personality disorders, poor impulse control, immature personalities, low frustration tolerance, dependency, developmental trauma, depression, addiction to alcohol, and various psychiatric illnesses.[48] Intrapsychic treatments have involved individual psychotherapy and group psychotherapy, usually led by one male therapist.[49] Psychiatrists have been the most visible proponents of intrapsychic explanations and treatment of male violence; some psychologists, sociologists, and therapists have also adopted this perspective.[50]

Intrapsychic interventions have 'proven unsatisfactory'[51] for two main reasons. First, intrapsychic clinicians have not been particularly adept at identifying violent offenders. Bradford, emphasizing the failure of many intrapsychic psychiatrists, notes that 'recent studies have shown that violent behavior does not have a higher incidence in psychiatric patients compared with the general population. Violence also has a low base rate in the mentally ill. These factors result in a high rate of false positives in the prediction of dangerousness given the present state of psychiatric knowledge.'[52]

Even among identified violent offenders, intrapsychic treatments have failed to produce a significant positive change. Marshall and Williams compared psychotherapy with behaviour therapy. Group psychotherapy was provided by a trained psychiatrist with several years' experience working with rapists and pedophiles. Marshall and Williams noted that the psychotherapy component was eclectic and provided psychodynamic interpretations of the offenders' attitudes and behaviours. After a series of two replications, not only was the psychotherapy less effective than the behavioural treatment, 'group psychotherapy actually made the patients worse on many measures including the measures of sexual preference.'[53]

Other studies support the findings of Marshall and Williams. Peters and Roether examined an analytically oriented hospital program with 167 sexual offenders. The program emphasized the intrapsychic causes of antisocial personality as the basis for sex offending. Peters and Roether found 3.2 per cent and 7.7 per cent recidivism rates in the untreated and treated offenders, respectively. Peters, in a ten-year follow-up study of the same groups, found a failure rate of 13.65 per cent for treated offenders. Among offenders who had not received the treatment, the rate was only 1.2 per cent.[54] Once again, the intrapsychic interventions not only failed to solve, but may have intensified, the problem.[55]

In summary, it must be said that intrapsychic therapists have to date provided only inadequate treatment. In focusing on individual physiological or psychological pathology, intrapsychic clinicians have avoided a thorough examination of society's role in creating violent men. Increased recidivism is just one price we pay for choosing to ignore the numerous factors external to the individual that may increase his propensity for violence. While intrapsychic interventions may have some application in treating an offender's ancillary issues, the perspective is of limited utility in reducing male violence.[56]

SUMMARY OF THE TRADITIONAL TREATMENT PERSPECTIVES

The treatments traditionally adopted to deal with male violence have failed to solve the problem. While some changes have occurred, they have been insufficient. We have yet to fully emerge, for example, from our lengthy legacy of legislated permissibility of male violence against women. While the advocates of physiological and intrapsychic treatments have not, of course, had any part in such overt endorsements of male violence, their restricted theoretical perspectives, which fail to integrate the role played by our existing social structures and gender relations in enabling male violence, permit its continuation. Their treatment methods have been of limited utility. For these reasons, traditional treatments came under critical review with the advent, in the 1970s, of the women's movement.

The Women's Movement and Social Constructionism

For years, women have been trying to focus attention on the issue of male violence. For example, Frances Power Cobbe was a prominent activist in late-nineteenth-century Victorian England, campaigning to end wife-beating.[57] Many other first-wave feminists 'were aware that behaviour that men considered "typical" was in fact exploiting many women, particularly poor and working women.'[58]

Yet, despite earlier efforts, it was the women's movement of the early 1970s that did the most to strip off the ancient and heavy blanket of denial over the issue of male violence against women. Feminists played a pivotal role. They helped shift our understanding of, and treatment for, male violence away from the various physiological and intrapsychic perspectives – which reinforce the gender status quo – and moved us toward social constructionism.[59] This process, which has yet to be completed, was precipitated through simultaneous work in three main areas: breaking the silence on the frequency and causes of male violence, questioning traditional survivor-victim therapy, and establishing pro-feminist services for victims.

BREAKING THE SILENCE

Female activists in the civil rights and counter-culture movements of the 1950s and 1960s had recognized that these movements were as thoroughly misogynist as the cultures they were attempting to supplant. By the early 1970s, as more women became politically conscious of the exploitation they were suffering as second-class citizens, they loudly questioned many basic premises of our social structures, challenged their male partners to change, and focused public attention on the numerous ways in which our male-dominated society abuses women.[60]

With this revival of feminism, male violence against women started to become identified as a significant social problem.[61] As women came together and shared their experiences, they developed a new awareness – a raised consciousness – of the plight of most women. Individual female victims of male-perpetrated emotional, physical, and sexual violence began to realize that they were not alone, and the stories of their sisters were strikingly similar. Gradually, as pieces of the puzzle were amassed and publicized, the frequency with which men abuse women became more apparent; the personal became political.[62]

Connecting with other women was essential. It enabled women to see how, both as individuals and collectively, they had been forced into accepting a role of powerlessness and victimization.[63] To rectify this situation, large numbers of women struggled to place the responsibility for the violence back onto the offender, identifying the numerous, and long-ignored, social factors that encourage men to be violent and women silent. Through demonstrations, leafleting, marches, protests, and a profusion of publications and writings, attention was focused on how the family, pornography, male and female socialization, the media, and other factors in society contribute to male violence against women.[64]

This largely grass-roots movement of women coalesced into a diversified social, political, and economic force for change. Within a few years, there accumulated a momentum strong enough to begin shifting our well-entrenched understanding and preferred treatment of male violence against women from the physiological and intrapsychic toward social constructionist. Women had succeeded at socially defining an existing condition (male violence against women) and its origins (social constructionism), and made it more difficult for either to remain ignored.[65]

THERAPY FOR THE SURVIVING VICTIM

Traditional therapies for surviving victims of male violence have been demeaning and exploitive to women. Theorists believed that male violence was rooted in individual pathology, thus perpetuating the prevailing myths about men not being able to control themselves. Typically, female victims were held responsible for provoking men's violence, for example, by arguing with men or tantalizing them by wearing specific types of clothing. This resulted in many women being labelled as masochists, and in men not being held accountable for their actions.[66] Traditional therapists offered little support for female surviving victims. Ironically, often the effects of male violence on women – such as anxiety, drug/alcohol abuse, and depression – were viewed as causes.[67]

Feminists identified several directions for change.[68]

Social Context. Within traditional clinical frameworks, the social context was not prioritized. In fact, women who struggled to alter their family structures – for example, by demanding changes by their male partners – were viewed as having a significant psychological problem.

The women's movement emphasized that many personal problems are inextricably linked to the social factors that create significant power differences between men and women. Any individual, to be fully understood, needs to be viewed within the context of his or her social system.

Feminist therapists argued that the roots of women's dissatisfaction are less likely to be found solely within individuals than within the various economic, political, familial, and social structures that systematically exploit women. Rather than limiting an individual's options to adjustment or adaptation to the existing system, feminists have advocated questioning, critiquing, and changing the social norms, customs, and political institutions that perpetuate women's second-class status.

Sex Roles. Traditional therapists often worked to reinforce women's prescribed role as mother and unpaid domestic worker. A woman who tried to break away from these roles frequently had her mental health under review.

The women's movement struggled to shatter the constraining, artificial, and socially created traditional hegemonic femininity. Proponents recognized that by valuing demure, polite, respectful, and deferential women, society helped perpetuate women's silence, servitude, and exploitation.

Feminists radically broadened the concept of femininity and encouraged independence, self-reliance, assertiveness, and a healthy self-image. Thus equipped, women would be less likely to endure abusive social contexts and better able to effect life change.

'Women's Work' Must Be Valued. Women traditionally were evaluated and graded according to male standards. This perpetuated their second-class status. Feminists emphasized that by cooking, cleaning, and nurturing, women through the ages have played the important role of keeping families together. The women's movement emphasized that these qualities should not be devalued simply because they have been of little interest to men. By affording value to many of the qualities and tasks traditional to women, feminist therapists have strengthened the ability of women to also undertake tasks traditionally reserved for men.

Client as the Expert. Traditional therapy emphasized the therapist – typically a male – as the expert. The counselling relationship thus maintained and often intensified the gender divisions of the larger society; this served to encourage client dependency.

Feminists struggled to affirm women's experience from a female perspective. They argued that women were the authorities of, and should value, their own experience. While a counsellor can facilitate a client's self-discovery and problem-solving, ultimately the client needs to decide for herself what changes, if any, are required in her life.

Affirm the Positive. Traditional therapies typically emphasized pathology. Feminist counsellors did not ignore the pathology (which, in any case, they were likely to define differently), but emphasized the client's strength and attributes. Feminists argued that if a client were to alter her life situation, first she would need to believe in her own abilities to effect positive change. Affirming the positive can help a client value qualities about herself she previously had not recognized or valued.

Collective Strength. Traditional treatments emphasized individual strength to counteract social hardship. Women were encouraged to take responsibility for problems that primarily were a function of the existing social structures. In this sense, traditional treatments have helped maintain the existing social order.

The feminist movement encouraged women to unite, in small groups, support networks, or *en masse.* Feminists recognized that women's individual and collective power to effect personal and political change would be increased when individuals felt supported, and not as if they were struggling alone. Unity could increase confidence and action.

PRO-FEMINIST VICTIM SERVICES

Feminists recognized that while critiques of traditional therapies were crucial, the system would not change overnight. Thus, during the 1970s and 1980s, it was feminists who were largely responsible for developing essential services for victims of sexual assault[69] and battering.[70] This was a response of unprecedented proportions; thousands of politically conscious women became involved. While many women lobbied for funds from existing state agencies, large numbers of women volunteered their time, energy, support, and skills to assist other women. Workers struggled against lack of money, physical space, and often the hostility of the existing mental health system to ensure that women-centred services were available, where women could feel safe to heal, and shift the responsibility for the violence onto the perpetrator.[71] Counselling and advocacy services were made available for women who, in an earlier period, would have been hard-pressed to find a counsellor willing to listen, support, and motivate, rather than label, blame, and victimize. Across North America, women were able to utilize the in-person counselling and crisis-line services provided for battered and sexually assaulted women. The fact that waiting-lists for feminist-based social services were consistently lengthy identified two obvious points:

the services were valued by their client populations, and the demand continued to exceed the supply.[72]

Feminists recognized that providing services to victims involved addressing the social constructionist forces which impaired a victim's recovery. Finding a balance between direct service and larger systems interventions remained a constant struggle. Yet, despite the difficulty, the movement did not back down from trying to effect social change to improve the status of women. Feminists recognized that numerous existing social forces increased the amount of time and energy expended by victims wanting to heal, and encouraged additional violence against future victims. Thus, the women's movement has focused on, among other things, changing numerous social traditions, including media portrayals of women and of male violence,[73] male control of public places, common myths about sexual assault and battering,[74] and women's difficulties in obtaining justice in the courts.[75] The struggle for services and social change has continued as women recognize they are fighting for their dignity, safety, and lives.

Effects of the Women's Movement on Male Violence

The women's movement inaugurated a new era in our society's treatment of male violence. While concentrating primarily on services for victims, the feminist critique precipitated a large-scale re-examination and revision of the assumption that male violence was natural and inevitable. The movement raised the popular consciousness about violence against women and shifted the outlook of millions of people from blaming women to holding perpetrators responsible for their crimes. Feminists made it clear that if male violence against women was going to be stopped, the social factors which encourage male violence would have to be changed.

The women's movement also created a demand for an equally radical revision of the treatment of male offenders.[76] Women realized that treating the effects of the problem would not, in the long term, bring about its abolition. Many feminist therapists became involved in the treatment of violent men. The major effort, however, was to demand state support and involvement in ending the crimes against women.

Turning to the state for assistance was a logical, but problematic, progression; funding was needed for treatment programs to help surviving victims and offenders. But significant sectors within the women's movement recognized that the state was not simply a neutral funder and arbiter of disputes between different sectors of the body politic. Through the perpetuation of misogynist laws, sexist education standards, military recruitment, and other means at its disposal, the state had played, and continued to play, an important role in the promotion of male violence. Thus women were turning for assistance to the very entity which was a very major part of the problem.

Because of the strength, magnitude, and determination of the women's movement, the state systems of most Western countries were forced into responding, though they did so slowly, haltingly, often out of political expediency, and generally on their own terms. The precise nature and extent of the Canadian and American state response to the feminist demands for an end to male violence against women is the focus of the next chapter.

5 / The State Response

Ralph Miliband, in *The State in Capitalist Society*, argues that 'the state' is not a thing, that it does not, as such, exist. What 'the state' stands for is a number of particular institutions which, together, constitute its reality, and which interact as parts of what may be called the state system.'[1] Miliband has identified five major state institutions whose interrelationship constitutes the state system: the government, the administration, the military and the police, the judicial branch, and sub-central government and parliamentary assemblies.

This chapter will examine the ways in which the various components of the state system have responded to the feminist-initiated demand to stop male violence against women. The state's approach to the problem has been based on two main perspectives for the treatment of male violence: family systems theory, and social constructionism. The internal theoretical contradictions of family systems intervention will be highlighted to reveal that it can actually increase, rather than decrease, the risk of violence for women. Meanwhile, social constructionism, the second perspective, will be shown to be only partly successful, despite its theoretical and clinical strengths, owing to inadequate implementation by the existing state system.

The state's support of a theory that is potentially dangerous to women and its ineffectiveness in implementing useful intervention to significantly decrease violence against women obviously invite criticism. The final section in this chapter will argue that currently, the state, far from being committed to using its full legislative and administrative powers to end male violence, is doing the bare minimum to simply contain feminist demands for change.

The Family Systems Approach

The family systems approach to male violence evolved in the mid-1970s in response to the feminist movement's critique of the physiological and intrapsychic treatment approaches, which blamed the victim or emphasized specific characteristics of the victim as potential causes, excluded external social factors, and implicitly sanctioned violence against women.[2] Family systems techniques, which involve conjoint therapy sessions, where the man and woman attend simultaneously, have been widely used in treating men who batter.[3] Popularity, however, does not necessarily signify effectiveness. Family systems approaches may ultimately facilitate, rather than abolish, male violence against women. Stordeur and Stille state that 'from the family systems perspective, violence is a relationship issue, with violence being one symptom of a disturbed or pathological relationship ... all members of the family participate in the system and carry the responsibility for family dysfunction. In this context, battering is no longer simply the responsibility of the batterer, but a behaviour that is maintained by the actions of all family or system members.'[4]

Michele Bograd's critique of the family systems approach, which supports that of Stordeur and Stille,[5] points out four major flaws.

SYSTEMIC APPROACHES TO VIOLENCE

Bograd notes that problems can occur if violence is considered as only one of many problems within a relationship and not given the priority it deserves. All too often, a couple's difficulties are inaccurately identified by clinicians as poor communication, substance abuse, finances, and then – almost as an afterthought – violence. Neglecting to perceive the man's violence as the major area needing work, and, indeed, the root of many other problems, allows it to be nudged from centre stage by somewhat superfluous secondary issues.

ALLOCATION OF BLAME

Inherently, the clinician's obfuscation of the primary role of violence in creating other problems gives the message to the couple that violence is not something about which they should be too worried. Presumably it will end once the man deals with his alcohol abuse, or once the couple sorts out their financial or communication difficulties. This belief excuses the man from accepting responsibility for his violence while increasing the woman's sense of self-blame. When violence is identi-fied as a relevant concern, typically its allocation within the family sys-tems approach is unclear and, at best, divided between the man and the woman. The implication is that the woman should know how to control her husband's feelings and actions; therefore, she must take responsibility for the man's violence. Family systems clinicians ignore differences in physical size and how men and women are socialized to feel about using physical force to defend themselves, and deny that men may learn violent coping skills before entering a relationship – even if they had not previously put them to use. Bograd notes that many family therapists are still unwilling to acknowledge that the woman may actually not have done anything to precipitate the vio-lence, and may truly have been an innocent victim.[6] Once again, the woman is blamed.[7] This can result in the woman constantly modifying her behaviour, trying to find ways to make it easier for her male part-ner not to drink, for example. Over time, the woman can become very stressed if all her efforts are in vain. Until she recognizes that it is up to the man to take responsibility for his violence, she will be on an unending search.[8]

SYSTEMS LANGUAGE AND MALE REALITY

Feminists have struggled hard to demonstrate the ways in which lan-guage can restrict women and men to certain prescribed roles, reduc-ing their creative and economic capacity to grow by venturing into new areas of endeavour, as they may appear appropriate to one sex only. Women in particular have been excluded from many areas that would allow them to increase their economic independence from men, because the existing language – which is a function of the larger soci-ety – favours men.[9]

Bograd acknowledges that the effects of the language used by family systems therapists are as destructive as any traditional counselling vocabularies. The use of 'neutral technical language of cybernetic and information theories' makes invisible many of the causes and effects of wife battering. Terms such as 'violent couple' or 'domestic violence' hide the fact that in the vast majority of the cases it is the men who are the offenders and the women who are the victims. Similarly, to argue that 'a woman remains in a relationship because abusive transactions satisfy needs at the systems level' neglects the possibility that the woman may be staying not because of the needs of the system, but simply because the man controls the physical and financial resources that would allow her to leave.[10]

There is also the issue of defining the problem solely from the man's point of view. All too often, wife-battering is portrayed as a result of the woman making demands of the man which apparently threaten his ability to cope. Examples might include a woman studying to earn a university degree, obtaining a higher-paying job than her husband, having a friendship with another man, or not being willing to be sexual whenever the man is interested. Frequently these are depicted as legitimate reasons for physical or sexual abuse. Bograd warns that if we do not take the assaulted woman's experience seriously into the formulation, we can provide support for the dictum that 'objectivity is man's subjectivity rendered unquestionable.'[11]

THE FAMILY AND SOCIETY

Family systems therapists tend to ignore the role of society in encouraging male violence, and to view the so-called battering or violent couple as a closed unit, removed from the social forces which contribute to male violence. Thus, the couple or family is identified as 'dysfunctional,' or 'deviant.' This, in turn, can encourage therapists to underestimate the prevalence in general of male violence against women. If it only occurs among deviants, surely the nice young middle-class couple sitting on the other side of the desk does not fit the type. Yet if one in four partnered women is battered, either we have a plethora of deviants or we are working with an erroneous and, because it allows violence to go undetected, dangerous concept.

Neglecting non-familial social factors reduces the explanation of wife-battering to intra-familial dynamics. Doing so limits the effectiveness of the intervention strategy. As Bograd states, while 'the individual family may be the stage of violent behaviour, it may not be its source.'[12]

The problems associated with family systems theory pose some very significant challenges for those working with male offenders and female victims. Compounding the situation is the practice of having the man and the woman attend therapy sessions together. If the therapist does not compensate for the internal weakness of the family systems approach, the intervention may be very dysfunctional. Bograd notes that the counsellor should be sensitized to four key issues.

The Therapeutic Alliance. Unless the woman feels safe in the counselling session, she is unlikely to receive the full benefit of the therapy. Very often, a man will attend sessions not from a desire to learn or change, but simply to placate his partner until she is firmly recommitted to the relationship – or else to monitor what is being told to her by the therapist. Under such circumstances, the woman may not wish to disclose anything, for fear of retaliation by her male partner. Thus, unless a non-violence contract is established and honoured, the conjoint sessions will likely do nothing to empower the woman, and may permit the man to avoid the central issue – ending his violent behaviour.

Violence as the Primary Treatment Concern. As stated earlier, if the therapist does not recognize the role of violence within a relationship, or relegates it to a secondary status, the effect can be to reinforce the woman's sense that she has done something wrong, that it is she who has – or is – the problem. Increasing the victimization of the woman thus is not likely to end the violence, and may even allow the man's battering or relationship rape to increase because it has gone unchecked. While family systems therapists would undoubtedly focus on homicide or suicide if those came up as clinical issues, they are not as likely to set male violence as a priority for treatment – despite the fact that because of it the woman's emotional and physical life may well be in jeopardy.

Perpetuation of Traditional Sex Roles. While the goal of conjoint therapy is to end the man's violence, the means of reaching that goal may be a therapy focusing on how the woman can change her behaviour. Predicated on the belief that both the man and the woman operate within a relatively closed system, whereby a positive change in one area results in a reaction (presumably positive) in the other parts of the system, and that the woman is the more malleable of the two systemic components, often it is she who is requested to change her behaviour. The thinking is that if only she could be a better woman or wife her man might not beat or rape her. While it is certainly advisable to ask a woman to modify her behaviour so as to protect herself, that is very different from implying that her actions caused the violence. As long as the woman can be blamed for the violence, the man is freed from taking responsibility for his actions and having to effect any changes in his life.

Preservation of the Marriage as the Goal of Treatment. Quite typically in therapy, men or women will request help to save their relationship. Counsellors must not get drawn into seeing this as the only positive outcome. If other options to the situation, such as a temporary, or a permanent, separation, are not considered, the man may never develop an awareness of the seriousness of his actions, which is essential to motivate changes in his behaviour. Similarly, if the woman is not given the opportunity to experience what it would be like for her to live apart from her abusive partner, she may not realize that this is something she would prefer. Structured separations are increasingly a part of family systems theory, but there are still many therapists who need to be cautious of their own biases and recognize that ending the relationship may need to be viewed as a clinical success if that is what is required to end the violence.

CONCLUSIONS ON FAMILY SYSTEMS THEORY AND PRACTICE

There is a real danger that the many internal structural and ideological weaknesses of family systems models can impair their effectiveness in ending male violence. The debate over family systems theory has long been polarized, with many critics advocating that it is completely unproductive.[13] It should be applied with the greatest of sensitivity, and only after both the man and the woman have done extensive individual, and preferably group, therapeutic work to deal with the numerous short- and long-term effects of the violence. Therapists should be alert to the pitfalls outlined above and be prepared to switch to an alterative method if it begins to derail.

Unfortunately, the family systems approach is seldom used with the required degree of sensitivity. For this reason, there is considerable anger in many sectors of the women's movement against family systems therapists who generally are well-paid and enjoy comfortable working conditions – and are completely ineffective, thanks to their practice of often missing cases of wife-battering, or holding the family responsible for the man's violence.[14]

By shifting much of the man's responsibility for violence to the female partner, family systems interventions replicate the problems found with the physiological and intrapsychic theories which they were intended to replace.[15] None of these approaches significantly reduces the risk of violence for women. Indeed, the methods can be used 'as agents of social control by constructing explanatory frameworks biased against women, supporting social structures oppressive to women, and defining stereotypically feminine traits (such as passivity and nurturance) as ideals of female mental health.'[16]

It should be recognized that family systems theory does mark an important transition point on the path to social constructionism. It rejects human physiology or intrapsychic factors as prime motivators for male violence. Where it fails, however, is in ignoring the multiplicity of factors involved in the creation of violent men. Typically, extra-familial causes of male violence are not adequately considered in the treatment of female victims and male offenders.

If counsellors and therapists are intent on ending male violence against women, it is clinically and politically dangerous to examine only the factors within a closed system – that is, the family – that are contributing to male violence. The role of pornography, the military, academia, and other agents of male socialization in encouraging and perpetuating violence against women needs to be recognized. Then again, if one wishes to maintain existing social structures and institutions, one might be more inclined to look only within the family for the causes for male violence. As long as the causes for the violence can be found within the family – and blamed upon the woman – we do not need to concern ourselves with the larger socio-political issues which contribute to, and perpetuate, male violence against women.

The internal flaws of the family systems theory and the manner in which it typically has been implemented have prompted feminist demands for further change in the methods of treatment of male violence. Feminists recognized the larger role of the multitude of social forces and institutions which participate in the creation of violent men and demanded treatment programs based on a more complete social constructionist approach. It is to those programs that attention must now be directed.

The Early 1980s Emergence of New State-Funded Social Constructionist Treatment Programs for Male Physical and Sexual Offenders

In the early 1980s, many concerned, politically active individuals worked to develop state-supported social constructionist treatment programs for male batterers and sexual offenders. They wanted a treatment perspective that would be free from the problems inherent in, and would address many of the factors ignored by, the physiological, intrapsychic, and family systems approaches. This section will review the various components of the social constructionist interventions for male offenders. These include: the examination of background issues, offender assessment and treatment, program content, program process, and post-group intervention. The final section of the chapter will critique the state system's implementation of social constructionism.

Admittedly, there are differences in the material conveyed in therapeutic settings to groups of batterers and groups of rapists. Any differences, however, are far outnumbered by the similarities between the two kinds of groups in the nature of therapeutic goals, content, and political ramifications. Those differences that do exist will be highlighted below.

BACKGROUND ISSUES

The Philosophy of a Social Constructionist Intervention

The philosophy of most social constructionist groups is grounded in six key principles. First, violence is a culturally and experientially learned behaviour. It is recognized that numerous agents of male socialization, which includes many of our society's major institutions, contribute to, and reward, the all-too-common belief that it is acceptable for individual men to choose to be violent toward women.[17]

Second, men must accept responsibility for their violence. A crucial clinical task is to help the man first accept responsibility for what he has done, and then establish and maintain the desire for change. Facilitators struggle to not let the man blame his anger on 'poor impulse control.' It is not a question of learning better control. Offenders already use violence to control those whom they – and our society – have deemed worthy of such abuse. Men do not simply lose control and proceed to rape and batter. They choose to do so because it serves a purpose. Don Long, from St Louis's RAVEN (Rape and Violence End Now), one of the first grass-roots groups created to work toward eradication of male violence, argues that male violence against women 'accomplishes something; whether it gets exactly what the batterer wanted or not is hardly the point. Violence shows those upon whom it is perpetrated that it can happen again, that the perpetrator is more physically powerful when "necessary," and that rebelling can lead to such violence at any time. Using violence to control a woman is not a question of "impulse." The act is consciously derived, it is purposeful, and it is – even if only temporarily – useful.'[18]

Accepting responsibility for one's actions involves not only making a statement promising non-violence, but undertaking significant change in many aspects of one's life. Barbara Hart has put together a comprehensive list itemizing numerous ways in which a man can become accountable for his actions. While written specifically for men who batter, the points are applicable to sexual offenders.

A Man Who Has Battered a Woman Becomes Accountable When ...
1. he has acknowledged to the battered woman and to her community of friends and family that he has assaulted and controlled a woman, and that he has committed acts of violence against her;
2. he has admitted the pattern of abusive control which tyrannized her;
3. he has admitted that his behaviour was *unprovoked* and *inexcusable*;
4. he knows his behaviour was criminal;
5. he understands his behaviour was not caused by stress, chemical dependency, or any other outside factor;
6. he knows he was *not* out of control;
7. he admits that he intended to control or punish her;
8. he deeply regrets his actions, and is horrified;
9. he recognizes the pain and suffering he visited upon her;
10. he accepts full responsibility for his acts;
11. he acknowledges this without expectations of approval from her;
12. he understands he is *not entitled* to her forgiveness;
13. he recognizes that the woman may never trust him again, and may remain afraid of him forever;
14. he can enumerate the losses suffered by her and her family;
15. he does not expect protection for his name;
16. he realizes he needs the help of his family, his friends and his community to prevent further use of violence;
17. he knows that he needs to find others to support him in non-violence;
18. he knows clearly that there is nothing in the relationship or the woman that *caused* the battery;
19. he knows he is at risk for battering any woman in the future;
20. he realizes that the battered woman should not have to hear any of the above points from him, unless *she* desires to hear it.

In addition, if the battered woman has left him,

21. he agrees to limit contact with her, her friends and her family;
22. he agrees to *stop* chasing and tracking her;

23. he agrees to avoid the places she frequents, and to provide her with plenty of space away from him;
24. he agrees to stop collecting information about her;
25. he understands he needs to pay restitution, which could mean child support and alimony, if she desires, and he agrees to support her in this restitution as long as she needs it, to replace the losses she has sustained;
26. and, finally, he refuses to manipulate their children to discredit her.[19]

A third principle guiding social constructionist work is the idea that if a man has used violence to achieve a certain goal, he may be lacking the skills necessary to be able to live a non-violent life. Thus, without outside intervention and assistance, he is unlikely to stop being violent. In all probability, the frequency and intensity of his cycle of violence will escalate.[20]

Fourth, ending the violence is the main focus of counselling. Maintaining the man's relationship is not a primary goal. It is in this sense that social constructionist approaches most obviously differ from family systems interventions.[21]

Fifth, when appropriate, group work can be more effective than individual counselling. Groups lessen the guilt, shame, and isolation of the offender. The intention is not by any means to protect the offender from experiencing these emotions; they may be powerful in motivating him to change. Rather, there is a recognition that unless these emotions are counterbalanced by support and encouragement, the individual may feel it is too hopeless to try what is, for him, a new way of life. Groups can facilitate emotional catharsis, insight, universality, instillation of hope, and positive peer identification. The group also provides a safe and immediate opportunity to model new behaviours.[22] The use of groups is widespread and endorsed by the vast majority of social constructionists.[23] A 1986 survey of American sex-offender treatments found that in 96 per cent of the 297 identified services, group treatment was preferred over individual work.[24]

Finally, social constructionism is an eclectic treatment philosophy with a pro-feminist foundation. Various professions, disciplines, and counselling schools of thought and approaches are integrated into social constructionist groups. Nicholas Groth, a therapist working with sexual offenders, emphasizes that 'we are obviously talking about an issue that is much broader than simply a clinical or psychological issue. It is a cultural, legal, a political, an economic, an educational, a medical, and a spiritual issue. And if we are going to be effective in combatting this problem, it really means approaching it from all of these perspectives.'[25] The multiplicity of approaches and roles incorporated into social constructionism is reiterated by others. Don Long notes that the counsellor 'strives most obviously to become teacher for and brother to the men who come for help, and occasionally slips into the role of cop, parent, and therapist.'[26] The work with sexual offenders, in particular, while taking a pro-feminist social constructionist perspective as a point of departure, incorporates behavioural, psychodynamic, cognitive, and biomedical elements and integrates a wide variety of educational and training components.[27]

The Goals of a Social Constructionist Intervention

The goals of social constructionist offender groups, which build upon the philosophical foundation, can be summarized as follows:
1. Helping the client recognize, acknowledge, and comprehend that he has a problem. This entails having him accept his need for treatment and understand the non-physiological origins of his behaviour.[28]
2. Ensuring that the client is willing to accept responsibility for his sexual or physical violence against women.[29]
3. Raising the man's consciousness of the effects of his violence on his victim(s) and others.[30]
4. Helping the man 'reevaluate his attitudes and values toward sexuality and aggression.'[31]
5. Working with the man to help him recognize and alter the various factors – emotional, cognitive, circumstantial, and behavioural – and the arousal stimuli in his progression toward battering and sexual violence.[32]
6. Ensuring the man has created and is using an effective control plan for non-violence (for more on control plans see pp. 147–50 and 161–2, below).
7. Providing a context for a major revision of the man's sex-role stereotyping.[33]
8. Having the man understand the need for, and providing him with, information about how to communicate more effectively and non-violently.[34]
9. Assisting the man in learning when and how to implement relaxation strategies.[35]
10. Improving the man's self-esteem.[36]

11. Facilitating the man's creation of a social support network to help him not reoffend.[37]
12. Making appropriate referrals for any other supplementary work (i.e., chemical dependency counselling, financial planning, parenting courses, etc.).[38]

Group Composition

Most groups for violent men continue to separate batterers from sexual offenders. Increasingly, this division appears to be rather arbitrary, as counsellors recognize that the populations are not as separate as previously presumed; both crimes are committed for many of the same reasons. Counsellors are struggling with the clinical issue of whether or not to keep the groups separate, as each option has certain very distinct advantages. Combining the two offender groups can increase the men's recognition of the similarities among the various ways men choose to be violent toward women. However, joint offender groups run the risk of significant internal polarization. The predominant myth that sexual offending is the most serious offence can allow batterers to feel superior, or vindicated that 'at least I didn't rape her,' and consequently the potential polarization, and the practical consideration that some of the content material for the two populations will differ, compel facilitators to continue running separate groups.

Meanwhile, many existing groups have dual offenders; some sex offenders may have battered their female partners and, conversely, many batterers have raped their wives. The result is an overlap between the groups for sexual and physical offenders. While this has not been an enormous problem to date, the number of identified dual offenders is likely to increase as assessment tools improve and public intolerance for male violence grows. In the absence of any combined sexual and physical offender groups, counsellors will most likely refer dual offenders to a group based on the offence which he is most likely to repeat. The preferable solution, of course, is to have the individual attend two groups.

How Do Offenders Get into a Group?

Unfortunately, very few male offenders come to a treatment group on their own initiative. Nicholas Groth lists the major reasons for this: '(1) They do not appreciate the seriousness of their behavior and do not recognize that they have a problem. (2) They do not know where to turn to receive dependable help. (3) They fear the adverse social and legal consequences of disclosure. (4) At times of stress they act out, rather than work out, their problems. (5) They perceive other persons, especially those in some position of authority, as obstacles, opponents, or objects in their lives rather than as sources of help and assistance.'[39]

An offender will present himself for treatment for at least five different reasons: his partner is threatening to leave; she has left; the man recently offended, and is feeling particularly remorseful and hopeful that he can change his behaviour; something was different about his last offence (i.e., he offended against a stranger, reached relatively greater levels of violence, or started hitting the children as well); various state or familial authorities have become involved and ordered him to do so.[40]

An offender can be referred, with varying levels of coercion, by a number of different agencies and individuals. These include: federal or provincial/state correctional institutions, local or federal courts, local or national (RCMP or FBI) police forces, lawyers, police departments, child welfare agencies, hospitals and mental health centres, social service agencies, mental health professionals, physicians, social workers, and the relatives, friends, or partner of the offender.[41] State-sanctioned referrals generally carry substantially more influence in providing the initial motivation to attend and in compelling men to stay in the groups; the negative repercussions of not following through with various legal requirements strengthen the incentive to remain involved.[42]

Cross-System Involvement Requires Close Work with the Criminal Justice System

There is some variation in the degree to which offender programs are connected to the criminal justice system. Some groups have been established and are operated by the criminal justice system. But even the more independent groups have some connection with it; many offenders are referred through the courts. A 1986 U.S. national survey of sex offender programs, for example, indicated that 28 per cent of all services were residential (of this, 87 per cent were public and 13 per cent were private), while 72 per cent of all services were community-based (out-patient) services (40 per cent were public and 60 per cent were private).[43] In Canada and the United States, the statistics on the exact relationship between each social constructionist program and the criminal justice system are not easy to compile. Neither country has thoroughly monitored or coordinated its response. Currently, groups exist somewhere along a continuum ranging from minimal connection to total involvement with the criminal justice system. For most groups that are closely involved with the system, it appears there is little difficulty in that connection. If there is any problem, it is that support from the system declines with inadequate state funding (see the critique of the state's response, below).[44]

Nicholas Groth notes that there are some disadvantages in actually providing a sexual offenders' group within a correctional institution. First, sex offenders often are emotionally, physically, and sexually abused within a prison by other inmates; thus, they are more likely to want to maintain a low profile rather than attend a group that publicly identifies their offence. Second, the very culture of prison is more likely to reinforce exactly those values and behaviours of violence that the group is intended to end. Groth notes that 'traits such as trust, warmth, sharing, and affection are lost to deception, manipulation, threat, intimidation, force, and assault.' Third, while the controlled environment of a penal institution ensures that a man will not reoffend, incarceration does not permit him any opportunity to try out the techniques and skills taught in the treatment program. Too often, the benefit of the program – and of its associated support system – lasts only as long as the offender's stay in the institution.[45] Not having had the experience of a practical application of the concepts of non-violence, the offender will find it difficult to implement them in his post-prison lifestyle.

If offender programs were more coordinated with the local or federal judicial system, such a situation would be less common than it is. Coordination would facilitate the smooth transfer of the offender into a program which offers the possibility of reforming his behaviour, in contrast to simply keeping him locked in a jail cell, where he is unlikely to learn non-violent interpersonal skills. As noted above, there are programs offered in correctional institutions as a part of an offender's sentencing; however, there is a growing consensus that offender programs are best delivered in a community setting. Thus, the offender may serve his time in jail, but the second portion of his sentencing may be conducted in a community-based treatment program. This allows for more effective implementation of the skills learned in the group. Clearly, if the individual is assessed as being an immediate danger to himself or others, other treatment modalities will be necessary.

The Issue of Acceptability

Largely because of the limited resources available for offender treatment programs, the question of who should be accepted into a program is fairly contentious.[46] When there are a specific number of openings within any individual program during a given period of time, does one admit each and every offender who presents himself requesting treatment? Nicholas Groth argues that all should receive an opportunity, even those who do not appear highly motivated.[47] Dreiblatt, however, argues that selectivity is important – particularly for community-based programs.[48] Given that many offender programs are fairly new, there is a built-in incentive to admit the most motivated men – either because group facilitators, uncertain of their skills, hope they will be easier to work with, or because clinicians want their statistics to be favourable in order to please sceptical administrators and funders.

A wide range of treatment services should be available in order to accommodate all offenders. The psychotic sex offender should be treated in a mental hospital; the client who has numerous offences beyond his crimes of violence should be treated in a correctional institution. The man whose criminal behaviour consists solely of physical violence against women should receive treatment in a security treatment centre specifically designed for such offenders, or else in a community-based program. Finally, the individual being released back into the community would be treated in an out-patient community-based program. The paucity of these services increases waiting-lists, decreases referrals, and maintains our current high levels of male violence against women.[49]

Gender of the Co-facilitators

Most commentators have recognized the need for two facilitators in order to attend to all that occurs within a counselling group. This has not been questioned. The point in dispute when offender groups were first emerging in the late 1970s and early 1980s was whether the facilitators should be both male, or a male and female pair. Some argued that offenders need to have two positive male role models; others countered that the men could also benefit from a positive female role model.[50] Some programs struck something of a compromise. Men and women would facilitate the offender and victim groups, respectively, and at some point during the treatment, the facilitators would switch for an evening.[51] By the late 1980s, the issue tended to be less ideological and more practical in nature. The chief concern, rather than the gender of the facilitators, was their level of qualification and skill.

OFFENDER ASSESSMENT

All clinical work requires that counsellors understand thoroughly the nature and extent of the client's presenting concern. This is particularly important if they are working with violent offenders – poor judgment by a therapist can put the lives of other women at risk.[52] This section will review the four major components involved in assessing a sexual or physical offender: the clinical interview, the psychometric evaluation, the physiological assessment, and the decision regarding acceptability for treatment.[53]

Clinical Interview

The interview is the primary assessment tool. While the psychometric evaluation and physiological assessment can turn up crucial pieces of information, these are supplementary in nature. During the clinical interview, which generally lasts several hours and may be spread over a couple of sessions, the counsellor's goal is usually to learn about three main areas: the offender's characteristics and cognitions, his victim's characteristics, and the mechanics of how he offends.

Offender's Characteristics

Counsellors need to determine the offender's age, religious beliefs, substance abuse,[54] cultural/ethnic background, mental and physical health, family history, educational history, personal relationships and support networks, employment history, criminal history, and beliefs regarding his rehabilitation and the possibility of recidivism.[55] In the last area, which is more subjective in nature than all the others, it is harder to obtain information required to assess a man's motivation to change, his probability of attempting or committing suicide and homicide, and an assessment of danger to the man's partner/community.

Motivation to Change. Violent men who present themselves for counselling vary in their commitment to doing the necessary work. Stordeur and Stille have identified five categories into which prospective clients might fit. First is the 'compliant mandated client.' This individual makes the counsellor's task somewhat easier. He is likely to be motivated to work at changing and, if his enthusiasm should wane, he has varying degrees of state support compelling him to continue.

A second client type is the 'belligerent mandated client.' While he is present physically, he often attempts to get the counsellor to do the work, rather than taking responsibility for his own actions.

A third category consists of men who have been charged and are awaiting a court appearance. Frequently, these men will present themselves with the intention, or that of their lawyers, of making a good impression in court; the defence will be strengthened by the evidence that the offender has accepted responsibility for his actions and is seeking help. The hope – and reality – is that this action will reduce the court sentence. Too often, however, these men disappear from counselling soon after the conclusion of court proceedings. Many offender programs refuse to see such men until their criminal judgment has been dispensed.

A fourth group of offenders seeking counselling is made up of men whose partner is in a crisis shelter. These individuals – like the men who have been criminally charged but not convicted – typically are motivated to change not because they feel they need to, but in order to achieve some desirable goal – in this instance, the return of their partner to the family home. Unfortunately these men generally drop out of counselling once the woman returns home. With their violence unchanged, they are likely to repeat the cycle.

A fifth group are the 'aware' or 'quasi-feminist' men. They tend to appear very intellectual and comfortable talking about sex-role stereotyping and other social constructionist issues, yet their actions indicate that they have not incorporated these concepts into their daily existence.[56]

The counsellor's task is to motivate individuals to do some very difficult work. Breaking through denial mechanisms is one of the most important methods for increasing motivation. As long as offenders do not believe there is a problem, they will not bother working at its resolution. Denial can be witnessed in various actions and in varying degrees of frequency. Violent men are likely to blame the victim ('if she didn't want it, why was she dressed like that?'), to justify their violence ('She provoked me'), to distort or minimize the extent of the problem or its effects on the victim ('Oh, I just slapped her a couple of times'), to externalize responsibility ('I was drunk,' or 'I was out of control'), or to omit and lie about their violence in general ('Well, we do argue, but I don't have a problem with my anger – I'm not a batterer' or 'She didn't say she didn't want it').[57]

The counsellor needs to assess the offender's level of violence very thoroughly. Most men will disavow much or even all of their violence at the beginning, and minimize it throughout the course of treatment as well. From the first contact with the offender, counsellors must establish the unacceptability of denying and trivializing the problem of violence. If they do otherwise, the offender could perceive it as support for a dangerous tactic.[58] The reality, however, is that counsellors, try as they may, will not pick up every instance of denial and minimization. Offenders generally are extremely skilled at hiding their violence; by doing so they can protect themselves from really facing up to what they have done, possibly minimize sentencing decisions, or preserve an advantage in child custody and access negotiations. Denial has important repercussions for the clinician trying to identify the areas requiring treatment. Unfortunately, it is not uncommon for new issues to be acknowledged or discovered during treatment.[59] High denial levels attest to the need to establish contact with, and obtain information from, other components of the offender's system, such as his partner or the police. Yet even these may not always be the best resource, as they too may have a certain interest in either minimizing or maximizing the true levels of the man's violence.

While counsellors can, with varying degrees of success, work with a man's denial, the fundamental prerequisite of being accepted into an offenders' program is that the man take responsibility for his violence.[60] While his violent history may not yet be known to the counsellor in its entirety, he needs at least to take responsibility for that which is known and acknowledge that it is he, and not his victim, who has the problem.

Assessment of Partner/Community Safety. A second crucial part of determining the offender's characteristics is the effort to calculate the threat the client may pose to his partner or community.[61] Counsellors need to consider several issues. First, what access does the offender have to potential future victims? Does he offend indiscriminately, or only against his partner? If it is the latter and she is in a shelter, the risk is temporarily diminished – but what threat will exist upon her return? Second, what is the degree of the state's involvement with the client? For many offenders, knowing that significant prison sentences could follow a reoffence reduces the probability of their resuming violent activities. Third, what family and community ties has the therapist established? If both are informed of the man's problem, more people can be involved in helping him remain non-violent.[62]

If the offence was perpetrated by the man against his female partner, the question arises as to whether the man should continue to live with her. While there is no definitive answer to this question, there are some guidelines that may be helpful. First, if there are any legal restrictions on their living together, clearly these will predominate. If not, it will be necessary to ensure that the woman has the freedom to reflect upon and choose what she would like to do. If she wishes to leave the relationship, either temporarily or permanently, she needs to be provided with the resources necessary to make her choice a reality. If she feels comfortable staying with the man, one should attempt to determine the probability of the man reoffending. If there are any concerns in this regard, it is important to outline the advantages of a separation, which may or may not be permanent. Separation can allow the man to work at integrating new skills into his life at a more manageable pace, and can allow the couple some time to take care of themselves individually before coming back together – if that is what they both want. When a decision is made to separate, the counsellor can help the couple negotiate the length of time away, the nature of contact (if any) during the separation, and options to lengthen or shorten the break, if both parties should be willing.

Offenders need to realize that the goal of treatment is not to repair their relationship – it is to end the violence. If, in the process, the relationship is rejuvenated, well and good. But the woman may decide she has had enough of the man's violence and may choose not to wait to see if he really changes this time – she has probably heard such promises many times before. The fear of permanently losing a partner makes many men reluctant to try a separation. The counsellor needs to remind the man that continually holding onto his partner, and not allowing her the time she may need to decide for herself if she will stay in the relationship, only perpetuates the abuse and may well, in the long run, cause the failure of the relationship. Thus, the short-term break may pay off in the long term – if there is a significant change in the man's behaviour; though there are no guarantees. This is a useful opportunity to try to determine why the man is entering treatment for violence. Is he doing it just to save his relationship? If so, his commitment to continue may disappear if his partner either returns to or permanently leaves the relationship. The goal is for the man to want to change his behaviour not for some immediate gain, but because he realizes it is unacceptable. If he understands this, the guilt, shame, or embarrassment over the pain he has inflicted on others, and the desire to live a happier life without hurting other humans, will motivate him to change. It is important that the wish to change originate with the offender himself. If counsellors try to impose this on a client, they are not likely to keep him in the program for very long. However, establishing an authentic motivation can take some time, and often requires reinforcement throughout treatment.

While these issues need to be considered when working with sexual offenders, the assessment of the safety or endangerment of others is more complex, particularly if they have offended against persons they do not know. As with batterers, there is a tendency by counsellors to underestimate. Counsellors can be under tremendous pressure for a favourable assessment from prosecutors, defence lawyers, other social service workers, the offender, and his family. Adding to this the client's propensity to minimize his violence, one recognizes the problems involved in accurately assessing offenders.[63]

It is a difficult balance trying to protect the rights of society and the rights of the offender. The result, particularly for many sexual offenders, is mandatory treatment in a security institution.[64] One useful way for counsellors to circumvent the problem is to actively involve the social service and criminal justice systems. Rather than just having the counsellor as the sole arbiter, input is required from the police, lawyers, partners, the courts, the prison system, and the mental health system. This is not to diminish responsibility for any errors, but to ensure that information from various areas is included in making treatment decisions. The information flow can be reciprocal. The man's support system needs to be contacted when he has dropped out, has been asked to leave the group, or appears to be escalating toward another offence.[65]

Likelihood of Suicide. The counsellor should determine whether the offender is considering harming himself in some manner. Most offenders seek counselling because of some important change in their lives. As a result of their violence, they may be dealing with a separation or divorce, arrest or detention, complicated legal processes, fears about incarceration, financial difficulties, child welfare officials, living alone, a disrupted social support system, demands for a change in behaviour from friends and family, or the fear of not being able to learn non-violent coping mechanisms.[66] Being inundated with such changes can result in many offenders being in a state of crisis upon presentation, or at various points throughout treatment.

Counsellors need to acknowledge to the client that it is normal to feel overwhelmed or apprehensive about his ability to cope with a difficult situation, and ask him if he has had past or current thoughts about suicide. If he has not, but is feeling generally unprepared for how he will get through the next segment of his life, the counsellor needs to help the man review his supports or identify what he needs to do to establish such supports if they do not exist. However, if the man acknowledges suicidal thoughts, the clinician needs to determine if the man has actually determined a plan of action and, if so, whether he has the means to carry it out. Dependent upon the man's responses, the clinician can assess if there is any immediate danger. If it is high, there may be a need for a temporary hospital admission. If that is unnecessary, the counsellor should review with the client all the possible alternatives to suicide. Time should be spent identifying the advantages and disadvantages of several options before any are chosen. Counsellors need to establish contracts with their clients, whereby it is agreed that they will contact specific persons before trying to harm themselve.[67]

Victims' Characteristics

The clinician should determine the types of victims sought by the offender and help him recognize these patterns to prevent future violent incidents. Victims' characteristics include age range, race, nature of relationship to the client (acquaintance, partner, stranger, etc.), the process of selecting the victim, manner in which the offender blames the victim for the offence, physical appearance, extent of substance abuse, offender's perception of the victim's view of the offence, and the perpetrator's perception of the trauma inflicted upon the victim.[68]

Mechanics of Offending and Establishing a Control Plan

Offenders who drop out of treatment can be a threat to all women's safety. Unfortunately, the drop-out rate after the first clinical contacts is fairly high. One study of batterers found that about 20 per cent of the men who attended the intake sessions never made it to the group;[69] another study found that 25 per cent dropped out during the first two group sessions.[70] The size of this lost population creates the challenge for counsellors of skilfully treading a fine line between rewarding the offender for wanting help – even if he was encouraged to do so by the judicial system – and confronting him on the unacceptability of his abusive behaviour. This task needs to be accomplished without minimizing the amount of work that he will need to do to change his behaviour. At the same time, therapists need to help clients recognize that the program has something essential to offer them. The goal is to keep the man long enough to establish one of the most crucial components of the social constructionist intervention – a control plan for nonviolence. This is a list of alternate activities which should be followed when the individual recognizes he is moving toward a violent offence. This technique has two main phases.

Identifying Thoughts, Images, and Feelings. The man should learn to identify the nature of his individual progression toward violence. What are the physical, emotional, and situational manifestations that occur prior to, during, and following a violent incident? Does a pattern exist as to when, where, or how a man offends? With what amount of force does he commit his crime? Does he use a weapon? What does he communicate during the attack? What are his thoughts and feelings before, during, and after the offence? What is his process for rationalizing the violence, and in what way does he blame his victim? What is the nature of his cycle of violence? Can he identify when he is at a specific phase?

Despite initial difficulty, many men eventually identify a habitual sequence of events in their escalation toward violence (see Figure 5.1). A batterer may recognize symptoms such as the following: he clenches his fists, his heartbeat accelerates, he grinds his teeth, he swears at his partner, or he visualizes how he is going to strike out at her. A sexual offender may recognize fuzziness in his visual perception, drying up of his salivary glands, a pounding sensation in his head, and a feeling of intense anger toward women while conjuring up myths of women's enjoyment of rape.

The next step is to have him identify the 'point of no return,' from which he feels it is too difficult to re-route his behaviour. Generally, it will be easier for an offender to choose non-violent behaviour at a point when he is, for example, anxiously pacing the floor than when he is punching holes in the wall. To help ensure non-violence, clients should never allow themselves to reach this point of no return. They need to identify several preceding stages in the escalation pattern, so that their occurrence is a signal to leave the situation.[71]

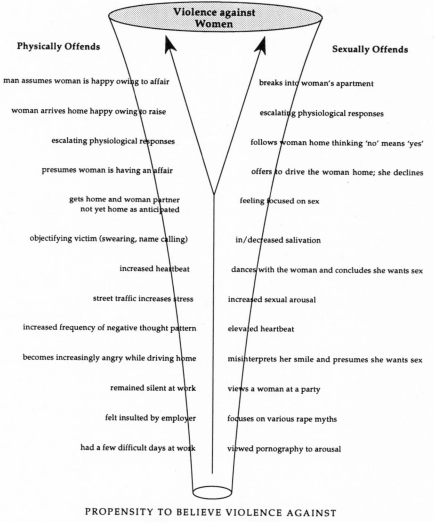

Physically Offends

man assumes woman is happy owing to affair

woman arrives home happy owing to raise

escalating physiological responses

presumes woman is having an affair

gets home and woman partner
not yet home as anticipated

objectifying victim (swearing, name calling)

increased heartbeat

street traffic increases stress

increased frequency of negative thought pattern

becomes increasingly angry while driving home

remained silent at work

felt insulted by employer

had a few difficult days at work

Sexually Offends

breaks into woman's apartment

escalating physiological responses

follows woman home thinking 'no' means 'yes'

offers to drive the woman home; she declines

feeling focused on sex

in/decreased salivation

dances with the woman and concludes she wants sex

increased sexual arousal

elevated heartbeat

misinterprets her smile and presumes she wants sex

views a woman at a party

focuses on various rape myths

viewed pornography to arousal

Violence against Women

PROPENSITY TO BELIEVE VIOLENCE AGAINST
WOMEN IS ACCEPTABLE

Figure 5.1
Sample violent offender escalations depicting situational, physiological, and emotional cues. (Note that each offender's escalation process may vary in length of time, include different cues, and proceed in a different order.)

Plan for Non-Violence. After identifying his pattern of escalation toward violence, each offender must establish for himself a strategy of prevention. The first priority should be to immediately leave any situation in which he recognizes that he is progressing toward violence; he can then follow a plan to halt and de-escalate his progression toward violence; ideally, this is accomplished through non-violent activities which encourage relaxation. Obviously, a batterer should not go chop wood; likewise, a sexual offender should not look at pornography. Preferable activities might include jogging, walking, talking to a friend, reminding himself he could face incarceration or lose his job if discovered, calling a crisis line, meditating, or whatever the individual feels is going to help him move away from violence.

Creating and implementing the control plan and time out is a crucial task for the man who wishes to change his abusive behaviour – and it can be one of the most difficult. Furthermore, to succeed, offenders need to realize that these means to non-violence will have to be constantly revised and amended as they learn more about the specific details of their escalation patterns, or as the patterns vary over time or in different settings. Each offender should monitor what fits for him and what needs to be changed. He must recognize that he alone is responsible for his violence or non-violence, and that excuses, such as that the woman was yelling at him and got him upset, or that he was too sexually aroused and lost control, are no longer acceptable. To help avoid such responses, thoroughness in establishing the control plan and the time out is essential. All potential scenarios for violence need to be considered to reduce the probability of a reoffence. Offenders should have several alternative plans for non-violence for use if for any reason the first plan cannot be put into action.[72]

Psychometric Evaluation

The clinical interview is often the most important part of assessment. In addition, a growing number of programs are using standardized psychological tests to provide new information or confirm information obtained from other sources. Testing covers areas such as drug and alcohol use and abuse, intelligence, physical and mental health, psychopathology, sexual history, sexual satisfaction, relationship status, passivity/assertiveness/hostility/aggression, social interaction skills, self-perception of abilities, and sexual attitudes – that is, knowledge, beliefs, attitudes toward women and children.[73] Clinicians use measures such as the Buss Durkee Hostility Inventory, the Conflict Tactics Scale, the Novaco Anger Inventory, the Brief Anger Aggression Questionnaire, the Hostility toward Women Scale, the Attitudes toward Women Scale, the Acceptance of Interpersonal Violence Scale, the Attitudes toward Wife Abuse Scale, the Clarke Sexual History Questionnaire, the Sexual Behaviour during Assault Self-Report Questionnaire; the Early Sexual Experience Self-Report Questionnaire, the Minnesota Multiphasic Personality Interview, the Tennessee Self-Concept Scale, the Ravens Progression Matrixes, and the Wechsler Adult Intelligence Scale.[74]

Physiological Assessment

This kind of assessment typically is reserved for sexual offenders. It is based on Zuckerman's work, which indicates that the most accurate indicator of physiological arousal in the adult male is penile tumescence.[75] Erectile responses are measured by a penile plethysmograph, which is a mercury-in-rubber strain gauge. The instrument is positioned so that it encircles the mid-shaft of the penis. As the penis becomes increasingly erect, the additional pressure reduces the capacity of the mercury column inside the plethysmograph to conduct a low-level electrical current. The resultant changes are mechanically charted and are extremely accurate.

The purpose is to determine what specifically arouses the offender. Very often, an offender who self-reports will, whether intentionally or unconsciously, minimize the range of arousing stimuli. The penile plethysmograph, when paired with a series of visual or auditory cues, enables the clinician and the offender to obtain a more accurate assessment. The slides presented typically include images of male and female children, adolescents, and adults. Accompanied by audiotapes, they can depict a range of sexual activities from consenting contact to violent assaults.

The utility of this tool cannot be overemphasized. In one study, Marshall et al. were able, with the penile plethysmograph, to detect in their programs twelve men who had denied any involvement in the sexual assault of children. The outcome of the testing resulted in seven of them acknowledging their abusive behaviour with children. Unfortunately, whether for reasons of limited funds, inadequate training of staff, or an aversion to technological measures, not all programs utilize this important resource. A 1986 survey of U.S. sex offender programs found that only 27 per cent of the 297 identified services used the penile plethysmograph.[76]

Decision

The next step in the assessment process is deciding whether the offender is eligible for treatment. Contrary to popular belief, few offenders suffer from serious mental disorders.[77] The majority of men who are not allowed into a group are rejected because of their low motivation to change.[78]

Significant chemical abuse is the second major reason why a client would be refused treatment. A survey of Canadian groups for batterers found that almost all groups decline such individuals.[79] A U.S. survey found that 30 per cent of refusals were based on candidates' alcohol and drug abuse.[80] Clients under the influence of drugs or alcohol are less likely to recognize the emotional and physical events and situations which might be used as cues to prevent violence. Such clients typically are referred to an outside agency to work on their chemical dependency. If appropriate, some clients will work with one agency on their violence and another regarding their drug/alcohol abuse.[81]

Referrals are also made if there is a need to address supplementary issues. This might entail relationship counselling, negotiating a separation, financial planning, obtaining birth control information, or employment counselling. The clinician operating the offenders' group should monitor the client's work in the supplementary programs.

Individual work may be required if the client is not quite ready for group work. Certain men may not yet fully recognize the need to change, or believe it is possible, or accept responsibility for their violence. Individual work also is important if the offender is in crisis, or exhibiting any significant suicidal tendency.[82]

Upon being assessed as acceptable for group work, an offender needs certain information. First, clinicians should explain the issues to be covered in the group. Clients need to understand how the material can help them establish and maintain a lifestyle of non-violence. Second, they need to be aware of group rules. Some typical rules are: no drugs or alcohol just prior to, or during, group sessions; no physical contact with another group member without first verifying with the intended recipient that it is acceptable; mandatory attendance (seldom may men miss more than one or two sessions without being expelled); and if a man is violent, this must be processed within the group. Third, clients need to know that there will be specific limits on confidentiality on the part of co-facilitators. For example, it cannot be maintained in cases where there are child welfare issues, fear for the safety of a potential victim, requests from corrections officials for information on attendance and participation, concerns that the partner does not know the offender is not attending or has been terminated from the group, or subpoenaed requests for testimony.[83] Informed consent to a group's rules and conditions is likely to increase the effectiveness of the treatment program.[84]

PROGRAM CONTENT

This section examines the content of the social constructionist group treatment programs. The issues listed will often be the focus of specific treatment sessions, but could also arise at any time throughout treatment.

Family of Origin

The goal is to help the offender recognize the positive and the negative effects that his family of origin have had on his personal development. Many men are unaware that they often repeat the lessons they learned as children about how to communicate their feelings, deal with anger, and relate to women. Sessions on family of origin can help offenders recognize that they need not even have witnessed violence; interpersonal patterns learned at home may have contributed to their violent behaviour.[85]

Key questions are used to facilitate discussion. Stordeur and Stille provide the following two sets of sample questions:

1. How were emotions expressed in your family?
2. How did individuals in your family handle anger?
3. How did people solve conflicts?
4. What methods of discipline were used?
5. How did you react to this discipline?
6. How did individuals in your family express love and affection?

1. As a child, what was the one phrase you remember hearing most often from your parents?
2. How were you praised? Criticized?
3. How is your present behaviour affected by your family of origin?
4. In what ways are you similar to your dad? Your mom?

5. What parallels are there between the way children were treated in your family of origin and the way you now treat children?[86]

Similar questions are asked of sexual offenders, though they can be supplemented with inquires into the familial values around sexuality, rape mythology, use of pornography, and general views on women.

Socialization Process

The intent is to help the offender recognize how he learned the acceptability of various forms of violence against women. The general purpose of the section is to re-educate and resocialize the group members to be non-violent. This can include:

1. revising their perceptions about male and female sex roles;
2. recognizing and changing their myths about male and female sexuality;
3. delineating appropriate and inappropriate sexual fantasies, expectations, and behaviour;
4. rewarding the expression of non-deviant sexual arousal;
5. working to understand and process the emotional, physical, and sexual abuse the client may have endured as a child;
6. rewarding empathic expression toward others and the development of sincere non-violent relationships;
7. increasing self-esteem;
8. learning and practising essential assertive communication skills rather than negative violent responses to difficult positive or negative feelings;
9. learning family and caretaking skills;
10. developing general occupational, interpersonal, and self-care skills;
11. recognizing how to control drug and alcohol use or abuse.[87]

Communication Styles

The objective is to identify functional and dysfunctional communication patterns.[88] Some of the major indicators of dysfunctional communication are as follows:

Ignoring Feelings. Our society has not encouraged men to feel or display the full range of potential human emotions; doing so would be perceived as being feminine. Anger has been the primary permissible emotion for men. Other than anger, a 'real man' does not have feelings;

he is tough and stoic. In the struggle to achieve this masculine ideal, men have been encouraged to sublimate the multiplicity of normal emotions under one or two broad categories. Even among men who express some emotions other than anger, frequently these have been funnelled into and expressed as a few generic emotions. For example, men are not encouraged to express feeling delighted, jubilant, or ecstatic. Even if a man remains able to identify these feelings to himself, he might only feel safe saying he is somewhat 'happy' – a rather inadequate description of his true state. Conversely, while a man may feel morose, depressed, or heartbroken, any of these various feelings may well be lumped under the broad category of feeling 'sad.'

Ignoring their feelings or masking their true emotions under more socially acceptable – but less accurate – generic labels can have disastrous consequences for men's ability to relate with others. Imagine the following hypothetical scenario between a man and a woman, Bob and Lois. Bob decides to pay Lois an impromptu visit; upon his arrival, Lois says 'thanks for coming – I'm happy to see you.' Lois may mean 'I'm thrilled you're here,' but Bob, listening to her actual response, may perceive it as 'Yeah, nice of you to drop by.' Both 'thrilled' and 'nice' fit under the broad category of happiness, but convey very different messages. For Bob, who may have put a lot of money and effort into making the visit, the perception that Lois feels merely 'nice' may lead him to feel that she is unappreciative or inconsiderate. Rather than identifying his feelings and checking them with Lois, Bob has made an assumption about Lois's true feelings regarding his visit. Bob may begin treating Lois in quite a different manner, becoming critical, for instance, or withdrawing. Unless the two individuals have a chance to discuss the difference in perception, their communication – and even their relationship – could be compromised.

Another outcome could develop from the same scenario. Bob gives Lois an expensive gift with the expectation that she will be ecstatic. Without accepting that Lois has the right to her own feelings about the gift, Bob may be quite disappointed by a less-than-enthusiastic response by Lois. Yet, Bob's disappointment is not the major problem. He, just as much as Lois, has a right to his feelings; his mistake is rather in how he deals – or does not deal – with them. If Bob lacks the skills to recognize that his expectations may have been somewhat unfounded, or the ability to communicate his feelings of disappointment, he may become angry and begin treating Lois abusively. Bob may become violent simply because Lois did not respond as anticipated. The escalation of many men toward violence often originates with something as trivial as this, or the previous, scenario.[89]

Taking Control in a Conversation. Men are more likely than women to take control of conversations. Many men will interrupt women who are speaking, ignore their attempts to enter a conversation, physically or visually invade women's personal space, change the topic to one they prefer, devalue woman's actual and potential contributions, remain intellectual and withhold emotions, and even raise their voices to drown out a woman's efforts to assert herself. Some men have been doing these things for so long that they are not even conscious of their actions. Others use such tactics quite intentionally. Both groups must recognize the abusive nature of their actions. They need to learn the value of listening to others, and to release their drive to dominate and control.[90]

Goal Fixation. Goal-oriented men tend to forget that there are some means of achieving a goal which cannot be justified. This is common with offenders, and particularly disturbing since they often use violence to attain their goals. A client accounting for a violent episode may claim, for example, that his objective was simply to finish a conversation with his female partner. However, upon questioning, it will become apparent that what he really wanted was for his partner to concede a point in an argument and admit that he was right. If, for whatever reasons, a woman is not willing to do this, the man may insist on continuing the conversation, rather than accepting that it is over, and escalate toward violence in order to make his point. Offenders frequently disregard the woman's right to choose her own agenda. While her choice may displease her male partner, the fact is that he does have several options besides violence. Offenders need to recognize that it is preferable to forsake a goal than resort to abusive methods in order to achieve it. Learning the acceptability of disagreement between two people – particularly a man and woman – is difficult – and essential – work for offenders.[91]

Engaging in Rampant Negative Self-Talk. Offenders typically spend inordinate amounts of time devaluing both their woman partner and themselves. They may perceive that they have been violated, ignored, or put down. Obviously, if convinced of this perception, they are likely to behave differently than if they had a positive self-image.

Many offenders feel inordinately resentful of their circumstances. At the same time, they need to learn that feeling offended when they truly have been mistreated or hurt is a normal, healthy reaction. Problems arise when offenders funnel such feelings into anger, which is expressed through violent behaviour, particularly towards women. Facilitators in treatment programs can help men understand that, while they certainly have a right to be angry and express anger, they do *not* have the right to be violent toward other people. Thus a man who has not had a relationship for several months, or did not have intercourse with his last date, may feel hurt, dejected, or even angry. But he does have choices as to how he responds to those feelings. Facilitators and other group members can help individual offenders develop the skills to identify and implement the necessary non-violent means.[92]

Lack of Assertiveness Skills. Assertiveness involves identifying one's feelings and thoughts on an issue and verbalizing them in a manner that is respectful of others. Offenders frequently lack this skill, and instead swing between extreme non-aggressiveness and unacceptable aggression. Rather than effectively dealing with feelings as they arise in situations, they ignore them, preventing their healthy expression. Over time, as more emotions are ignored, the pressure builds. When it gets too high, the self-depreciating offender convinces himself that he has endured too much and is entitled to blow up. This tendency, when combined with the belief that violence against women is acceptable, often results in an abusive episode.

To non-violently resolve discrepancies in interpersonal communications, offenders need to learn to identify feelings, to recognize how, and when, to best express those feelings, to effectively handle criticisms, to make constructive requests, to calmly say no if they so desire, and to work to a compromise.[93]

Inadequate Paraphrasing, Summarizing, and Listening. People will often draw incorrect conclusions from comments made by other individuals. We internalize what has been said to us, process it, and choose a response. Frequently, however, this is done without our having first verified with the other person what we thought we heard. They may actually have meant something different from what we have concluded. This can lead us to inappropriately respond to the original comment simply because of a breakdown in communication that could easily have been avoided.

Offenders, in their attempts at controlling or devaluing women, will often fail to, or will choose not to, listen. They should work at understanding what has been said, remain alert for self-depreciating thoughts, and not take personally things not intended to hurt them. Even when another's comments are inappropriate or hurtful, the offender need not respond with violence. He should relinquish his desire for power over others and direct his energy toward recognizing the power within himself to make non-violent responses.[94]

Drug/Alcohol Use and Abuse

Offenders with significant chemical abuse habits are typically referred to special treatment to deal with that issue. However, even where abuse is not chronic, treatment programs attempt to increase awareness of the part drug and alcohol play in violence. Because the social support network of many offenders is centred around drug and alcohol use, group members are confronted to examine their consumption patterns in relation to their violent behaviour towards women; they are supported to discover how else they might socialize and build support networks if drugs and alcohol are making non-violence difficult to implement.

When discussing this issue in the group, facilitators may recognize that some members, not detected earlier, require referral to another agency to deal specifically with their drug/alcohol use or abuse.[95]

Parenting

This is an important area for at least three reasons. First, men in the group may have been, as children, emotionally, physically, or sexually abused. Second, since our society traditionally has not encouraged active participation of men as parents, their knowledge of effective parenting may be very limited. Third, group members may have been abusive toward their children.

This session complements the earlier one on family of origin. Offenders will have examined the influence of their family on their development. Now the focus is on the offender's influence on his own children. Having acknowledged what it felt like to grow up in an abusive home, the offender will find it harder to excuse the inappropriateness of his own abusive parenting. If the offender should trivialize the difficulty his children may be experiencing, the facilitators and members of the group can confront him on the discrepancy between his earlier comments during the session on family of origin. The combination of the two sessions can be very effective in addressing child abuse, in that it significantly increases the offender's empathy for his children.

For individuals with significant parenting difficulties, it may be necessary for child welfare authorities to be contacted to intervene on the child's behalf. If the child is not at risk, a referral of the offender to a parenting group may be appropriate.

The men review various parenting styles, have an opportunity to talk about the difficulties of parenting, and can recognize how the skills for non-violence against women can also be used when parenting. Being aware of one's self-depreciating thoughts and taking time out can be crucial factors in preventing child abuse and making parenting less frustrating.

All group members – even those without children – can benefit from examining parenting issues. At the very least, the material can help the men further develop an understanding of the parenting styles prevalent in their family of origin.

PROGRAM PROCESS

The following is a brief review of the major techniques utilized in offender treatment programs.

Cognitive Restructuring (Self-Talk)

Cognitive restructuring is based on Meichenbaum's work. It is 'a therapeutic approach whose major mode of action is modifying the patient's thinking and the premises, assumptions, and attitudes underlying his cognitions. The focus of therapy is on the ideational content involved in the symptom, namely, the irrational inferences and premises.'[96]

Offenders are particularly prone to negatively interpret the actions of women in their lives. By cognitively restructuring their external reality in a negative light, they legitimize their violence against women. For example, a man who has a high degree of acceptance of rape myths (i.e., no means yes, or a certain style of dress means the woman wants sex) sees a woman walking down the street wearing a short skirt; in interpreting this event, he may ascribe specific intentions to her (i.e., she is asking to get raped) and choose his actions accordingly.

Most people are unaware that they are, either positively or negatively, filtering their external reality (see Figure 5.2).[97] Their perception is

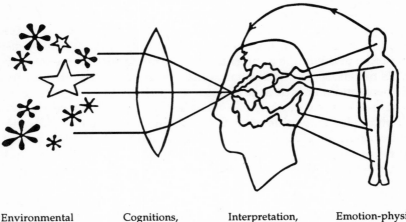

| Environmental events | Cognitions, perceptions (sensory input) | Interpretation, self-talk (irrational ideas) | Emotion-physical system |

Example

A. Facts and events

A mechanic replaces a fuel pump he honestly believed was malfunctioning, but the car's performance doesn't improve. The customer is very upset and demands that he put the old fuel pump back.

B. Mechanic's self-talk

'He's just a grouch – nothing would please him.'
'Why the hell do I get all the tough jobs?'
'I ought to have figured this out by now.'
'I'm not much of a mechanic.'

C. Emotions

Anger and resentment
Depression

Figure 5.2
Cognitive filtering and restructuring of social reality (from Martha Davis, Elizabeth Eshelman, and Matthew McKay, *The Relaxation and Stress Reduction Workbook* [Oakland, CA: New Harbinger 1982], 100)

that what they think and feel is the true external reality. With offenders, this kind of subjective distortion, when combined with their relatively greater acceptance of rape and battering myths and their
willingness to use violence, can be very dangerous. Offenders also
tend to be particularly quick to negatively process their external reality. Ellerby notes that offenders are likely to cognitively distort their
self-perceptions (which contributes to low self-esteem), the nature and
reasons for the offence, their responsibility, and the victim's role (by
extensive blaming).[98]

The objective is for the men to recognize that there exists an interme-
diate processing step between experiencing and responding to their
external reality. This step involves how they explain and ascribe meaning to what they experience. For example, if a man's female partner is
late coming home from work, he has many choices as to how to interpret this fact: she may have been delayed because of a busy day at
work, a traffic jam, or a last-minute decision to purchase some groceries. Without actually knowing the correct reason, the man may talk
himself into a negative belief – that his partner is having an affair with
another man, for instance – to be abusive or violent upon her arrival.
Offenders must become aware of how they cognitively filter their perceptions of what they see occurring around them prior to responding.
By learning how he can change the way in which he processes reality,
an offender can come to recognize and re-route, in a positive manner,
his negative self-talk and thinking, and thus avoid being violent. For
this to happen, the man needs constant feedback, challenging, and
supportive, non-judgmental confrontation both within himself and
from other group members, as well as the group facilitators. It is essential to maintain a balance between confrontation and support so that
the man will remain motivated to complete this often difficult work –
and so that he will not choose to leave the group because of feelings of
frustration and failure.[99]

Control Plan Modifications/Improvements

Control plans have two components: a list of the physical, emotional,
and situational cues preceding a violent incident, and a list of non-
violent activities for use during a time out from violence. In most
programs, control plans are established during the initial clinical
assessment (see above, Mechanics of Offending and Establishing a
Control Plan, pp. 147–50).

Control plans are constantly evolving. Over time, as offenders gain more understanding of their problem, they will recognize additional emotional, physiological, and situational events that are part of their escalation toward violence. These can be additional cues to be integrated into the control plan and make it more thorough and accurate. Ideally, offenders will establish a number of viable contingency plans for a multitude of potentially violent situations. Group time needs to be allocated throughout the duration of the offender group for feedback and modification of each man's control plan.

Aversion Therapies

Aversion therapies are used to help offenders in choosing non-violent behaviour. The intervention entails pairing aversive, or unpleasant, stimuli with stimuli which have led to violence, in an attempt at modifying the offender's responses. The most commonly used aversion therapies use electrical and olfactory techniques. Since certain men will respond to one technique and not the other in certain situations, many therapists utilize both techniques. Aversion therapies are used primarily with sexual offenders to alter their reactions to preferred sexual stimuli.[100]

Puffs of ammonia fumes (smelling salts), for example, are paired with brief aural and/or visual presentations of the offender's deviant-arousal object. Repeated pairings are intended to make the offender cease to associate the stimulus with a pleasant response. The advantage of the olfactory approach is that an offender can carry with him several ammonia capsules and use them as needed to prevent arousal and erection responses.[101]

High drop-out rates and a desire to break the offender's pattern as quickly as possible are the two reasons why therapists generally introduce aversion therapies during the initial assessment period. Once in the group, some offenders may need additional time to strengthen the connection between the two stimuli. If only a few men require additional work, focusing too much on the needs of one or two individuals may be disruptive to the group process. In such a case, one-on-one sessions with the therapist, while requiring additional time, are likely to be more effective.

The application of aversive techniques is not without controversy. Because clinicians can easily cross the boundary between using such interventions to curb the client's criminal sexual tendencies, and inflicting aversive stimuli as a punishment, there is a serious concern about abuse. While the ethical conduct of the therapist is an issue with any counselling technique, the use of the chemical or electrical stimuli makes this technique more vulnerable to criticism. One Canadian survey of programs for sex offenders found that they were more likely to use aversion therapies (75 per cent of Canadian programs) than their American counterparts. The difference was attributed to Canada being 'a relatively less litigious society,' with a less-developed clients' rights movement. The report noted that despite this national tendency, jurisdictional differences exist. Hospital by-laws in the Alberta Hospital in Edmonton, for example, forbid the use of aversive procedures.[102]

Covert Sensitization

Covert sensitization involves the association of unpleasant imagined events with the offender's deviant stimuli. By not using physical entities such as ammonia or physical shock, covert therapies circumvent the legal and ethical difficulties associated with aversive interventions. Since the rationales of aversion and covert therapies are identical, frequently the former can be used instead of the latter. Covert sensitization, being fairly easy to implement, lends itself to use with populations other than sex offenders; it is also used with battering groups.

The client must first identify the physical, emotional, and situational cues involved in his progression toward violence, and identify the points he must not pass if he is to interrupt the process by taking time out. These points in the escalation process are paired with one or more unpleasant imagined events. The imagery can be aversive either physiologically – thoughts about vomiting, for instance – or psychologically – such as imagining what it would be like to have his partner leave him because he has been violent, or spending time in jail for a sexual assault.[103]

Role-Modelling

In a group setting, therapists are important role models. Clients see them identify and express thoughts and emotions, communicate effectively, and practise non-violent problem-solving techniques. Offenders witness a consistent implementation of the theory and skills discussed in the group. Role-modelling helps the men incorporate new, non-violent components into their lifestyles.

Since role-modelling is an important learning tool, many therapists prefer mixed-gender co-facilitation. It allows group members to view interactions between a man and a woman that are based on trust, respect, and equality. They witness an informed, intelligent, assertive female co-leader, they hear two facilitators handling conflict or differences of opinion, they observe the respect with which the male facilitator treats his equal female partner, and they see the male facilitator taking risks in identifying and expressing his feelings, without feeling his masculinity is being compromised. Witnessing the components of healthy masculinity, femininity, and a positive and productive relationship between the two facilitators can contribute significantly to the value reformation desired of offenders. By changing the values associated with certain actions (i.e., it is good or admirable, and not cowardly, to be able to walk away from a situation in order to avoid being violent), the facilitators can help individual offenders consider new modes of behaviour.

Role-modelling also can be used in another, more active, manner. Working as a large group or in smaller clusters, offenders themselves can role-play difficult situations from their lives. For men who have had problems communicating effectively, avoiding self-depreciating thoughts, or implementing a control plan for non-violence, this is a safe setting in which to attempt new and different responses. Role-playing helps the men appreciate the difficulty of putting theory into practice and to develop their skills and confidence.[104]

Confrontation and Encouragement

Facilitators must not let offenders minimize, trivialize, or ignore their violence. With confrontive, probing, clarifying, but non-argumentative questions, facilitators can help offenders to learn more about their violence and to take responsibility for it. Insufficient confrontation will expose only half-truths. An offender may acknowledge his violence by saying 'Yes, I slapped her a few times.' With more confrontive questioning, the facilitators may discover that he also vandalized the house, repeatedly punched the woman, and tried to strangle her.

Despite the importance of confrontation, it is virtually pointless unless it is balanced with encouragement. The two need not compromise each other. Avoiding confrontation – by not stating categorically that all violence is unacceptable or by providing insufficient encouragement (by not helping offenders deal with the frustrations of the new demands placed upon them) – may prevent offenders from believing they can change their behaviour, and consequently from staying in the group long enough to achieve their goal of non-violence. While a court-mandated client might remain, his level of commitment could plummet, affecting the motivation of the remaining members. Offenders have a great deal of difficult work to do to effect change in their lives; this requires constant support and reassurance.

Ellerby's term for encouragement is 'relapse prevention.' He notes three factors which must not be ignored. First, offenders need to be made aware that old escalation patterns will occur. This does not mean the offender has failed; rather, it indicates that work still remains, for the reality is that maintaining non-violence is a lifelong task. Second, if a man should reoffend, he needs to be encouraged to learn from his mistake and revise his control plan, if need be. As Ellerby states, 'one lapse does not need to become a complete fall off the wagon.' Third, the men need to remember that violent urges will arise, but that each of these will pass over time, and also that to maintain non-violence, they may need to implement a form of covert sensitization (i.e., reviewing the negative ramifications of following through with their violence).[105]

Therapists who fail to maintain the necessary balance between confrontation and support can indirectly endanger the safety of additional women.[106]

Monitoring

Since offenders often will minimize or deny their violence, therapists need to supplement what is reported to the group by the individual offender with information from other sources. The personal contacts established during the assessment phase to ensure partner safety can be used to determine if the client is secretly reoffending. These contacts might include lawyers, neighbours, partners, work colleagues, and parole officers. At least one program in the United States trains people from the offender's support system to raise their awareness, maintain surveillance on the offender, and inform the clinician should the client appear to be heading toward a reoffence. These supports can be maintained and utilized even after the group therapy has ended.[107]

The information flow, however, should not be just from the support system to the therapist; clinicians have an ethical responsibility to contact the offender's support system whenever they have reason to believe the client is soon likely to reoffend. Daniel Sonkin has identified eight important guidelines for determining whether to warn or protect potential victims:

1. if violence is escalating in frequency or severity during the course of treatment;
2. if explicit or implicit threats are made;
3. if the client is in crisis and is unable to assure the therapist of his ability to control himself (even with assurance, the therapist may need to issue a warning);
4. if the victim expresses fear for her own or another's safety;
5. if there is a escalation in the client's use of drugs or alcohol;
6. if the client refuses to cooperate with the treatment plan;
7. if the therapist discovers that the client has not talked about acts of violence committed while in treatment;
8. if the client has committed life-threatening acts of violence or made specific threats to kill prior to entering treatment (not discovered until in treatment) or during treatment.[108]

Victim Empathy

Removing many of the myths about female sexuality, sexual assault, and battering from an offender's belief system can sensitize him to the painful effects of his violence. This awareness can diminish the ease with which he will reoffend.

Clinicians use a variety of techniques: films such as *A Scream from Silence*, which convey the horrors of sexual assault;[109] guest speakers, such as women facilitators from groups for the female victims of male violence, or sexual assault counsellors; role-playing; and guided imagery (a type of visualization process in which clients observe their feelings in hypothetical scenarios). If one or more of the group members was victimized as a child, for example, it may be helpful for him to share the memories of his experiences with the group.[110]

Relaxation Techniques

In order for offenders to successfully maintain a lifestyle of non-violence, it is essential that they know how to relax, both physiologically and emotionally. The social constructionist literature stresses the integral role of relaxation techniques. Daniel Saunders, for example, advocates the combination of relaxation therapies with cognitive restructuring to increase the effectiveness of each.[111]

Relaxation techniques include listening to audiotapes of guided imagery or nature, exercise, meditation, biofeedback, and Jacobson's progressive relaxation. Early in their treatment, offenders need to be informed of the importance of relaxation and taught techniques for it. Offenders should develop an awareness of the physical and mental components of a relaxed state, and recognize that deviations toward anxiety, frustration, or violence may indicate the need to implement their control plan. Relaxation therapies should be integrated into the offender's daily routine.[112]

Sharing

A large portion of the time within an offender group is allocated to instructive information transfer in order to expand offenders' knowledge and awareness of the various issues associated with their problem. The next largest portion of group time is set aside for members to share their experiences in an open group discussion. Topics might include: an offender's most violent incident;[113] a recent violent incident; the effort involved in integrating the new group material into their lives; how they modified the material for greater success; or how certain components of the program have not worked for them. Most offenders are socially isolated or lack ongoing close contact with any support system; the peer experience, by providing such support, is thus a vital element in the success of these programs. The benefits include: the opportunity for offenders to hear the experiences of other men; mirroring and feedback; a context in which to normalize their own difficulties, successes, and failures; and the solidarity of their peers in the continuing struggle to effect significant behaviour change. The men learn more about themselves and each other, and about men in general. These discussions generate disclosure of information that later is useful either in acknowledging and supporting a man through a difficult learning process or in confronting the man on his action (or lack thereof) by reminding him that earlier he had identified something he wanted to change.

The importance of the peer group in providing feedback cannot be overemphasized. Some thoughts and suggestions, coming from the facilitators, very often will not carry the same weight they would when expressed by another offender. The peer has the credibility of having 'been there' and of wrestling with the same issues. This component, obviously, is absent in individual counselling.

To get the best use of sharing time, facilitators maintain several important limits. Stordeur and Stille have itemized five points for consideration: (1) retain a focus on the issue at hand; (2) avoid long, intro-spective journeys; (3) recognize when a man needs more than sharing time; (4) be willing to be directive when necessary; (5) when possible, partition sharing time according to demand.[114]

POST-GROUP INTERVENTION – FOLLOW-UP GROUPS

Follow-up groups have evolved for two main reasons. First, offenders need a setting in which to continue developing their skills of non-violent conflict resolution. Joining a follow-up group can reduce an offender's likelihood of recidivism. Second, many offenders who have persisted with a program often simply do not want it to end. They have taken significant risks with the other members, established strong emotional bonds, and come to appreciate the supportive learning envi-ronment.

Such groups are modelled roughly on a self-help principle. Facilita-tors are either always in attendance, or will drop in from time to time to ensure the follow-up group has not become dysfunctional – for example, by neglecting the practice of confronting individuals on their abuse. The group format is similar to the sharing time previously expe-rienced in the treatment group. If the group deems it necessary, a speaker may come in to deliver a presentation on a specific issue. Notwithstanding the occasional presence of a facilitator, these groups – compared with the initial treatment group – can foster in their mem-bers a greater feeling of autonomy, concern for others, and a sense of mastery and ownership of the group.

SUMMARY OF THE SOCIAL CONSTRUCTIONIST OFFENDER GROUP INTERVENTION

When one examines the components of the social constructionist approach to working with offenders, the intervention – at least in theory – appears promising. Social constructionism integrates a variety of clinical approaches. While the emphasis is on how our society cre-ates violent men, physiological components are taken into account as well; for example, in the identification of physical cues to help the offender determine his emotional state and forestall a violent incident.

Yet as with any intervention, it is necessary to determine how well it works in practice. This entails a critical analysis of the state response to male violence against women.

Critique of the Current State of Response

Prior to 1980, offender programs were virtually non-existent. In Canada, programs for batterers grew from four in 1981 to over thirty in 1984 and 114 in 1989.[115] Programs for sexual offenders increased from twelve in 1984 to twenty-five in 1990.[116]

American statistics are somewhat more difficult to obtain.[117] Greater legislative control by individual states – as compared to a national coordination of efforts – has caused fragmentation of services and decreased the general awareness of what work is being done across the country. The available U.S. statistics reveal a significant increase in the number of treatment programs for offenders: in 1977, in Boston, one of the first U.S. programs for batterers was started; by 1987, one American directory listed 185 programs for men who batter,[118] and by 1990, an additional 307 groups had been formed, bringing the total number to 492 groups.[119] U.S. programs for sexual offenders also increased in number: in 1984, Knopp identified 197 service programs for sex offenders;[120] by 1986, Knopp, Rosenberg, and Stevens listed 297 programs.[121]

The proliferation of groups is certainly encouraging, though it does not tell us very much about their effectiveness. The key question is whether the state response, as it exists now, can succeed in thoroughly ending male violence against women. This section, therefore, will examine two components of the current state response: internal problems of offender programs; and the role these services play in the larger social structure.

INTERNAL PROBLEMS

Most Groups Focus on Men Who Batter

The figures given above indicate that there are significantly more groups for batterers than for sex offenders. This difference is compounded by the typically longer duration of most sexual offender group programs, which means that even if the quantities of groups were comparable, the number of sexual offenders served would always be lower. While the number of sex offender groups is growing, the few that do exist are located in the larger urban areas. Short of relocating an offender so that he might attend the program, which would be prohibitively expensive, the other option is to imprison the individual. While this certainly will bring the individual to the program, many clinicians argue that incarceration for treatment is not always the best intervention strategy; the nature of the prison environment may reinforce the very behaviour that the treatment is trying to change. Consequently, sex offenders who are not near a large urban centre or in jail – which is to say, the vast majority – do not receive treatment. At best, they may have a probation officer, with whom they periodically are obliged to meet.[122]

There is no mention in the literature of treatment groups for emotionally abusive men. This deficiency exists despite evidence indicating that the emotional abuse of women may be the most difficult behaviour to change.[123] Presumably, an emotionally abusive male, in the absence of treatment groups, could pursue individual counselling. But such a proposition has several drawbacks. First, the client will never reap the benefit of a group dynamic (i.e., peer confrontation and support). Second, because waiting-lists at publicly funded agencies are long, and fees are high for private therapists, he may not be able to find someone to work with him. Third, many counsellors, when faced with numerous demands for services, will institute a form of clinical triage. If a sex offender, a batterer, or an incest victim is seeking treatment at the same time as a man who has been emotionally abusive, treatment of the latter's problem may well be considered a lower priority and deferred.

Urban Bias

In North America, urban areas are served better than rural areas by the existing social services system. This continues to be the case despite the evidence that male violence against women is not only an urban problem. In 1986 in Canada, only six of the ten provinces had established programs for sex offenders; some of these programs were, in fact, only 'in the latter stages of planning.' Most of the programs were in large urban centres or in smaller adjacent communities.[124] The situation is not considerably better for batterers' groups. In Prince Edward Island, for example, in 1989, there was only one. Some men were driving more than 140 kilometres in each directon to attend. Unfortunately many men will not be sufficiently motivated to overcome obstacles of time or distance in order to attend.[125]

Similar problems exist in the United States. A 1984 national survey of U.S. batterers' programs indicated that at least 60 per cent were located in major urban areas and that there exist significant regional variations. The north central United States had 35 per cent of the groups; the Northeast, 31 per cent; the Northwest, 15 per cent; the Southwest, 13 per cent; the south central, 3 per cent; and the Southeast, 3 per cent.[126]

Services rarely exist in rural areas. Often, people with specialized skills simply are not available within small communities. When there is a skilled individual living and working in the area, he or she may be confronted with numerous problems. These include a heavy generic counselling load, isolation from other therapists who work with offenders, and divided community support for the program.

Compounding the problem of getting rural offenders into treatment is the low profile of existing offender groups outside of their immediate community. Since the groups are not well known to rural therapists, few men outside of an offender group's immediate catchment area are referred to it.[127]

The Intervention Is Too Brief

Short Duration of Groups

In 1988, the Canadian Council on Social Development surveyed approximately 100 groups for men who batter. From the forty-five respondents, they determined that the majority of programs consisted of twelve to sixteen weekly meetings and acknowledged that some were shorter.[128] A U.S. survey found that 36 per cent of the programs lasted four to twelve weeks, 31 per cent thirteen to twenty-four weeks, and 20 per cent twenty-five to thirty-six weeks.[129]

Jerry Finn's 1985 review of thirteen batterers' programs in North Carolina found the duration ranged from six to sixteen sessions.[130] A program operating in Windsor, Ontario, in 1983, consisted of eight sessions and included men who had already gone through the program.[131] Another Canadian program would start whenever there were ten referrals, running for only six sessions. The researchers noted that although a chief goal of these programs was to connect these men with other – presumably longer-term – services, they ignored the potential for a high drop-out rate when clients transfer from one service to another.[132]

A similar disparity of duration can be observed among treatment groups for sex offenders. Howard Barbaree and William Marshall, in an overview of Canadian programs, found a significant variation in the length of programs, with some lasting more than two years.[133] The implication is that the two-year program appears more to be the exception than the rule.

There is growing evidence that approximately nine months of intense work is required to change a man's violent behaviour.[134] Clearly, then, the numerous six-to-eight-week, even the twelve-to-sixteen-week, programs are not providing adequate time to cover the necessary content and to process issues, or for the men to practise their new skills. With so brief a therapeutic intervention, many of the offenders will not even have had time to go through their full cycle of violence while in the group. A participant's learning process might thus take place only on the theoretical level, without the powerful experiental learning afforded by practical applications. Cycles of violence are various; there are men who can violently offend, be put in a group, graduate, and be back on their own, all during the honeymoon phase of intense remorse and good behaviour after a violent incident. Then, at the point when the honeymoon phase begins to pass into the escalation phase and it is most essential for them to be in the group to receive coaching and support, they will have great difficulty choosing non-violence.[135]

Minimal Individual Tracking or Follow-up Group Work

Most offenders programs have either few established follow-up mechanisms, or none at all.

Follow-up Evaluation. The purpose of follow-up is twofold: it allows clinicians an opportunity to evaluate the effectiveness of the intervention, and it maintains contact where recidivism is likely.[136] Follow-up does not typically occur. The majority of U.S. programs do not follow up. Among those that do, the median amount of time between termination and follow-up is four months; only half perform more than two follow-ups.[137] A 1985 Canadian review of sex offender programs notes that 'like their American counterparts, the Canadian programs were weakest in the area of evaluation and follow-up.'[138] This is a common concern.[139] Browning emphasizes that there is a need for 'tightly-designed demonstrations of treatment effectiveness, rather than for descriptive or "process" evaluations. Only the former can provide assurance to women's groups, corrections officials and other referral sources that treatment is a desirable option for assaultive men.'[140]

Few Follow-up Groups. Ongoing follow-up support groups are a critical factor in the maintenance of non-violence.[141] Yet, as lately as 1988, follow-up groups were still the exception rather than the rule.[142]

Among the programs that provide follow-up services for offenders, some counsellors note the difficulty of maintaining contact with the clients, or of finding the time to do so. Others, citing staff shortages, have not even availed themselves of external agents that would be amenable to doing the work. University campuses are a resource that could be utilized. Many graduate students in psychology or social work, for example, would appreciate the chance to gain experience by assisting various offender programs. But the demand for their services has not been high.[143]

There also is the problem that follow-up work often is poorly implemented. Some facilitators, lacking any other option, are compelled hastily to recruit and train volunteer counsellors to ensure that the offenders' group receives support. While theoretically this could be a viable solution, the time required to meet the volunteer counsellors' supervision needs could easily consume any time saved (for the facilitator) by the volunteer program. Other counsellors, who may view operating an offenders' follow-up program as a lower priority than working with men who have just presented themselves for counselling,[144] will not put any effort at all towards creating such a group.

Some programs initiate and maintain contact with the offenders' female partners, who often can provide a more accurate and detailed report on the offenders' behaviour than he himself will. Yet the reality is that this frequently is not even attempted – or if it is, is not maintained.[145] This occurs despite awareness of its importance.[146]

Dropping Out

Few offenders remain in treatment for very long. In the United States, 60 per cent of the programs for batterers claimed dropping out to be a significant problem, with rates ranging from 50 to 75 per cent.[147] One study found a drop-out rate of 25 per cent after the first two sessions.[148] It appears that the lengthier the program, the higher the drop-out rate.[149] This correlation is disturbing, in light of the evidence that to change a violent offender's behaviour requires approximately nine months of intense work.[150]

Effectiveness

Successful programs should end a man's violence. Robert Longo has developed the following criteria for assessing an offender's progress:

1. Responsibility
2. Behavioural control
3. Accepts Feedback
4. Self-disclosure
5. Stress management
6. Use of leisure time
7. Insight into the offense

8. Social maturity
9. Empathy
10. Self-esteem/concept
11. Impulse control
12. Self-expression
13. Self-awareness
14. Participation[151]

Appraising an offender's performance in each of these areas may be complicated and time-consuming. The clinician who does so, however, will obtain a fairly accurate indication of how successfully the client has modified his behaviour, and which areas will require additional work before treatment can be concluded.

Program success, however, is not always equated with stopping each offender's violence. Objectives commonly are formulated in terms of reducing the threat to the public.[152] Yet 'threat' is often inadequately defined. Does the offender only beat his wife once a month rather than three times? This may indeed be some kind of improvement, but the original problem remains, even if its frequency of manifestation has diminished. As for the victim, she must continue to live in fear, knowing that an attack is still likely to occur at some point. Clinicians struggle with this issue of reduced threat, not wanting either to minimize or to overestimate an offender's progress.

Most researchers measure effectiveness by the recidivism rates of group members. Yet, even here, the figures are anecdotal, wide-ranging, and not too impressive. The following are a few examples of studies of effectiveness.

Batterers' Groups
- Jeffrey Edleson, David Miller, Gene Stone, and Dennis Chapman evaluated a twelve-week program during a follow-up period of forty-six weeks and found that with seven of the nine men, physical abuse ended and 'substantially curtailed another man's abuse.' They acknowledge that there was one man on whom the program did not have much of an effect.[153]
- In a program with 5 court-ordered and 165 voluntary offenders, where the men averaged 7.8 sessions, the men and their female partners were contacted six months after treatment. Seventy-five per cent of the couples were still living together. Of those, 59 per cent

reported an end to sexual or physical violence. Only 14 per cent reported no emotional abuse.[154]
- In a U.S. national survey of batterer programs, 67 per cent reported that up to 25 per cent of the offenders returned to battering; 15 per cent of the groups said that no client reoffended. The average reported recidivism rate was 16 per cent.[155]
- David Currie of Toronto's Family Service Centre, the facilitator of the first batterer group in Canada, reports that for 33 per cent of clients, his programs do not work.[156]

Sexual Offenders' Groups
- Nicholas Groth evaluated his offender program at the Connecticut Correctional Institution and found a 19 per cent and 36 per cent recidivism rate among those attending and not attending treatment, respectively.[157]
- W. Prendergast evaluated 324 clients in one program and found a 9.3 per cent recidivism rate over a one- to ten-year follow-up period.[158]
- M. Saylor studied one group of 402 offenders that had a 22.1 per cent reoffending rate after being released from prison for up to twelve years.[159]

CONCLUSIONS ON THE INTERNAL PROBLEMS

The paucity of the research is a recurring problem in the study of the various internal problems of social constructionist interventions. Unfortunately, most research to date has been narrow in focus, and lacking in valid and reliable experimental design.[160] The result is that many important questions have yet to be adequately answered. Among them are the following:

1. What is the optimum program length?
2. What are the clinical factors affecting program length?
3. Can the variability in statistical effectiveness be attributed to the differing lengths of the follow-up period?[161]
4. Will longer follow-up periods always reveal higher recidivism rates?[162]
5. Do clinicians need to become more selective during the intake process? Would it be advantageous, when forming a group, to select individuals according to variables of demographic or offence history?[163]

6. What inaccuracies ensue when studies are based only upon: graduates of offender programs;[164] offender reports of recidivism – when this population is notoriously unreliable for acknowledging the frequency and intensity of their violence;[165] or court reports – when it is known that most offenders do not come in contact with the police or courts?[166]

7. How can the offender's social supports be better utilized to help him from reoffending?[167]

8. Which offenders should be treated in an institution, and which within the community?[168]

9. Is there utility in mixing court-mandated and voluntary clients in the same group?[169]

10. Since many programs implicitly expect strong verbal and reading skills, is the current treatment approach best suited to the general offending population?[170] If not, in what ways should it be modified?

11. For how long, realistically, do offenders need to be monitored, both for the safety of their victims and the assessment of the clinical intervention?[171]

12. How can we best treat men who diminish or end their physical or sexual violence against women, but become significantly more emotionally abusive?[172]

With so many questions unanswered, some observers might challenge the utility of social constructionism in facilitating an end to male violence against women. They might even be moved to question whether social constructionism is not, in fact, a bankrupt philosophy.

THE BANKRUPTCY OF SOCIAL CONSTRUCTIONISM?

It is obvious that there are fundamental problems in the delivery of services to end male violence against women. Yet, it seems equally true that the continued existence of those problems cannot be attributed to any theoretical flaw inherent in the concept of social constructionism – it is unquestionably true that our society does create violent men and encourage male violence against women. The fault lies rather in that the state has attempted to implement social constructionism in a truncated version. The existing state response is more of an attempt at containing the demands of feminists for change than a serious effort at ending male violence. This is most evident when one examines two issues: current state funding of social constructionist programs, and the insufficient use of legislative power by the state to end male violence.

Funding

Programs to end male violence against women are woefully underfunded. A survey of U.S. programs for batterers found that 57 per cent claimed funding to be a problem. They noted that while federally funded U.S. programs are more secure, significant financial difficulties are experienced by 31 per cent of state-funded programs, 40 per cent of United Way–funded programs, 50 per cent of local government programs, 61 per cent of those supported by client fees, and 73 per cent of volunteer-operated programs. 'The common theme repeated by respondents in response to many of the survey items is that there is a critical need for additional funding.'[173] A 1984 review of Canadian batterer programs found that 80 per cent of program leaders reported that their programs were inadequately funded.'[174]

Inadequate funding can result in diminished quality of treatment, fewer offenders receiving treatment, expanded waiting-lists, a bias towards urban services, inadequate follow-up, fewer ongoing support groups, worker burn-out, reduced contact with an offender's support system, shortening or elimination of programs, and – most important – women being placed at risk.[175]

The current funding process has reflected two patterns: splitting the opposition and poor planning.

Splitting the Opposition. While support in Canada for men's programs has increased through the federal justice department, the solicitor general's office, and provincial justice departments, too often the money is provided at the expense of counselling services and shelter programs for women. Bev Lever, assistant to Ontario's provincial coordinator of family violence initiatives, notes that 'right now there are more support groups for men who batter in Metro Toronto than there are groups for women who are battered. A lot of women's groups are getting angry at the diversion of funds.' One worker at an Ottawa shelter stated, 'these days you can't apply for a grant unless you have an activity for men.'[176]

It is a deplorable situation. It is valid to argue that unless services are provided for men to learn to be non-violent, their cycles of violence will remain unbroken. But the money should not be provided at the expense of already underfunded women's services. This is a strategy useful to the state: pit activists working with men against those working with women to impede the two from joining to pit themselves against the state. As long as the forces are split, the overall demand for services will be weakened.[177]

Inadequate Planning and Coordination. The allocation of funds for treating male violence has been poorly planned and coordinated. In Canada, the Director of Health and Welfare's Family Violence Prevention Division, for example, has acknowledged that while funding for work with male offenders has increased substantially in the last decade, the government does not know how much has been allocated.[178] While money has been provided and many programs funded, there has not been a thorough review of how best to invest the money. Rather than supply adequate resources to a limited number of well-designed programs, the government has appeared more willing to provide lower-cost programs in greater quantities. This has encouraged the development of inadequately staffed programs of short duration – for which one cannot hold the program planners completely responsible. Many facilitators recognize the problems with their programs and do the best with the limited funds provided. Donald Dutton, a Canadian researcher and therapist, admits that the existing groups for men are a band-aid solution but until one gets something better, one uses what one has.[179] It appears the increasing public demands for an end to male violence have resulted in the government tossing money into programs without first developing an overall strategy for ending male violence or thoroughly assessing the clinical strength of the programs that have been funded.

Providing money for programs helps the government counter the charge that it is ignoring the problem. In Canada, for example, on 7 June 1989, Health and Welfare and the Status of Women announced – with considerable media fanfare – a series of initiatives to deal with 'family violence.' (Their use of the more generic label, which masks the major role of men as offenders, is noteworthy.) Six federal departments – Health and Welfare, Canada Mortgage and Housing Corporation, Justice, Solicitor General, Indian and Northern Affairs, and Secretary of State – were to receive $40 million over the following four years to improve services related to family violence – primarily for short-term accommodation for battered women.[180] This initiative, while much needed, was only moderately impressive. In today's economy, and for a national program, $40 million does not buy very much. The $40 million, however, could provide the perception that the government was resolving the problem. Responding to the initiative's announcement, Joan Gullen, of the Ottawa-Carleton Family Services Centre, stated she was 'very, very skeptical about their commitment [i.e., to ending male violence] ... of the Prime Minister and some of the men in cabinet.'[181]

In addition to being stingy with funding, governments have also been reluctant to provide leadership in development of programs and delivery of services. While money has been provided, most programs have been started by grass root workers. James Browning notes that 'while some programs have received direct federal or provincial funding, the majority have been initiated at the community level by concerned individuals in women's shelters, mental health settings, family counselling settings, probation and parole services or on a private basis.'[182] Because of inadequate federal support, most of the initial grass-roots programs have had to be taken over or absorbed by larger agencies whose funding was already limited. These agencies have had to siphon off money from other areas or programs for which they receive financing more readily, in order to provide funding for offenders' programs.[183]

Generally, the government appears content to maintain the perception that it is resolving the problem of male violence, and does not really invest the full effort that is required. Admittedly, there have been some changes. In 1989, the Canadian Justice Department announced it was sponsoring an evaluation of men's battering programs. The department was to create an inventory listing programs that had been provincially evaluated, and to identify what information was missing. It was to examine numerous questions: What constitutes success? Does stopping physical assault equal success? How does one end psychological abuse? What prevents men from returning to violence? How can feminists' demands to 'completely stop domineering attitudes toward women' be reconciled with the state's more limited notion that 'success may mean stopping repeated violence'?[184] The individuals responsible for initiating this review deserve credit. Yet, state agency report-writing has not always led to action. Conducting research does not automatically result in the wide-sweeping changes necessary to deal with male violence against women; this will not occur without the necessary political will.

The situation is not much different in the United States. Jerry Finn argues that many programs were created by numerous social service agencies and not so much by central government decree. He advocates establishing coordinating mechanisms to collect and disseminate information on treatment issues, connect agencies that provide complementary services in order to prevent isolation and duplication of services, increase program evaluation, and use existing programs to assist in the efficient creation of additional services in other communities.[185]

Increased state coordination of services need not result in a system of rigid, centrally dictated edicts to which all facilitators must adhere. Greater coordination entails streamlining the system to increase its effectiveness, establishing – in consultation with numerous clinicians and researchers – a series of guidelines for offender intervention.[186] The absence of standards can allow significant numbers of highly motivated, but not necessarily skilled people to do this work. Many operate a group approach but their philosophical perspective may include, for example, family systems theory. The discussion in chapter 4 noted how ineffective – even dangerous to women – this approach can be with male offenders.

The tenuousness of the funding for numerous programs, the playing off of men's against women's programs, and the failure to develop an effective plan to end male violence cannot be attributed solely to the typical slowness of the state machinery. It appears to be more a function of unwillingness to acknowledge the magnitude of the problem, the role the state has played in encouraging and legitimizing – while minimizing the seriousness of – male violence against women, and the extent of the effort needed to end the crimes. Merely containing feminist demands for change, rather than seriously undertaking to stop male violence, seems to be the focus. This fact is borne out when one examines other areas where state action has yet to be mobilized to end male violence against women.

Inadequately Utilized Opportunities for State Intervention

The state system has at its disposal tremendous legislative and investment capacity to influence and direct national economic, political, and social policies. The following are some examples where state involvement could be increased to help eliminate the factors which contribute to and allow male violence against women.

Education of the Judiciary. Members of the judiciary need to be thoroughly educated about male violence. Many individuals within the system subscribe to the popular myths and misconceptions about the causes and treatment of male violence. There are numerous 'prosecutors who refer to the raped woman as [for example] a "silly bitch" and brazenly ask the victim of a brutal gang rape whether she enjoyed forced anal intercourse, and judges conducting rape trials who remark that "boys will be boys." Incredibly, one judge stated for the record that he himself could not conceptualize how a truly innocent woman could allow herself to be raped; unless there is evidence of extensive physical trauma, "a hostile vagina will not admit a penis."'[187] A Montreal woman who charged her assailant after a sexual assault was asked by the defence attorney: 'Was it violent?'[188] A Northwest Territories man was acquitted on a charge of assault causing bodily harm. Judge Mark de Weerd stated that his wife's decision to wear a T-shirt depicting three cartoon polar bears engaged in sexual activities was 'calculated to arouse alarm, fear and anger in [the] other spouse, with clearly foreseeable consequences.'[189]

Judgments often reflect the legacy of physiological and intrapsychic theories, and the influence of family systems perspectives.[190] The minimization of the man's responsibility by an uninformed judiciary can reduce the sentences passed down and decrease the likelihood the judge will recognize the utility or availability of treatment programs. This results in many offenders not being sent to treatment as a component of their sentence. All too commonly, among the judiciary and the general public, the focus, particularly with sex offenders, is on incarceration.

The evidence indicates that prison sentences may in fact increase the offender's violence so that he leaves the institution with a greater likelihood of reoffending. Robert Freeman-Longo favours more treatment programs, arguing: 'They come out with more violence, they are more angry, and oftentimes their crimes escalate so that more harm is done to their victims. Prison is not a cure for this problem, and if we are going to use it as a cure, we had better make laws that say "You are locked up for the rest of your life until you die," because, outside of a specialized treatment program for sex offenders, that is the only way to prevent these men from reoffending.'[191]

Nicholas Groth, director of the Sex Offender Program at the Connecticut Correctional Institute in Somers, Connecticut, echoes Freeman-Longo's call for services. From his experience in Connecticut, approximately 30 per cent of prison inmates are incarcerated as a result of a sexual offence (this figure has also been noted in Florida, Kansas, North Dakota, and Vermont). Groth argues that if one in three inmates were incarcerated for an alcohol-related crime, the state would promptly institute an alcohol treatment program. Unfortunately, fulfilling the need for more offender programs is not so clearly a priority to state funders. Nor is the limited utility of incarceration evident to some members of the judiciary.[192]

Some court officials go beyond just minimizing the problem of male violence or promoting incarceration over treatment. As in any largely male population, within the ranks of the judiciary itself, there are men who actively practise violence. When they are brought to light, important questions arise. The following example is illustrative. Nova Scotia provincial judge Ronald A. MacDonald pleaded guilty to assaulting his wife. He was taken off the bench until he was sentenced. Yet his job status remained fairly secure. For the provincial judicial council to examine whether he was fit to stay on the bench, it was required that the judicial council – composed entirely of other judges – be ordered to meet by the chief provincial judge. This never took place. For offenders in other occupations, it might be debated whether they should lose their jobs for a crime of violence. However, an individual in a judicial position is in a different category. To what degree will a judge like MacDonald intentionally or unconsciously trivialize the violence – and the resultant sentences – of offenders entering his courtroom? As long as there is any chance of this, it seems inappropriate that he should continue his duties.[193] That he was so readily able to do so is a clear indication of the sensitivity of the judiciary to this fact.

Obviously, not all judges are offenders or minimize male violence. Whether for reasons of financial expediency – prison sentences are expensive – or a sincere belief in the value of treatment, many judges are requiring offenders to attend treatment. Yet even here, additional education is required. Problems have occurred when judges were not precise in their recommendations. Many offenders are charged and informed that they must seek counselling; however, without specifics on which agency to go to, when they need to start, and for what duration, an offender can attend one counselling session at an agency that does not focus on male violence and, technically, have fulfilled his court obligations – he did attend counselling.[194]

Educating the judiciary about male violence myths and the importance of treatment is crucial to helping end male violence. A study of U.S. offender programs found that the origin of a referral to treatment appears to affect completion. Results were broken down into two categories – programs with low and high attrition rates. Of the referrals for low attrition rates, the offenders who completed treatment were referred from the following sources: judges, 72 per cent; self-referrals, 63 per cent; wives, 57 per cent; social workers, 50 per cent. In programs with high attrition rates, those who were likely to leave were referred from the following: clergy, 76 per cent; shelter, 65 per cent; friends, 64 per cent; alcoholism counsellors, 60 per cent; police, 60 per cent; and relatives, 55 per cent.[195] With referrals from judges resulting in the greatest number of offenders completing treatment, it is vital that judges be appropriately informed of the issues and the available resources.

An informed judiciary could also facilitate the revisions necessary in our current legal system to obviate the current need for individuals to spend large amounts of money and time extricating themselves from the aftermath of male violence. Linda MacLeod and Cheryl Picard have identified three components that would assist battered women: a 'multi-door' courthouse that would house mediators and counsellors to provide assistance in resolution of disputes; pre-trials, if appropriate, which could help reduce the length involved in a full court process; and mediation services to assist people in resolution of conflict.[196]

Increasing Police Awareness and Training Programs. A major impediment to increasing the number of victims of male violence who report the crime is the low expectation that the police will be of assistance. In one survey, 27 per cent of the sample group had been raped or sexually assaulted; only 10 per cent of the victims reported to the police.[197]

A 1979 study of 13,706 battering cases in Ohio revealed that of the cases reported, 67 per cent did not result in any official police action, that criminal complaints were initiated in 24 per cent, and that only 16 per cent of the offenders were arrested. Daniel Bell, the researcher who compiled the data, concluded that victims who do not initiate criminal complaints do not receive adequate protection or services from the criminal justice system.[198] The same author, in a later study, emphasized that police officers are largely untrained and unwilling to deal with woman abuse, and are reluctant to arrest offenders or make referrals to social agencies for follow-up without any court backing. Bell concludes that 'the police have perpetuated domestic violence by their inappropriate action, as well as their inaction, in domestic dispute intervention. Consequently, the family members' right to protection has been abridged by the police system's unwillingness to cope with domestic violence.'[199]

There have been improvements in many jurisdictions. For example, some areas have passed legislation enabling the state to bring charges against an offender, rather than waiting for the victim, who may be too afraid of the repercussions from her assailant, to do so.[200] As important as such legislation may be, it does not directly address how attending officers should respond to 'domestics' and deal with sexual assault victims. Police officials, as products of our current society, perpetuate many of the myths about male violence against women. Workers in battered women's shelters and sexual assault centres across North America can recount numerous true horror stories, where officers could not comprehend why a woman might want to return to live with a violent partner, or excused a man's violence, or trivialized it as 'just a domestic dispute' rather than a crime of violence, or blamed sexual assault victims for what they were wearing or where they were walking. This is utterly unacceptable.

Police officers can play a key role in helping end male violence against women. One study by Sherman and Berk is illustrative of this: it indicated that police action may significantly affect batterer recidivism. Sherman and Berk found that an arrest resulted in the lowest recidivism rate, while advice resulted in a significantly greater rate. The least effective tactic was an order for the man to leave for eight hours.[201]

Funding Social Service Worker Awareness and Training Programs. Social service workers can often play an important role in identifying and assisting victims of violence and working with offenders – but workers in fields not directly related to male violence are rarely trained to recognize symptoms of violence. Too often, women are put down for returning to an abusive relationship, rather than being assisted to establish contingency safety plans, or determine what other options are open to her.

Leaders of self-help groups at Alcoholics Anonymous, to give one example, deal with many victims and offenders in their programs. Unfortunately, the myth that male violence frequently is caused by alcohol compels many to believe that if the alcohol problem is treated, the violence will disappear. Typically, alcoholism and violence are two separate problems. Even in those instances where it appears that violence and alcohol consumption are inextricably linked, offenders should be referred to separate treatment programs to resolve each issue.[202]

Positive Image Advertising. The majority of offenders do not self-refer or get caught, and so do not receive treatment. Only 2 per cent of rapists, for example, are charged, and just 1 per cent are convicted.[203] The stigma against seeking help, and the ease with which the silence is maintained, keep hidden, and away from treatment, the vast majority of offenders.[204] This majority is not reached by the existing approach to ending male violence. One way to reach them, their support system, and the violence-supporting value system they live by is through a barrage of positive, healthy images of men and women.

A multitude of themes or messages could be covered. Among other scenarios the media campaign could portray: men disagreeing with women and dealing with it non-violently by taking a time out; men counteracting the multitude of sexual assault supportive myths, emphasizing that men are responsible for their actions and that violence against women is a crime; men struggling with and communicating their feelings in a manner that does not jeopardize their sexual identity; men interacting with each other and expressing feelings without threatening their status within the peer group; or men talking about the availability and utility of services for victims and offenders.

As long as most men continue to believe it is acceptable to be violent, or view violence as an integral component of true masculinity, it will continue. Joan Gullen argues that 'the main instrument in curbing domestic violence is to raise the taboo.' 'Public exposure,' she says, 'That's going to deter them.'[205] Extensive positive image advertising through television, radio, and print media would serve to introduce alternative models of how men and women can interact. Such images would empower children, women, and men to recognize that the violence is unacceptable and alternatives can be chosen.

A positive image campaign would have both immediate and long-term effects. Existing research clearly indicates that most offenders acquire their violent supportive values, and start offending, early in life. Sex offenders, for example, very commonly start offending during adolescence.[206] Waiting until numerous offences have occurred, in light of the statistical improbability that the man will end up in counselling, is a reactionary approach of limited utility. Clinically, it is much easier to work with a young individual whose value system is not firmly entrenched. Waiting until offenders are in their late twenties or early thirties only increases the number of victims, and the amount of work the offender must do to change his behaviour.

The state could easily be taking the initiative in this area. It has the

essential funds at its disposal, and experience in conducting such public relations campaigns. While some state-funded media programs
have been provided, the scale of investment does not fit the magnitude
of the problem. Conceivably, the response among other state planners
might be to claim that the cost is prohibitive. Yet we need to recognize
the cost to women and society if significant value changes do not
occur. And even if money were the only important criterion, current
investment could reduce future expenditures. While we do not know
enough about the full monetary cost of male violence to society, some
statistics are available. The Canadian Advisory Council on the Status
of Women, for example, indicates that 18 per cent of emergency cases
in hospitals are battered women.[207] That is a heavy load for an already
overburdened health-care system. Increasing public awareness of these
social costs could make it harder for state officials to block funding of
programs to end male violence.

The Education System. Public education can initiate change in social values. In relation to male violence against women, improved education
is an important tool, and one that is preferable to many other methods.
Banning pornography, for example, reduces the supply but does little
to decrease demand. In fact, it may even encourage the underground
market. However, appropriate education campaigns could reduce the
demand for pornography and its incumbent misogyny and perpetuation of rape mythology. Education efforts are also less likely to raise
the civil liberty issues involved in censorship.

In recent years, school systems have been under considerable community pressure to supplement the provision of basic education with
increased awareness and prevention of numerous social issues. Areas
of focus have included streetproofing, AIDS, suicide and depression,
human sexuality, and child sexual abuse. To these could be added similar programs to help end male violence against women. Issues could
include assertiveness training, effective communication skills, non-violent conflict resolution, human rights, sex-role acquisition, and myths
surrounding male violence and rape.

Programs to end male violence could build upon existing school services in other areas. Improved communication skills and assertiveness
training, for example, are pertinent to many social issues. While programs to end male violence have been conducted in some communities, the main initiative has been from motivated, but often isolated,
individuals. The response has not been as extensive or systematic as

necessary. Programs could be introduced into the curriculum at kindergarten and continued through university.[208]

Existing programs for ending male violence provide some indication of the utility of a comprehensive expansion of current education efforts.[209] One area of activity has been the creation of programs aimed at reducing the incidence of men sexually assaulting women by increasing the social stigma against male violence.[210] Most programs have been instituted at the university level, but – with age-appropriate modification – are transferable to the primary and secondary school setting. The existing programs focus on several key areas.

1. *Statistics.* By reviewing the level, types, and contexts for sexual assault, the facilitators can increase awareness that sexual violence is a significant and frequent crime, perpetrated generally by men on female victims. This can make it more difficult, for example, for men to downplay or make light of, often out of ignorance, the frequency with which women are assaulted.[211]

2. *Myths.* The discussion on the frequency of sexual assault can lead directly to the myths that obfuscate the frequency and horror of sexual assault. Many men still need to be informed, or reminded, that women do not ask to be assaulted or that a man's testicles will not turn blue and be damaged if he is sexually aroused and does not immediately achieve orgasm.[212]

3. *Male socialization and rape.* Time is spent identifying how male socialization encourages men to sexually assault women. For many participants, this information may be very new, and possibly threatening. Facilitators work at turning around a disbelieving or hostile crowd.[213]

4. *Personalizing rape.* One of the most effective ways to get many men to recognize the horror of sexual assault is to have them think about what it would be like for *them* to be sexually assaulted – as, indeed, does happen to many men in prison. This approach can be successful. Some participants, however, become defensive and adamantly proclaim that it just would not happen to them. This provides an opportunity to review the myth that people want to be sexually assaulted.

Another approach for personalizing sexual assault uses the men's socialization to the advantage of ending rape. The men are asked to consider how they would feel if any of the women in their personal lives (wives, mothers, female partners, etc.) were sexually assaulted. The resultant anger can be significant. The next step is to remind them that the woman they may attempt to fondle at a crowded party is likely to be someone else's friend, lover, or daughter. By personalizing the crime, and humanizing potential victims, it can be more difficult for many men to verbally or sexually offend; the victim may no longer be viewed as some nameless, isolated entity, but instead as someone with a name, a life, and relationships with others.

5. *Alternative behaviours.* Groups for male offenders outline options to help the men not reoffend. This necessity also exists for those who have yet to commit, or to be charged for, a crime. They need a plan of non-violent action ready to put in place should it be needed.[214]

The men also could be encouraged to brainstorm to come up with how they can help change the oppression of women, and what they might do instead of the traditional activities of encouraging sexism and violence against women. The aim is to have the men engage in a practical problem-solving session, not a theoretical, philosophical discussion. Each man should work to identify at least one significant way in which he wants to change his behaviour, and outline the steps he considers necessary in reaching that goal.

6. *Working with other men.* Workshops on ending male violence can be an opportunity for individuals to meet other men who are questioning significant aspects of the traditional hegemonic masculinity most rewarded by our society. In beginning to break down this isolation, these men may learn that they can work cooperatively with like-minded men for larger projects and gain support in an often lonely task.

The systematic introduction of such programs into educational curricula is a necessity if we are to live up to our rhetoric of being opposed to male violence against women. Such programs could significantly increase the social stigma against male violence.[215]

Pressuring the Private Sector. There are numerous opportunities for the state to compel the business sector to end its contributions to male violence against women. While many unions have pushed for, and many companies have instituted, sexual harassment guidelines to supplement the existing state prohibitions, these efforts need to be increased and made more uniform. Too many women continue to suffer sexual harassment or exploitation on the job in their efforts at making a living. Corporations could be required to review and strengthen existing policies, provide the necessary mechanisms to process complaints, and conduct awareness workshops to raise the taboo against this as yet too common – and too often trivialized – crime.[216]

Pay equity is another example in the workplace. As long as women continue to earn less than their male counterparts for the same work, women are more likely to remain financially dependent upon men. This dependency is a common reason why many women return to a violent partner.

Companies could be required to have and train human service workers so that they are familiar with the issues involved in male violence against women. Such individuals could play an important role in helping female victims, or offenders, connect with the necessary services.

The state also could insist that corporations not use images which demean women or encourage male violence to sell their products. The production and sale of war toys is another area requiring examination. As long as we continue to encourage young boys to play with violent toys, we should not be surprised to find that when they reach adulthood they continue to deal with their external reality by violent means.

Conclusions on the State Response to Male Violence against Women

Despite its numerous efforts and activities, the state is as yet not trustworthy as an ally in the struggle to end male violence against women. The family systems approach, while an improvement over the earlier physiological and intrapsychic perspectives, often obfuscated the high incidence of, and men's responsibility for, violence against women. Similarly, while the existing social constructionist offender groups are improving the lives of many victims and perpetrators, the changes they effect are but a portion of what is really required. At best, the current state response is a truncated version of social constructionism. Despite important changes in program funding and legal statutes, the state has, by and large, avoided the major issues. Providing some money for research, shelters, and treatment programs is easy, but what is really needed is substantially increasing treatment availability, utilizing the school system to improve communication and non-violent conflict resolution skills, pressuring the private sector to end its abuse of women, and examining how best to end the creation of violent men. To date, the state has failed to sufficiently change the existing social milieu that encourages, legitimizes, and then minimizes or ignores male violence against women.

One reason why the state has restricted its potential response is that the traits that are at the root of the social creation and perpetuation of violent men continue to be valued in other areas of our society. Many fear that if competition, for example, is diminished, our economic and military security could be threatened. Thus women's safety continues to be viewed as a disposable commodity, something that can be ignored in order to perpetuate the nature of masculinity which is the foundation of the existing social, political, and economic order.

Contrasting what has been done with that which could be exposes the state system's limited enthusiasm over ending male violence against women. Rather than approach the problem with all the resources at its disposal, the major emphasis has been to sort out the motivated clients from the already minority population of offenders that are discovered and jam them into poorly funded treatment programs. This will not end male violence against women. As one critic has noted, 'it is naïve to assume that we will end patriarchy by working with a dozen men every Wednesday night.'[217] It has been a band-aid approach to a major social problem.

Not only has the state system's movement toward social constructionism fallen short of what is required, the existing gains are not secure. Current funding levels are not guaranteed. In an era of conservative fiscal policies, budgets are being slashed when, in fact, more money is needed to end male violence against women. Similarly, existing legislative changes can be rescinded if the movement toward social constructionism is weakened.

The reality is that it is not just additional funding that is required. We can only expect so much from poorly funded programs that are operating in a society that largely ignores the larger, more expensive and politically difficult social, economic, and ideological changes. Until we address these larger issues, we will continue to produce more violent men. As David Currie notes, 'The solution to stopping the violence is not simple. A single approach is not going to work. We need more transition houses, more comprehensive community resources, more public education, more groups for men and more social action. None of them by themselves will be effective in stopping domestic violence. But all together, we might have a chance.'[218]

As the majority of people remain silent about the war that many men are waging against all women – as long as male violence remains marginalized as a 'women's issue' – the political pressure for a more complete social constructionist state response is lessened, and the state system can avoid implementing the necessary solutions to end male violence.

To date, the state has displayed an appalling lack of political will to seriously deal with the existing problem on a scale commensurate with its magnitude. The question remains as to what is needed to success-fully shift the state response closer toward a more complete form of social constructionism. As indicated in the previous chapter, the women's movement was the initial and the major catalyst for the move from physiological and intrapsychic explanations of male violence. In turning to the state for support and assistance, feminists have met with several successes and many failures. This chapter has examined the state system's untrustworthy commitment to ending male violence. The next chapter will examine the responses among men – as the third force in the movement toward, and away from, social constructionism – to discern how they have reacted to the demands of women for change. As the largest portion of the infamous silent majority, men – provided they so choose – can play a crucial role in demarginalizing male violence against women and exerting the additional pressure necessary for the state to produce a completely social constructionist response.

6 / Responses among Men

This chapter establishes a context for understanding male responses to demands for an end to male violence against women. It examines three main types of response: reinforcement of the status quo, avoidance or wilful ignorance of the issues, and working for positive change. While some men may fit into two or all of these categories, ultimately, either they are working for an end to male violence, or they are part of the problem.

Reinforcement of the Status Quo

This is the response of men whose main goal is to limit or reverse the advances of feminism, and is characteristic of four groups: offenders, conservative ideologues, men's rights advocates, and male terrorists.

OFFENDERS

Reviewing how men have responded to the demands for an end to male violence against women makes us aware that very little has changed. The population of offenders remains large and intimidating. As we look for signs of positive change among men, the continued existence of this group reminds us of the tremendous amount of work necessary before women achieve equality and safety of person in our society.

CONSERVATIVE MASCULINISTS[1]

Conservatives believe that traditional sex roles for men and women are the most appropriate. They believe that it is part of men's nature to be dominant politically and socially. Kenneth Clatterbaugh, in an article that examines the numerous so-called men's movements, notes that these consist of two varieties – moral conservatives and biological conservatives.[2]

Moral Conservatives

Moral conservatives believe that men are innately violent and unruly, and that the family, church, and community work to civilize and domesticate male nature. To question or attack these institutions, therefore, is to threaten the fragile stability of our civilization.

Clatterbaugh cites the many writings of George Gilder, including *Sexual Suicide* and *Men and Marriage*, as characteristic examples of moral conservative masculinist philosophy. Gilder affirms the traditional image of men as providers and protectors, while asserting that women excel as caregivers and nurturers. He masks his support for male supremacy by arguing that men exercise power only in the social and political spheres, and since it is the domestic and sexual spheres – where, Gilder states, women are dominant – which are presumably more important to human happiness, he reasons that ultimately women possess greater power than men. Gilder contends that violence in our society is caused primarily by single men who have been deprived of the civilizing benefits of a wife and family. Men who use pornography or are violent are seen as cases where socialization has failed; such men have not been sufficiently tamed.

From the moral conservative perspective, then, for existing institutions to adopt more liberal policies is highly threatening; moral conservatives, therefore, strive to strengthen and reinforce the traditional status quo of genders. They fear that feminism is to blame for many of our society's problems, and see feminists as ripping up the essential fabric of an order which, it would seem, has always worked fairly well. Moral conservatives may thus view organizing to achieve such non-traditional goals as reproductive freedom, gay rights, equal employment opportunities, or shelters for battered women as anti-family, even anti-civilization.[3]

Many of the fundamentalist religions that fuelled the 1980s revival of conservative politics throughout the Western industrial nations have been an important buttress for moral conservatives in their attempts to reverse what they consider to be significant gains for feminists at the expense of the social order. Moral conservatives have worked extremely hard to try to return and confine women to their traditional role as childbearers, subservient to their husbands.[4] They have attempted to do this in two key areas.

Objecting to State Funding for Day Care. State funding for child care is anathema to the moral conservatives' vision of the proper social order. Typically they attribute numerous social ills, such as juvenile delinquency, teen pregnancy, and drug abuse, to the absence of the mother from the home.[5] Moral conservatives ignore evidence which shows that children of working mothers are often no less well-adjusted – in fact, are even slightly more socially independent – than those of their stay-at-home counterparts.[6] Conservatives also ignore the financial necessity – economic recession is one example – that often compels both parents to seek paid employment.[7] Moral conservatives tend to blame individual families – particularly women, as the major consumers – for an inflated consumer lifestyle.[8] There are some middle-class families which could – and do – forgo the second income so that parents might spend more time with their children, and blaming the woman is an evasive attempt to create a culprit while ignoring the failings of the current economic and political system.

Fighting against Women's Reproductive Freedom. Many of the men marching at rallies to protest against abortion are moral conservatives.[9] With the support of various fringe and established churches, they continue to make a lot of noise; meanwhile, statistics indicate that approximately 70 per cent of Americans and Canadians believe that abortion is a personal, medical matter and not a criminal one.[10]

With the 1980s rise of neo-conservative politics, the campaigns in the United States and Canada over reproductive freedom experienced significant setbacks. Reacting to the 1970s shift toward liberalization of abortion laws and a relative increase in the availability of legal abortions, the moral conservatives lobbied effectively to pull back the pendulum, with the result that once again democratic access was being jeopardized.

In the United States, *Roe vs. Wade*, the 1973 landmark case eliminating all legal impediments to women's right to abortion, was being challenged across the country. The U.S. Supreme Court's 1973 judgment in favour of *Roe* was a watershed victory for the numerous groups and individuals who had lobbied throughout the 1960s to establish the reproductive freedom of American women. Despite the euphoria among pro-choice supporters after the Supreme Court ruling, many acknowledged that the decision was in reality more a compromise than a victory. While allowing abortions, the ruling was no guarantee of secure, democratic access to or funding for abortion in the United States. It did 'too little to help poor women, teenage women, and many others.'[11]

Roe vs. Wade was problematic in other ways. While established with the purpose of protecting the health and welfare of the woman faced with an unwanted pregnancy, it also perpetuated state involvement in the abortion debate.[12] As long as the state was willing to grant a woman the right of access to abortion, that same state could – with a change of planners and an increase in political pressure – reverse the decision.

Since 1973, Roe vs. Wade has been under attack. Clinics have been picketed and bombed; employees and clients have been threatened and assaulted and clients, in the protesters' vernacular, 'street counselled,' or dissuaded from choosing abortion. The increasingly conservative political and economic climate of the early 1980s significantly encouraged such activities.

Ronald Reagan's and George Bush's Republican administrations played an important role in strengthening, and often directing, the moral conservative backlash against reproductive choice. One of the leading figures was William Bradford Reynolds, 'the administration's "hit man" for civil rights, most notable for his attack on affirmative action.'[13] Reynolds encouraged Missouri State Attorney General William Webster to include overruling Roe vs. Wade in the case of Webster vs. Reproductive Health Services. Webster emerged after the Missouri state legislature, declaring that life begins at conception, restricted abortion in three ways. It 'preclude[d] public facilities or employees from assisting in abortion; ... impose[d] a gag rule on counselling about the abortion option by any program or person paid with public funds; ... and require[d] doctors to perform a battery of useless tests on women to determine fetal viability.'[14]

One day after the November 1988 U.S. presidential election, the outgoing Reagan administration filed a submission encouraging the Supreme Court to hear the Webster case. The Bush administration later submitted one of the most substantial anti-choice briefs received by the court.[15]

When the U.S. Supreme Court (filled primarily with Republican-appointed chief justices) went to rule in July 1989, it had three options.

First, it could have completely overruled *Roe vs. Wade*. This while possible, would not likely have been well-received by the three or four out of five Americans who favour a woman's reproductive freedom.[16] Second, the court could have decided, as happened in New Hampshire, that 'the state shall not compel any woman to complete or terminate a pregnancy.'[17] This would have enabled legislators who might not want to choose between the two sides in the debate to avoid the issue. The government would, in effect, remove itself from the debate. Yet, if it would not ensure funding for clinics, the availability of abortion services would be seriously curtailed.[18]

In its ruling on *Webster*, however, the U.S. Supreme Court legislated the third option: upholding the restrictive Missouri law. The court, therefore, did not overturn *Roe vs. Wade*, but left it dramatically weakened and vulnerable to future court and legislative challenges. The *Webster* decision was a victory for opponents of abortion and moral conservatives; it created opportunities for increased state regulation in two key areas: viability testing and public funding.[19]

Despite a consensus within the medical and scientific communities that fetal viability is, and will likely remain for some time, at twenty-four weeks, the *Webster* ruling invited doctors to test fetal viability at twenty weeks. Such tests will likely delay, and increase the cost of, abortions. They also further involve the state in the control of a woman's reproductive freedom. As Howard Schwartz, a Kansas City obstetrician-gynecologist, states, 'They're making us add extra roadblocks, extra costs, and extra interventions to prove that the baby isn't mature, which we already knew.'[20]

Public funding was the second area attacked by *Webster*. By upholding the Missouri decision to curtail state support for abortion services, the Supreme Court effectively threw back to each state and municipal legislature the issue of whether to fund abortion services. This resulted in a multitude of statutes being proposed in various state legislatures – over 400 in 1990 and most of them restricting choice – and a patchwork quilt of contradictory laws across the United States.[21] Some states have since legally ensured women's choice; many others have severely curtailed and even blocked what had been law prior to the *Webster* ruling.[22]

The Supreme Court decision was part of, and further fuelled, the moral conservative backlash against the reproductive freedom of American women. Justice Harry A. Blackmun, author of the *Roe* decision, observed that the *Webster* ruling 'is filled with winks, and nods, and knowing glances to those who would do away with *Roe* explicitly.'[23]

In the wake of *Webster*, moral conservatives launched renewed efforts in three areas. First, many legislative initiatives were undertaken to compel minors seeking abortions to inform, or have the consent of, one parent.[24] Ignoring the potential dangers of such a requirement, many states began legislating parental consent. One such law in Indiana, for example, contributed to the death of at least one young woman, seventeen-year-old Becky Bell. Afraid to tell her parents that she was pregnant, apparently Becky procured an illegal abortion and died of complications resulting from the infection in her womb.[25]

Abortion clinic licensing standards were the second issue pursued by moral conservatives after *Webster*. The campaign for increased restrictions was politically – rather than medically – motivated, and intended to make it harder for free-standing abortion clinics to legally remain open. This would increase women's dependence on approved hospitals – many of which, following *Webster*, were being denied public funds,[26] and thus unable to offer full service in the area of abortion.

Federal financing was the third area attacked by moral conservatives following *Webster*. On 23 May 1991, in *Rust vs. Sullivan*, The U.S. Supreme Court upheld federal regulations (introduced in 1988) that prevented workers in federally funded family planning clinics from discussing abortion. Henceforth, if an agency wanted to retain federal aid, pregnant women automatically would be referred for prenatal care. If a woman enquired about ending an unwanted pregnancy, she was to be informed that 'the project does not consider abortion an appropriate method of family planning.' Were a clinic to not comply with the ruling, the federal government would withdraw the Title X funding provided under the 1970 Public Health Service Act.[27]

Rust vs. Sullivan had significant implications. It affected over 4,500 clinics that served nearly four million women annually. Most of the clients affected by this legislation were young (one-third were under twenty years of age), had a low or marginal income, and did not yet have children.[28]

Opponents responded swiftly to the Supreme Court ruling. Many clinics threatened to ignore the legislation. Others quickly complied with the regulations and divided their services – programs mentioning abortion as an option needed to be housed separately and funded privately.[29] The American Medical Association and the American College of Obstetricians and Gynecologists continued the lobby they had organized against the ruling. They argued that it would be unethical for doctors to withhold information from clients, and that to do so could make practitioners susceptible to malpractice suits. Constitutionalists and free speech advocates also rallied against *Rust*. Justice Blackmun, for example, recognized that 'while suppressing speech favorable to abortion with one hand, the [*Rust* ruling] compels anti-abortion speech with the other.' Their significant opposition to the ruling notwithstanding, pro-choice advocates had suffered yet another blow.[30]

These renewed battles over abortion reflect the rise of moral conservative strength and influence in the United States. Weakening *Roe vs. Wade* was an open attack on the rights and freedoms of American women. *Webster* and *Rust* effectively put the gains of twenty years of feminist struggle under siege, and most of the victories would have to be reclaimed.[31] In North America, this phenomenon was not confined to the United States.

In Canada, relative to the United States, the moral conservative reaction took longer to consolidate; nonetheless it was equally threatening to women's reproductive control. Throughout the 1970s, thousands of women had rallied to demand access to safe therapeutic abortions. Abortionist Dr Henry Morgentaler, a popular media focus for the Canadian movement for reproductive choice, had fought for decades for a woman's right to decide for herself whether to carry a pregnancy to term. Despite repeated attempts to close his clinics, Morgentaler won numerous court battles.[32] But by the end of the 1980s, the resistance appeared to be strengthened. The Canadian Supreme Court's 1988 decision to strike down the 1969 federal abortion law appeared to fortify the moral conservatives' resolve.[33] They continued to accost women walking into abortion clinics and to harass and attack the doctors that performed abortions. These efforts were supplemented by a new strategy: supporting court challenges by individuals to block a woman's reproductive freedom.

In July 1989, lawyers on behalf of a Toronto man, Gregory Murphy, submitted an affidavit to the Supreme Court of Ontario to prohibit Murphy's partner, Barbara Dodd, from having an abortion. While the injunction eventually was set aside by the Supreme Court, for a brief period there was considerable uncertainty as to which way the court would rule. Had the case not been dismissed, Barbara Dodd, who wanted to terminate her pregnancy, would have been required by law to follow through and carry the child to term. It would have been a pregnancy and delivery enforced by the state at the request of the father.

The Ontario Supreme Court decision to set aside the injunction was not a clear victory for pro-choice advocates in Canada. The presiding judge, Justice W. Gibson Gray, emphasized that he was not ruling on whether court injunctions should be used in Ontario to prevent abortions. Instead, the injunction was blocked owing to the fact that Barbara Dodd 'was not given sufficient notice of the hearing and that there were elements of fraud [by Gregory Murphy] in the depositions put before Mr Justice John O'Driscoll of the same court a week earlier.'[34] Despite this statement, Clayton Ruby, Barbara Dodd's lawyer, felt a victory had been scored. He noted: 'What we have seen is a taste of life if the right-to-life [groups] have their way. Women who want an abortion will have to go to court, they will have to argue, they will be under the threat of criminal prosecution and jail.'[35]

Barbara Dodd was not the only woman to struggle with the judicial system and the accompanying national media attention. Chantale Daigle, a twenty-one-year-old secretary from Chibougamau, Quebec, faced a similar struggle.

Chantale had been in a relationship with Jean-Guy Tremblay since November 1988. Shortly after they started sharing an apartment, Jean-Guy became emotionally abusive. By late March 1989, when Chantale learned she was pregnant, Jean-Guy, a former nightclub bouncer, had escalated to using physical violence.[36]

Jean-Guy Tremblay admitted that Gregory Murphy's actions against Barbara Dodd prompted his decision to procure a court injunction to prevent Chantale from having an abortion. Tremblay obtained a temporary, and then a permanent, injunction on 7 and 17 July 1989, respectively. Chantale cancelled the abortion she had scheduled and sought legal counsel. Her case soon went to the Canadian Supreme Court.

On 8 August 1989, as the Supreme Court justices were about to deliver their ruling, it was discovered that Chantale had gone to, and received an abortion in, a Boston clinic. She had been afraid that Canada's highest court would require her to carry through with the pregnancy. Upon hearing of Daigle's abortion, the Supreme Court judges briefly reconvened in their private chamber, then returned to announce their decision. Unanimously they overturned the Quebec Superior Court's injunction.[37]

The Dodd and Daigle cases were nominal victories in the pro-choice battle; the war, however, was not over. On 29 May 1990, for example, the Canadian House of Commons – dominated by Brian Mulroney's Conservative Party – passed new legislation, known as Bill C-43, to replace the old Abortion Act struck down in 1988. The government called it a compromise solution though it satisfied no one on either side of the abortion debate. Opponents of abortion felt it was too lenient; pro-choice advocates, meanwhile, found it unacceptable because it recriminalized abortion, removing the decision from individual women and placing it in the hands of doctors – most of whom are men; it also further restricted access to abortion, and enabled third-party intervention by disgruntled husbands or male partners.[38]

To the surprise of many people on both sides of the issue, on 31 January 1991, Bill C-43 was defeated in the Senate by a tied vote of 43:43. Despite 'unbearable ... pressure from the Prime Minister's Office,' the government's lobbying efforts had failed.[39] Abortion, had once again become legal in Canada, and many pro-choice proponents were claiming it would remain so for at least a generation.[40]

While it was major step toward ensuring the reproductive freedom of Canadian women, the narrow defeat of Bill C-43 by no means ended the debate over abortion. The federal government's Bill and efforts to have it passed demonstrate the strength of the moral conservative ideology at the federal level, or at least a recognition in Ottawa that moral conservatives are a force to be reckoned with for any party hoping to maintain political power. Although for moral conservatives the demise of Bill C-43 was a setback, it is unlikely that they will abandon their agenda. One can anticipate, in addition to continued public protests, attempts to recriminalize abortion and to limit democratic access through restrictions on funding and periodic publicity, in various media from full-page newspaper ads to bumper stickers, promoting the right-to-life perspective and appealing to the individual woman's conscience to follow through with an unwanted pregnancy. While the numerical strength of moral conservatives is unknown, they remain a strong influence on the collective consciousness of Canadian society and, therefore, a significant obstacle to women's freedom to choose abortion.

Conclusions on Moral Conservatives. Moral conservatives encourage, through political and social pressure, the belief that a woman's primary function is to bear and nurture many children. At the heart of this ideology is the issue of control over women's lives and bodies. For women to lose this control could mean being increasingly restricted to the traditional mothering role. While potentially rewarding for many, this occupation must be one that is chosen – not dictated by an absence of options. It was precisely the basic lack of options that was a driving force behind the 1970s revival of the women's movement; women were tired of being confined to a traditional socially prescribed role.

During the 1980s, moral conservatives were trying to return to that earlier period, and succeeded in placing many obstacles in the path of feminism.

The reinforcement by moral conservativism of the belief that a woman's primary function is to bear children creates a context where it is easier for men to justify retaliation, punishment, or legal and physical restriction of women who attempt to deviate or break away from such a restrictive norm. It is not uncommon for men to begin assaulting their wives when they make such an attempt – for example, by announcing that they are going to start attending university, or obtain paid employment outside the home.[41]

What moral conservatives wilfully ignore is that their philosophy is built upon, and perpetuates, unequal power relationships between many social groups. As Kenneth Clatterbaugh states, 'the conservatives' ready acceptance of inequalities – between men and women, among men, or by race – opens them to the charge of being a voice for white male supremacy.'[42] Clatterbaugh's point is appropriate. The images and values advocated by moral conservatives are strikingly similar to how the family was officially portrayed in Nazi Germany from the 1920s through to the end of the Second World War.[43] A second notable parallel exists here: German moral conservatives received considerable support and encouragement from numerous biological conservative theorists, and such links were being replicated in the 1980s and 1990s.

Biological Conservatives

Biological conservative masculinists contend that men will dominate over women because of their innate aggressive advantage. For example, 'the central fact is that men and women are different from each other, from the gene to the thought to the act, and that emotions that underpin masculinity and femininity, that make reality as experienced by the male eternally different from that experienced by the female, flow from the biological natures of man and woman ... Women who deny their natures ... are condemned – to paraphrase Ingrid Bengis's wonderful phrase – to argue against their own juices ... roles associated with gender have been primarily the result rather than the cause of sexual differences.'[44] Biological conservatives also believe that women's physiology endows them with greater overall importance: by their essential child-bearing and nurturing capabilities, they ensure the continuity of the species. Goldberg notes: 'Perhaps this female wisdom comes from resignation to the reality of male dominance; more likely it is a harmonic of the woman's knowledge that ultimately she is the one who matters. As a result, there are more brilliant men than brilliant women and more powerful men than powerful women, there are more good women than good men. Women are not dependent on male brilliance for their deepest source of strength, but men are dependent on female strength. Few women have been ruined by men; female endurance survives. Many men, however, have been destroyed by women who did not understand, or did not care to understand, male fragility.'[45]

Biological conservatives place considerable responsibility for men's failings – and presumably their violence – at the feet of women who have somehow failed to understand, accommodate, and lovingly correct the frailty of men. This belief underpins most battering and sexual assault myths. If only the woman had been more sensitive and recognized that her male partner had had a bad day at work, if only she had not withheld from him her nurturing support, she could have avoided the black eye or push down the two flights of stairs. Similarly, had she only remembered male fragility, she would not have worn that specific 'provocative' outfit and tempted her rapist. Such a perspective absolves men of their responsibility for their crimes of violence and blames women.

Clatterbaugh notes that there are some biological conservatives who go even farther in their beliefs than does Goldberg. As described earlier in chapters 3 and 4, Edward Wilson argued that traditional masculine dominance, aggression, sexual assault, and promiscuity are seen as ways of increasing the survival rate of specific gene pools in environments that are often difficult for human survival.[46] What Goldberg and other biological theorists ignore or minimize is the human capacity for cognitive intervention in our actions. Even if we do have specific physiological drives, we also have the capacity to make specific choices about whether, how, or when we try to satisfy them. Male violence is *not* inevitable – it is socially constructed.

Conclusions on Moral and Biological Conservatives

The political climate of the late twentieth century encouraged cynicism regarding the prospect for an end to male violence against women. With a revival of conservative ideology following the economic recession of the late 1970s, there came a relatively lengthy period characterized by the continuous dismantling of various social policies which had been established to protect the rights and freedoms of the many groups exploited and abused by the traditional social and economic system.[47] In this context, maintaining women's rights became an uphill battle, severely complicated by the political strength of conservative concepts about masculinity and femininity.

From the conservative perspective, feminism, in its efforts at redressing the social, political, and economic power imbalance between men and women, is doomed to fail; it simply defies the laws of nature. While conservatives often respond to feminism as if it were a frivolous and mistaken waste of time, the force of their often virulent attacks is telling: the current vitality of neo-conservative ideology (notwithstanding its frequent lack of logical cohesion) is doubtless to a great extent based on a fear that the claims of feminism are legitimate and that it consequently will appeal to significant sections of the population.

What was different about the 1980s compared to the early 1970s, when the current feminist movement first emerged, was that opposition to feminism appeared to be strengthened. Not since the 1930s had conservative ideology, policies, and programs enjoyed such popularity.[48] In the United States, the Republican party, under Reagan and then Bush, succeeded in threatening the gains made by the women's movement in the 1970s. This phenomenon was not limited to the United States; it manifested itself in other countries around the world.

Conservative masculinists have played a significant role in the revival of the political right wing. In becoming more vocal, they helped legitimize the violence against women perpetrated by millions of male offenders. They served to strengthen the prevalent, albeit somewhat nebulous, perception among many men that women had always 'had it pretty good' and were having an even easier time since the advent of feminism. In encouraging such resentment, the conservative masculinists are a fundamental force contributing to the high levels of male violence against women. While officially they may not condone individual acts of violence, their belief that aggression and violence are natural male qualities ensures that women will continue to be hurt and killed.

THE MEN'S RIGHTS ADVOCATES

Background

The origins of the men's rights perspective are easy to find. As discussed earlier in chapter 3, many men became resentful of the restrictions inherent in the hegemonic masculinity of the 1950s. In traditional marriage, playing the compulsory role of breadwinner left many men feeling they were holding the short end of the stick.[49]

The 1970s revival of feminism exacerbated existing tensions and encouraged a more organized male response. Many men felt threatened or confused; they also began to reflect on issues that had long been ignored. Many joined consciousness-raising groups to examine the feminist questioning and challenging of male roles as breadwinner, soldier, or leader; men's degradation and abuse of women; and the dangers of hegemonic masculinity.

This reaction from men began – as did the feminist movement – primarily in the United States, where the media, for lack of a better term, labelled it 'the men's movement.' The activity soon spread across the United States and Canada, then to Western Europe and beyond. By the mid- to late-1970s, many men's groups were putting together and publishing proclamations of their principles as personal and political statements. This flurry of activity, while still extremely small when compared to the women's movement, was significant. Many men were examining what had previously been unspoken, and many were hopeful for potential changes ahead.[50]

The next natural step was for organizers to pull together groups for regional and even national gatherings to continue raising the consciousness of men and to spark discussion for solutions to the many problems confronting men and women. At these conferences, the differences within the movement, which had just started to emerge at the local level, became unavoidable. While many of the individuals and groups may have been united as men responding to the demands of feminism, dissimilarities in their class, race, and ideology quickly resulted in political analyses and actions that moved in very different, and often contradictory, directions. The movement that had barely begun appeared to be falling apart.[51]

In the early 1980s, several commentators within the men's movement, such as Joe Interrante and Ned Lyttelton,[52] portrayed the division as between two main groups: men's rights advocates – those struggling to extend the rights of men – and pro-feminist/anti-sexist men – those struggling to end the violence men perpetrate against women. In general, this categorization remains correct, even though by the end of the 1980s, additional, smaller sectors also were evident. Despite the creation of these other factions (discussed below), the number and strength of the men's rights advocates, or male liberationists, have remained significant, and since they generally have reinforced male violence against women, this has further jeopardized women's safety.

Philosophy and Practice of the Men's Rights Advocates

The men's rights advocates are fundamentally opposed to feminism.[53] They contend that feminism misrepresents the reality of men's and women's lives. Proponents would argue that men and women are abused equally by the current norms of social relations, or that men are, in fact, more abused because of the extremely restrictive traditional male sex role. They contend that feminism has become a force not only to empower women but to seize power over men as well. They see the women's movement as promoting negative images of men, male guilt, and distortions of the power relations between men and women. From their perspective, feminism has actually created a new sexism, one that makes men the primary victims.[54]

Men's rights members have been working to create male-run organizations with a variety of agendas; they might provide legal protection and counselling support for fathers engaged in divorce or custody proceedings, or monitor and critique advances made by the women's movement, or study and highlight how women abuse men. Typically the men's rights masculinists move beyond protectionism into attacking gains made by women for equality. This has left men's rights proponents open to censure; they have given a new name to some very ancient and traditional practices of replicating and protecting the patriarchy.[55]

One of the best published examples of men's rights masculinism is Francis Baumli's *Men Freeing Men: Exploding the Myth of the Traditional Male*.[56] It is a compilation of thoughts, comments, and position papers from the Coalition of Free Men, Divorced Dads Incorporated, The Men's Experience, Men's Rights Association, Men's Rights Incorporated, and others intent on improving the status of men. The focus ranges from the informative, such as why male sperm counts have decreased in the last fifty years (industrial toxicity), to the personal, such as accounts of what it felt like to be called a faggot and queer throughout school. Baumli's work reflects the resentment men's rights members have toward traditional hegemonic masculinity. Men's rights advocates recognize and advertise the potentially disastrous health, financial, and emotional consequences of striving to fulfil the traditional male role.[57] They emphasize that being the breadwinner or the soldier is often a lot less than what it is made out to be.

While men's rights advocates deserve some credit for their critique of hegemonic masculinity, their analysis is woefully incomplete. In exposing the failings of hegemonic masculinity and its effects on men, the men's rights advocates conveniently either ignore or minimize two key factors: first, the enormous advantages which historically have accrued to men adopting traditional hegemonic masculinity; and second, the disastrous effect this particular form of masculinity – and its incumbent acceptance of male violence – has had on the lives of millions of women. By ignoring these crucial realities, the men's rights proponents make the extremely self-centred claims that men are oppressed, and that the women's movement only serves to compound the problem. Men's rights activists believe, and work hard to prove, that men have had to suffer just as much as – if not more than – women. This philosophy is evident in several key areas in Baumli's *Men Freeing Men.*

Sexuality. A typical example of the men's rights perception of male-female sexuality is the submission by Robert Sides, 'Male Anger and Male Sexuality.' While it is extremely brief, in two paragraphs he clearly shows both his anger toward women and his uncritical acceptance of rape mythology. He is upset because he feels that it is no longer socially permissible for men to feel resentful of sexually attractive women – in this case, fashion model Brooke Shields. He states: 'What irks me most is the fact that women cannot believe men would get p.o.'d seeing this 16-year-old yank them around who then whispers, on talk shows, that she really is still a virgin! So why is she sticking her ass in our faces? I mean, don't taunt us unless you're going to deal with the heat, too, sister![58] Once again, it is a reversion to the old biological determinist belief that men have uncontrollable sexual urges and cannot contain themselves when aroused by the sight or presence of a woman. While Sides does not specify if 'the heat' involves sexual assault, he is intimating that it is the woman who is responsible for anything that may occur. This is a replication of the victim-blaming which women have endured for centuries.

Two articles on prostitution, David Morrow's 'You Pay for Every Piece You Get' and Herb Goldberg's 'Prostitution as Male Humiliation,' maintain the tone established by Sides. Morrow could easily have written *Playboy* magazine's editorial policy in the 1950s. He contends that men are used by women who plot to steal whatever they can from men. He proclaims one rule: 'only if a woman has several suitors of the highest socioeconomic standing which her body and personality can attract will she choose the one who is most gentlemanly. But if she has as suitors a prominent asshole and a gentleman of lesser economic means, she will choose the asshole. Later she can easily divorce him, sue for alimony, and still be maintained in his economic lifestyle.'[59] This is Morrow's explanation for why 'women marry jerks and pricks despite their insistence that they want thoughtful, gentle, considerate husbands.'[60] Morrow's advice to men is to be sure to establish themselves professionally and personally before getting married. 'A man who waits until after he is established before thinking about marriage will have the economic bait to attract quality females, but since his properties are in his name and were acquired before marriage, a woman's major temptation to divorce is absent. Too, a job steadily and conscientiously performed by a man before marriage will be fairly secure even in the event of a divorce, since the boss would blame the wife for any disruption.'[61]

Herb Goldberg's article is not much of an improvement. Goldberg, one of the most prolific and published advocates of men's rights,[62] in 'Prostitution as Male Humiliation,' reiterates the men's rights perception that men are continually being victimized by women. He implies that prostitution is equally degrading for women and men. Admittedly, it can be a less-than-rewarding experience for a man to purchase the services of a prostitute, but two issues – power and choice – are largely ignored by Goldberg. Being the purchaser, rather than the one who is purchased, automatically gives the man a power advantage. While the transaction may be humiliating for both people, typically the man has considerably more choice: it is the man who chooses when to walk into, and out of, the transaction. While some women may consciously choose to prostitute themselves, too often this decision is dictated by limited economic opportunities or a perception, developed after years of emotional, physical, and sexual abuse by men – often from early childhood – that being sexual with men is the only means of receiving love or appreciation. Goldberg conveniently forgets to mention that men who pay for a prostitute seldom are physically or sexually abused during the transaction, yet this commonly occurs to women providing the service. Goldberg ignores the relative freedom and power of the men in such situations and pursues a different train of thought. He notes that married men are 'starved for a moment of spontaneous, nonobligating, aggressively free sexual abandon.' Another rape myth: wives are not putting out, and men are entitled to do whatever they must in order to fulfil their needs. This is the same excuse offered for many sexual assaults. Maybe, instead of purchasing a prostitute's services, the men to whom Goldberg alludes should consider why their relationships do not meet their emotional and sexual needs. Then again, it is a lot easier to pay for a receptacle for their presumably unrestrainable sexuality than to do some critical self-examination.

Pornography. The writings about pornography in Francis Baumli's *Men Freeing Men* maintain the tone established in the section on sexuality. Robert Sides proclaims that women have choices, 'whether they want to be responsible for them or not'; women involved in the pornography industry are there of their own free will, and men cannot be held responsible for their actions. He contends that any man who would assume such a responsibility is clearly a victim of 'the bamboozlement of Femthink.'[63]

Eugene Martin, meanwhile, sets himself up as a great conciliator: 'just as I make access to pornography symbolic of sexual freedom, I can guess that my sisters are seeing in pornography all the threats of sexual slavery of every sort.'[64] Not denying women's claims, he argues that men have a right to their freedoms. Not surprisingly, this is the very perspective often used by pornographers to defend their industry. Baumli indicates that even among men's rights masculinists there is diversity. He implores Martin not to try to obtain his sexual knowledge from pornography, for it humiliates and hurts both men and women equally. Baumli's approach, in keeping with the central thesis of men's rights ideology, is to trivialize the violence perpetrated against women and instead focus on how men and women are hurt equally.[65]

Parenting. During the 1980s, in much of the Western world, there was an increase in the participation of men as parents.[66] While the verb 'to father' typically still is viewed as being the equivalent of 'to sire' or 'to procreate,' many men are striving to change that perception so that comforting, soothing, cleaning, and all the other necessities of child care often associated with 'mothering' will be recognized as skills that can be practised successfully by men. Though it is commendable that our society currently acknowledges men who are actively involved as parents, it is a sad reflection that we view this more as an oddity – or at best a novelty – rather than the norm. Nevertheless, numerous men have begun to deviate from the norm of traditional hegemonic masculinity by being present at the birth of a child, or staying at home to raise their children, or even just having a conversation with a co-worker about the attributes of cloth versus disposable diapers.

Men's rights advocates have worked hard to turn to their political advantage this very positive change among men. Men's rights proponents emphasize that men are discriminated against by a legal system that favours women and works to separate children from their fathers.[67] With such a plank in their platform, it follows that they would receive a significant portion of their support from disgruntled fathers either separated from, or sharing custody of, their children.[68]

Susan Crean provides an excellent exposé of the intentions behind the men's rights groups. She argues that by pressing for some very legitimate demands, such as paid paternity leaves and tax deductions for unmarried fathers who do not live with their children but contribute to their upkeep without court pressure, men's rights activists have been able to gain significant public attention and sympathy for their larger agenda.[69]

Men's rights advocates view the gains of feminism as a direct assault 'on the rights and authority of men in the family.'[70] They focus their endeavours on narrowing the legal interpretations of mothers' rights and ensuring fathers' custody rights clauses in family law reform.[71] They contend that such an agenda is important, as men are sincerely concerned about their children's welfare and are highly desirous of joint or full custody.[72] Yet the statistics indicate otherwise. Crean notes that in Manitoba, Canada, for example, only after the provincial government legislated a support enforcement program did the default rate drop to 15 per cent. Prior to the legislation, 85 per cent of the men reneged on their support payments. Furthermore, the vast majority of men have not contested custody and do not appear to want it. Crean states that 'only 15 per cent of all divorce cases in Canada involving children are contested and women initiate the action in 72 per cent of those cases.'[73]

Crean notes that many men's rights advocates are so determined to ensure men's access to their children that batterers' and sex offenders' crimes frequently are minimized.[74] Many men's rights advocates do not want to break the 'strong bond between the child and abuser.'[75]

Men's rights activists can be found across North America, with groups in most major cities. In smaller centres, such a group may be little more than one individual who staffs a phone line or monitors an answering machine, but usually it is connected to another organization in a larger centre. Crean correctly points out that while the actual number of activists may be small, they do hold the sympathy – spoken or otherwise – of many influential men in society. She recognizes the connections: 'Some have called the fathers' rights phenomenon the "equality backlash" but in reality it is the "patriarchal backlash," through which the male establishment has been quietly letting the fathers' rights activists fight feminism for its proxy.'[76]

Violence. In the area of violence against women, meanwhile, the men's rights movement errs by omission rather than overzealous commission. Baumli's anthology *Men Freeing Men*, for example, completely avoids the issue of male violence against women. Instead, the reader is treated to six articles about female violence against men. First there is Suzanne Steinmetz's 'Battered Husbands: A Historical and Cross-Cultural Study.' Her intention was to reveal the extent to which men are abused by women; she indicates an approximate ratio of twelve or thirteen women for each male who is abused. To Steinmetz's credit, she acknowledges that not only the frequency but also the levels of abuse experienced by men can be significantly lower than those endured by women. Steinmetz emphasizes that husband abuse often is underreported and that efforts in this area need to be augmented.

Steinmetz ignores the causes of the violence against men. Many instances involve defensive action before an attack by a male partner. The statistics on women committing murder unquestionably contain many cases of women killing in self-defence – and Steinmetz does not inform the reader that there is lively debate about the exact proportion (see above, chapter 1). If the self-defence/offence issue is factored in, the difference increases between the number of male and female victims significantly.[77]

Dan Logan's 'Men Abused by Women,' Ken Pangborn's 'Family Violence and Women's Lib,' and several other articles on how men are portrayed in the media express considerable anger at the women's movement for focusing on the abuse of women. The men's rights activists attempt to demonstrate from this that feminists are interested in abused members of our society only as long as they are female.

The tactics of the men's rights advocates appear to be based on discrediting the opposition in order to improve their own image. They are the self-styled champions of any and all men who have been abused.

They seem intent on producing one abused man for every abused woman so that they can claim that the sexes are in fact equal. Naturally, this would reduce the pressure on men to change their values, beliefs, and actions. A brief look at *Transitions*, a newsletter of a group known as the American Coalition of Free Men, illuminates this point. Cover-story titles include 'Sexual Molestation by Females,' 'Woman Charged with Sex Abuse,' 'Women and the Media Contributing to Sexual Harassment.'[78]

The choice of the articles for Baumli's book clearly reveals the political intent of the men's rights advocates. If they truly were committed to improving the lives of male abuse victims – as opposed to discrediting feminism – men's rights advocates would be addressing the fact that the vast majority of violence experienced by men – on the street, in the home, or in jail – is at the hands of other men.[79]

Conclusions

Men's rights advocates gain some credibility by using concepts such as role theory, which is partly compatible with a social constructionist approach. Yet rather than encouraging men to examine and to take responsibility for their violence, men's rights proponents work to shift the focus toward examples of women's economic, emotional, and physical dominance over men. Equally useful for deflecting men's responsibility for violence is a certain simplistic variety of feminism which views men as inherently violent and, unless controlled by traditional institutions, the cause of most of our social problems. As long as there are individuals who pretend that power imbalances occur only along gender lines and ignore all the divisions resulting from factors of race, class, religion, and sexual preference, men's rights activists will be better able to argue their case. For example, they will always be able to find instances of wealthy women exploiting male workers to demonstrate the oppression of men. The underlying intention of the men's rights proponents is to thoroughly discredit feminism. The obvious benefit for these men and many others is that if this is accomplished, feminist demands – such as the one for an end to male violence against women – will be easier to ignore.[80]

The men's rights philosophy upholds the gender status quo. It reinforces a tendency within hegemonic masculinity for men to perceive primarily their own victimization as men and to minimize or ignore the effect hegemonic masculinity has had on others – particularly women.

Individuals working for a reduction of male violence against women must be prepared for the obstacles created by the men's rights advocates. They are a formidable group of men who clearly feel very threatened by the changes they see occurring around them. While most might not openly advocate violent behaviour towards women, significant portions of their theory and practice reinforce traditional misogynist values, and thus contribute to male violence against women.

MALE TERRORISTS

Like all offenders, male terrorists practise violence against women; what makes them particularly malevolent is that they specifically target women who, as feminists, strive to empower themselves and their sisters. Two recent Canadian examples illustrate this disturbing – and universal – tendency.

The Montreal Massacre

Late in the afternoon of 6 December 1989, twenty-five-year-old Marc Lépine entered the engineering building of the Ecole Polytechnique at the University of Montreal, carrying a green garbage bag containing two 30-clip magazines and a .223-calibre semi-automatic rifle. Going directly to the second floor, Lépine shot and killed his first victim, Maryse Laganière, age twenty-five, an employee of the school's finance department. From there he moved to a classroom, Room 303, where Eric Chavarie, an engineering student, was conducting a presentation. Lépine entered the room and ordered the men and women into opposite corners. At first he was not taken seriously; the students thought it was a practical joke. After he fired a shot at the wall, however, the gravity of the situation became obvious. Lépine ordered the men out of the room, and proceeded to shoot the women. Four of them were seriously wounded; six were killed. From Room 303, Lépine descended to the cafeteria, fatally shooting three more victims and wounding others, and then returned to the third floor. He went to a second classroom, Room 311, where upon entering, he started shooting. The students scrambled for cover; Lépine jumped on top of several desks to fire at the women hiding underneath. Four more women were killed and several wounded. Lépine then turned his rifle on himself and blew off the top of his skull.

This was the worst civilian massacre in Canadian history: fourteen dead and thirteen seriously injured. As people tried to make sense out of the horror, one thing became clear. Marc Lépine came to the Ecole Polytechnique intent on killing women. In Room 303, he had shouted 'You're all a bunch of feminists, and I hate feminists.' François Bordeleau, an engineering student, heard Lépine say 'I want the women.' All the dead and most of the wounded were women; specifically, these victims were part of a larger movement of women penetrating the bastions of male dominance. Though it was not likely his intention when he undertook his murderous rampage, Marc Lépine drew public attention – even if only temporarily – to the issue and levels of misogyny in our society. His actions horrified and shocked millions of people, and motivated many to increase their efforts to end male violence.

Yet, increased political activism was not the only public response. Despite the fact that fourteen women were slaughtered, that Lépine – by his own comments – was an extreme misogynist, and that his suicide note contained a hit list of fifteen prominent Quebec women, many do not view him as a male terrorist. Many commentators tried to reduce Lépine's action to the work of one madman rather than a symptom of the misogyny of our culture. Doing so was possibly easier than admitting the entire fabric of the society needs reworking if male violence against women is to end.

While Lépine may have acted in a manner more violent than would many other men, his escalation process was similar to those of other violent offenders. Friends and neighbours, questioned after the massacre, described Lépine as friendly but extremely withdrawn, and noted he felt unsuccessful in his relationships with women, and had failed in many career attempts – one of which had involved applying to, and being rejected by, the Ecole Polytechnique, the site of his eventual rampage. Rather than dealing with his emotions, Lépine evidently ignored them and allowed the tension to increase. Eventually he exploded under the self-inflicted pressure.

Too many commentators have missed the fact that while Lépine did react to what he perceived to be serious threats to himself, he could have exercised several options. Instead of reaching out for help and support, for example, Lépine chose to enter the Ecole Polytechnique with a gun and hunt down women. The process is the same for the millions of other men who decide to sexually or physically assault known and anonymous women. But Lépine was not only a misogynist – his hatred had an additional refinement – he was anti-feminist, a reactionary; he felt deeply threatened by the advances of women and was determined to make them suffer for their gains.[81]

While the insane brutality of Marc Lépine's actions shocked Canadians, his opposition to feminism is by no means an isolated phenomenon.

The Queen's University Anti-Rape Campaign

In the fall of 1989, a committee of the student union at Queen's University in Kingston, Ontario, launched a campaign against date rape in order to raise awareness of the issue, dispel many of the myths, and reduce its frequency. A major component of the program was a 'No Means No' slogan intended to challenge one of the most common rape myths that women are always ready for, and wanting, sex but often play coy and pretend otherwise in order to test the sexual desirability of the male partner; a 'real man' will not accept no for an answer. The posters were displayed around campus.

By the first week of October, several signs mocking the anti-rape campaign had appeared in windows of the Gordon House men's residence. Their aggressive wording betrayed the fear that many women know often lies beneath male bravado. 'No Means Yes,' 'No Means More Beer,' and 'No Means Kick Her in the Teeth' reflect the tone of the response among these men.[82] On 11 October 1989, a group of women organized, painted 'No Means No' on the side of Gordon House, and sent letters to the parents of students with signs in their windows, informing them their sons were engaging in misogynist activities. The next day, after more signs appeared in the windows of Gordon House and other campus residences, the dean of women ordered the signs removed by 2:00 p.m. the following day.

On October 13th, the signs indeed disappeared; the issue, however, was by no means resolved. An open struggle continued for the next few weeks. The dons in Gordon House held a gender awareness week, providing seminars on sexual assault, rape, and the effect of the signs. On October 26th, the Alma Mater Society assembly discussed the issue but chose not to take any action because the Main Campus Residence Council (MCRC) was to examine the issue on the same day. While the MCRC did hold an open meeting, they chose not to punish the offenders. Instead, they advocated a gender awareness week for all residences. On November 2nd, the issue began to draw national attention, with the media giving the story top billing.

It is telling that during all this time, there had been no formal response from the university administration. At 9:00 a.m., on November 9th – well over a month after the men's signs appeared – thirty women staged a sit-in at Queen's principal David Smith's office, demanding an apology for the administration's inaction, the retention of the dean of women, and the institution of a sexual assault awareness campaign by the administration for the entire campus. Only then did the administration finally respond. Within a day, it called for a joint open meeting in January 1990 of the Gender Issues Board, the Alumni Weekend Board, and the Orientation Review Board (ORB). The administration also requested the ORB to establish an annual open meeting in September to deal with misogynist activities during 'Frosh week,' an initiation period for new students. On the afternoon of November 10th, the thirty women left the principal's office noting they had succeeded in raising the awareness of sexual assault issues at Queen's University. Yet because of their brave and admirable efforts – and their victory – these women were confronted by men on the street and received harassing phone calls.

The Queen's scandal indicated that despite gains made by feminists since the 1970s, not much has changed in our society. While nine of the men who had displayed signs in their windows did send a letter of apology to the *Toronto Star* and the *Kingston Whig-Standard* admitting that their 'humour was in bad taste,' the question remains why they would ever have thought in the first place that rape was a laughing matter. If the initial actions of these nine repenters are to be explained as a function of peer pressure – i.e., to fit in with their male peer group, they felt they had to display the posters – there is especial cause for concern. After all, it is this same pressure to conform to the male group and hegemonic masculinity that, at its most extreme, results in gang rape, and also plays a large part in acquaintance and stranger rape as well. Furthermore, the nine men who publicly apologized, and the others who did not, were not the only offenders who likely increased the fear of rape in most women hearing this story; the men of the Queen's university administration need to be held accountable for its dilatory response. There was no need to wait until thirty women took direct action. Would the administration have continued to ignore the issue if the sit-in had not occurred? While this will never be known, their month-long delay is an appalling and frightening sign. By choosing not to respond – and inaction is a conscious choice – until they were coerced, the administration in effect provided support and encouragement to the Gordon House offenders. If university administrations, at Queen's and elsewhere, really want to reduce date rape – which has been termed a 'campus epidemic'[83] (see chapter 1, above) – there are numerous proactive steps that could be implemented. Mandatory gender awareness seminars, permanent anti-rape campaigns directed at changing male – as opposed to female – behaviour, improved lighting and escort services on campus to enable women to walk around safely at night, and established policies to promptly respond to misogynist material or activities are just a few of the possible options. Unfortunately, the Queen's scandal verifies that such programs – and thus the safety of all women – receive a low priority indeed.

What happened at Queen's is just another example of how men have responded negatively to demands for an end to male violence against women. Clearly, the mentality of the men in Gordon House who displayed the signs and of the men who confronted in person or harassingly telephoned the thirty women involved in or associated with the sit-in at Queen's, was one of violence towards women. Like Marc Lépine (though not as extreme), the poster writers in Gordon House went a step beyond; they also directed attacks at what they perceived as a threat – women working to improve conditions for other women.

In the early 1970s, when a renewed feminist movement was emerging, there existed at times a naïve belief, which has continued through to the current period, that younger men were conscious of, and sympathetic to, feminist concerns. 'Male chauvinist pigs,' as they were often called in that earlier time, were portrayed in the media as balding, fat, middle-aged men in cheap business suits. The Queen's scandal reminds us, among other things, that the 'old guard' of traditional, patriarchal masculinity can be very young. Carrying on the dishonourable tradition of their predecessors, these men are the shock troops of a threatened and reactionary mindset that strives to ensure the preservation of the inequalities between men and women. Sensing that such an agenda cannot be stated so openly in the current period, such male terrorists may try, when confronted, to trivialize their actions as 'a bad joke' – but violence against women is under no circumstances a laughing matter.[84]

CONCLUSIONS ON THE REINFORCERS OF THE STATUS QUO

Reinforcers of the status quo go to great lengths to ensure that the traditional social order is maintained. They see little wrong with the existing divisions between men and women, and strive to protect them. While not all reinforcers may directly practise violence towards women, their theories and values help legitimize the violence of men in general. In the struggle to end male violence against women, reinforcers are one of the most difficult obstacles, though certainly not the only one. Men who simply avoid the issue of male violence are also an impediment.

Avoidance

THE SILENT MULTITUDES

A large number of men continue to be silent about male violence against women. Men need to recognize that by not criticizing their sexist and abusive male peers, they help perpetuate the tradition of male violence.

Male silence makes it difficult to know where many men stand on the issue of violence against women. No percentage estimates exist, for example, to tell us how many of the silent multitudes actively practise violence, how many might be aware of the problem but not involved in working to effect change, or how many individuals, though they are not offenders, remain oblivious to the problem of male violence. Compounding such ignorance is the tendency within contemporary popular culture encouraging individuals to remain uninformed and silent about many important social issues; a perspective exemplified in the 1970s by the popular phrase, 'If it feels good, do it,' and in the 1980s by 'Don't Worry, Be Happy.' People are encouraged to pursue individual happiness, and are not rewarded for developing a strong sense of social responsibility and a willingness to get involved.

We have yet to reach a stage where it is common, or, better still, commendable, for men to speak out against violence against women. Granted, there is a historic tradition within the current concept of hegemonic masculinity of protecting women, but it is a custom based in paternalism and repressive notions of women either as physically inferior, men's chattels, or both. And – as is evident from the types and frequencies of male violence examined above in chapter 1 – it has done nothing to end the problem; there are those who argue that it has contributed to the situation. What has yet to emerge among many men is a willingness to see male violence as a crime that they should be involved in ending.

There are two important reasons why large numbers of men do not assert their opposition to male violence against women. First, and foremost, is that many men benefit from being violent toward women. By exerting physical and emotional terror, many men can easily have their needs met: the victim will often comply out of fear. While many men who go for counselling claim that they have recently developed empathy for their victim(s), they also acknowledge that for many years they never really cared at all about how their violent behaviour affected her.

Offenders, of course, are not the only men who remain silent about male violence. Many non-offenders also do not speak out. While statistical evidence has yet to be gathered, it would appear that many men are afraid to risk suspicion among their peers that they are not hegemonically masculine men. Speaking out against male violence demands a critical approach to one's real and mythical peer group, and indicates that one views women as equals rather than as second-class citizens. Thus, many men, fearing such behaviour will jeopardize their membership in peer groups, maintain their position – and risk the safety of women. Such men succumb to the considerable pressure for men to laugh at a male friend's, co-worker's, or employer's misogynist joke, for instance, or to objectify and whistle at women walking down the street. Too many men continue to fear opposing this pressure.[85]

There do exist men who succeed in speaking out without feeling their masculinity is threatened. Too often, however, this occurs only within a select, safe group of friends or co-workers. While they may not welcome sexist remarks in such a context, in various other male peer groups these individuals will remain silent and make no attempt to effect change. Thus, the important changes remain localized and less significant.

It is also common for many men, aware of the values of one peer group or social milieu, to act differently according to various settings. Thus, for example, a three-piece-suited executive may express very appropriate ideas at work, but choose to be a misogynist when he hangs out with his friends at the bar or gymnasium in the evening.

An additional problem is that many men continue to be ignorant of how they are being violent and the effects on their victims. This is most evident with emotional abuse. Jeers, insults, and sexual innuendos typically are viewed as harmless jokes, or merely in bad taste.[86] As long as men who are aware of the effects of these jokes remain silent, nothing will change. Men who hear these 'jokes' go unchallenged may internalize the violent values they promote, and feel pressured to repeat similar jokes themselves in order to look like 'real' or hegemonic men. The cycle repeats itself as it has for thousands of years; male silence contributes to male violence.

LIBERAL CRITICS OF TRADITIONAL MASCULINITY

Since the mid-1970s, there has been a major increase in the amount of material published by male liberal academics examining men and masculinity. Regrettably, this material is notable more for its quantity than its quality. The majority of the works, while expanding our awareness of various aspects of masculinity, either avoid entirely or address but inadequately the issue of male violence against women. While many women have written, researched, and repeatedly focused on male violence against women, a similar effort has not been forthcoming from men. This near-silence clearly indicates the value assigned to the issue by many men. Considering the magnitude of the problem, writers and publishers should be, whenever possible, addressing, rather than avoiding, the issue. Male violence against women should not be ghettoized in specialized works on abuse. The multitude of books on masculinity published in the 1970s and 1980s failed to recognize how central the mentality of male violence against women has remained to hegemonic masculinity. This failure is evident in four areas typically discussed by liberal critics of masculinity: men's health, sexuality, parenting, and male sex roles.

Health

Thanks to an emerging awareness of the lower life expectancy of men relative to women, considerable attention has been afforded to examining men's health and lifestyles to account for this statistical difference. Issues under examination include hazardous work environments, high stress, minimal self-care, fewer or less intimate friendships, and poor physical and cardiovascular health.[87]

While high stress levels, for example, may be an acknowledged factor in damaging men's health, the emphasis tends to fall too much on the external, situational stresses in lives – such as the demands of work. While this is valid for many men, it is also evident that raised levels of physical and emotional stress can be related directly to an individual's self-induced cognitive distortions of external reality.[88] Thus, it is not always the specific stressor that is significant; rather, it is how the individual perceives and interprets, and chooses to react to, the event. Impairment in a person's capacity to non-violently interpret his external reality is compounded further if his value system contains many rape and battering myths. The result can be a greater, and more frequent, escalation toward violence, which can negatively affect the health of the man, not to mention the safety of women with whom he comes into contact.

Information on men's health, therefore, should be accompanied by a critique of hegemonic masculinity's acceptance of male violence against women. Many writers might justify their failure to provide this with the argument that this would not concern the general male audience that they are writing for. Yet according to the statistics on male violence (chapter 1), the offender population is not nearly as insignificant, or as distinct from the general male population, as we might like to believe.

Part of learning to be non-violent involves significant value changes, as well as a close monitoring of one's physical and emotional state. Awareness of physical responses can help a man recognize whenever he is escalating toward a violent episode. To halt this progression, the offender can implement a prepared non-violent control plan, which is likely to include various forms of physical activity, be it walking, running, swimming, or something else. Information on positive ways of avoiding violence is of crucial importance and, given the pervasiveness of the problem, should be disseminated as widely as possible. Individuals should not have to go to a specialized book on abuse to learn these techniques. For any author purporting to examine male health, it is a serious omission to ignore male violence against women, the effects of repeatedly escalating toward and practising violence, maintaining misogynist value systems, and the potential role of physical activity in averting a violent episode.

Sexuality

The tendency to ignore male violence against women can also be observed in most material pertaining to male sexuality. Derek Llewellyn-Jones has provided a thorough overview of the types and availability of such resources. He notes that in 1981 there were over fifty sex manuals in circulation and twelve of them had sold more than one million copies each. He submits that since most were written by American men, the focus of the subject-matter has been distorted. The tone of most of the works, for example, is very goal-oriented. Men and women are encouraged to determine what best suits their partner's desires in order to induce more frequent, enjoyable, and intense orgasms. Not that there is anything inherently or morally wrong with wanting to have an orgasm, of course; the problem is that in being so focused on the goal, individuals may ignore the process. Specific activities become techniques for achieving orgasm rather than pleasurable in and of themselves. To achieve success – read orgasm – couples must study, discuss, and of course frequently practise, sex. Unfortunately, sex manuals often seem more like introductions to basic acrobatics. It is not uncommon for their authors to acknowledge that many of the positions demonstrated are best suited for young, physically fit individuals.

One result of being highly goal-focused is that to a great extent, the pursuit of pleasure is turned into difficult work; that work, furthermore, often is not evenly shared. Llewellyn-Jones states that the vast majority of manuals replicate the traditional notion that it is the man who must orchestrate the entire sexual production (if not extravaganza). Such an approach is likely to reinforce the performance anxiety from which many men are already suffering; the result is that most books devote an inordinate amount of time addressing the problems of premature ejaculation and impotence.[89]

Encouraging men to control an event as highly charged as sexual intercourse is not necessarily a good idea, particularly in the case of violent men, who already have very significant control issues. But being in control of oneself and of one's environment is an important component of hegemonic masculinity; rather than seriously addressing the desire of many men to control people and situations, sex manuals typically encourage men to do so more expertly, at least in the sexual arena, by communicating with their partners to determine their needs and desires, instead of being unaware, or assuming they already know the answers. However, considering the statistics on battering and marital rape in relationships, on acquaintance and stranger rape, and on emotional abuse, many male readers are unlikely to suddenly start communicating effectively with women, since their history has been to do anything but. Even if such men were to start using these skills, if they have not used them extensively – or at all – in the past, their female partners may not feel truly safe to comment honestly on their male partners' sexual techniques. While the authors of sex manuals deserve credit for repeatedly emphasizing the importance of men communicating with their female partners, they must be faulted for their extreme vagueness about the element of violence that contaminates so many male-female encounters. By not dealing with the issue of male violence against women, they are preserving a deadly secret.

A much more critical and open approach is essential if men are to come to terms with their sexuality and how they relate to others.

Avoiding the issue of male violence against women only impedes the growth of such awareness. Writers on male sexuality need to talk about how to recognize what is healthy and, conversely, what is abusive behaviour. Generally, current manuals take it as a basic principle that 'anything goes' as long as those involved agree to it; however, this sanction is unworkable and potentially quite dangerous in an abusive relationship. A dynamic of subtle and overt coercion obviously will preclude a balanced and equitable sexual discussion and practice for the couple.

Regrettably, rather than addressing the frequent links between male violence and male sexuality, many of the most popular sex manuals only reinforce existing myths. One example is *The Joy of Sex*, which has sold more than 4.5 million copies; *New York Magazine* noted that it 'may be the best thing of its kind ever published.'[90] The book is over 250 pages in length, but affords less than one-quarter of a page to rape (on page 248, no less). The book's editor does admit that rape 'is a frightening turn-off,' and encourages women to repel the attacker by defecating (as if this can be done at will). Fighting back is not encouraged, as it may be 'provocative.' The clincher, though, is 'Don't get yourself raped – i.e., don't deliberately excite a man you don't know well, unless you mean to follow through.' Another rape myth perpetuated – this time in a publication sold not in pornography shops, but nationwide in mall bookstores.[91]

The currently available sex manuals appear to have been written in a vacuum. They presuppose a safe, non-violent, equitable, open relationship between two people when, for large numbers of individuals, this simply does not exist. Although discussions of sex or sexuality are an ideal context in which to address the issue of male violence, none of the authors of these manuals has done this. The result is that the silence on male violence is maintained.

Parenting

This is another example where male liberal critics of traditional masculinity typically ignore male violence against women. Throughout the 1980s, there was a veritable avalanche of books, articles, and media images dealing with men as effective, creative parents.[92] As already noted, some of the interest in men as parents was generated and used for specific political purposes by men's rights advocates. Yet much of the attention afforded the issue evolved from the simple fact of men –

in an era when for many families two incomes were becoming an economic necessity – who spent more time with the kids and came to recognize the potential pleasures of parenting. The media picked up and publicized the issue. For example, Kodak ran an advertisement that typified the new male image. A very fit and muscular young man, clad only in tight jeans, was pictured sitting in a warm and sunny windowseat with his knees pulled up and his head tucked down – almost as if in an upright fetal position. In his arms he cradled a very young baby. The photo reflected a perfect blending of strength and sensitivity, the values increasingly demanded of contemporary men.

Undoubtedly, more images like the Kodak advertisement are required. Men need to believe that they can be effective parents. For too long – whether by choice, or because of the obligation of the breadwinner role, or both – males have been involved very little in the tremendous responsibility of child care, usually only playing a disciplinarian role. Men need to realize they are capable of nurturing, encouraging, loving – and toilet-training – their children as well.

In the media's portrayals of men as wonderful fathers, two points must not be forgotten. Some critics believe the media has seriously overrepresented the actual degree to which men are taking responsibility for child care.[93] They argue that while men have become somewhat more involved as parents, the distribution of labour is still far from equitable, with women continuing to be responsible for most of the hard work. While more fathers are taking their children to play in the park, not all of them also scrub the diaper pail.

A second point must not be ignored amid the media hype of idealized fatherhood. There are many fathers who are extremely abusive within the home environment. By abusing the mother and/or children, whether emotionally, physically, or sexually, too many men have directly and indirectly destroyed the lives of other family members. The media's underreporting of such abuse, and simultaneous promotion of idealized images of fatherhood, is more than just hypocritical; it is a failure to address reality, which allows male offenders to avoid responsibility for their violence, and which can complicate recovery for many victims.

Men need to learn the art of being parents; this is not an idea that was ever emphasized for most contemporary adult males when they were children. Part of teaching men how to be good fathers involves clearly demarcating the demands of the job. Advertisements and articles on fathering need to emphasize that it is not always a pleasant and rewarding experience. It can be extremely frustrating and isolating, not to mention exhausting. Parenting can also exacerbate any pressures existing within a relationship, and create new ones as two adults try to adjust to the emotional, physical, and financial stresses of raising a child. A popular perception that ignores the strains of being a parent, implies that the experience is always blissful, and ignores the issue of men needing to learn how to deal non-violently with their emotions can be a prescription for disaster. It can mean setting many men up to fail – with potentially disastrous ramifications for all family members.

Men need to learn the signs and symptoms of their escalation toward violence, what to do to get out of a potentially violent situation, and how to get help to deal with their problem. They should not have to search out a book on abuse to acquire such information. The very nature of parenting requires that people know how to deal with their negative emotions effectively without violence. However, most of the material to date appears focused on a picture of the rewarding and appealing aspects of parenting, almost as if to coax reluctant men into undertaking the position – if only on a part-time basis. This approach must be complemented with an appropriate handling of the reality of male violence within families.

Male Sex Roles

Considering the concern during the last hundred years over the degree to which men adopt a version of masculinity compatible with the needs of the economy and the nation, and approved by those who control both (see chapter 3), it is not surprising that the male sex role is the issue that has received the most attention from liberal academics, writers, and public commentators.[94] The main focus of most of their work has been to address the vast number of challenges to traditional hegemonic masculinity during the 1970s and 1980s. They emphasize that adopting the breadwinner role, so highly valued in the 1950s, is no longer sufficient. While contemporary men may still be required to provide an income for themselves or a family, there are increasing demands for them to become more skilful in recognizing and communicating their feelings, more involved in family maintenance and activities, and less goal-oriented and self-centred in their interpersonal and sexual relations. These expectations have placed considerable pressure on men to be more critical of traditional masculinity. Most of the liberal critics examining the origin and nature of these demands focus on the ease – or difficulty – which men experience in integrating these activities with their perceptions of healthy masculinity.

Despite the importance of liberal sex-role research in addressing the need for the development of a new, less traditional, more flexible masculinity, generally it does not occur within a context which illuminates the high levels of male violence against women. These works do not reflect the reality that many men refuse to implement change, or have difficulty doing so, and use violence as a vehicle of protest. Many men will still beat their partners because they forgot to buy the groceries or dared to go back to college. The liberal critics rarely acknowledge male violence against women. When it is discussed, it is seldom afforded a degree of attention commensurate with the size of the problem.

Liberal sex-role theorists also fail to recognize the limits of male sex role (MSRI) theory. As discussed in chapter 3, MSRI theory is not sufficiently rooted within a social context. Roles are often treated as if they existed as a distinct entity, as if they were tangible or permanent, rather than as theoretical models created by individual human beings trying to explain a fluid and socially constructed reality. The gaps in MSRI theory are a reflection of the society in which it was produced. Since male violence against women continues to be largely ignored by society, it is hardly surprising that MSRI theorists should perpetuate this criminal ignorance. They devote considerable time, meanwhile, to examining more socially valued components of masculinity, such as the strength of the work ethic, or male sexuality. Dealing with the problem of violence against women has no priority. While much energy is expended by liberal critics in debating the angst of many contemporary men having to struggle with the demands placed upon them by the new male roles, it is not the men who are the major victims in our culture. It is certainly true that there are pressures to modify the traditional male role – and for many men this would entail some difficult self-analysis and change – but the larger issue must not be forgotten. It was men who created the traditional roles, and used their ensuing positions of greater power, relative to women, to extract many benefits for themselves. It is frightening that a fairly large body of literature could examine the pressures compelling a revision of contemporary hegemonic masculinity and almost completely obviate one of its most integral components – male violence against women. If one were to examine only the material generated by the liberal critics of masculinity, male violence would appear to be an insignificant fringe issue, relevant only to a small minority of men. Yet the statistics examined in chapter 1 attest to the inaccuracy of such an impression. The reality is that one cannot properly and thoroughly examine contemporary masculinity without also focussing on and examining male violence against women.

Conclusions on the Liberal Critics of Traditional Masculinity

The explosion of material relating to men's issues in the 1970s and 1980s was a positive development. The information helped spark a discussion on contemporary masculinity which continues to evolve. Unfortunately, to date insufficient attention has been afforded the subject of male violence against women. Reflecting the society in which these works were produced, writers about male concerns have reinforced the silence on the issue, which consequently remains largely invisible.

NEW AGE MEN

In many western industrialized countries, there emerged during the 1980s a philosophical perspective directed toward rediscovering and synthesizing pieces of astrology, psychology, Western and Eastern philosophies and medicine, pre-Christian spirituality, metaphysics, and environmentalism. Advocates believed that much of this information and knowledge would be essential for individuals trying to live on our highly industrialized, war-torn, overpopulated, resource-limited planet. Presumably, the renaissance of the various bodies of knowledge into a new perspective was to facilitate our transition into what proponents termed the New Age. For men of this New Age, liberation and personal growth involve coming to terms with and knowing their inner energy, or life force.[95]

The quest to connect with their inner masculine essence involves all-male gatherings, often several days long and situated outside an urban context to enable the participants to leave behind traditional roles and patterns of interacting with others. Commonly the settings and activities are chosen in an effort to create a primordial atmosphere. The body as well as the spirit is nurtured: food is often prepared by the men themselves and consumed collectively. Men gather in groups to build and then wear masks depicting their 'inner man.' Drums of all sizes either are constructed or available for ceremonial drumming – intended to dispel the spirits of contemporary masculinity and invite the reawakening of a long-lost, and undiluted, masculine essence.

Poetry readings and small group discussions are a common component of these retreats. New Age men want to move away from traditional hegemonic masculinity, toward a more healed and powerful, and less wounded and defensive sense of masculinity. Robert Bly, an American poet, has become one of the most important leaders of New Age men, and has developed a significant following that appears, at times, to border on idolatry.[96]

Bly has introduced the concept of the 'wildman,' the name he gives to the true, powerful, sensitive, energetic, and life-giving essence deep within men. Bly argues that when men are connected with their wildman they have boundless energy and exuberance. Sensitivity is encouraged in New Age men; at the same time, it is to be coupled with a stronger sense of confidence and belief in the rightfulness of their inner masculinity. New Age men reject the traditional hegemonic masculinity of 1950s corporate America for having damaged the inner male essence.[97]

New Age men work very hard to help other men break out of their old roles. Significant portions of their workshops focus, for example, on critiquing the failings of traditional hegemonic masculinity, while also helping participants appreciate and empathize with what their fathers and grandfathers had to do to 'be a man' in their respective times. New Age men encourage other men to heal the rift between themselves and earlier generations of men. They argue that the split between men often has been compounded by generations of men being absent from the home. Young males, according to New Age theorists, long for the presence of their father's masculine essence.[98]

New Age masculinism is very appealing to many men. The retreats provide a safe and supportive environment for men to experiment with discarding old, and adopting new, interpersonal communication and behaviour patterns. For this, the New Age men deserve considerable commendation.

They also deserve credit for emphasizing that the wildman – the true inner male essence – is not a violent entity. The wildman purportedly operates from a point of strength, while offenders, being disconnected from the wildman, are weakened and insecure, and thus more likely to strike out.[99]

The New Age men's philosophy, however, does suffer from some significant weaknesses. An initial problem is the extensive use of mythical tales and Freudian and Jungian presuppositions. While these add a compelling mystic dimension, often associated with New Age masculinism, they are not very strong theoretical foundations upon which to build a theory of personality development.[100]

There are also problems inherent in Bly's concept of the wildman. By arguing that the wildman is intrinsically good, powerful, and – most important – nonviolent, Bly takes a position which is the opposite of that of moral conservatives and in fact somewhat simplistically parallels social constructionism. Moral conservatives argue that male nature is inherently violent; it is essential that it be tamed by traditional social institutions. According to the New Age and social constructionist perspectives, meanwhile, it is actually the society that creates violent men. But New Age men diverge from a social constructionist perspective in two important ways – both of which lay the movement open to considerable criticism.

New Age men focus primarily on how men have been wounded. Paralleling the men's rights advocates, New Age men emphasize the price men have paid by accepting the traditional male role – heart attacks, shorter life expectancy, and fewer intimate friendships. While the New Age men may lack much of the vehemency and resentment evident in the men's rights movement, they share many of the same concerns. It is interesting to note that Jed Diamond, in *Inside Out: Becoming My Own Man*, a salient example of New Age male philosophy, readily acknowledges his respect for the work of Herb Goldberg, one of the leading men's rights masculinists.[101]

Like the men's rights advocates, New Age men fail by minimizing the part men have played in creating hegemonic masculinity and enjoying its numerous benefits. They do not recognize that being a hegemonic male can be a conscious choice. For instance, men will restrict the full range of human emotions, sacrificing their emotional development, in order to maintain power over others, or to perpetuate the illusion of being in control of themselves. In their efforts to expand the range of acceptable masculinities, New Age men often criticize women for the limits they have put on men. Women, particularly mothers, are blamed for coming between fathers and sons, and blocking the natural flow of male energy.[102] Such a stance is somewhat reminiscent of the men's rights position. Thus, the credibility of New Age masculinists exposing the price of hegemonic masculinity for men is lost when they do not simultaneously acknowledge and emphasize its price for women.

New Age men also fail to advocate a collective responsibility for ending male violence. While not completely ignoring the fact that women have been abused by men, typically it is mentioned almost in passing. Violence is something practised by other men – those not connected with their inner essence. While New Age men do not approve of male violence against women, neither do they cultivate a strong sense of shared responsibility toward changing other men or the system that encourages them to be violent. The New Age men's philosophy essentially is based on internal, individual work and does not seriously address the need for significant political action to end male violence. While the positive qualities of men need to be emphasized, and many men may need to undertake considerable individual self-analysis, these should not preclude participation in a cooperative effort to alter the social forces that create violent men. By not affording at least an equal priority to changing the social institutions such as the media, pornography, the military, and others that create violent men, New Age men essentially leave intact the existing misogynist system.

CONCLUSIONS ON AVOIDANCE

While silent multitudes of men remain an enigma, the liberal critics and New Age men have played an important role in loosening the restrictions on acceptable masculinities. This change was indeed long overdue.

Where these groups fall short is in acknowledging the extent and degree to which men are violent toward women. Since they ignore or minimize this key aspect, it follows that they must not be too actively involved in eradicating the social institutions which create violent men. Liberal critics and New Age men are unlikely to be found picketing stores selling war toys, or campaigning for a reduction of violence on television. If they do participate in such activities, it is more likely in order to oppose certain social realities which encourage a specific, restricted masculinity, rather than out of a primary concern for the effect these realities have on the lives and safety of women. However, with statistics indicating that one in two women is sexually or physically assaulted at some point in her life, to ignore or minimize male violence against women in any way is completely unacceptable.[103]

Working for Change

Men working to eliminate crimes of violence against women can be divided into four categories.

MEN IN OFFENDERS' PROGRAMS

The commendable efforts of men who would like to end their violence are repeatedly hampered. Typically, funding for offender programs is insufficient, and follow-up and support group services are inadequate (see chapter 5); meanwhile, of course, the social forces which encourage, legitimize, and reward male violence largely continue to flourish as well. Also, those men who do succeed in changing their violent lifestyles are an important resource, one that is yet to be fully exploited both in society at large and among the offender population. Greater public attention to their successes increases recognition and validation of the issue of male violence against women, and their example encourages other offenders to believe that change is possible. As well, men who have undergone such a transformation can make an invaluable contribution by sharing their experience of the process with others attempting to do likewise.

INDIVIDUALS

A man's motives for changing violent behaviour may range from an ultimatum from his female partner that if the violence does not end she will leave, to being confronted by friends who demand a radical change in his behaviour, to an individual recognition and acknowledgment of his violence against women, comprehending the unacceptability of it, and resolving to change. One of the major problems with acting individually is that men trying to develop different behaviour may lack the essential support or information necessary to effectively achieve, and maintain, a lifestyle of non-violence. As well, while change is positive, if it takes place in only one individual, the effects on his male peers may be minimal.[104]

NON-HEGEMONIC MASCULINISTS

Many non-hegemonic men – i.e., gay men, men of colour, and the poor – have been dissatisfied with the restrictions traditional hegemonic masculinity has put on men's options. They have known first-hand the effects of homophobia, racism, and classism.[105] Such prejudices – or what Ned Lyttelton has called the major dividing lines[106] – serve to narrow the ranks of men to whom money, power, and status are accorded down to white, middle-class heterosexuals. With the emergence of men's groups composed primarily of white heterosexual middle-class males, non-hegemonic men recognized that their interests were unlikely to be promoted. New Age and men's rights advocates have sought to broaden the scope of acceptable masculinities – wanting, for example, freedom for men to be more emotionally expressive, and less career-bound, and to develop more intimate friendships – but there are very clear limits as to how far. Many men's rights advocates are extremely homophobic;[107] few men with limited income can afford a weekend retreat to beat drums and make masks, and neither group – without being overtly racist – has ever made ending racism a major political objective. For these reasons, many non-hegemonic men either have never been attracted to these movements or, if they have, have soon defected and established their own critiques of hegemonic masculinity.

Such theoretical and political contributions have provided diversity and vitality to the debate on masculinity. They have challenged existing institutions, as well as the supposedly progressive new men's groups, to examine their own homophobia, racism, and classism. The non-hegemonic men have increased the complexity of the issue; no longer is the discussion focused just on gender.[108]

Yet even the non-hegemonic masculine perspective contains a serious contradiction: despite its egalitarianism, it fails to promote the equality of the sexes. Many examples exist of gay men, men of colour, and socialist men placing their needs above women's rights. For example, Gay Republicans in the United States support a political party that has restricted funding for day care and abortion services and, discriminating against the poor as well, has cut back on food stamps.[109] Many men of colour, while intent on ending racism, have perpetuated significant gender divisions within their families and social organizations.[110] For example, Stokely Carmichael, the leader of the Student Non-violence Coordinating Committee (SNCC), an important American black civil-rights group in the 1960s, stated that 'the only position for women in SNCC is prone.'[111] Numerous socialist organizations are no less notorious for ignoring the rights and demands of women. Many classical Marxists continue to view the women's movement as secondary to the class struggle; they believe that once all vestiges of the class society have been abolished, distinctions based on sex will disappear.[112] Non-hegemonic men who focus on the single issue of advancing their rights and opportunities as members of specific minorities, while ignoring or discounting gender-based exploitation, parallel the efforts of those men working primarily for an expansion of acceptable masculinities.

Both groups ignore the misogyny that is the basis for the exploitation and abuse of women. Non-hegemonic masculinists who do so may want to loosen the restrictions on membership in the 'boys' club,' but they still want it to be all-male.

There are, however, many other non-hegemonic men striving to end misogyny and male violence against women. These men are an important locus of change. Many gay men, owing to an awareness and experience of the often violent expressions of homophobia, have been in the forefront of men's groups focusing attention on male violence.[113] Numerous men of colour also have come to realize that an end to racism will not yet mean equality for non-white women. Thus, many native Indian, black, and Hispanic men have worked side by side with their female counterparts struggling to improve the status of their respective minorities.[114] Similar cooperative efforts have been made among socialist men. After the 1970s revision of the New Left's position on feminism, there was general acknowledgment that a socialist *and* a feminist revolution were needed to end oppression and sexism. Many socialist men have been organizing women workers or integrating feminist theory and practice into their personal and political lives.

Each of the pro-feminist non-hegemonic groups has made important contributions to the theoretical debate and practical understanding of our social reality. Without an examination of homophobia, for example, many men would be hard-pressed to understand why, despite their best intentions and efforts, they are failing to develop deeper, more significant friendships with other men. Men of colour have emphasized the particular difficulty of integrating certain feminist principles within minority communities. Sharing of the breadwinner role and division of the domestic responsibilities equitably can be a trying process in any household; for many native Indian or black people, it is further complicated by racism, since discrimination results in significantly lower rates of employment and pay. To maintain economic solvency, a couple may have no other option than to settle for a fairly traditional division of labour. It is not that all rectification of gender imbalances should be put on hold until the family income is higher, but until then, some role-reversal options simply do not exist.[115]

Pro-feminist socialist men also have made some valuable contributions. One of the most important is the framework for a better understanding of numerous components within feminism. Liberal analysts are unlikely to examine the relationships between class and gender; the result is a difficulty explaining the various often divergent strands of feminism. The preponderance in numbers and political clout of middle- and upper-class women within feminism has skewed the focus of many programs and policies toward the relatively more affluent population.[116] This helps explain why many working-class males would find conservative and men's rights philosophy appealing. From their class position it might appear that there are many options and programs for middle-class women that are not available for working class individuals. A pro-feminist non-hegemonic perspective recognizes the influence of both class and gender. Working-class men need not be opposed to feminism; rather, they should be critical of bourgeois feminists, and recognize their own allegiance to their working-class sisters. However, such solidarity can be difficult to establish – particularly when others are working to thwart it. Conservative and men's rights activists encourage and manipulate misogynist values among men in order to discredit feminists and feminism. Similarly, the history of the trade union movement provides numerous examples where the ruling classes have exploited differences between male and female workers in order to accentuate and perpetuate divisions within, and thereby maintain control over, the working class.[117]

In highlighting the important contributions of pro-feminist non-hegemonic men, one cannot ignore that there exist undeniable contradictions which limit these men in effecting social change. Not all individuals have incorporated into their personal and political lives a theory which crosses all the dividing lines. Thus there are, for example, racist pro-feminist gay men, pro-feminist socialist men who are homophobic, and gay black men who despise the poor. Transcending the various dividing lines in one's ideology and work can be very difficult.

The integration of multiple issues is problematic not only for individuals. It can operate at a national level as well. In Cuba, for example, while socialist and feminist policies have immeasurably improved the lives of millions of Cubans, gays continue to be persecuted.[118] Cuba serves as an important validation of the arguments of non-hegemonic men. To ignore misogyny, homophobia, racism, or any other dividing line can perpetuate the historic abuse and exploitation of various groups of people.

It is encouraging that there are men who are working toward integration of multiple issues; such a holistic approach helps us to develop a vision of a society free of all forms of discrimination. Of course, considerable work remains before this is a reality, and the possibility of a broadly based multiple-issue social movement is still extremely uncertain. However, this hopeful vision of a world without exploitation, abuse, or persecution is one that was being spoken about more and more during the late 1980s. During the 1970s, when many individuals in the West had become disheartened with the apparent inability of socialism to resolve many of the world's problems, there was a greater amount of energy devoted to single-issue causes. A virtually endless list of examples includes saving the whales, stopping nuclear power, ending world hunger, overthrowing apartheid, ensuring gay rights, and ending violence against women. What became increasingly evident to numerous lobby organizers is that while the issues may differ, the process was the same – gaining power from those who maintain control. Many of these groups and movements were working for the same goals – peace, prosperity, equality, and ecological survival. Non-hegemonic men played an important role in identifying the various dividing lines and emphasizing that for the exploitation of power to end, alliances are essential. Putting their theory into practice, many non-hegemonic men worked in conjunction with the pro-feminist men's groups.

THE PRO-FEMINIST MEN'S RESPONSE

Philosophy

Pro-feminist masculinism, like many of the responses among men, emerged in the wake of the 1970s revival of feminism. Pro-feminist men acknowledge that the hegemonic male role has many disadvantages. They admit that heart attacks, relatively earlier deaths, fewer intimate friendships, and a generally impaired ability to effectively communicate feelings are significant costs to pay for being male in our society. What sets the pro-feminist male response apart from others, however, is the emphasis on the privileges men receive by adopting hegemonic masculinity and, more important, the harmful effects this has on women. Through emotional, physical, and sexual violence, men maintain control over women. Raising awareness about male violence and working toward its eradication are major goals for pro-feminist men. Contrary to the conservative or the New Age men's perspective, pro-feminist men argue that male dominance of women is not a function of suppressed male essence, genes, natural selection, or inadequate socialization. From a pro-feminist perspective, male violence is caused by a society in which male violence against women is generally encouraged and legitimized and its effects minimized. Pro-feminist men, adopting a social constructionist approach, criticize social forces and institutions like pornography, the military, the media, and the family for creating violent men.[119] Their perspective is pro-feminist, gay affirmative, and male-supportive. They emphasize that the existing masculinities and femininities are socially created and thus have the potential for change.

Pro-feminist men argue that every man needs to develop effective, non-violent communication skills, share domestic responsibilities, and balance competitive drive with adequate self-care. They recognize that it is insufficient if these changes occur only within a limited sphere. Focusing upon the individual without altering the social structures which contribute to the individual's value formation allows the collective violence to continue largely unchecked. At the same time, altering the society without encouraging individual changes could permit some very abusive situations within individual homes to continue. Thus, men must effect not just personal but also collective, social structural changes. The truly radical act – at least in regard to its effect on the patriarchy – is not just to change oneself, but to speak out against male violence against women.

The collective responsibility of men for creating and, consequently, for ending male violence against women is central to the philosophy of pro-feminist males. They recognize that the average man may not have bashed in a woman's teeth, raped a female acquaintance, forced a woman's sterilization, paid a prostitute for services rendered, or practised any other obvious form of violence. Yet when one reflects on our culture, it seems inconceivable that there could exist a man who has not, at some point in his life, even if only in his ignorant adolescence, somehow put down, violated, or abused a woman, or accrued monetary benefits, power, or status through some form of exploitation and subjugation of women.

The simple fact of being male in our society confers certain rights and privileges that are unknown to many women. Men's acknowledgment of this reality can induce a tremendous sense of collective guilt, which, in turn, can make some feel either ashamed about being male, or resentful toward women for highlighting men's abuse of power. This guilt, in part, has contributed to the growth of the men's rights and New Age men's groups – both work to assuage male guilt. They seek to resurrect and affirm positive masculine qualities, but often end up discrediting feminism.

Pro-feminist men recognize the importance of men feeling good about their masculinity. However, they argue that one of the most important vehicles for developing a positive masculine self-esteem is for men, rather than ignoring the alarming levels of male violence against women, or pretending it is someone else's problem or responsibility, to become individually and collectively involved in ending male violence against women. The following is an outline of some of the major efforts of pro-feminist men.[120]

Areas of Activity

Prevention of Rape. The traditional basis for prevention of rape has been to teach women how to defend themselves. The result has been a proliferation of books and articles recommending a variety of measures – encouraging women never to walk without an escort at night, to take self-defence courses such as karate or Wen-Do, to ensure they are never alone with a male in an elevator, to keep their keys handy in order to avoid wasting time outside of a locked car or apartment door if being pursued, or to gouge the eyes of an assailant. While such techniques are useful, this traditional approach to rape prevention does not deal directly with the problem. Since it is men who are the offenders, it should be men – not women – who change their behaviour. Pro-feminist men have been active in trying to change men's beliefs about rape through individual and collective efforts.

Individual efforts. A multitude of options exist. Here are but a few of the actions pro-feminist men are requesting of individual men:

1. Putting a *Stop Rape* bumper sticker on one's car.
2. When walking behind a woman late at night on the street, keeping one's hands visible, moving to the other side of the street, and maintaining a significant distance from the woman, so that she does not feel she is being followed. If walking with a group of men, these tactics are particularly important.
3. Confronting potential rapists. If witnessing a potential rape scene, asking the woman if the man is bothering her – and being prepared for a retaliation from the attacker. (This can allow the woman time to escape.) If one fears physically intervening, calling the police or other people nearby is helpful. Creative tactics also can be implemented – for example, if driving a car, aligning it so the headlights shine on the attacker, and repeatedly honking the horn.

4. Confronting the rape-supportive jokes or conversation of friends and co-workers.
5. Exposing rape mythology.

Collective efforts. Numerous collective actions also can be implemented.

1. Lobbying for better street lighting, escort services to cars, or improved security in apartment buildings and other spaces where women are vulnerable to attack.
2. Criticism, when appropriate, of local police handling of sexual assault cases.
3. Exposure and criticism of inappropriate media coverage of assaults. Also pointing out the numerous endorsements of rape mythology provided by media images in general. Boycotting companies that portray images of women enjoying rape.
4. Organizing public meetings to inform co-workers, community residents, and politicians about sexual assault. Working on ending their support of rape mythology.
5. Offering to provide support services or child care for Take Back the Night marches.
6. Working to make rape prevention programs a required part of school and university curricula.
7. Producing and distributing literature debunking the various rape myths.[121]

Speaking out against Pornography. Pro-feminist men have also been active in the struggle against pornography. They argue that the industry profits from the degradation of women through the perpetuation of sexist stereotypes and the reinforcement of rape mythology. Direct action against pornography has included picketing pornographic bookshops and movie theatres, distributing pamphlets to people on the street explaining how pornography is dangerous to women, and acts of civil disobedience – throwing eggs at buildings, spray-painting theatre marquees, or breaking windows. Pro-feminist men have also been active in writing letters to newspaper editors, doing research verifying the harmful effects of pornography, conducting discussion groups with friends, co-workers, or the general public, and lobbying legislative leaders to restrict or prohibit the sale and distribution of pornographic material.[122]

Working to End Battering. Pro-feminist men have organized to raise public awareness about the levels and effects of male violence against women. Through discussion groups, leafleting, and rallies, men have been broadcasting a slogan central to the pro-feminist philosophy – 'Men breaking silence about male violence.'

One such effort is of particular interest. In 1985, the Ending Men's Violence Task Group of the National Organization for Men against Sexism, an American pro-feminist men's group, created and organized BrotherPeace, an annual international day of action to end male violence. Organizers designated 3:00 p.m. (Central) on the third Saturday in October as a common time when men, through a moment of silence, could 'recognize those who have died from, or suffered and survived, male violence.' The synchronization of the action was important. Not only were organizers emphasizing that male violence was a global phenomenon, they were also encouraging concerned individual men to realize they are not alone in their desire for change.[123]

By the third BrotherPeace, in 1987, activities were taking place in at least fifty-six cities in the United States and Western Europe. Approximately sixty organizations in the United States and in nine other countries in Asia, Europe, South America, and Central America supported the actions. 'This represent[ed] more people in more cities with the endorsement of more local, national, and international organizations publicly demonstrating against men's violence against women than ever before in history.'[124]

Efforts such as BrotherPeace reduce the emotional isolation between men which has helped perpetuate the silence about male violence. Most men do not talk about male violence or other important personal issues. Yet knowing men are asserting themselves and, at some level, risking their position with other men can free some men to speak out. Pro-feminist advocates encourage men who do so to establish supports for themselves; the process of becoming critical of all forms of male violence against women can result in distancing by male friends who are not prepared to examine their own violence.[125]

Programs for Physical and Sexual Offenders. During the 1970s, numerous men working from a pro-feminist perspective struggled to establish treatment programs for male physical and sexual offenders. While many of these counsellors would not have identified their actions as part of a movement of pro-feminist men, their theoretical approach and practical applications placed them firmly within the realm of pro-feminist masculinism – whether or not they were card-carrying members. Their motivation for providing offenders' treatment programs stemmed from a concern over the limited availability and the poor quality of existing services. Among the first pro-feminist offenders' programs were: RAVEN (Rape and Violence End Now) in St Louis, Missouri; EMERGE in Boston, Massachusetts; AMEND (Abusive Men Exploring New Directions) in Denver, Colorado; DAP (Domestic Abuse Project) in Minneapolis, Minnesota; and Evolve in Winnipeg, Manitoba.[126]

These programs, along with the women's movement, have played an important role in shifting our understanding and treatment of violent offenders from physiological and intrapsychic pathology toward social constructionism. Integral to the treatment approach was a critique of hegemonic masculinity and of the social forces which encourage male violence against women.[127] Other, more traditional, therapists may agree that violence is not genetic, but they have failed to emphasize the concomitant point that violent men are socially constructed. The theoretical and clinical strength of the original pro-feminist offender programs resulted in their being important models for other agencies and communities wanting to establish their own groups.

The process of developing the original programs was not easy. Many were designed and implemented prior to the establishment of any official state support.[128] As indicated above in chapter 5, many state planners display a significant reluctance to provide a leadership role in the treatment of male violence. Pro-feminist men have helped take up the slack.

Men working from a pro-feminist perspective have also been active in some very traditional settings in an effort to effect significant treatment modifications within the existing system. Many clinicians employed with state corrections departments, for example, in working with batterers or sex offenders are reshaping the available treatment modalities to address the social construction of violent men. Other men establishing independent treatment programs, or those involved with existing agencies, have been doing a great deal of the front-line work with offenders. They deserve, though like many front-line workers often do not receive, tremendous credit. Part of their reward for doing this difficult work is the sense of personal and political satisfaction they experience in knowing that they are helping to end male violence against women.

Opposing the Military. Many pro-feminist men have been actively critical of the military's role in perpetuating hegemonic masculinity through training men to kill. While various military establishments increasingly advertise their recruitment of women, pro-feminist men recognize that extending the opportunity to become killers equally to women has nothing whatsoever to do with solving the problem.

Pro-feminist men active within the peace movement have criticized the military for its tremendous drain on the civilian economy and for its contribution to various foreign-policy decisions that exploit people abroad to serve the interests of a domestic ruling elite. From the pro-feminist men's perspective, hegemonic masculinity and militarism are mutually supportive evils. While economic and political forces often are crucial factors in international and interpersonal violence, pro-feminist men emphasize that they are exacerbated by the competitive, violent, aggressive, untrusting, and individualistic values of military organizations and hegemonic masculinity. As noted above in chapter 3, descriptions of military goals, objectives, or manoeuvres are often couched in metaphors of violence. The army does not simply march through foreign wheat fields. It ravages virgin enemy territory, invincibly thrusting forward, penetrating to the heart of its victim. Variations of such aggressive imagery are heard daily in the media and reflect how hegemonic masculinity uses, and is used by, the military to achieve often similar goals – the subjugation of other human beings.

Pro-feminist men do not support such goals. Their hope is that by establishing a less violent variety of masculinity as ideal, the freedom of men and the military to rape, pillage, control, and destroy could be significantly reduced.[129]

Organizing in Support of Women's Reproductive Freedom. Pro-feminist men have been active in the struggle for women's reproductive choice. They have attended rallies, signed petitions, and held discussion groups to help explain the importance of, and promote the support for, reproductive freedom. Pro-feminist men, to date, have played a largely supporting role. There exist, however, at least two notable exceptions. The first, and most obvious, example is the many male physicians that have been conducting therapeutic abortions over the years. While being an abortionist does not automatically make a doctor pro-feminist, many either started their work with, or soon developed, that perspective. This occurred despite the restrictions that might be placed on a medical career by anti-choice supporters within the medical establishment. Ironically, it has been the vehement opposition of the anti-choice movement that has been responsible for the development of some ardently pro-feminist doctors who choose to perform abortions.[130]

A second example of active male support for women's reproductive freedom was the organization, in Canada, of Men for Women's Choice. The main catalyst for the creation of this group was the Canadian federal government's initial release of Bill C-43 (see above, pp. 199–200) that would turn back the clock on the freedom of Canadian women to make their own personal choices about abortion. A small organization of pro-feminist men, based in Toronto but with support from men across the country, on 23 November 1989 ran a full-page advertisement in the *Globe and Mail*, a nationally distributed newspaper.[131] That advertisement received considerable local and national media coverage and allowed the group to emphasize that not all men want to control women's bodies and lives. The group noted that an Environics Research poll found that 61 per cent of Canadian men oppose the federal government's decision under Bill C-43 to put abortion back into the Canadian Criminal Code. Only 30 per cent of Canadian men support such a move.[132]

The publicity afforded to Men for Women's Choice and similar groups indicates the potential fruitfulness of pro-feminist men organizing. One advantage is that men campaigning in support of feminist goals is still a media novelty. National media attention is not easy to attract. After twenty years of women making demands, there is something of interest in men making these same requests. Admittedly, sexism is one of the factors at play: our society generally affords greater attention to men. Yet there is something creative in utilizing the misogynist system to promote greater freedom for women.

Structure of the Canadian and American Pro-feminist Men's Response

Many men with a pro-feminist perspective work as individuals, possibly not recognizing they are part of a larger social force. The more formal pro-feminist men's response is composed primarily of numerous small groups of concerned men. Paralleling the structure of the feminist movement, pro-feminist men recognize the power of a small group setting – it is a context where men are more likely to feel comfortable taking risks, sharing personal feelings, thoughts, and experiences.[133] Individuals may also be more able to skilfully question or confront, without intimidating, other group members.

Essential for the success of the small group – and one of its greatest attributes – is its increased potential for supporting individuals. While large groups also provide support, they are unlikely to be as effective; individuals get lost in the crowd. Small groups can better provide the mutual support integral to the pro-feminist men's philosophy. Being a numerical minority within the total population of all men, and often widely dispersed over substantial geographic distances, pro-feminist men recognize the need to connect with and support one another.[134] In the existing society, there remain many disincentives for men to speak out against male violence. Pro-feminist men emphasize that without encouragement and support for men who do so, the movement is unlikely to grow and to reach its goals of dismantling hegemonic masculinity and ending male violence against women. Isolation can breed despair; support and networking can foster and sustain the energy needed to tackle the patriarchy.[135]

Pro-feminist men have also been active in organizing local, regional, and national workshops and conferences to discuss issues and ideas, formulate strategies, and learn from the successes and failures of other pro-feminist men working to effect change. Topics for discussion include understanding and prevention of rape and battering, the effects of the military on masculinity, the media and masculinity, organizing men for political action, homosexual and heterosexual friendship and intimacy, and abortion, choice, and men. Such meetings provide an important opportunity for pro-feminist men to connect with each other. They are an encouraging respite from the general population of men, many of whom still think rape – or some other form of male violence – is acceptable, funny, or just not a big deal.

The small groups, local events, and national conferences also serve a function for those men not attending. Knowing that there are men who are organizing to overhaul hegemonic masculinity and end male violence against women may cause other men to examine their own misogyny and, at some future point, join in the process. 'In Canada, it is estimated that there exist approximately 200 groups, representing about 5,000 men.[136] In 1989, there were groups in Newfoundland, Prince Edward Island, and New Brunswick. Several were operating in Quebec. Ottawa had eight groups, Toronto nine. There was a group each in Hamilton, St. Catharines, Kitchener, North Bay, and two in London. Moving west, there were three in Winnipeg; two in Regina and one each in Aberdeen and Saskatoon, Saskatchewan; and one in Olds, Edmonton, and Sherwood Park, Alberta. Calgary and Vancouver each had three. In Victoria, British Columbia, fifteen groups were operating.'[137]

Part of banding together has involved the creation of structures for coordinating the many groups and pooling limited resources. By the end of the 1980s, pro-feminist men had established men's forums in every major Canadian city. While a national body has yet to be created in Canada to coordinate men's pro-feminist organizations, one that already comes close to playing that role is Partners in Change, an Ottawa-based group formed in 1988. The organization views its function as providing 'a forum for men wishing to negotiate the transition from "power-over" to "power-with."'[138] Other national men's groups have emerged to deal with specific single issues. One example is the aforementioned Men for Women's Choice, a group of pro-feminist men supporting women's right to reproductive freedom.

The existing organizational structures serve as clearing-houses encouraging an information flow among groups and across the country. These organizations also have helped organize national conferences. Kingston and Grindstone, two communities in Ontario, have hosted pro-feminist men's conferences since the mid-1980s.[139]

In the United States, the situation is somewhat different. The pro-feminist men's movement, while numerically larger than in Canada, has had to contend with the significant strength of both the men's rights and the New Age men's groups. During the 1970s there was little differentiation between the emerging men's groups. This changed dramatically in the early 1980s as the divisions between the various groups became more clear.[140] More and more, separate organizations were being developed to coordinate the different responses. In 1982, at the Seventh National Conference on Men and Masculinity, held in Boston, men's rights activists indicated an intention to become more independent. Some pro-feminist men, wishing to ensure the future of the annual Men and Masculinity conferences, formed the National Men's Organization (NMO).[141]

NMO's National Council met in August 1982 in San Francisco, established a series of pro-feminist principles, created *Brother* as a national newsletter, and identified *M.: Gentle Men for Gender Justice* – an existing magazine – as 'the forum for the national men's movement.'[142]

Since its formation, the National Men's Organization has twice changed its name. Initially, the pro-feminist NMO was often confused with a New York–based men's rights organization with the same name,[143] so in 1983 the name was changed to the National Organization for Changing Men. After some continuing concern that the name was still inadequate in indicating the direction in which members presumably were changing, the organization became, in 1990, the National Organization for Men against Sexism (NOMAS).[144]

The various name changes notwithstanding, the organization has continued to flourish, to more clearly separate itself from the men's rights advocates, and to serve as a clearing-house and national coordinating body for American – and to some extent, Canadian – pro-feminist men.

Aside from continuing to publish *Brother* as its national newsletter and maintaining a supportive relationship with *Changing Men* (previously *M.: Gentle Men for Gender Justice*), NOMAS has been involved in numerous activities to help end male violence against women. One example, mentioned above, is the BrotherPeace Annual International Day of Actions to End Male Violence.

NOMAS also has developed several task groups which focus on specific issues. These are: Child Custody Issues, Ending Men's Violence, Fathering, Gay Rights, Homophobia, Male-Female Relationships, Men and Aging, Men and Mental Health, Men and Spirituality, Men's Culture, Men's Studies Association, Pornography, and Reproductive Rights.[145] The task groups enable men with specific interests to become involved. Certainly, some groups are more active than others.[146] Yet each has formulated a pro-feminist perspective and works at ending the oppression, misogyny, and discrimination which hegemonic men typically perpetrate against minority groups.

In the United States and Canada, the pro-feminist men's response has been nurtured and strengthened by the still small but nevertheless growing number of academic and popular books,[147] journals and magazines,[148] articles about the movement in mainstream publications,[149] resource directories,[150] protest singers,[151] and the emergence of men's studies as an academic discipline.[152] These resources have provided crucial information and awareness about hegemonic masculinity, and about how to effect change and end male violence.

Will the Pro-feminist Men's Response Succeed?

Of all the organized activities among men, pro-feminist groups have been the most involved in working to end violence against women. The growing numbers of men criticizing male violence and encouraging sweeping changes in the currently hegemonic masculinity is a unique historic phenomenon. While they are still small in numbers, the intent of their efforts parallels that of other social activists. Nineteenth-century American white abolitionists, or twentieth-century white South Africans working to end apartheid, are just two examples. In each situation, while belonging to a group that exercised considerable power and control over others, individuals have struggled to end the exploitation. Pro-feminist men have a crucial role to play in ending the abuse of women. By working with misogynist males – many of whom will be more willing to listen to men than to women – pro-feminist men can accelerate a move toward male non-violence.

Despite its important work, its encouraging potential, and its increasing numbers, the pro-feminist men's response, relative to that of all men, is quite small. The reasons are quite clear. Part of the problem is that pro-feminism is as yet a relatively new attitude among men. Another contributing factor is that many men simply do not want to change. Addressing this obstinacy – or ignorance – remains a major challenge.

The pro-feminist men's response also contains some significant internal contradictions that will limit its growth and future success. When positive responses among men toward ending male violence are so few, one is tempted not to be overly critical. Yet, if pro-feminist men ignore these contradictions and delay their resolution, the depth and scope of the success in ending male violence against women could be seriously limited. The following comments are made in the spirit of helping rather than hindering these efforts.

A basic problem is that pro-feminist men are not unified behind a single form of feminism; reflecting the divisions among feminist women, they are split into two main groups. While theoretical unanimity is not essential, in its absence consistent policy decisions and political actions can become more difficult to formulate and enact.

One group of pro-feminist men follows radical feminist thought while another works from a liberal feminist philosophy. According to the radical feminist perspective, men should work to end sexist behaviours in their own lives and those of other men, and take only a supporting role in the women's movement. Men should never be overly assertive in the feminist context, as that would be replicating traditional male behaviour. While men will lose some privileges, they also will lose the burdens of being a man in the move toward a non-sexist society.[153]

The liberal pro-feminist men, meanwhile, recognize the limiting nature of the traditional male sex role and view feminism as an excellent catalyst for men to critically examine their own lives. The focus is

246 Ending the Silence

less on the role of patriarchy than on the economic and legal oppression of women. It is believed that men need to work together to liberate themselves from the constraints of the male role and that a feminist revolution is insufficient to help men change. Men need to do much of the work of establishing working groups and national forums to promote information-sharing and change.[154]

The debate over pornography is one area where the underlying theoretical divisions may be clearly observed. While there appears to be a general agreement among feminists that heterosexual pornography perpetuates misogynist values in men, there is disagreement over what should be done about it. Pro-feminist men, working from a radical feminist perspective, advocate banning or restricting pornography, while those working from a liberal feminist perspective fear that censorship could be manipulated to silence gays, women, and other oppressed groups.

Within both segments of the pro-feminist men's response, the discussion on pornography inevitably brings up the issue of gay pornography. While misogyny as well is a concern,[155] the most heated debate concerns whether or not gay male pornography perpetuates a hegemonic masculinity among gay males. While some argue that the non-violent material simply is erotica, others contend that the images portray a certain masculine ideal that denies or restricts the reality of other gay men.[156]

Other significant debates within the pro-feminist men's response are a reflection of its still-evolving theoretical foundation and relatively narrow demographic composition. Despite the involvement of many non-hegemonic men,[157] pro-feminist men's groups remain predominantly white, middle-class, and heterosexual.[158] This significantly limits their theoretical outlook and, concomitantly, the direction of their policies. Currently, the major focus of pro-feminist men is on gender-related issues: to broaden the scope of acceptable masculinity, and to end male violence against women. Accomplishment of these goals is, undeniably, crucial; however, by limiting their efforts to redressing exploitation resulting from gender-based power differences alone, pro-feminist men are in fact less likely to attain their goals.

Non-hegemonic men have repeatedly pointed out that oppression is not limited to gender. There exist numerous other dividing lines – class, race, sexual preference, able-bodiedness, religion, and others – by which people are disempowered and limited in their potential. An unemployed black woman, for example, exploited on the one hand by the patriarchy and its misogyny, is also likely on the other hand to be a victim of classism and racism. Her employment prospects are limited not just because she is female – though that most definitely is one obstacle for her in this society. Employers may refuse her request for work because she is black and/or poor as well. If she does succeed in finding a job, it will likely be for lower pay than her white or male counterparts would receive. Non-hegemonic men stress that exploitation and abuse are not single-issue concerns; gender is just one of many possible dividing lines. To date, most pro-feminist men have not accorded these other dividing lines equal recognition; gender has been prioritized as the primary basis of exploitation. The result is a reverse variation on Old Left socialism, which emphasized class struggle and relegated gender issues to the post-revolutionary agenda. Many pro-feminist men, while deserving credit for their willingness to question male privileges, have not displayed the same enthusiasm for examining, and dispensing with, the benefits accrued to them simply because they are straight, white, and middle-class. If all forms of violence are to end, a movement is needed that strives to eliminate every power imbalance; all the dividing lines need to be erased.[159] The pro-feminist men's response, while moving in the right direction, has yet to embrace this comprehensive ideal.[160]

It remains to be seen whether pro-feminist men will succeed in addressing the various divisions among themselves as well as in the general population. There are numerous individuals working to erase all dividing lines, but this struggle will not easily disappear, as the various prejudices are often both inextricably intertwined and individually strong – as are the vested interests of those who want to prioritize only gender issues. Still, without the abolition of the dividing lines within individual groups, and ultimately society at large, violence will never be eradicated.

So where does the pro-feminist men's movement go from here? Despite its limitations, it remains an important vehicle for social change. Men concerned about violence against women – be it motivated by gender, race, class, or anything else – need to become active. It is to be hoped that, with sufficient pressure from within as well as from external political movements, the pro-feminist men's movement will expand its focus beyond the issue of gender. If it is unwilling to do so, other political formations may be necessary to fill the gap.

The pro-feminist response among men is at a crucial juncture, and there are at least three potential outcomes. The first is that internal contradictions will induce a paralysis that will cause it to collapse. At present, this appears unlikely; the recent expansion of the pro-feminist perspective would indicate that there are many men who want to end violence against women. The second possibility is that the response will continue with its current structure, addressing primarily issues of gender, but with greater numbers of supporters. Even if pro-feminist men can accomplish nothing else, this could provide a significant impetus toward ending the violence in our society. The third and most difficult possibility is the creation of a broadly based movement that accords equal priority to all forms of violence and works to erase all dividing lines between human beings. It is difficult to say which of these three possibilities will prevail. Ultimately, the actual outcome of the movement will be determined by the philosophy and hard work of the men within it and the strength of the internal and external resistance to it.

Conclusions

The prospects for an end to male violence against women in the near future, while better than they were twenty years ago, still look appallingly grim. Hegemonic men, as the major offenders, and the social structures which help create them, remain formidable obstacles. This reality must be confronted individually and collectively and changed if women are ever to achieve equality and safety in this society. Many individuals may believe that significant changes have occurred among men in the wake of the 1970s revival of feminism; this chapter has indicated this to be an inaccurate and even dangerous conclusion. The major reactions among men have been to fight to maintain traditional gender divisions, or to dismiss male violence against women as an insignificant problem. Both attitudes perpetuate the problem. Each helps ensure that the social forces which encourage male violence against women will not be seriously questioned or threatened; that state support for treatment services for women, children, and men will not substantially increase; and, most seriously, that women's lives, emotionally, physically, and sexually, will continue to be viewed as unworthy of protection, and thus will remain in jeopardy.

This intolerable situation must not continue. It can be rectified. While the amount of work which lies ahead is tremendous, the task is not an impossible one. In the next chapter, several concrete suggestions are offered for those individuals who want to help break the silence, and end the violence.

7 / Where Do We Go from Here?

There still exist many obstacles to ending male violence against women. Men continue to commit an appalling number of emotionally, physically, and sexually violent crimes of every description against women. The statistics – which typically underrepresent the actual number of crimes – are, unfortunately, ignored and minimized; indeed, male violence against women more often than not is glorified. Substantial effort is necessary to publicize and criticize male violence. The silence on men's violence must be permanently broken.

The suffering of victims, of course, has been largely ignored. Victims' reactions vary considerably according to such factors as the nature of the attack, its duration, the victim's relationship to the offender, and the woman's previous history of abuse. Listening to victims' accounts, many counsellors have begun to realize that the effects of abuse are not necessarily linked to specific varieties of violence. Victims of different forms of violence may experience identical effects – diminished self-esteem and anger are just two examples. Victims' stories are helping a growing number of individuals recognize that verbal putdowns, sexual harassment, date rape, battering, femicide, and other crimes against women are all variations on the same theme – a fundamental misogyny in our culture. Efforts at raising awareness of male violence should not be aimed just at increasing the public's familiarity with the statistics. People also need to recognize the links between the numerous crimes against women, and that most offenders are men, and that the majority victimize women they know. Men need to be held responsible for their crimes; women must no longer be blamed for male violence.

Increasing knowledge about male violence against women inevitably leads to the question (posed in chapter 3): Why are men violent? The answer is complex. Despite our recurring tendency to look for physio-logical reasons, or blame it all on the family, such explanations are not supported by the evidence. While the family is a crucial component, the media, the military, male peer groups, sport, and pornography are key elements in the social construction of violent men. Any serious revision of these social institutions will involve a tremendous amount of work, and provoke significant opposition from those wanting to maintain the status quo.

Fundamental changes must also occur in the treatment of male vio-lence. Chapter 4 examined the limitations of treatments emphasizing physiological and intrapsychic pathology. The women's movement was identified as the catalyst which removed male violence from social and clinical obscurity and placed it firmly on the political stage. The women's movement, as the first major force to challenge the reality of male violence, shifted our conceptualization and treatment of it from the traditional approaches toward social constructionism. The strength and determination of millions of women, unwilling to preserve the silence about male violence, and committed to rectifying the power imbalance between women and men, compelled the state to respond.

The state, as the second force in the struggle to end male violence, has been reluctant to fully implement a social constructionist solution. Many positive changes have occurred in the treatment of male vio-lence; yet, with the current limits on funding and an apparent unwill-ingness on the state's part to take serious and significant initiatives toward ending the creation of violent men, the state cannot address the full magnitude of the existing crisis. It seems generally content to pro-vide inadequate treatment services for the relatively few offenders who happen to get caught or the even fewer who seek help voluntari-ly. This laissez-faire attitude reveals the limited degree to which one can expect the state to end crimes against women.

State funding must be increased. The difficulty of this task is com-pounded in the Western world by two main factors: economic reces-sion, and a political climate in which state and corporate policy-makers are rapidly dismantling the welfare state. Still, such obstacles do not preclude future victories by feminist women and men; with signifi-cantly increased lobbying, they could compel the state to legislate rad-ical changes to hinder or reduce the number of structural facilitators of male violence in our society. It is unacceptable for the state to take pride in the woefully inadequate treatment of a handful of male offenders while ignoring the many who are not in treatment as well as the social forces which help create violent men.

Yet without significant pressure from the grass roots, the state is unlikely to implement substantial social constructionist reforms, particularly any which might threaten the vested interests, for example, of corporations that exploit traditional masculinities and femininities to sell their products.

To induce state action, women and men must break the silence on male violence. To its credit, the women's movement has never relaxed its campaign for change. Most men, however, have done nothing to pressure the state to act more boldly. In fact, many men have been active in trying to block state concessions to feminist demands. Other men either continue to offend, or try to ignore the violence perpetrated by their peers, or remain silent. From the victim's perspective, these various male responses are indistinguishable – it inevitably means more women end up being beaten or raped.

Pro-feminist men, as a potential third force in the struggle to end male violence against women, have an obligation to become more vocal and to promote change among their male peers. The women's movement has achieved several victories against misogyny since the early 1970s. But to protect these gains, and to build on them, additional help will be needed. All men must take responsibility for male violence. The following sections outline how men can become involved.

If You Are a Violent Offender

- Do not minimize or deny your violent behaviour. Do not try to convince yourself it will never happen again. The research on offenders indicates that if a man has been violent, unless there is outside intervention, his violence is likely to increase in frequency and severity.
- Get yourself out of, and stay away from, dangerous situations (i.e., leave the house or your relationship) to avoid reoffending.
- Get help immediately: open the phone book and call a local crisis centre, women's shelter, or men's group, or contact the court office for a list of services for offenders in your area.

If Your Know Someone Who Has Offended

- Ensure that the victim is safe, supported, and made aware of appropriate options and services for help.
- Talk to the offender about his violence. Do not perpetuate it by keeping it secret. Do not pretend the violence did not happen or that it was not a big deal. Clearly inform this person that you do not

believe it acceptable for a man to be violent towards a woman – regardless of the situation, he has other options. Let him know you think he needs help; however, be sure to strike a balance between confrontation and encouragement. While men must be confronted about their violence, they also need to be encouraged that changing their behaviour, while difficult, is not impossible.

- Find out what services exist for offenders, and pass on the information. Talk about the advantages of change. Offenders are particularly receptive to help during the so-called honeymoon phase following a violent episode.
- Inform the offender that you will be letting others know about the violence. Friends, family, and co-workers need to be informed, particularly if they are in regular contact with the offender.
- Do not forget to follow up. The violent individual may at some point decide to ignore his problem. Remind him that it is unlikely to disappear without outside help.

Identify Your System(s)

In the process of becoming politically involved to end male violence, each individual needs to identify the systems within which he wants to effect change. Some men will work within several. Others may want to focus their energy in specific areas until they become more familiar with and experienced in the work. Any effort is an important contribution to the goal of ending male violence against women. The systems in which one may become active include:

- family
- friends
- workplace
- organizations and unions
- clubs and fraternities

- school/university
- community
- city
- province/state
- country

Identify Your Area(s) of Interest/Concern

Select one issue or area about which you feel quite strongly. An emotional commitment to an issue is important: it will help you deal with the considerable resistance, both external and internal. The following items, not in any order of priority, are some initial areas requiring work.

AMONG MEN

- Reject and boycott misogynist humour; confront men on their violence.
- Take every opportunity to speak out against violence against women.
- Confront homophobia; inform others about how it discriminates against homosexuals and can hinder friendships among heterosexual men.
- Challenge racism and expose the harmful effect of racist jokes.
- Try to change the consciousness and habits of friend(s), rather than giving up on the friendship(s).
- Organize workshops, conferences, and town hall meetings exposing male violence against women and discussing how it can be stopped.
- Encourage erotica; expose and reject pornography and the misogyny integral to it.
- Do not feel compelled to maintain hegemonic masculinity. Take risks with your peers; lying about sexual exploits, for example, can perpetuate myths about male and female sexuality. Dishonesty may reinforce the perception that one is a hegemonic male; it also precludes true intimacy between friends.
- Emphasize that while hegemonic masculinity may pose many disadvantages to men, it poses deadly risks to women. Acknowledge the fact that hegemonic masculinity has never been foisted upon men; they have chosen to adopt it and to reap the benefits. Highlight the advantages in embracing other varieties of masculinity that do not accept violence against women.

LARGER-SCALE POLITICAL ACTIVITIES

- Demand additional and extended programs for victims and offenders. Raising public awareness about the crime of male violence is likely to result in an increased demand for services.
- Ensure that funds for offenders' programs are not siphoned off from services for victims.
- Campaign to change the court system to decrease the number of offenders who escape prosecution.
- Support more severe legal sanctions against male violence.
- Work to end discrimination against homosexuals and all visible minorities.

- Lobby for an expansion of services within correctional institutions. While many offenders need to be incarcerated for their crimes, values learned in jail often only compound offenders' existing problems. Thus, in-house and second-stage treatment programs need to be developed – particularly with sexual offenders – to ensure the acquisition of new, non-violent skills.
- Challenge misogynist comments made by any elected and appointed officials, or public figures.
- Hold fund-raising events to generate money to establish, maintain, or expand a local rape crisis centre, battered women's shelter, or offender program.
- Work to improve day-care services to promote the economic independence of women from their male partners.
- Lobby for equal pay for work of equal value.
- Support the movement for reproductive choice. Democratic access to safe abortion services is crucial.
- Investigate whether your local government monitors alimony payments. If so, what percentage of men are maintaining their payments, and how does the government respond to those who do not?
- Request state and private funding for public service announcements identifying the varieties and effects of male violence against women, stressing the criminal nature of the acts, and indicating how to get help.
- Participate in the debate on pornography. Erotic material that does not perpetuate rape myths and misogyny can be endorsed as an alternative.
- Expose the military's drain on the civilian economy and the resultant reduction in social-service expenditures. Critique the military's role in perpetuating hegemonic masculinity and encouraging men to use violence to solve problems.
- Expose the parallels between misogyny and environmental degradation. Many of the same values supporting violence against women contribute to the exploitation, rape, and plunder of our planet as well.

WITHIN THE EDUCATION SYSTEM (SCHOOLS, UNIVERSITIES, AND COLLEGES)

- Lobby for courses on assertiveness, effective communication, and conflict resolution. Such skills are essential to assist victims and to reduce the numbers of potential victims.

- Request that critiques of battering and rape mythology be required components of family life programs and ethics courses. Such courses need also address, and to counter the effects of, homophobia, racism, and classism.
- Encourage administrators to make women's history and rape prevention courses mandatory.
- Petition for courses on human sexuality which will address all its aspects – not just basic biology and reproduction. Birth control information is crucial. Also, such courses might help to reduce the frequency of sexual assault by helping males to develop effective, non-violent communication styles and an increased awareness of male/female sexuality.
- Examine and critique the material used in schools to ensure that male violence against women is presented appropriately and truthfully. Material perpetuating or trivializing male violence against women and other forms of violence needs to be removed or used as a teaching tool to demonstrate myths and inaccurate information concerning male violence.
- Pressure your local schools and universities to educate their staff to end the transmission to students of racist, sexist, homophobic, classist, and other values which reinforce dividing line values in society.
- Insist that rape prevention courses (ones which focus on changing men's thinking and behaviour) be required for all males.

WITHIN THE PRIVATE AND STATE BUSINESS SECTORS

- Lobby for change in the media portrayal of various masculinities and femininities. Hegemonic varieties most often are rewarded while non-hegemonic varieties receive minor parts or are the brunt of malicious stereotypes. Letter-writing (i.e., to the editor, the company president, or one's elected government representative), demonstrations, and boycotts can be effective. If the offender is a corporate manufacturer, appeal to the television network, magazine company, or radio corporation. If the media company is to blame, work to have sponsors remove their ads.
- Encourage affirmative action programs for women, homosexuals, and visible minorities.
- Negotiate extended paternity leaves to encourage the sharing of parenting responsibilities between mothers and fathers.

- Emphasize that men should be able to have time off work to care for sick children.
- Lobby for quality day-care services or for subsidies for existing private day-care centres.
- Have your employer provide taxi vouchers to enable female employees to ride home more safely at night, rather than having to take public transit or walk to their cars in deserted parking facilities.
- Demand improved lighting on company grounds and the provision of escort services for women to their cars, especially if parked at some distance.
- Coordinate or provide workshops on sexual assault, battering, and emotional abuse. For the men who participate, the task will be to examine, question, and alter behaviour. For the women, the goal will be to become empowered and familiar with resources available to help them deal with abuse.
- Lobby for extensive training of social, or human service, workers in corporations so that they can assist victims and offenders of violence. Skills would include:
  1. Discreetly approaching employees suspected of being abuse victims or offenders, encouraging them to look at their situations, and emphasizing the availability and importance of getting help.
  2. (a) *For victims*: offering protection at the workplace by screening phone calls when appropriate and alerting security staff to the possibility of intrusion by the abuser.
     (b) *For offenders*: as is often done with alcoholics, inform the offender that he may lose his job if treatment is not pursued. Time off work may be provided as an incentive.
  3. Establishing a liaison with the local domestic violence shelter, rape crisis centre, and offender treatment program.
  4. Be aware of resources that will acquaint battered or sexually assaulted employees with the options of recourse within the criminal justice system.
  5. Ensure a workplace free of any materials or references that perpetuate rape myths, sexual harassment, or stereotypes of women, or minimize the effects of violence.

While it is not the function of human resources staff to solve employees' problems, increased awareness, the desire to intervene, and referral to appropriate outside resources can help victims and offenders help themselves.[1]

CLINICAL AND SOCIAL SERVICE NECESSITIES

Research how best to improve treatment of offenders and victims. Enlist direct service workers in lobbying for additional state funding. While all citizens need to be involved and are useful in such an effort, they may lack the knowledge, confidence, and credibility to emphasize the need for improved services. Request that social service workers (social workers, psychologists, psychiatrists, para-professionals, teachers, doctors, police officers, and administrators) conduct workshops for their working peers on racism, homophobia, classism, and sexism within the social services. For too long we have complacently ignored, for example, the stories of native people being beaten by police officers, or homosexuals having to 'stay in the closet' to keep their jobs. Encourage employers to take disciplinary action against employees who continue to perpetuate the various dividing lines.

- Critique the work of academics and writers who ignore or minimize male violence against women.
- Confront social service workers who ignore or minimize male violence against women.
- Insist that men be held responsible for their violence. Counteract the all-too-prevalent victim-blaming.
- Establish sexual harassment prevention codes for the workplace.

Avoid Reinventing the Wheel

The above list is just an initial inventory. There are other issues or areas of concern not mentioned in it which should be pursued. To prevent burn-out or the wasting of time and energy, it is essential to first determine in which areas other individuals or community groups are already active. Contact them and determine where work is needed rather than duplicating what is already being done.

Many of the items listed in the previous section can be addressed within the context of existing trade or professional organizations. Teachers' and civil service unions and community groups (e.g., Lions Clubs, parent-teacher associations) can be mobilized to effect change within their systems and to use their political power to elicit a more effective state response to male violence.

Some of the items on the list may be best addressed within a pro-feminist men's group. Participation in such a group, however, is dictated to a great extent by geography. Large urban centres generally have several groups that often have workshops, gatherings, and film screenings that gain them a fairly high profile within the community. Often there are counselling centres known to specialize in men's issues that can connect the individual with an existing group. In smaller centres, the task may not be so easy. Since many groups, for financial or other reasons, meet in the homes of individual men, they are unlikely to be listed in the phone book under a group name. Thus, telephoning a local counselling service or crisis centre may provide the required information. To facilitate this process, Appendix 1 lists contact addresses for the pro-feminist men's groups in the United States and Canada.

Small communities – and even some big cities – may require concerned men to create their own pro-feminist men's group. Such individuals should search for like-minded men among their immediate peers and co-workers, and within their community. Ideas for establishing a pro-feminist men's group are outlined in Appendix 2; these may help individuals avoid some of the pitfalls that earlier groups have encountered.

Be Creative

Working to end male violence need not involve only letter-writing and protesting. For example, while male violence is no laughing matter, humour and satire can be used to convey a point that otherwise might not be readily received by the targeted audience. Social change is required; this begins with education and if humorous skits and plays can accomplish the goal, they need to be part of the strategy. Traditional hegemonic men possess many characteristics that could be parodied quite humorously – and to great effect. Visual artists and musicians also could be active in portraying the type of world we want to leave behind and the one we want to work toward.

The Importance of Self-Care

Battling the status quo to bring about change is not easy work. Individuals need to identify their loci of support: where are they going to be affirmed, nurtured, and encouraged to maintain their work for an end to male violence? Possibilities include friends, family, a men's group, the workplace, school or university, the community, or other individuals within various national organizations. These supports should be established and maintained to ensure their vitality when required. Hegemonic men act as if they were completely self-sufficient and independent of all others; in reality, it is a sign of strength to be able to acknowledge that one needs, and values, support.

To succeed in the eradication of male violence requires establishing far-reaching goals while celebrating small gains. The struggle is a formidable one; feminists who have been involved in it for years can attest to that. While disillusionment and despair that these crimes against women continue virtually unimpeded are normal, individuals must remain angry – and active. Those committed to eliminating crimes against women must recognize that it will be a long haul – and never give up. Men's crimes of violence against women must end.

North American Pro-Feminist Men's Group Contacts

In the United States

The best listing of American men's groups and services has been compiled by RAVEN (Rape and Violence End Now) in *The Ending Men's Violence National Referral Directory* (St Louis, MO: St Louis Organization for Changing Men 1986). The directory can be ordered through RAVEN. Address enquiries to: RAVEN (Rape and Violence End Now), P.O. Box 24159, St Louis, MO, USA 63130, or phone (314) 725-6137.

In Canada

The best listing of Canadian men's groups and services has been compiled by the Glebe New Men's Group. See Kenneth Fisher, for the Glebe New Men's Group, *Men's Groups: Toward a National Listing* (Ottawa: Glebe New Men's Group 1988). Address purchase inquiries to: Ken Fisher, 32 Morris Street, Ottawa, Canada K1S 4A7, or phone (613) 233-7376. For a map of contact people across the country, see Figure A.

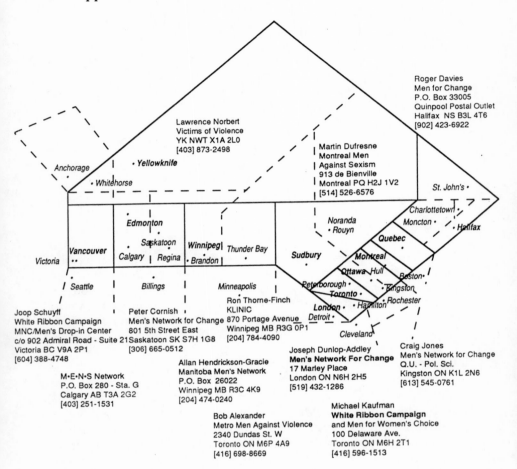

Figure A

Toward a national men's network

Produced by Ken Fisher, Ottawa-Hull Men's Forum against Sexism, 32 Morris Street, Ottawa K1S 4A7 (phone: 613-233-7376; Fax 613-233-3037). Reproduced with permission.

Suggestions on Forming a Pro-Feminist Men's Group

Forming a pro-feminist men's group can help individual men find support, an environment in which to develop effective communication and interpersonal skills, and connection with other men in a political process. By facilitating changes among men, pro-feminist men's groups can play an important role in the effort to end male violence.

Pro-feminist men have created groups which parallel the consciousness-raising model developed during the early 1970s by the women's movement. This has afforded pro-feminist men the advantage of learning about group structures and processes which facilitate individual and collective growth. They also have become acquainted with some of the potential problems.[1]

Bill Dare has compiled a useful resource which identifies how best to use the consciousness-raising model in the context of a pro-feminist men's group.[2] Dare acknowledges that the process of forming or entering a group can be rewarding, as well as very different from what most men have experienced – and frightening. Dare reviews the process numerous North American men have been undertaking, and offers guidelines to alert individuals who are engaged in creating or running a group regarding what to look for and what to avoid.

Forming a Group

There are many valid ways to form a group. One is to ask friends or co-workers who may be sympathetic to the idea and, if necessary, have them enquire further through their circle of friends and associates for other interested individuals. Making such enquiries can be uncomfortable. To minimize this, some men advertise in the classified section of an appropriate newspaper or post a notice on a suitable bulletin board.

If you know of a group, you might contact one of its members about the possibility of joining. If you believe a group exists in your area but do not know how to make contact, connect with a crisis centre, women's group, or a local resource/counselling service for referral information. Finding an existing group can involve a little legwork, telephoning, and sleuthing, but it may well be worth the effort.[3]

Dare notes that a group works best when each person knows at least one other participant. This connects members and accelerates the period required in a group to establish trust. If another member is a friend or acquaintance, a man is more likely to open up to the group, and not simply engage in superficial, and safe, conversation. If everyone knows someone else, this brings a history or camaraderie into the group, which can make the gatherings more rewarding.

Dare emphasizes the importance of limiting the size of the group to between six and ten members. In larger groups, individuals may not have sufficient opportunity to thoroughly express themselves. Dare also advises that it is advantageous to have an all-male group, for two reasons. First, it may be easier for some men to open up and discuss previously unmentioned aspects of their personalities. In a mixed-gender group, there can be a tendency for men to maintain intact hegemonic male roles. Second, a males-only group encourages men to be active listeners and caregivers within the group. If women are present, many men can quickly assume – often without noticing it – a more traditional leadership role and expect the women to take care of the group by becoming its major source of nurturing, support, and acceptance. This relieves the men from responsibility for these functions.

Getting Started

The following factors should be dealt with early in the group's formation and attended to throughout its existence.

Expectations. All group members need to clarify their expectations. What is it that they hope to obtain, and to contribute, to the group? What are their needs? Do individuals feel that enough of their needs will be met by the group? If there appear to be significant incongruities between the needs of one individual and the rest of the group, negotiated compromises may resolve the differences. If not, the individual may choose to connect with another group.

Ground Rules. Confidentiality is a crucial issue. For the emotional security of all members, it is important that individuals agree not to take specifics of what was said or done, or any names and identifying details, beyond the confines of the group. If this agreement is not honoured, the sense of safety within the group will be impaired, and the risks individual men might otherwise be willing to take to share certain aspects of themselves will be fewer. For some men, the group can be a testing-ground on which to try out new skills or ways of interacting. While it is hoped that they will eventually take these changes to the world outside of the group, this is not likely to happen if they never feel secure enough in the first place to try.

There are, however, some limits to confidentiality. When a group member makes reference to something that may jeopardize his life or safety, or that of another individual, the secret cannot be maintained. The appropriate people (i.e., police, hospital staff, or family members) need to be informed.

Location. Location can affect the frequency with which members attend and the degree to which they will feel safe to reveal their innermost thoughts and emotions. Many groups prefer to rotate the location among members' homes in order to avoid any one individual's feeling like a permanent host, while others do less work.

Time and Commitment. Before starting a group it is important to clarify group members' expectations regarding frequency and duration of meetings. Some groups meet every one or two weeks, particularly when the group is just forming. Other groups vary; when something of importance requires extended discussion, they may meet more frequently than at other times of the year. Depending upon the commitments of the group members, they may decide to meet more or less often. It is important to clarify how people feel about other members missing meetings. Is it acceptable, or intolerable? How frequently must one attend? Group members should clarify these issues at the beginning to avoid future difficulties.

Decision-Making. Decision-making processes can significantly affect the strength, vitality, and longevity of the group. Options include: consensus (all members support a decision arrived at by a synthesis of everyone's ideas), majority rule, accepting a facilitator's decision; or unanimous support. Of these, the consensus approach, while possibly more difficult and time-consuming in the short term, may be the best in the long run. If individuals start imposing their will on the group and leaving some men out of the decision-making process, internal animosity and resentment may build up, and ultimately tear apart the group.

At the end of each meeting members might summarize what has been agreed upon. At the next meeting they can review the conclusions and determine if in the intervening time there remains a common vision and purpose with regard to them. This also is an appropriate time for members to identify new issues and determine if other members are interested in integrating these into the group agenda. Periodic reviews and revisions should take place throughout the group's existence to ensure that individuals feel they have an input into the group's direction.

Not a Therapy Group. Throughout the life of the group, members need to be clear on their limits as helpers. Issues may be brought to the group by one member that are really beyond its scope. Specific meetings may focus on one individual if in his current situation he might benefit. If, however, this need persists and the group begins skewing its activities and time to help just one person, the individual may need encouragement to seek additional help outside of the group.

Preliminary Activities

The following are some exercises suggested by Dare that can be used to help members begin working together as a group.

- Each member talks about his life history, focusing on earliest memories, or adolescence, or adulthood, or giving a general review. While possibly requiring a few meetings to accomplish, this allows members to become acquainted with one another's backgrounds, values, and goals.
- Each person discusses how he feels about being in a men's group. This can be an opportunity for individuals to acknowledge that considerable diversity of backgrounds, personalities, and interests is possible, acceptable, and to be valued.
- Each member talks about feelings or events that make him happy, or upset.
- Each member talks about an agreed topic – what it means to him and to the community he represents. Members might also provide some

explanation of how their interpretation and value of a specific issue has changed throughout their lives.

- All group members read a specific article or book and discuss it at the next meeting.
- External resource people are invited to present seminars on specific issues on which group members have decided they need some additional information.
- Members conduct role-plays of various issues to help sort out personal and political positions.
- Each member traces his body on a large piece of paper and talks to the group about his relationship with his body and its various parts.
- Members do non-verbal exercises to develop a wider variety of communication skills.

Group Process Issues

It is very important to be alert to group process and do the work necessary within a group to keep it functioning smoothly. Being aware of the following can help in this task.

Group Facilitation. The group should determine how it will be directed. Many groups operate without any facilitator. Others find it helpful to have someone responsible for coordinating activities (i.e., discussions, readings, or demonstrations). If a person is chosen to facilitate, it is advantageous to rotate this responsibility. Doing so encourages group members to feel equal within the group, which increases the possibility of individual participation. People need to be wary of any members who want to take control of the group. While this can be convenient in the short term – he or they may do most of the work – in the long term, other individuals will start losing input toward, control of, and interest in the group's direction.

Checking In / Checking Out. At the start of each meeting it can be helpful to have each person spend a few minutes relating what has happened in his life since the group last met. This permits members to reconnect with each other, and serves to identify issues or subjects that need to examined and discussed in more detail later in the meeting.

At the conclusion of a meeting, it is important for each person to reflect on the time spent with the others. Did he learn anything new? Did he sort out an issue? Did he relate how he was feeling about something that occurred in the group? Group members' comments do not necessarily require any response, but if further discussion appears necessary, members may agree to address the issue at a future meeting. The 'check-out' should be seen as a time when members can honestly express their sentiments and accept that often there will not be a consensus.

Honesty and Risk-Taking. Being honest about oneself can be an intimidating challenge, particularly when one does not know how the group will respond. Other risk-taking (i.e., nurturing or confronting others) can also be frightening. Yet if individuals are to grow beyond their traditional masculinities, they will need to stretch beyond what feels comfortable.

If, however, men do not sense a strong basis of trust and security within the group, honesty and risk-taking may be limited; individuals may feel inhibited from speaking or acting. If such tension exists, members should talk it over with the group and, ideally, work toward a positive resolution. At the same time, group members should respect the wishes of individual members who choose not to take risks.

Listening. This skill is crucial in maintaining a healthy group. Many men need to become better listeners. All too often, individuals are already formulating, for example, a facetious reply or a piece of advice without sincerely attending to what the speaker is saying. By not listening attentively, they are not respecting the other person. Inattentive listening also prevents one from comprehending and respecting the depth of another's disclosure. This lost information can easily aggravate existing divisions within the group.

Feedback and Constructive Criticism[4]

Being able to give and receive feedback and constructive criticism can be very difficult. Yet these are two of the most important tools for individual and collective growth and group cohesion. The following are some guidelines.

HOW TO GIVE FEEDBACK AND CONSTRUCTIVE CRITICISM

When giving any criticism, individuals need to examine their motives. Why does one want to tell something to another person? Is it to practise more honest communication and to clarify the relationship between the two people? Is it to help – or to hurt them? Individuals need to ask themselves if the criticism is justified. If so, then ...

Step One: Be Concrete. Be very specific. Can you succinctly describe, with clear examples, what it is about an individual that is objectionable? Separate out the vague, sweeping generalizations and negative sentiments from the actual behaviour or event on which you want to comment.

Step Two: Describe How the Situation Makes You Feel. Identifying our feelings is often the first step in recognizing that something is wrong and that we need to speak up. It also helps us focus more clearly on the problem. It prevents individuals from ignoring concerns and suppressing them in resentment and silence until they surface in destructive ways. Clarifying feelings helps get things out in the open and draws the other person's awareness to the fact that an action or statement of his has had certain, possibly unanticipated or undesired, effects.

Step Three: State What You Want the Other Person to Do. If there is a particular person or action by a person that is causing difficulty, point it out to him either privately or within the group setting – but be specific. Addressing it in the group as a general issue is less likely to effectively resolve the problem. The person for whom the comment was intended may not recognize that the statement was directed towards him. He may assume the comment was intended for another group member, and pay no attention.

Step Four: Identify the Purpose. Identify to the individual why a change in his behaviour may be helpful. Indicate how the change may benefit the individual and/or the group.

Summary. Identify to the person that when he does A(observation), you feel B(emotion) and want him to do C(action-want), because of D(purpose).

HOW TO RECEIVE FEEDBACK AND CONSTRUCTIVE CRITICISM

Two skills are important. We need to be able to paraphrase, or put into our own words and repeat back to the person what was just said to us.

This ensures that the message received is the one the person intended. If there is some discrepancy, the two people may need several exchanges back and forth, paraphrasing each other, until there is a clear understanding of the real comment or criticism. It is important that one person not respond until he is clear about what the other is saying. This procedure underlines the importance of effective listening.

Before and after the point has been established, each person needs to empathize with what the other may be feeling. Taking the other person's perspective enables us to recognize the effects of our words and actions, or the absence of either.

Problems to Avoid in Groups

Intellectualizing. This is one of the most significant hurdles for men to overcome. They tend to get locked into a mode where they theorize and hypothesize about ideal situations, talk about how others should change, and do not look at the great deal they could be doing in their our own lives to effect change. Intellectualizing, in and of itself, is not evil; it is a problem when it is divorced from the real life of the individual and his personal support system. It can be a helpful discipline for the men to talk in the first person, using 'I' instead of 'they, them, we, us,' or 'you.' As well, the men should try to fit their theories with their concrete, rather than some abstract, reality. One way to reach this goal is to have men recognize the difference between the 'I think' perspective, located in the head, from the 'I feel,' which is more emotive and felt at the 'gut' or intuitive level. Historically, hegemonic male culture has devalued feelings as non-hegemonic, typical of women or gay men. Men need to reclaim their full range of feelings if they are to be able to change and end their sexist behaviour. Otherwise they are unlikely to empathize with women, and thereby to really understand why the violence must end.

Domination. Certain people inevitably talk more than others. This is not a problem unless the verbosity of some is silencing others. Groups need to consider why some members are always, and others never, silent. While no individual should be forced to speak, groups can make it a little easier for him. Tactics include asking all members to talk briefly about a specific issue before opening up a more general open discussion. Second, individuals can directly ask a silent member for his thoughts on a specific issue. Third, a speakers' list might be kept to ensure that people speak in turn, and that the more boisterous members are kept in check and do not interrupt and dominate. The issue of internal competition might be brought forward for discussion. The point is not to expect all to speak equally, but rather to keep in check those who want to verbally steamroller others, and encourage those who repeatedly allow others to speak for them to assert themselves.

Judging. As much as possible, judging – or coming to definitive conclusions about others – is something that should be discouraged within the group. The problem with judging is that we may make inaccurate conclusions about other group members and preclude development of deeper relationships with them. Judging can also restrict change within others, as we may expect a prescribed or habitual set of actions from an individual, making it difficult for him to broaden his repertoire. While feedback and constructive criticism, when used appropriately, can be beneficial to the group process, judging is not helpful. Recognizing and identifying when one is judging others can help group members halt this destructive practice.

Group in a Stall. Members need to be alert to when the group has reached an impasse. It may seem as if the group is not going anywhere. There may be some interpersonal dynamics between a couple of the members that are impairing the whole group. When an impasse occurs or member apathy toward the group is increasing, it is important to address the problem by talking about it and then resolving it in a constructive manner. If members feel it is necessary, or would be easier, they may choose to have an outside mediator come into the group and help it through this difficult time.

Challenging and Confronting Sexist Behaviour and Attitudes

Men's pro-feminist groups provide a forum for men to challenge themselves and other group members to look at how men contribute to the oppression and exploitation of women. This task often prompts discussions about how to avoid such complicity. Such discussions, while sometimes difficult, are essential to the success of the group in contributing to the end of male violence against women. Confrontations – both within and outside of the group – must be clear but supportive. If the intent is to humiliate an individual, one may well achieve that goal but miss the more important one of helping him change his behaviour. Members need to balance confrontation of members with affirmations of their positive qualities.

The following is an initial list of topics for discussion. The goal is to raise individual and collective awareness of male violence as a crime against women and to help formulate and implement solutions.[5]

1. Men and children
2. Parenting
3. Men and birth control
4. Divorce and child custody
5. Family planning/values and goals
6. Men's sexuality
7. Women's sexuality
8. Homosexuality/bisexuality
9. My sexuality
10. Fantasies, sexual and other
11. Men's gender roles
12. Relationships with others
13. Monogamy/fidelity
14. Alternatives to marriage
15. Men doing housework
16. Sports culture
17. Sexism, male privilege
18. Men and work, jobs
19. Men and aggression; rape
20. Anger
21. Anger toward women/men
22. Violence and alternatives to it
23. Men's power over women
24. Men's mid-life crises
25. Death and dying
26. Body awareness
27. Men and dance/movement
28. Expressing emotions
29. Homophobia/heterophobia
30. Feminism
31. Women's issues
32. Fear of being 'feminine'
33. The men's movement
34. Men and guilt
35. The good things about men
36. Stress and men's health
37. Women's history
38. How to enact new male roles
39. Gains and losses of changing
40. Intimacy
41. Myth, dreams, and symbols
42. Peer group vs. the 'lone wolf'
43. Aloneness vs. loneliness
44. Self-actualization and self-esteem
45. Independence and inter-dependence
46. Men and spiritual values
47. Creativity
48. Competing/supporting
49. Growing up male
50. Our fathers

Conclusions

Attending to the needs and process of the group and its individual members is an important requirement for encouraging the growth and life of the group. While each group will be unique, the aforementioned suggestions can help protect and strengthen the group and encourage the ability to confront and end male violence against women.

Notes

Introduction

1 A fairly concise definition of feminism is as follows: 'a feminist is a person who favors political, economic, and social equality of women and men, and therefore favors the legal and social changes that will be necessary to achieve that equality.' The definition was written by Janet Shibley Hyde in *Half the Human Experience: The Psychology of Women*, 405–6.

Chapter One

1 Within the literature and also segments of the women's movement, there is considerable contention over the use of the terms 'victim' and 'survivor.' Those opposed to the use of the term 'victim' typically argue that we should not, as the term tends to, imply that the individual is helpless and unable to overcome the effects of the crime. Often those using the term 'survivor' reserve it for women who, in therapy, have worked through their experiences of abuse. Yet this excludes women who have not, for whatever reason, done so. After all, the simple fact of being alive makes a person a survivor, even if in order to live with the abuse over a long time one had to deploy coping mechanisms that might be described as self-destructive. Those preferring the word 'victim' do not view it as debilitating, arguing that it acknowledges the perpetration of a criminal act against the person, which should not be forgotten.

  One feminist counsellor, Anne Merrett, has proposed the use of the term 'surviving victim' as a compromise of the two positions. Her term skilfully acknowledges that a woman was indeed victimized but also acknowledges that she has survived – by whatever means. (Anne Merrett, conversation with the author, 6 October 1989.)

Yet, while the term 'surviving victim' is a significant improvement, it too fails – as Merrett acknowledges – to cover all the possible permutations. Not all victims survive. For this reason, and for the purpose of literary variety, 'victim' and 'survivor' will be used as well. It should also be noted that not all victims are female. In the context of this project, however, one can assume that the gender of the victims, unless specifically stated otherwise, will be female.

2 The revival of feminism, which originated in the Western industrial countries, continues to have repercussions throughout the world. Yet women's gains have not been globally uniform. Material wealth, availability of education, religious codes, and other factors affect the national and international spread of feminism. Some women in India, for example, thanks to their wealth, may be significantly less oppressed than a working-class woman in North America. The greater strength of feminism in First World countries is not, as it is sometimes assumed, primarily a function of First World men being more tolerant or sophisticated than their counterparts elsewhere.

3 See, for example, Beneke, *Men on Rape*.

4 For a discussion on the advantages and disadvantages of the continuum, see, for example, Liz Kelly, 'The Continuum of Sexual Violence,' in Hanmer and Maynard, eds., *Women, Violence and Social Control*, 46–60.

5 Ibid.; Kelly, despite commenting on the potential and existing problems with the continuum, adheres to a linear format.

6 Peltoniemi, 'Family Violence'; Kuhl, 'Community Responses to Battered Women'; Oppenlander, 'Coping or Copping Out'; Buzawa, 'Police Officer Response to Domestic Violence Legislation in Michigan'; Pelton, 'Family Protection Team'; Loeb, 'A Program of Community Education for Dealing with Spouse Abuse'; Brown, 'Police Responses to Wife Beating'; Worden and Pollitz, 'Police Arrests In Domestic Disturbances'; Berk, Berk, Newton, and Loseke, 'Cops on Call'; Dutton, 'Interventions into the Problem of Wife Assault'; Homant and Kennedy, 'Police Perceptions of Spouse Abuse'; Bell, 'Domestic Violence'; Buchanan and Perry, 'Attitudes of Police Recruits towards Domestic Disturbances'; Bowen and Sedlak, 'Toward a Domestic Violence Surveillance System'; Waaland and Keeley, 'Police Decision Making in Wife Abuse'; Bandy, Buchanan, and Pinto, 'Police Performance in Resolving Family Disputes'; Dolon, Hendricks, and Meagher, 'Police Practices and Attitudes toward Domestic Violence'; Anderson and Bauer, 'Law Enforcement Officers.'

7 Janet Bagnall, 'Wife Beaters: Few Culprits Undergo Therapy; Even Fewer Give Up Violence,' *Montreal Gazette*, 16 Nov 1987

8 Kaye, 'The Battle against Men Who Batter'
9 Murray Straus, 'Wife-Beating: How Common and Why?' in Straus and Hotaling, eds., *The Social Causes of Husband-Wife Violence*, 23–36
10 William Stacey and Anson Shupe, *The Family Secret: Domestic Violence in America* (Boston: Beacon 1983), 2–3, cited in Guberman and Wolfe, *No Safe Place*, 44
11 Walker, *The Battered Woman*, 19, quoted in Pirog-Good and Stets-Kealey, 'Male Batterers and Battering Prevention Programs'
12 For material on physical violence during dating, see Bogal-Allbritten and Allbritten, 'The Hidden Victims'; Miller and Miller, 'Self-Reported Incidence of Physical Violence in College Students'; O'Keefe, Brockopp, and Chew, 'Teen Dating Violence'; Sigelman, Berry, and Wiles, 'Violence in College Students' Dating Relationships'; Mathews, 'Violence in College Couples'; Roscoe and Benaske, 'Courtship Violence Experienced by Abused Wives'; Makepeace, 'Life Events Stress and Courtship Violence'; and Roscoe and Kelsey, 'Dating Violence among High School Students.'
13 Walker, 'The Cycle Theory of Violence'; chapter 3 in *The Battered Woman*, 55–77
14 Jouriles and O'Leary, 'Interspousal Reliability of Reports of Marital Violence'; and Edleson and Brygger, 'Gender Differences in Reporting of Battering Incidences'
15 Shields and Hanneke, 'Attribution Processes in Violent Relationships'
16 Fitch and Papantonio, 'Men Who Batter'
17 Eberle, 'Alcohol Abusers and Non-Users'
18 Leonard et al., 'Patterns of Alcohol Use and Physically Aggressive Behaviour in Men'
19 Deschner, *The Hitting Habit*, 31; Okun, *Woman Abuse*, 57–8
20 Toufexis, 'Home Is Where the Hurt Is,' *Time*, 130/25 (21 Dec 1987); and MacLeod, *Battered But Not Beaten*, 21
21 Dobash and Dobash, 'The Nature and Antecedents of Violent Events'
22 Mathias, 'Lifting the Shade on Family Violence'
23 The research was conducted by the National Clearinghouse on Family Violence, Health and Welfare Canada, and was noted in Janet Bagnall, 'Wife Beaters: Few Culprits Undergo Therapy; Even Fewer Give Up Violence,' *Montreal Gazette*, 16 Nov 1987.
24 The unnamed study was referred to in Toufexis, 'Home.'
25 The two estimates, respectively, are from Toufexis, 'Home,' and Saunders, 'When Battered Women Use Violence.'
26 Toufexis, 'Home'

27 Neidig, Friedman, and Collins, 'Attitudinal Characteristics of Males Who Have Engaged in Spouse Abuse'
28 Goldstein and Rosenbaum, 'An Evaluation of the Self-Esteem of Maritally Violent Men'
29 Balswick and Peek, 'The Inexpressive Male'; A.L. Ganley and L. Harris, 'Domestic Violence: Issues in Designing and Implementing Programs for Male Batterers' (Paper presented at American Psychological Association meeting, Toronto 1978); Balswick, 'The Inexpressive Male'; B.E. Carlson, 'Battered Women and Their Assailants,' Social Work, 22 (1977), 455–68, cited in Ponzetti, Cate, and Koval, 'Violence between Couples'
30 Summers and Feldman, 'Blaming the Victim versus Blaming the Perpetrator'
31 Kalmuss and Seltzer, 'Continuity of Marital Behavior in Remarriage'
32 Okun, Woman Abuse, 49
33 For more on the contradictions in the literature, see ibid., 42–3.
34 Richard J. Gelles, 'No Place to Go: The Social Dynamics of Marital Violence,' in Roy, ed., Battered Women, 46–62, quoted in Guberman and Wolfe, No Safe Place, 46
35 Walker, The Battered Woman, 1979, cited in Stordeur and Stille, Ending Men's Violence toward Their Partners, 223
36 Hoffman, 'Psychological Abuse of Women by Spouses and Live-In Lovers,' 37
37 Not a Love Story: A Film about Pornography, National Film Board of Canada, Studio D, 1981
38 Walker, The Battered Woman, 42–54
39 The experience of being repeatedly, and often, subtly abused emotionally so that it causes a reduction in self-esteem, sometimes to the point of its extinction, is not limited to women. Children are abused in the same way. A child who is unremittingly told that he or she is bad or stupid may begin to believe it. All of us have scars from our childhood that impair our ability to function as happy, healthy, confident, and assertive adults. For many children, the abuse has been too extensive, the wounds too deep; every year, thousands of adolescents kill themselves before reaching adulthood, while many others are severely emotionally handicapped.
40 Examples were culled from Klinic Community Health Centre, Evolve, part B-5; and Stordeur and Stille, Ending Men's Violence, 237. Stordeur and Stille adopted theirs from Biderman's Chart of Coercion, presented originally in an Amnesty International publication.
41 Purdy and Nickle, 'Practice Principles for Working with Groups of Men Who Batter,' cited in Edleson, 'Working with Men Who Batter'
42 Murray Straus, 'Wife Beating: How Common and Why?' Victimology, 2/3–4 (1978), 443–59, cited in Okun, Woman Abuse, 130

43 Hoffman, 'Psychological Abuse'

43a B.M. Jenkins, 'Hostage Survival: Some Preliminary Observations,' speech given at the Psychological Association Annual Conference, 1981

43b C. Hatcher, 'The Adult and Child Hostage Experience: A Conceptual Framework,' paper presented at the Annual Meeting of the American Psychological Association, 1981

44 Hoffman, 'Psychological Abuse.' For an excellent examination of the effects of the female socialization process on women, and how to counteract them, see Sanford and Donovan, *Women and Self-Esteem.*

45 See, for example, Cameron and Frazer, *The Lust to Kill,* 5.

46 M. Wolfgang, 'Family Violence and Criminal Behaviour,' *Bulletin of American Academy of Psychiatry and the Law,* 4 (1976), 316–27, cited in Barnard et al., 'Till Death Do Us Part'

47 Dobash and Dobash, 'Wives'; Martin, *Battered Wives,* cited in Okun, *Woman Abuse,* 36

48 Kaye, 'The Battle against Men'

49 Cameron and Frazer, *Lust to Kill* (1987)

50 Stanko, *Intimate Intrusions*

51 Canadian Council on Social Development, 'The Global Injustice: Family Violence – and What's Being Done about It – Around the World,' *Vis-à-Vis: A National Newsletter on Family Violence,* 7/1 (Spring 1989), 1–2, 8–9

52 Ibid., 8–9

53 Ibid.

54 'Witness 1': U.S.A. 'Violence against Women,' in Russell and Van de Ven, comp. and eds., *Crimes against Women,* 144–6. The word 'femicide' was coined by Carol Orlock, and the list of femicide cases was compiled by Louise Merrill from various San Francisco newspapers.

55 Stanko, *Intimate Intrusions*

56 'Witness 1'

57 This is a reworked and expanded version of Diana Russell's definition. See her *Sexual Exploitation,* 67.

58 Shotland and Stebbins, 'Bystander Response to Rape'

59 Renner and Wackett, 'Sexual Assault'; John Briere, Shawn Corne, Marsha Runtz, and Neil Malamuth, 'The Rape Arousal Inventory: Predicting Actual and Potential Sexual Aggression in a University Population' (Paper presented at the Annual Meeting of the American Psychological Association, Toronto 1984); White and Mosher, 'Experimental Validation of a Model for Predicting the Reporting of Rape'; Mahoney, Shively, and Traw, 'Sexual Coercion and Assault'

For information on sexual murderers see: Burgess et al., 'Sexual

Homicide'; Ressler et al., 'Sexual Killers and Their Victims'; and Ressler
et al., 'Murderers Who Rape and Mutilate.'

While sexual assaults exist between other combinations of the two
genders, the most prevalent form involves men assaulting women.
Estimates are that approximately 90 per cent of incest and sexual abuse
victims are women (Gillian Chase, 'An Analysis of the New Sexual
Assault Laws,' *Broadside*, 4/4 [n.d.], 53–4). Of the annually arrested
perpetrators of sexual assault in the United States, only 0.8 per cent are
women (FBI *Uniform Crime Report*, cited in Russell, *Sexual Exploitation*, 67).

60 For more information on sexual assault myths, see below, chapter 3.
61 Karen Barrett, 'Date Rape: A Campus Epidemic?' *Ms.*, Sept 1982, 50–1, 130
62 Ellen Sweet, 'Date Rape: The Story of an Epidemic and Those Who Deny
It,' *Ms.*, Oct 1985, 56–9, 84–5
63 Russell, *Sexual Exploitation* (1984)
64 For more information on date rape see, among others, Costin, 'Beliefs
about Rape and Women's Social Roles'; Byers and Wilson, 'Accuracy of
Women's Expectations Regarding Men's Responses to Refusals of Sexual
Advances in Dating Situations'; Shotland and Goodstein, 'Just Because
She Doesn't Want to Doesn't Mean It's Rape'; Muehlenhard, Friedman,
and Thomas, 'Is Date Rape Justifiable?'; Kanin, 'Date Rapists'; Muehlenhard and Linton, 'Date Rape and Sexual Aggression in Dating Situations';
Fischer, 'College Student Attitudes toward Forcible Date Rape.'
65 Shotland, 'A Preliminary Model of Some Causes of Date Rape'
66 Within the literature there exists a debate as to whether marital sexual
assault should be considered a manifestation of domestic violence or one
of the various types of sexual assault. This split reflects the two areas in
which this crime was 'discovered.' For more on this debate, see Hanneke and Shields, 'Marital Rape,' and Hanneke, Shields, and McCall,
'Assessing the Prevalence of Marital Rape.'
67 Cited in Bidwell and White, 'The Family Context of Marital Rape,' 278
68 Prince Edward Island Advisory Council on the Status of Women, *Believe
Her!: A Report on Sexual Assault and Sexual Abuse of Women and Children*, 6.
See chapter 4 for the changes to the Canadian sexual assault laws.
69 The U.S. figures are from Finkelhor and Yllo, *License to Rape*, cited in
Hanneke, Shields, and McCall, 'Prevalence of Marital Rape,' 350.
70 Diana Russell, 'Rape In Marriage: A Case against Legalized Crime'
(Paper presented at the Annual Meeting of the American Society of
Criminology, San Francisco, Nov 1980) and 'The Prevalence and Impact
of Marital Rape in San Francisco' (Paper presented at the Annual Meeting
of the American Sociological Association, New York, Aug 1980), both
cited in Bowker, 'Marital Rape: A Distinct Syndrome?' 347–8

71 Pagelow, 'Double Victimization of Battered Women: Victimized by Spouses and the Legal System' (Paper presented at the Annual Meeting of the American Society of Criminology, San Francisco, Nov 1980), cited in Frieze, 'Investigating the Causes and Consequences of Marital Rape,' 535

72 Julie Doron, 'Conflict and Violence in Intimate Relationships: Focus on Marital Rape' (Paper presented at the Annual Meeting of the American Sociological Association, New York, Aug 1980)

73 Frieze, 'Investigating the Causes and Consequences of Marital Rape,' 532–55

74 Sonkin, Martin, and Walker, *The Male Batterer*, cited in Stordeur and Stille, *Ending Men's Violence*, 22

75 In this study, the phrase 'drug and alcohol use/abuse' is used, despite its redundancy and awkwardness, for two reasons. First, because of the relatively thorough integration and normalization of alcohol consumption in our society, and the resultant desensitization to its social effects, alcohol often is not viewed as a drug, despite the pharmacological evidence to the contrary. Second, use and abuse are relative terms. Combining them can eliminate any semantic obstacles that might impede an accurate assessment of the problem.

76 Bowker, 'Marital Rape,' 347–52

77 Finkelhor and Yllo, *License to Rape*, 6–7, 204, 213–19

78 A.G. Johnson, 'On the Prevalence of Rape in the United States,' *Signs: Journal of Women, Culture, and Society*, 6 (1980), 146, cited in Bidwell and White, 'Family Context of Marital Rape'

79 Regrettably, many of the other works suffer from serious methodological problems. The following are three examples. Sutherland and Scherl, 'Patterns of Response among Victims of Rape,' used a sample of thirteen white middle-class young women who worked in mixed-race core-area community projects and reported their assaults. This hardly constitutes a random sample. Burgess and Holmstrom, 'Rape Trauma Syndrome,' while using a larger sample size ($N = 109$), once again only worked with reported assaults. A similar approach was used by Clark and Lewis, *Rape: The Price of Coercive Sexuality*. In using police records, they were working only with the reported cases. This is not to say that the observations of these authors, and others utilizing similar techniques, are not useful; rather, that they must be kept in perspective and within certain limits. Each of these works provides an excellent summary of the possible symptoms exhibited by victims, but they become unreliable when they start making statements about victims in general. In essence, these studies can only give us small and sometimes conflicting pieces of what is a much larger picture, the totality of which we have yet to delineate.

80 Russell, *Sexual Exploitation*, 34
81 Russell states that San Francisco was chosen because it is larger than nearby Berkeley or Oakland, and thus could increase the perceived credibility of the results. Possibly to avert any homophobic concerns, Russell notes that while San Francisco has a large gay population, this does not affect the prevalence of heterosexual sexual assault or – contrary to another popular myth – the sexual abuse of children. San Francisco's sexual assault rate per 100,000 (1978) was comparable to those of other American cities (San Francisco, 86; Los Angeles, 83; Boston, 84; Cleveland, 88; and Dallas, 91). The interviews, which were conducted in-residence, were private, confidential, and, on average, one hour and twenty minutes long. See Russell, *Sexual Exploitation*, 34–6.
82 See, for example, Burgess and Holmstrom, 'The Rape Victim in the Emergency Ward.' While extremely informative and useful with the population sampled, it is not generalizable outside of the hospital setting.
83 Russell uses the phrase 'acquaintance assault' in two different contexts, causing some confusion. In the narrow sense, acquaintance rape refers to sexual assaults committed by an individual known to the victim, but not a date, friend, relative, etc. Acquaintance rape in the larger sense, applying the definition more commonly used, implies that the woman was assaulted by someone she knows. This could include friends, dates, and family members. Russell, *Sexual Exploitation*, 283–5.
84 Ibid.
85 Ibid. The variety in the totals is caused by several women having been victimized more than once.
86 Kamini Maraj Grahame, 'Sexual Harassment,' in Guberman and Wolfe, *No Safe Place*, 112. Grahame cites the following as central to the creation of her definition: MacKinnon, *Sexual Harassment of Working Women*; and *Report of the Presidential Advisory Committee on Sexual Harassment* (Toronto: York University 1982).
87 Marlene Kadar, 'Sexual Harassment as a Form of Social Control,' in Fitzgerald, Guberman, and Wolfe, eds., *Still Ain't Satisfied*, 170
88 M.A. Largen, *Report on Sexual Harassment in Federal Employment* (Boston: New Responses 1979); Working Women United Institute, *Sexual Harassment on the Job: Results of a Preliminary Survey* (New York 1975); and B.C. Errington and A. Davidson, *Sexual Harassment in the Workplace* (Vancouver: British Columbia Federation of Labour and the Vancouver Women's Research Centre 1980), cited in Cammaert, 'How Widespread Is Sexual Harassment on Campus?' 389
89 See Stanko, *Intimate Intrusions*, 59–69. Russell, in *Sexual Exploitation*, 281,

also speaks highly of the statistical validity of the Merit Systems study.
90 See Stanko, *Intimate Intrusions*, 59–69. Stanko gathered her information from Susan E. Martin, 'Sexual Harassment in the Workplace: From Occupational Hazard to Sex Discrimination' (Paper delivered at the Law and Society annual meeting, Amherst, MA, 1981); Collins and Blodgett, 'Sexual Harassment'; and Cooper and Davidson, *High Pressure*, 100. For the Liverpool survey results, Stanko cites Ann Sedley and Melissa Benn, *Sexual Harassment at Work* (London: NCCL Rights of Women Unit 1982), 11; for the results of the Alfred Marks Survey, she cites Nathalie Hadjifotiou, *Women and Harassment at Work* (London: Pluto Press 1983), 10.
91 Walker, Erikson, and Woolsey, 'Sexual Harassment'
92 See, for example, Sheila Kitzinger, 'Sex and Power: Sexual Harassment,' in *Women's Experience of Sex*, 264–9; Jensen and Gutek, 'Attributions and Assignment of Responsibility in Sexual Harassment'; and Powell, 'Effects of Sex Role Identity and Sex on Definitions of Sexual Harassment.'
93 See, among others, MacKinnon, *Sexual Harassment*; Kitzinger, *Women's Experience of Sex*, 265–70; Rhodes and McNeill, eds., *Women against Violence against Women*.
94 While not commonly practised in the West, female castration is a common experience for many women in the Third World. It includes clitoridectomy (the removal of the clitoris), excision (the removal of the clitoris and the adjacent parts of the labia minora or all the exterior genitalia except the labia majora), and infibulation (excision followed by the sewing of the genitals to annihilate the entrance to the vagina, except for a tiny opening to allow for the passage of blood and urine). These surgical procedures generally are done without anaesthetic, causing untold pain, infection, and death to many women. One report indicates that in Guinea, 85 per cent of women undergo excision. Clitoridectomy reportedly is practised in Saudi Arabia, Yemen, Sudan, Egypt, Ethiopia, Syria, Iraq, the Ivory Coast, and among many African peoples. For more on female castration, see Russell and Van de Ven, *Crimes against Women*, 150–3.
95 Many Third World women are manipulated to undergo sterilization through state-sponsored advertising campaigns which identify over-population as the sole cause of Third World poverty. By ignoring other factors, such as excessive state militarization, corrupt ruling elites, and an international monetary system that encourages Third World under-development, such campaigns have sent thousands of women to state-sponsored clinics. In Colombia, 40,000 women were sterilized between 1955 and 1965; in Brazil, 1,000,000 between 1961 and 1971. Puerto Rico has the highest sterilization rate in the world: one 1968 study revealed

that 35 per cent of Puerto Rican women of childbearing age had been
sterilized. The comparable figures for India and Pakistan (both have
public sterilization programs) were 5 and 3 per cent, respectively. The
Puerto Rican rate was the result of 19 clinics, working at maximum
capacity to sterilize 1,000 women per month. Ninety per cent of the cost
of the sterilization program was financed through the U.S. Department of
Health, Education, and Welfare. See Russell and Van de Ven, *Crimes
against Women*, 27–9, and Morgan, ed., *Sisterhood Is Global*.

96 Surgical mutilation includes all operations provided for women so that
they might fulfil an existing stereotype of traditional feminine beauty. In
the nineteenth century, the common practice was for women to have ribs
removed, so that they could cinch their corsets more tightly at the waist,
thus producing the ideal hourglass figure; in the twentieth century, more
sophisticated techniques are applied: women undergo liposuction, which
involves first dissolving and then suctioning out supposedly unsightly
cellulite from almost any unwanted location. The long-term safety of this
procedure is not known. Other techniques to achieve beauty include
implantation of silicone into the breasts, or, less commonly, breast reduction. There also exist a multitude of fad diets by which many Western
women are endangering their lives in order to lose a few pounds –
despite mounting evidence that such diets often result in an increase in
weight over the long term, which creates for many women a vicious cycle
of dieting, losing, and gaining. For information on how the medical
establishment regularly discriminates against women see Mendelsohn,
Male Practice.

97 We also need to remind ourselves of the extent to which women who
choose to act on their attraction to other women are abused by men who
believe that all women must automatically desire men. See, for example,
Blackridge and Gilhooly, *Still Sane*.

98 See, for example, Silbert, 'Prostitution and Sexual Assault.'

99 For more on the history of the availability of contraception and abortion
in Canada, as well as the Canadian abortion debate, see: Morgentaler,
Abortion and Contraception; McDonnell, *Not an Easy Choice*; Collins, *The Big
Evasion*; and McLaren and McLaren, *The Bedroom and the State*.

In the late 1980s, the debate over a woman's right to control her body's
reproductive capacity was highlighted by several court challenges to a
woman's right to proceed with an abortion when her male partner was
opposed. See, for example, Downey, 'Dodd Wins Bid to Have Abortion:
Notice of Hearing Insufficient, Court Sets Aside Injunction Order.'

100 In the Peoples' Republic of China, state family planning policy, in the

interests of improving the standard of living, dictates an official standard of one child per family. Pressure to conform to this norm is considerable; should a woman choose to proceed with a second pregnancy, she forfeits all one-child benefits, such as preferential access to food, housing, education, and employment, and risks economic penalties. In 1979 alone, approximately five million abortions were performed. See Greer, *Sex and Destiny*, 364–72. For the number of abortions, Greer cites *Population Bulletin* (Population Information Centre, Sri Lanka).

101 For an excellent introduction to many of the abuses women endure in our current physical and mental health institutions see Chesler, *Women and Madness*.

Chapter Two

1 Cohen and Roth, 'The Psychological Aftermath of Rape'; Lenox and Gannon, 'Psychological Consequences of Rape and Variables Influencing Recovery'; Popiel and Susskind, 'The Impact of Rape'; Warshaw, *I Never Called It Rape*, 65–82; and Stewart et al., 'The Aftermath of Rape'

2 MacKinnon, *Sexual Harassment of Working Women*, 47–55

3 MacLeod, *Battered But Not Beaten*, 11–18

4 Finkelhor and Yllo, *License to Rape*, 117–38; Dowdeswell, *Women on Rape*, 75–98; Yassen and Glass, 'Sexual Assault Survivor Groups'; Lenox and Gannon, 'Psychological Consequences of Rape and Variables Influencing Recovery'; Sharma and Cheatham, 'A Women's Center Support Group for Sexual Assault Victims'; and Colao and Hunt, 'Therapists Coping with Sexual Assault'

5 Turner and Shapiro, 'Battered Women'

6 Frank and Stewart, 'Treating Depression in Victims of Rape'; Becker et al., 'Depressive Symptoms Associated with Sexual Assault'; Santiago et al., 'Long-Term Psychological Effects of Rape in 35 Rape Victims'; Lenox and Gannon, 'Psychological Consequences of Rape'; Judith Becker, Linda Skinner, and Gene Abel, 'Sequelae of Sexual Assault: The Survivor's Perspective,' in Greer and Stuart, eds., *The Sexual Aggressor*, 240–66; and Dowdeswell, *Women on Rape*, 75–98

7 MacLeod, *Battered But Not Beaten*, 11–18

8 Walker, 'Psychosocial Theory of Learned Helplessness,' in *The Battered Woman*

9 Martin, *Battered Wives*, 141–7

10 Most of the information on the physical and emotional effects of abuse still is classified by the different varieties of male violence. For informa-

tion on the effects of sexual violence, see: Burgess and Holmstrom, 'Rape Trauma Syndrome'; Medea and Thompson, *Against Rape*, 101–11; Russell, *The Politics of Rape*; Sharon McCombie and Judith Arons, 'Counselling Rape Victims,' in McCombie, ed., *The Rape Crisis Intervention Handbook*, 145–72; Ellen Bassuk, 'A Crisis Theory Perspective on Rape' in McCombie, ibid., 121–30; Flora Colao and Miriam Hunt, 'Therapists Coping with Sexual Assault,' in Robbins and Siegel, eds., *Women Changing Therapy*, 205–21; Katz, *No Fairy Godmothers, No Magic Wands*, 21–33, 63–75; Hutchinson and McDaniel, 'The Social Reconstruction of Sexual Assault by Women Victims'; and Renner and Wackett, 'Sexual Assault.' Standard resources on the effects of physical violence are: Walker, *The Battered Woman* (1979); Armstrong, *The Home Front*; and Martin, *Battered Wives* (1981).

An excellent Canadian resource that successfully integrates the various types of abuse against women of all ages is Guberman and Wolfe, eds., *No Safe Place*.

11 Russell, *Rape in Marriage*, 193
12 Becker et al., 'Sexual Problems of Sexual Assault Survivors'
13 Finkelhor and Yllo, *License to Rape*, 117–38
14 Ibid.
15 Dowdeswell, *Women on Rape*, 75–98; Colao and Hunt, 'Therapists Coping'; and Becker, Skinner, and Abel, 'Sequelae of Sexual Assault,' in Greer and Stuart, eds., *The Sexual Aggressor*, 240–66
16 MacKinnon, *Sexual Harassment*, 47–55
17 Warshaw, *Ms. Report on Rape*, 65–82
18 Miller, Williams, and Bernstein, 'The Effects of Rape on Marital and Sexual Adjustment'
19 Jehu, in association with Gazan and Klassen, *Beyond Sexual Abuse*, 108
20 Colao and Hunt, 'Therapists Coping'; Girelli et al., 'Subjective Distress and Violence during Rape'; and Santiago et al., 'Long-Term Psychological Effects of Rape in 35 Rape Victims'
21 Santiago et al., 'Long-Term Psychological Effects'
22 MacKinnon, *Sexual Harassment*, 47–55
23 Becker, Skinner, and Abel, 'Sequelae of Sexual Assault,' 240–66; Warshaw, *Ms. Report on Rape*, 65–82
24 Scheppele and Bart, 'Through Women's Eyes'
25 Frank and Stewart, 'Treating Depression,' 95–8; Scheppele and Bart, 'Defining Danger,' 63–81; Resick, Veronen, and Calhoun, 'Assessment of Fear Reactions in Sexual Assault Victims'; and Girelli et al., 'Subjective Distress during Rape'

26 MacLeod, *Battered But Not Beaten*, 11–18

27 Wetzel and Ross, 'Psychological and Social Ramifications of Battering'; Finn, 'The Stresses and Coping Behaviour of Battered Women'; and Guberman and Wolfe, *No Safe Place*, 46

28 For more on the fear resulting from battering, see, for example, Wetzel and Ross, 'Psychological and Social Ramifications of Battering.'

29 For example, see Lynn Pacela, *Self-Defense* (Santa Monica: Goodyear 1980).

30 Walker, *The Battered Woman*, 42–54; Sutherland and Scherl, 'Patterns of Response among Victims of Rape'

31 Dowdeswell, *Women on Rape* (1986), 75–98; Finkelhor and Yllo, *License to Rape*, 117–38

32 Lorraine Parrington, Counsellor, Sexual Assault Crisis Program, Klinic Community Health Centre, Winnipeg, interview with the author, 12 April 1990. For a clear explanation of the hurdles impeding the prosecution of sexual offenders in Canada, see Victoria Women's Sexual Assault Centre, *Working with Survivors of Sexual Assault.*

33 While focused on helping incest survivors, one recent work skilfully encourages women not to denigrate themselves for having adopted specific coping mechanisms. See Bass and Davis, 'Coping: Honouring What You Did to Survive,' in *The Courage to Heal*, 40–54.

34 MacKinnon, *Sexual Harassment*, 47–55

35 Finkelhor and Yllo, *License to Rape*, 117–38

36 Colao and Hunt, 'Therapists Coping,' and Yassen and Glass, 'Sexual Assault Survivor Groups'

37 Warshaw, *Ms. Report on Rape*, 65–82

38 MacLeod, *Battered But Not Beaten*, 11–18

39 Victor Frankl, *Man's Search for Meaning: An Introduction to Logotherapy* (New York: Touchstone 1962); Romero, 'A Comparison between Strategies Used on Prisoners of War and Battered Wives'

40 Dinkmeyer and McKay, *Parent's Handbook*

41 Ibid.

42 Modlin, 'Traumatic Neurosis and Other Injuries'

43 Guberman and Wolfe, eds., *No Safe Place*, 41–60; MacLeod, *Battered But Not Beaten*, 11–18

44 Hanmer and Maynard, eds., *Women, Violence and Social Control*

45 For example, Education Wife Assault, a non-profit community organization in Toronto, reports that a 1984 study on suicide attempts concluded that battered women are far more likely to attempt suicide than other women (cited in Kaye, 'The Battle against Men Who Batter'). Others have had similar findings; see Walker, *The Battered Woman*, 174.

46 Russell, *Rape in Marriage*, 193–5
47 Finkelhor and Yllo, *License to Rape*, 117–38
48 Kilpatrick et al., 'Mental Health Correlates of Criminal Victimization'
49 Colao and Hunt, 'Therapists Coping'; Dowdeswell, *Women on Rape*, 75–98
50 Guberman and Wolfe, *No Safe Place*, 46
51 See, for example, *The Burning Bed* (American Broadcasting Corporation).
52 For more on the issue of women killing their male attackers, see Browne, *When Battered Women Kill*, and Gillespie, *Justifiable Homicide*.
53 Russell, *Sexual Exploitation*
54 Colao and Hunt, 'Therapists Coping'; and Yassen and Glass, 'Sexual Assault Survivor Groups'
55 Warshaw, *Ms. Report on Rape*, 65–82
56 MacLeod, *Battered But Not Beaten*, 11–18; and Wetzel and Ross, 'Ramifications of Battering'
57 Chandler and Torney, 'The Decisions and the Processing of Rape Victims through the Criminal Justice System'
58 Renner, Wackett, and Ganderton, 'The "Social" Nature of Sexual Assault'; Martin et al., 'Controversies Surrounding the Rape Kit Exam in the 1980s'
59 Colao and Hunt, 'Therapists Coping'
60 Blume, 'Alcohol Problems in Women'
61 Turner and Colao, 'Alcoholism and Sexual Assault'
62 Burgess and Holmstrom, 'Rape Trauma Syndrome'; DiVasto, 'Measuring the Aftermath of Rape'
63 Wooley and Vigilanti, 'Psychological Separation and the Sexual Abuse Victim'
64 *Glamour* survey, February 1984, cited in Marlene Boskind-White, 'Bulimarexia: A Sociocultural Perspective,' in Emmett, ed., *Theory and Treatment of Anorexia Nervosa and Bulimia*, 113–26
65 For more on eating disorders, see also Orbach, *Fat Is a Feminist Issue*, and Chernin, *The Obsession*.
66 Burgess and Holmstrom, 'Rape Trauma Syndrome'; and Hoffman, 'Psychological Abuse of Women by Spouses and Live-in Lovers'
67 Burgess and Holmstom, 'Rape Trauma Syndrome'; Becker et al., 'The Effects of Sexual Assault on Rape and Attempted Rape'
68 MacLeod, *Battered But Not Beaten*, 11–18
69 Finkelhor and Yllo, *License to Rape*, 117–38; Warshaw, *Ms. Report on Rape*, 65–82
70 Burgess and Holmstrom, 'The Rape Victim in the Emergency Ward'
71 Ron Schwartz, counsellor, telephone interview with the author, 7 May 1990

72 Boston Globe, 'Rape Victims Suffer Diseases,' *Winnipeg Free Press*, 21 Mar 1980, 31. The article summarized a report published in *New England Journal of Medicine*, during the week of 19–23 March 1990.

73 Dowdeswell, *Women on Rape*, 75–98

74 McGregor, 'Risk of STD in Female Victims of Sexual Assault'; Warshaw, *Ms. Report on Rape*, 65–82

75 Ruch, Chandler, and Harter, 'Life Change and Rape Impact'

76 DiVasto, 'Measuring Rape'; Walker, *The Battered Woman*, 61

77 Colao and Hunt, 'Therapists Coping'; Dowdeswell, *Women on Rape*, 75–98; Warshaw, *Ms. Report on Rape*, 65–82

78 For an examination of the relations between crisis theory and sexual assault trauma (SAT) or rape trauma syndrome (RTS) see Ruch and Hennessy, 'Sexual Assault: Victim and Attack Dimensions'; Kilpatrick, 'Rape Victims'; Lenox and Gannon, 'Psychological Consequences of Rape'; Colao and Hunt, 'Therapists Coping'; and DiVasto, 'Measuring Rape.'

   For information on the appropriateness of SAT/RTS as diagnostic tools and the lengthy struggle for their admissibility in court, see Raum, 'Rape Trauma Syndrome as Circumstantial Evidence of Rape'; Burgess and Holmstrom, 'Rape Trauma Syndrome,' 981–6; Bristow, 'State v. Marks'; Lauderdale, 'The Admissibility of Expert Testimony on Rape Trauma Syndrome'; and Frazier and Borgida, 'Rape Trauma Syndrome Evidence in Court.'

   The argument against the use of RTS in court (presumably because it is indistinguishable from post-traumatic shock) is presented by Wright, 'Of Slithy Toves, Rape-Trauma Syndrome, Burn-out, etc.'

   For information on the cycle theory of violence and learned helplessness see Walker, *The Battered Woman*, 42–70

79 For information on the long-term effects of marital rape, see Finkelhor and Yllo, *License To Rape*, 117–38.

   For information on the long-term effects of sexual assault, see, among others, Santiago et al., 'Long-Term Psychological Effects of Rape.'

   An important article about the effects of sexual assault often lasting longer than the duration of the resources provided by most rape crisis centres is Gilmartin-Zena's 'Rape Impact.'

80 While it may be difficult to accurately estimate the cost, one example is illustrative of the magnitude of the problem. A Canadian report on wife-battering notes that '70% of the women who stayed in shelters in 1985 came with children: 26% with one child, 27% with two, and 17% with three or more children. This means that, based on this study's previous estimates of the numbers of women who probably stayed in all 230 shelters across

the country in 1985, at least 55,000 children stayed in crisis shelters which accepted battered women. As well, at least another 55,000 were the children of mothers who requested shelter but could not be accommodated. This means that, in 1985, at least 110,000 children were living in homes where the mother sought emergency shelter. Of these, the mothers of at least 86,000 children requested shelter explicitly because they were battered. Most of these children were young. Fifty-two per cent were under five years of age, 32% between five and ten, and 16% between 11 and 18.' See MacLeod, *Battered But Not Beaten*, 32. These numbers exclude the children whose mothers do not even attempt to use the existing shelters.

Chapter Three

1 Shibley Hyde, *Half the Human Experience*, 56
2 Edward Wilson, *Sociobiology: The New Synthesis* (Cambridge, MA: Harvard University Press 1975), and David Barash, *Sociobiology and Behavior* (New York: Elsevier 1982), cited in Shibley Hyde, *Half the Human Experience*, 56
3 Shibley Hyde, *Half the Human Experience*, 56
4 Williams, *Psychology of Women*, 131
5 Ibid.
6 Shibley Hyde, *Half the Human Experience*, 57
7 Williams, *Psychology of Women*, 131
8 Wilson, *Sociobiology*, 125, cited in Williams, *Psychology of Women*, 131
9 Barash, *Sociobiology and Behavior*, cited in Williams, *Psychology of Women*, 132
10 Ruth Bleier, *Science and Gender* (New York: Pergamon 1984), 23, quoted in Williams, *Psychology of Women*, 132.
11 Williams, *Psychology of Women*, 132
12 Ibid.
13 Ibid.
14 Bleier, *Science and Gender*, 46, cited in Williams, *Psychology of Women*, 133. (Italics in Williams.)
15 Shibley Hyde, *Half the Human Experience*, 62
16 Stearns, *Anger: Psychology, Physiology, Pathology*; Thiessen, *The Evolution and Chemistry of Aggression*; Averill, *Anger and Aggression*, 44; Frank Elliot, 'The Neurology of Explosive Rage: The Dyscontrol Syndrome,' in Roy, ed., *Battered Women*, 98–109; Frank Elliot, 'Biological Contributions to Family Violence,' in Barnhill, ed., *Clinical Approaches to Family Violence*, 36–58; and John R. Lion, 'Clinical Aspects of Wife-Battering,' in Roy, ed., *Battered Women*, 126–36

17 S.P. Grossman, *A Textbook of Physiological Psychology* (New York: Wiley 1967), cited in Robert Franken, *Human Motivation* (Pacific Grove, CA: Brooks/Cole 1988), 316

18 Franken, *Human Motivation*, 316

19 H. Persky, K.D. Smith, and G.K. Basu, 'Relation of Psychologic Measures of Aggression and Hostility to Testosterone Production in Man,' *Psychosomatic Medicine*, 33 (1971), 265–77, cited in Shibley Hyde, *Half the Human Experience*, 240

20 L.E. Kreuz and R.M. Rose, 'Assessment of Aggressive Behaviour and Plasma Testosterone in a Young Criminal Population,' *Psychosomatic Medicine*, 34 (1972), 321–32, cited in Franken, *Human Motivation*, 322. Kreuz and Rose's results have been supported elsewhere. See: J. Ehren-kranz, E. Bliss, and M.H. Sheard, 'Plasma Testosterone: Correlation with Aggressive Behaviour,' *Medicine*, 36 (1974), 469–75; and R.T. Rada, D.R. Laws, and R. Kellner, 'Plasma Testosterone Levels in the Rapist,' *Psychosomatic Medicine*, 38 (1976), 257–68, cited in Franken, *Human Motivation*, 322.

21 For a review of the evidence, Shibley Hyde (p. 240) refers to Robert Rubin, J.M. Reinisch, and R.F. Haskett, 'Postnatal Gonadal Steroid Effects on Human Behaviour,' *Science*, 211 (1981), 1318–24.

22 Shibley Hyde, *Half the Human Experience*, 240

23 Franken, *Human Motivation*, 320

24 Russell, *Sexual Exploitation*, 285

25 Stordeur and Stille, *Ending Men's Violence against Their Partners*, 17–54; and Ron Schwartz, counsellor for Evolve, a men's program at the Klinic Community Health Centre, Winnipeg (telephone interview with the author, 7 May 1990).

26 Ron Schwartz, telephone interview with the author, 7 May 1990

27 Browning, *Stopping the Violence*, 1-2

28 Deschner, *The Hitting Habit*; M. Faulk, 'Men Who Assault Their Wives,' *Medicine, Science, and the Law*, 14/3 (1974), 180–3, and 'Men Who Assault Their Wives,' in Roy, *Battered Women*, 119–26; Lion, 'Clinical Aspects of Wife-Battering'; L. Schultz, 'The Wife Assaulter,' *Corrective Psychiatry and Journal of Social Therapy*, 6 (1960), 103–11; N. Shainess, 'Psychological Aspects of Wifebattering,' in Roy, *Battered Women*, 126–36; J. Snell, R. Rosenwald, and A. Robey, 'The Wifebeater's Wife: A Study of Family Interaction,' *Archives of General Psychiatry*, 11 (1964), 107–12; and A. Symonds, 'Violence against Women: The Myth of Masochism,' *American Journal of Psychotherapy*, 33/2 (1979). Cited in Stordeur and Stille, *Ending Men's Violence*, 23–4.

29 Browning, *Stopping the Violence*, 1–2
30 Ibid.
31 Knopp, *Retraining Adult Sex Offenders*, 27
32 Ibid.
33 Joanne Greer, 'The Sex Offender: Theories and Therapies, Programs and Policies,' introduction to Greer and Stuart, eds., *The Sexual Aggressor*, viii; and Watts and Courtois, 'Trends in the Treatment of Men Who Commit Violence against Women'
34 Greer, 'The Sex Offender'
35 Dutton, 'Wife Assaulters' Explanations for Assault,' paraphrased in Stordeur and Stille, *Ending Men's Violence*, 23–4. For an example of the problems associated with the use by traditional clinical researchers of small sample populations to verify their theories, see Faulk, 'Men Who Assault Their Wives,' in Roy, *Battered Women*.
36 R. Maiuro, T. Cahn, P. Vitaliano, B. Wagner, and J. Zegree, 'Anger, Hostility, and Depression in Domestically Violent versus Generally Assaultive Men and Nonviolent Control Subjects,' *Journal of Consulting and Clinical Psychology*, 56/1 (1988), 17–23, cited in Stordeur and Stille, *Ending Men's Violence*, 23–4
37 Bograd, 'Family Systems Approach to Wife Battering,' cited in Stordeur and Stille, *Ending Men's Violence*, 23–4
38 Zacker and Bard, 'Further Reading on Assaultiveness and Alcohol Use in Interpersonal Disputes'; D. Coleman and M. Straus, 'Alcohol Abuse and Family Violence' (Paper presented at the Annual Meeting of the American Sociological Association, Boston, Aug 1979); and Eberle, 'Alcohol Abusers and Non-Users,' cited in Browning, *Stopping the Violence*, 1–2
39 See, for example, Faulk, 'Men Who Assault Their Wives,' Lion, 'Clinical Aspects of Wife-Battering,' and Shainess, 'Psychological Aspects of Wife-Battering,' all in Roy, *Battered Women*.
40 Nicholas Groth, 'Juvenile and Adult Sex Offenders: Creating a Community Response' (Training lecture sponsored by the Tompkins County Sexual Abuse Task Force, Ithaca, New York, 16–17 June 1983), quoted in Knopp, *Retraining Adult Sex Offenders*, 27
41 Knopp, *Retraining Adult Sex Offenders*, 26
42 For more on the debates pertaining to the existence, dominance, and passing of various matrilineal societies, see Lerner, *The Creation of Patriarchy*; and Paula Webster, 'Matriarchy: A Vision of Power,' in Rayna Reiter, *Toward an Anthropology of Women* (New York: Monthly Review Press 1975), 141–56.
43 Brownmiller, *Against Our Will*

44 Ned Lyttelton, 'Men's Liberation, Men against Sexism and Major Dividing Lines,' in Nemiroff, ed., *Women and Men,* 472–7

The additional dividing lines become apparent in different contexts; for example, women of all classes and racial groups may unite in a protest against sexual assault by men, but two days later may be found, divided into two groups on opposite sides of a bargaining table, fighting over an attempt to unionize a textile factory. While the majority of factory owners may be male, some women do own businesses and oppress other women. In this specific example, the major issue is one of class, not gender.

45 Stordeur and Stille, *Ending Men's Violence,* 23–36

46 Joseph Pleck, a psychologist who has done extensive sex-role research, dates its 'initial formulation' or 'explicit development' to the 1930s, but acknowledges that 'the cultural concerns about masculinity' had developed during the previous century. For an excellent brief history of the male sex-role identity theory, see Joseph Pleck, 'The Theory of Male Sex-Role Identity: Its Rise and Fall, 1936 to the Present,' in Brod, ed., *The Making of Masculinities,* 21–38.

47 Ibid. The popular linking of effeminacy and homosexuality reflects our society's misogyny. Both women and gay men are viewed as lacking masculinity, and thus of less value. As long as women are devalued in our society, many straight men will consider labelling a man as effeminate to be a serious insult. If femininity were highly valued in our society, the insult would become a compliment.

48 Ibid.

49 For more on the feared feminization of men throughout several periods, see Michael Kimmel, 'The Contemporary "Crisis" of Masculinity in Historical Perspective,' in Brod, *The Making of Masculinities,* 121–53.

50 Bruce Kidd, 'Sport and Masculinity,' in Kaufman, ed., *Beyond Patriarchy,* 250–65

51 Lord Baden-Powell, a commanding hero of the Boer War, was the founder of the Boy Scouts. His *Aid to Scouting* handbook, originally written to help train British soldiers for the Boer War, was adapted for young boys in 1907–8. The difficulty the British had had in recruiting a sufficient number of able-bodied males and in obtaining a decisive victory in this war no doubt contributed to the enthusiastic official support for Baden-Powell's program.

For more on the role of scouting in counteracting the perceived feminization of American men, see Hantover, 'The Boy Scouts and the Validation of Masculinity.'

52 Kimmel, '"Crisis" of Masculinity in Historical Perspective.' For more on

masculinity during the nineteenth century, see Dubbert, *A Man's Place*,
13–190.

53 Anne Fausto-Sterling, in *Myths of Gender*, 129, notes that the difficulty
most countries have had in recruiting men for the military contradicts
much of the mythology that men are innately violent, and thus would
relish the opportunity to fight in a war. While status is accorded to those
who excel in the military, it seems many men would rather find it
elsewhere. It also should be noted that the class positions of many of the
glorifiers of war typically prevent them from serving in the military, or at
least keep them at a safe distance from the front lines.

54 Pleck, 'Male Sex-Role Identity Theory,' 21–38

55 For more information on the post-1945 American political climate and the
accompanying international context, see: Robert and Michael Meerapol,
We Are Your Sons: The Legacy of Ethel and Julius Rosenberg (Boston:
Houghton Mifflin 1975); Walter LaFeber, *America, Russia, and the Cold
War: 1945–1975* (New York: Wiley 1976); John Chabot Smith, *Alger Hiss:
The True Story* (New York: Holt, Rinehart, and Winston 1976); and T.E.
Vadney, *The World since 1945*.

56 Lopata and Thorne, 'On the Term "Sex Roles",' 720

57 For more on what hegemony entails, see Tom Carrigan, Bob Connell, and
John Lee, 'Toward a New Sociology of Masculinity,' in Brod, *The Making
of Masculinities*, 94.

58 The MSRI focus has been reinforced in the contemporary period through
the numerous experiments based on extremely unrepresentative sample
populations – university students in introductory psychology classes.

59 Pleck, 'Male Sex-Role Identity Theory'

60 Connell, 'The Concept of "Role" and What to Do with It,' 15

61 Pleck, 'Male Sex-Role Identity Theory'; and Connell, 'Concept of Role'

62 Tim Carrigan, Bob Connell, and John Lee, 'Toward a New Sociology of
Masculinity,' in Brod, ed., *The Making of Masculinities*, 63–100

63 Ibid.

64 For a review of the literature on the intergenerational transmission of
violence, see Okun, *Woman Abuse*, 59–63.
    For an excellent examination of the effects on children witnessing male
violence against women in their family of origin, see Jaffe, Wolfe, and
Wilson, *Children of Battered Women*. Jaffe et al. also outline how society
could better respond to the needs of these children.

65 Richard Gelles, *Family Violence* (London: Sage 1979), quoted in Segal, *Slow
Motion*, 255

66 Roy, 'A Current Survey of 150 Cases,' in *Battered Women*, 24–44

67 Straus, Gelles, and Steinmetz, *Behind Closed Doors*, cited in Okun, *Woman Abuse*, 61

68 Stordeur and Stille, *Ending Men's Violence*, 25, cite the following family systems examples: S. Hanks and P. Rosenbaum, 'Battered Women: A Study of Women Who Live with Violent Alcohol-Abusing Men,' *American Journal of Orthopsychiatry*, 47 (1977), 291–306; M. Elbow, 'Theoretical Considerations of Violent Marriages,' *Social Casework*, 58 (1977), 515–26; A. Symonds, 'Violence against Women: The Myth of Masochism,' *American Journal of Psychotherapy*, 33/2 (1979), 161–73; L. Hoffman, *Foundations of Family Therapy* (New York: Basic Books 1981); J. Geller, 'Conjoint Therapy: Staff Training and Treatment of the Abuser and Abused,' in Roy, ed., *The Abusive Partner*; D. Everstine and L. Everstine, *People in Crisis: Strategic Therapeutic Interventions* (New York: Brunner/Mazel 1983); P. Neidig and D. Friedman, *Spouse Abuse: A Treatment Program for Couples* (Champaign, IL: Research Press 1984); J. Weitzman and K. Dreen, 'Wife Beating: A View of the Marital Dyad,' *Social Casework*, 63 (1982), 259–65; and Cook and Frantz-Cook, 'A Systemic Treatment Approach to Wife Battering.'

69 Walker, 'The Cycle Theory of Violence,' in *The Battered Woman*, 55–70

70 Potential reasons for the existence of more research on the effects of television include: the presence of the TV in the home, the greater number of hours spent watching TV relative to viewing movies or reading magazines, and the corporate concern over consumer spending habits. The traditional distinctions between the various media have been significantly reduced, however, with the advent of home video rentals and music videos.

71 For more on the limited male roles presented in the media, see Mike Messner, 'Why Rocky III,' *M.: Gentle Men for Gender Justice*, 10 (Spring 1983), 15–17; Ian Harris, 'Media Myths and the Reality of Men's Work,' *Changing Men*, 16 (Summer 1986), 8–10, 44; Richard Dyer, 'Male Sexuality in the Media,' in Metcalf and Humphries, eds., *The Sexuality of Men*, 28–43; and Durkin, 'Television and Sex-Role Acquisition 1.'

72 Eron et al., 'Age Trends in the Development of Aggression, Sex Typing, and Related Television Habits'; Gunter and Furnham, 'Personality and the Perception of TV Violence'; Gunter, 'Do Aggressive People Prefer Violent Television?'; Pierce, 'Television and Violence'; Gunter and Furnham, 'Perceptions of Television Violence'; Huesmann, Lagerspetz, and Eron, 'Intervening Variables in the TV Violence-Aggression Relation'

73 Cobb, Stevens-Long, and Goldstein, 'The Influence of Televised Models on Toy Preference in Children'

74 See, for example, Mattern and Lindholm, 'Effects of Maternal Commentary in Reducing Aggressive Impact of Televised Violence on Preschool Children.'

75 Liebert, 'Effects of Television on Children and Adolescents'

76 Neil Postman interview, 'Media File,' CBC Radio, 17 Feb 1990

77 For more on the effects of television advertising, see: Eisenstock, 'Sex Role Differences in Children's Identification with Countersterotypical Televised Portrayals'; Schwartz and Markham, 'Sex Stereotyping in Children's Toy Advertisements'; Moschis and Moore, 'A Longitudinal Study of Television Advertising Effects'; Gutman, 'The Impact of Advertising at the Time of Consumption'; Rak and McMullen, 'Sex-Role Stereotyping in Television Commercials'; and Cobb, Stevens-Long, and Goldstein, 'The Influence of Televised Models on Toy Preference in Children.'

78 Phillips, 'The Impact of Mass Media Violence in U.S. Homicides'

79 Loye, Gorney, and Steele, 'An Experimental Field Study'; Rubinstein, 'Television and Behavior'; Phillips, 'The Impact of Mass Media Violence'; Pierce, 'Television and Violence'; Freedman, 'Effects of Television Violence on Aggressiveness'; Potts, Huston, and Wright, 'The Effects of Television Form and Violent Content on Boys' Attention and Social Behavior'; Friedrich-Cofer and Huston, 'Television Violence and Aggression'; Eron and Huesmann, 'Television as a Source of Maltreatment of Children'; and Leonard Berkowitz, 'The Effects of Observing Violence,' in Aronson, ed., *Readings about the Social Animal*, 235–46
  One study has provided greater detail for the debate by differentiating between the various types of television programming and assessing their respective levels of violence. See Williams, Zabrack, and Joy, 'The Portrayal of Aggression on North American Television.'

80 S. Feshbach, 'The Stimulation versus Cathartic Effects of a Vicarious Aggressive Activity,' *Journal of Abnormal Social Psychology*, 63 (1961), 381

81 Comstock, 'Sexual Effects of Movie and TV Violence.' Another, equally critical, study was done by Russell Geen, David Stonner, and Gary Shope, 'The Facilitation of Aggression by Aggression: Evidence against the Catharsis Hypothesis,' in Aronson, *Readings about the Social Animal*, 247–56.

82 Rubinstein, 'Televised Violence'

83 Baxter et al., 'A Content Analysis of Music Videos'

84 Sherman and Dominick, 'Violence and Sex in Music Videos'

85 Tara Ferguson, Account Executive, MuchMusic Inc., Toronto, states that though MuchMusic has not surveyed its audience for verification, it

assumes most adolescents view rock videos with their friends and not their parents.

As of 1 September 1989, MuchMusic was available on 90 per cent of Canadian cable networks and entered approximately five million households. (Tara Ferguson, telephone interview with the author, 23 April 1990.)

86 D. Millar and S. Baran, 'Music Television: An Assessment of Aesthetic and Functional Attributes' (Paper presented to the International Communication Association, San Francisco, May 1984), cited in Sherman and Dominick, 'Violence and Sex in Music Videos'

87 Although women are recruited into the military organizations of many countries, men comprise the vast majority of recruits (Gwyn Dyer, *War: Anybody's Son Will Do*, a National Film Board of Canada Production, 1983). While the role of women in the military requires examination, this section focuses on what the military experience does to men.

88 Arkin and Dobrofsky, 'Military Socialization and Masculinity.'

For excellent work on the links between masculinity, the military, and science, particularly in the atom bomb project as the culmination of three centuries of masculine, destructive, and conquering science, see Easlea, *Fathering the Unthinkable*, and 'Patriarchy, Scientists, and Nuclear Warriors,' in Kaufman, ed., *Beyond Patriarchy*, 195–215.

89 Dyer, *War: Anybody's Son Will Do*

90 Ibid.

91 Ibid.

92 Arkin and Dobrofsky, 'Military Socialization and Masculinity,' 160

93 Doyle, *The Male Experience*, 226

94 For a description of the U.S. military as a meeting ground for gay men and lesbians during the Second World War, and the beginnings afterwards of gay neighbourhoods in cities like San Francisco, see D'Emilio, *Sexual Politics, Sexual Communities*, 23–39.

One book focusing particularly on the wartime period is Bérubé, *Coming Out under Fire*.

95 There are observations on male violence as being linked to homophobia (specifically, men's fear of being perceived as feminine, and the stereotyping of gays as sharing feminine attributes) in Michael Kaufman's 'The Construction of Masculinity and the Triad of Men's Violence,' in *Beyond Patriarchy*, 12, 17, 19–22.

96 Gay-bashing, or the direct physical assault against someone who is presumed – for whatever reason – to be gay, is the most extreme manifestation of homophobia, which involves a more general emotional,

financial, physical, sexual, political discrimination against individuals perceived to be gay. For more details, see Kelner, *Homophobic Assault.*

97 Arkin and Dobrofsky, 'Military Socialization and Masculinity,' 162
98 Donna Warnock, 'Patriarchy Is a Killer: What People Concerned about Peace and Justice Should Know,' in Pamela McAllister, ed., *Reweaving the Web of Life* (Philadelphia: New Society Books 1982), 32, quoted in Dorothy Goldin Rosenberg, 'Feminism and Peace,' in Nemiroff, ed., *Women and Men,* 518–19.
99 C.J. Levy, 'ARVN as Faggots: Inverted Warfare in Vietnam,' *Transaction,* Oct 1971, 18-27, quoted in Arkin and Dobrofsky, 'Military Socialization and Masculinity,' 163
100 Lt. Col. James McLellan, Canadian Armed Forces, Ottawa; telephone interview with the author, 23 April 1990
101 Ibid.
102 Even if all the data were available, it would be particularly difficult to arrive at a total figure, as many individual items can have both military and civilian uses. For example, the massive interstate highway system that the United States built in the post-1945 period was designed to allow for rapid troop transport and civilian evacuation in the event of a civil, conventional, or nuclear war.
    Noam Chomsky argues that while considerable amounts of information often are available in the West, the existing structures within the media do not encourage, and often appear to impede, its distribution. See Noam Chomsky and Edward S. Herman, *The Political Economy of Human Rights,* vol. I: *The Washington Connection and Third World Fascism* and vol. II: *After the Cataclysm: Postwar Indochina and the Reconstruction of Imperial Ideology* (Montreal: Black Rose 1979).
103 For more on the difficulties experienced by the 1980s peace movement, see: Dorothy Nelkin and Michael Pollak, *The Atom Besieged: Antinuclear Movements in France and Germany* (Cambridge, MA: MIT Press 1982); New Left Review, eds., *Exterminism and Cold War* (London: Verso 1982); Ernie Regehr and Simon Rosenblum, *Canada and the Nuclear Arms Race* (Toronto: Lorimer 1983); Diana Johnstone, *The Politics of Euromissiles* (London: Verso 1984); Barbara Harford and Sarah Hopkins, eds., *Greenham Common: Women at the Wire* (Toronto: Women's Press 1985); and Dimitrios Roussopoulos, *The Coming of World War III,* vol. I: *From Protest to Resistance / The International War System* (Montreal: Black Rose 1986).
104 Gwyn Prins, *Defended to Death: A Study of the Nuclear Arms Race from the Cambridge University Disarmament Seminar* (Harmondsworth: Penguin 1983)

105 For more on how traditional male values have perverted the issue of national security, see Helen Caldicott, *Missile Envy: The Arms Race and Nuclear War* (Toronto: Bantam 1985).

106 Sivard, *World Military and Social Expenditures 1986*, 3–7. For more on the strains the military places on domestic economies, see, among others, Seymour Melman, *The Permanent War Economy: American Capitalism in Decline* (New York: Touchstone 1974), and Roussopoulos, *The Coming of World War III*, vol. I.

107 Arkin and Dobrofsky, 'Military Socialization and Masculinity,' 153

108 For more on the implications of our glorification of specific male heroes, see Gerzon, *A Choice of Heroes*.

109 In 1986, war toys generated $1.2 and $16 billion, respectively, in Canada and the United States. The U.S. figure was up from $10 billion just six years earlier. See John Barber, 'Warfare in Toyland,' *Maclean's*, 99/50 (15 Dec 1986), 38–41. The Stop War Toys Campaign indicates that 'for every boy aged 5–12 in the US, 2 G.I. Joe products are sold yearly.' See the Stop War Toys Campaign, quoted in Kimmel and Messner, *Men's Lives*, 215.

110 Michael Kidron and Dan Smith, *The War Atlas: Armed Conflict – Armed Peace* (London: Pan 1983), part 2: The Weaponry, subsection 13

111 Donna Warnock, cited in Goldin Rosenberg, 'Feminism and Peace,' in Nemiroff, *Women and Men*, 518–19

112 Erich Fromm, quoted in Kohn, 'Make Love, Not War'

113 Dyer, *Anybody's Son Will Do*, an NFB Canada Production, 1983

114 A. Eagly and L. Carli, 'Sex of Researchers and Sex-Typed Communications as Determinants of Sex Differences in Influenceability: A Meta-Analysis of Social Influence Studies,' *Psychological Bulletin*, 90 (1981), 1–20; G. Javornisky, 'Task Content and Sex Differences in Conformity,' *Journal of Social Psychology*, 108 (1979), 213–20; and S. Feldman-Summers, D. Montano, D. Kasprzyk, and B. Wagner, 'Influence Attempts When Competing Views Are Gender-Related: Sex as Credibility,' *Psychology of Women Quarterly*, 5 (1980), 311–20. Cited in Aronson, *Readings about the Social Animal*, 12–55. Aronson notes that women conformed more than men only when the researcher was male or when the group task was male-oriented.

115 Richard Cohen, 'Men Have Buddies, But No Real Friends,' *For Men*, Spring 1987, 7; and Paul Kivel, 'The Fear of Men,' *Changing Men*, 17 (Winter 1986), 19

116 Adolf Hitler's Nazis recognized the 'educational potentialities' of the emerging organizations for adolescents and sought to exploit them by creating the Hitler youth. See Grace Longwell Coyle, *Group Work with*

American Youth: A Guide to the Practice of Leadership (New York: Harper 1948), 11. Coyle cites: Edward Hartshorne, *German Youth and the Nazi Dream of Victory* (New York: Farrar and Rinehart 1941); Erika Mann, *School for Barbarians* (New York: Modern Age 1938); and Marianne Welter, 'A Lost Generation' (Master's thesis, Western Reserve University 1944).

117 Hantover, 'The Boy Scouts and the Validation of Masculinity'

118 J.E. West, 'The Real Boy Scout,' *Leslie's Weekly*, 1912, 448, quoted in Hantover, ibid., 191

119 The list is from the back cover of Zilbergeld's *Male Sexuality*. While Zilbergeld's list was not intended specifically for adolescent males, it does provide a good summary of what many young males are taught to value.

120 Longo, 'Sexual Learning and Experience among Adolescent Sexual Offenders'; Joyce Thomas and Carl M. Rogers, 'A Treatment Program for Intrafamily Juvenile Sexual Offenders,' in Greer and Stuart, eds., *The Sexual Aggressor: Current Perspectives on Treatment*, 127–43; and A. Nicholas Groth, 'Treatment of the Sexual Offender in a Correctional Institution,' in Greer and Stuart, *The Sexual Aggressor*, 160–76

121 Jullian Wood, 'Boys Will Be Boys,' *New Socialist*, 5 (May–June 1982), 41–3

122 Don Long, RAVEN, St Louis, MO, 1991

123 Ibid.

124 One recent study has indicated that at age nine or ten, boys and girls are equally close to their best friends. By ages eleven or twelve, boys scoring high on the masculine items of Self-Perception Inventory (a sixty-item version of the BEM Sex Role inventory) were significantly less close to their best friends than girls of the same age. These boys were also less close to their friends than other boys who scored equally on masculine and feminine items on the Self-Perception Inventory. The Gerald Jones and Myron Dembo study was published in *Merrill-Palmer Quarterly*, 35/4: 445. A synopsis was published in *Growing Child Research Review*, Apr 1990, 2.

125 A sample escalation toward violence is depicted in chapter 5, p. 149.

126 'Daddy's Pride and Joy,' advertisement in *Baby Talk*, 52/10 (Oct 1987), 34

127 Feigan Fasteau, *The Male Machine*

128 Unger, *Female and Male*, 167–91

129 Barber, 'Warfare In Toyland'

130 Wilson and Daly, 'Competitiveness, Risk Taking, and Violence'

131 David Rice-Lampert, Probation Officer, Community and Youth Corrections, Department of Justice, Province of Manitoba; telephone interview with the author, 24 April 1990

132 Aronson, *Readings about the Social Animal*, 19
133 Solomon Asch, 'Opinion and Social Pressure,' in Aronson, *Readings about the Social Animal*, 13-22; originally appeared in *Scientific American*, 193/5 (1955)
134 Aronson, *Readings about the Social Animal*, 12–55
135 Stanley Milgram, 'Behavioral Study of Obedience,' in Aronson, *Readings about the Social Animal*, 23–36; originally printed in *The Journal of Abnormal and Social Psychology*, 67/4 (1963)
136 There are numerous histories of pornography. See, among others, Dworkin, *Pornography*, and Kendrick, *The Secret Museum*.
137 Ehrenreich, *The Hearts of Men*, 29–41
138 Ibid.
139 For a critique of *Playboy*'s role in accelerating pornography's exploitation of women, see ibid., 42–51.
140 Ibid.
141 *Not a Love Story: A Film about Pornography*, National Film Board of Canada, Studio D, 1981. In 1977 the California Department of Justice estimated the industry's profits at four billion dollars. It is safe to assume they currently are much larger. For more, see Schipper, 'Filthy Lucre: A Tour of America's Most Profitable Frontier.'
142 Kate Millett interview in *Not a Love Story: A Film about Pornography*
143 For more information on the emergence, and areas of activity, of the women's movement, see below, chapter 4, p. 120–6.
144 *Not a Love Story*
145 Andrea Dworkin and Catherine MacKinnon are the two most prominent feminists in the anti-pornography/pro-censorship debate. See: Dworkin, *Pornography*; Andrea Dworkin, 'I Want a 24 Hour Truce during Which There Is No Rape,' *M.: Gentle Men for Gender Justice*, 13 (Fall 1984), 2–3, 44–5; and eds., 'An Interview with Andrea Dworkin,' *Sexual Coercion and Assault* 1/1 (Jan 1986), 17–19. For more on the social conservative philosophy and contribution to the pro-censorship debate, see Klatch, *Women of the New Right*.
146 See Burstyn, ed., *Women against Censorship* and 'Porn Again'; and Kinsman, *Regulation of Desire* (1987).
147 Gary Kinsman, 'The New Sexual Censorship Legislation: Just as Bad as before if Not Worse,' *Fuse*, 45 (Spring 1987), 19–20; and Klatch, *Women of the New Right*, 201
148 Neil Malamuth and Edward Donnerstein, 'The Effects of Aggressive Pornographic Mass Media Stimuli,' in L. Berkowitz, ed., *Advances in Experimental Social Psychology*, 15 (1982).

Edward Donnerstein and Daniel Linz, in 'The Question of Pornography,' warn that we must not draw too narrow a definition of pornography. The effect could be that we might ignore the misogynist values portrayed in the more general media. From their research they conclude 'that violence against women need not occur in a pornographic or sexually explicit context to have a negative effect upon viewer attitudes and behaviors' (p. 60).

149 Linz, Donnerstein, and Penrod, 'The Effects of Multiple Exposures to Filmed Violence against Women'

150 Neil Malamuth, 'Erotica, Aggression and Perceived Appropriateness' (Paper presented at the 86th annual convention of the American Psychological Association, Toronto, Sept 1978)

151 Donnerstein, 'Pornography and Violence against Women'

152 Mayerson and Taylor, 'The Effects of Rape Myth Pornography on Women's Attitudes and the Mediating Role of Sex Role Stereotyping'

153 Malamuth and Ceniti, 'Repeated Exposure to Violent and Nonviolent Pornography'; Berkowitz, 'Some Thoughts on Anti and Prosocial Influences of Media Events'; and W. Josephson, 'The Effects of Violent Television upon Children's Aggression: Elicitation, Disinhibition or Catharsis?' (PhD diss., University of Manitoba 1984)

154 Among many others arguing that pornography reinforces previously held views about women, and thus reinforces violence toward women, are: Gray, 'Exposure to Pornography and Aggression toward Women'; Zillmann and Bryant, 'Pornography, Sexual Callousness, and the Trivialization of Rape'; Leonard and Taylor, 'Exposure to Pornography, Permissive and Nonpermissive Cues, and Male Aggression toward Females'; Linz, Donnerstein, and Penrod, 'Multiple Exposures to Filmed Violence'; and Malamuth and Check, 'The Effects of Aggressive Pornography on Beliefs in Rape Myths.'

155 In a study of a sample population of university males, Dano Demaré, John Briere, and Hilary Lips found that 81 per cent of the subjects consumed non-violent pornography in the last year, while 41 per cent and 35 per cent used violent and sexually violent pornography, respectively. See their 'Violent Pornography and Self-Reported Likelihood of Sexual Aggression.'

156 Palys defined 'triple-X' as: (a) material created primarily for the portrayal of explicit sexual activity; (b) items, or the stores in which they were available, which have been the target of various protest and lobbying groups; (c) the material in 'sex specialist' shops; and (d) videos that frequently are cited under the obscenity provision of the Criminal Code

of Canada. Palys defined 'adult' or 'single-X' material as videos that may be labelled pornographic but (a) are available over the counter at most video rental shops (one did not need to go to a specialty shop); (b) were not an embarrassment for the rental store; and (c) have not been targeted for lobbying or media attention. For more information on Palys's coding and selection of the videos, see his 'Testing the Common Wisdom.'
157 Ibid.
158 Russell, *Sexual Exploitation*, 140–2, 284–5
159 Canadian Advisory Council on the Status of Women, *Rape and Sexual Assault: Fact Sheet #4* (Ottawa), reprinted in Porteous, Loptson, and Janitis, *Let's Talk about Sexual Assault*, 4. For works dealing with female socialization and sexual assault, see: Clark and Lewis, *Rape: The Price of Coercive Sexuality*; Griffin, *Rape: The Politics of Consciousness*; Pauline Burt, 'A Study of Women Who Both Were Raped and Avoided Rape,' *Journal of Social Issues*, 37/4 (1981), 123–37; Riger and Gordon, 'The Fear of Rape'; Sutherland and Scherl, 'Patterns of Response among Victims of Rape'; and Julia Schwendinger and Herman Schwendinger, 'Studying Rape: Integrating Research and Social Change,' in Carol Smart and Barry Smart, eds., *Women, Sexuality, and Social Control* (London: Routledge & Kegan Paul 1978), 104–18.
160 White and Mosher, 'Experimental Validation of a Model for Predicting the Reporting of Rape'; Turner and Colao, 'Alcoholism and Sexual Assault'; and Renner and Wackett, 'Sexual Assault'
161 Clive Seligman, Julie Brickman, and David Koulack, 'Rape and Physical Attractiveness: Assigning Responsibility to Victims' (Winnipeg: University of Manitoba, draft copy, undated); and Porteous, Loptson, and Janitis, *Let's Talk about Sexual Assault*, 6
162 Brownmiller, *Against Our Will*, 315–17, 319; Smart and Smart, 'Accounting for Rape: Reality and Myth in Press Reporting,' in Smart and Smart, *Women, Sexuality, and Social Control*, 89–103; Riger and Gordon, 'The Fear of Rape' and Marlene Radar, 'Sexual Harassment: A Form of Social Control,' in Fitzgerald, Guberman, and Wolfe, eds., *Still Ain't Satisfied*
163 See, for example, C.G. Abel, J.V. Becker, and L.J. Skinner, 'Aggressive Behaviour and Sex,' *Psychiatric Clinics of North America*, 3 (1980), 133–51, cited in Check and Malamuth, 'An Empirical Assessment of Some Feminist Hypotheses about Rape,' 415.
164 Briere, Malamuth, and Check, 'Sexuality and Rape Supportive Beliefs,' 398. (Italics in the original.)
    For information on the pervasiveness of sexual assault myths, see,

among others: Smart and Smart, *Women, Sexuality and Social Control*; Burt, 'Cultural Myths and Supports for Rape'; H.S. Field, 'Attitudes toward Rape: A Comparative Analysis of Police, Rapists, Crisis Counsellors, and Citizens,' *Journal of Personality and Social Psychology*, 36 (1978), 156–79, cited in Burt, 'Cultural Myths,' 217; Schrink, Poole, and Regoli, 'Sexual Myths and Ridicule'; Bunting and Reeves, 'Perceived Male Sex Orientation and Beliefs about Rape'; Briere, Malamuth, and Check, 'Sexuality and Rape-Supportive Beliefs'; Check and Malamuth, 'An Empirical Assessment of Some Feminist Hypotheses about Rape'; and Smith, *Fear or Freedom*.

165 Briere, Malamuth, and Check, 'Sexuality and Rape-Supportive Beliefs'; and Brownmiller, *Against Our Will* (1980)

166 See, among others: Brownmiller, *Against Our Will*; Walker, *The Battered Woman*; Dobash and Dobash, *Violence against Wives*; Griffin, *Rape* (1986); and Schechter, *Women and Male Violence*.

   Check and Malamuth, in 'An Empirical Assessment of Some Feminist Hypotheses about Rape,' have worked to statistically verify earlier literary hypotheses about sexual assault.

167 Burt, 'Attitudes Supportive of Rape in American Culture' and 'Cultural Myths and Supports for Rape'

168 Briere, Corne, Runtz, and Malamuth, 'The Rape Arousal Inventory: Predicting Actual and Potential Sexual Aggression in a University Population' (Paper presented at the Annual Meeting of the American Psychological Association. Toronto 1984)

169 Briere and Malamuth, 'Self-Reported Likelihood of Sexually Aggressive Behavior'

170 Briere et al., 'The Rape Arousal Inventory'

171 Demaré, Briere, and Lips, 'Violent Pornography and Self-Reported Likelihood of Sexual Aggression'

172 Don Sabo, 'Feminist Analysis of Men in Sports,' *Changing Men*, 18 (Summer–Fall 1987), 32

173 For a critique of this perspective see Dunning et al., 'The Social Roots of Football Hooligan Violence.'

174 Mike Messner, 'Sports and the Politics of Inequality,' *Changing Men*, 17 (Winter 1986), 27–8

175 Mike Messner, 'Jocks in the Men's Movement,' *Changing Men*, 14 (Spring 1985), 34–5, notes that 'since the late 1960s the left/counterculture has denounced organized competitive sports because of its extreme Lombardian ethic that "winning is everything."'

176 Team owners, whether individuals or a corporation, often are involved

because of the commercial spin-offs for their company. The tendency for involvement of beer and liquor corporations appears less than coincidental. They profit from the association of their product with activities, such as sport, which are thoroughly imbued with values of traditional masculinity. It is the gender equivalent of the lengthy tradition of companies wrapping themselves in the national flag and avowing their nationalism in order to boost sales. (Mitzel, *Sports and the Macho Male*.)

177 Mike Messner, 'Ah, Ya Throw Like a Girl!,' *M.: Gentle Men for Gender Justice*, 11 (Winter 1983–4), 21–2

178 Mitzel, *Sports and the Macho Male*; the Kennedy quote was cited in Feigen Fasteau, *The Male Machine*, 101, who cites Nancy Gager Clinch, *The Kennedy Neurosis* (New York: Grosset & Dunlap 1973), 266.

179 Rozee-Koker and Polk, 'The Social Psychology of Group Rape'

180 Mitzel, *Sports and the Macho Male*

181 For an example of how a game could be better structured to develop individual pleasure and skill, see Max Rivers, 'Mainly Men Football: An Example of Cooperative Competition,' *Changing Men*, 18 (Summer–Fall 1987), 32.

182 For more on homophobia in sports, see Mike Messner, 'AIDS, Homophobia, and Sports,' *Changing Men*, 19 (Spring–Summer 1988), 30.

183 For more on the positive and negative effects of sport on self-esteem and masculinity, see Michael Messner, 'The Meaning of Success: The Athletic Experience and the Development of Male Identity,' in Brod, *The Making of Masculinities*, 193–209; and Stein and Hoffman, 'Sports and Male Role Strain.'

184 Sutherland, 'Olympic Ideals Seem to Be Fading Further Away'

185 Messner, 'Sports and the Politics of Inequality'

186 Bruce Kidd, 'Sports and Masculinity,' in Kaufman, *Beyond Patriarchy*, 250–65

187 Messner, 'Sports and the Politics of Inequality'

188 Ken Dyer, 'Female Athletes Are Catching Up,' *New Scientist*, 22 Sept 1977, 722–3, cited in Fausto-Sterling, *Myths of Gender*, 219

189 Bryson, 'Sport and the Oppression of Women'

190 Mike Messner, 'Redefining Courage and Heroism,' *M.: Gentle Men for Gender Justice*, 12 (Spring–Summer 1984), 32–3.

    Michael Kimmel, calling it 'macho-mouth rhetoric,' emphasizes that 'politicians have always tried to appear tough and manly, using their military accolades or athletic prowess to prove that they possess the ability to govern.' For some examples of macho-mouth rhetoric in the

1988 U.S. presidential campaign, see: Kimmel, 'Macho Mouth on the Campaign Trail: The Winning Strategy in '88, Talk Like a Man,' *Psychology Today*, 22/10 (Oct 1988), 27.

191 For more on violence in sport, see Coakley, *Sport in Society*, and Smith, *Violence and Sports*.

192 While jokes abound about many women being sports widows, the statistics on the estimated number of hours men spend viewing sports are not easily available. But glimpses of the larger picture do exist. During the 1988–9 NHL hockey season, for example, 1,173,000 men (18 years and over) watched each regular season game broadcast on the Canadian Broadcasting Corporation (CBC). The figure was expected to increase to approximately 1,891,000 men (18 years and over) during the Stanley Cup play-offs, according to *Sportstime/Gametime: 1989* (Toronto: CBC Television Network Sports Sales 1989).

Statistics also indicate that 78 per cent of Canadian men 20 years and over spend over three hours per week for over nine months of the year engaged in physical activity during leisure time, according to the Canadian Fitness and Lifestyle Research Institute, 'Time Spent on Physical Activity in Leisure Time' (Ottawa: CFLRI 1988).

193 See, among others: Goldberg, *The Hazards of Being Male*; Grimm and Yarnold, 'Sex Typing and the Coronary-Prone Behavior Pattern'; and Lipton, 'Masculinity in Management.'

Chapter 4

1 Dobash and Dobash, *Violence against Wives*, 31–2

2 For more detailed analysis of the history of the subjugation and exploitation of women, see Dobash and Dobash, chapter 3, 'The Legacy of the "Appropriate" Victim,' 31–47. The book is well written and skilfully integrates much of the available material.

3 Julia O'Faolin and Lauro Martines, eds., *Not in God's Image: Women in History* (Glasgow: Fontana/Collins 1974), 70–88, quoted in Dobash and Dobash, 35

4 Dobash and Dobash, *Violence against Wives*, 31–2. Dobash and Dobash cite O'Faolin and Martines, 53–6, 67–9.

5 O'Faolin and Martines, *Not in God's Image*, 72, quoted in Dobash and Dobash, 39

6 Dobash and Dobash, *Violence against Wives*, 40

7 Ibid., 46 quoting Fuero Jusgo, cited in Julia O'Faolin and Lauro Martines, *Not in God's Image*, 191

8 Dobash and Dobash, *Violence against Wives*, 46, quoting Statuti di Perugia, quoted in O'Faolin and Martines, 191

9 Dobash and Dobash, 46, citing Coutumes de Beauvaisis, cited in O'Faolin and Martines, 188

10 Dobash and Dobash, *Violence against Wives*, 46, quoting Coutumes de Beauvaisis, quoted in O'Faolin and Martines, 189

11 L. Finkelstein, quoted in de Beauvaisis, cited in O'Faolin and Martines, *Not in God's Image*, 189, cited in Dobash and Dobash, 47

12 Martin Luther, quoted in O'Faolin and Martines, 209, cited in Dobash and Dobash, 53

13 John Smyth recorded this saying in *The History of the Hundred of Berkeley*, ed. J. Maclean (Gloucester, 1885), 32, quoted in Dobash and Dobash, *Violence against Wives*, 55.

14 Dobash and Dobash, 60

15 Matthew Hale, *History of the Pleas of the Crown* (1736), quoted in Russell, *Rape in Marriage*, 17

16 Finkelhor and Yllo, *License to Rape*, 2–3 and 139–40; and Estrich, *Real Rape*, 5, 28

17 Martin, *Battered Wives*, 31

18 The expansion of capitalist markets in the sixteenth and seventeenth centuries spurred significant development in the sciences which, in turn, initiated a shift from the more divinely inspired assumptions about the world and human relations toward more secular, and presumably 'scientific,' explanations (see Mortimer Chambers, Raymond Grew, David Herlihy, Theodore K. Robb, and Isser Woloch, *The Western Experience* [New York: Alfred Knopf 1974], 505–45). From the evidence provided by Dobash and Dobash, it would appear that as regards male violence against women, this transition was not nearly as swift as changes in areas such as astronomy or physics (see, for example, Dobash and Dobash, *Violence against Wives*, 50–64). The current frequency with which individuals continue to cite religious explanations for gender divisions attests to the enduring appeal of this tradition.

In sixteenth- and seventeenth-century Europe, important changes occurred in the understanding of science and human physiology. The application of this information to justify male violence was encouraged after Charles Darwin released *On the Origin of Species* in 1859 – see Shibley Hyde, *Half the Human Experience* – and reached new heights following numerous twentieth-century technological advances.

19 Hucker et al., 'Cerebral Damage and Dysfunction in Sexually Aggressive Men'

20 Frank Elliot, 'The Neurology of Explosive Rage: The Dyscontrol Syndrome,' in Roy, ed., *Battered Women*; and Frank Elliot, 'Biological Contributions to Family Violence,' in Barnhill, *Clinical Approaches to Family Violence*. See also John Lion, 'Clinical Aspects of Wifebattering,' in Roy, *Battered Women*.

21 Averill, *Anger and Aggression*

22 Ibid., 44

23 G.J. Cullington, 'Psychosurgery: National Commission Issues Surprisingly Favorable Report,' *Science*, 194 (1976), 299–301; and P.K. Bridges and J.R. Bartlett, 'Psychosurgery: Yesterday and Today,' *British Journal of Psychiatry*, 131 (1977), 249–60. Cited in Fred Berlin, 'Sex Offenders: A Biomedical Perspective and a Status Report on Biomedical Treatment,' in Greer and Stuart, eds., *The Sexual Aggressor*, 83–123. The quote is Berlin's.

24 Carol Bohmer, 'Legal and Ethical Issues in Mandatory Treatment: The Patient's Rights versus Society's Rights,' in Greer and Stuart, *The Sexual Aggressor*, 3–21

25 Heim, 'Sexual Behavior of Castrated Sex Offenders.' Heim notes that castration has been used most extensively in Europe. He cites H. Plenge's figure of over 10,000 castrates in the region of Zurich alone since 1910. See Plenge, 'Die Behandlung erhelich ruckfalliger Sexualdelinquenten, vornehmlich der Homosexuellen, unter Berucksichtigung der Kastration.' Even some feminists support castration. One writer, Isabelle Lyle, has several proposals for an end to male sexual violence against women. These include: castration, curfews for adult males, and areas designated as off-limits to men. See Isabelle Lyle, 'Rape Is a Male Problem and Men Won't Like the Solution,' *Broomstick*, 9/2 (n.d.), 10–11 (reprinted from *The Daily Californian*).

26 Heim, 'Sexual Behavior of Castrated Sex Offenders'

27 Barbaree and Marshall, 'Treatment of the Sexual Offender,' 16

28 Heim cited F. Cornu, *Catamnestic Studies on Castrated Sex Delinquents from a Forensic-Psychiatry Viewpoint* (Basel: Karger 1973), referenced in N. Heim and C.J. Hursch, 'Castration for Sex Offenders: Treatment or Punishment? A Review and Critique of Recent European Literature,' *Archives of Sexual Behavior*, 8 (1979), 281–304; and A. Langeluddeke, *Die Entmannung von Sittlichkeitserbrechern* (Berlin: de Gruyter 1963). See Heim, 'Sexual Behavior of Castrated Sex Offenders,' and Barbaree and Marshall, 'Treatment of the Sexual Offender,' 16–17.

29 Heim, 'Sexual Behavior of Castrated Sex Offenders,' and Barbaree and Marshall, 'Treatment of the Sexual Offender,' 16–17

30 Heim, 'Sexual Behavior of Castrated Sex Offenders,' 19
31 Ibid., 11–19
32 Barbaree and Marshall, 'Treatment of the Sexual Offender,' 17. They are referring to Ford and Beach, *Patterns of Sexual Behavior*.
33 Thiessen, *The Evolution and Chemistry of Aggression*, 55
34 J. Money, 'Use of an Androgen-Depleting Hormone in the Treatment of Male Sex Offenders,' *Journal of Sex Research*, 6/3 (1970), 167, cited in Thiessen, *The Evolution and Chemistry of Aggression*, 82
35 Knopp, *Retraining Adult Sex Offenders*, 41–8. For examples of other clinicians using Depo-Provera, see Bradford, 'Research on Sex Offenders,' and Berlin and Meinecke, 'Treatment of Sex Offenders with Antiandrogenic Medication.'
36 Bradford, 'The Hormonal Treatment of Sexual Offenders.' While males may not react in the same way as females to various drugs, it is worth noting that significant health concerns have been expressed over the use of Depo-Provera as a contraceptive drug for women. See: Berer, *Who Needs Depo-Provera?* and Goodman, 'The Case against Depo-Provera.'
37 Barbaree and Marshall, 'Treatment of the Sexual Offender,' 16
38 Berlin, 'Sex Offenders,' in Greer and Stuart, *The Sexual Aggressor*
39 Sherman, 'The Stuff That Men Are Made Of'
40 Bradford, 'The Hormonal Treatment of Sexual Offenders'
41 Barbaree and Marshall, 'Treatment of the Sexual Offender,' 14–15
42 A. Nicholas Groth, 'Treatment of the Sex Offender in a Correctional Institution,' in Greer and Stuart, *The Sexual Aggressor*, 160–76
43 Lorraine Parrington, counsellor, Sexual Assault Crisis Program, Klinic Community Health Centre; interview with the author, 12 April 1990
44 Ibid.
45 Knopp, *Retraining Adult Sex Offenders*, 43–8; Barbaree and Marshall, 'Treatment of the Sexual Offender,' 15–16; and Bohmer, 'Legal and Ethical Issues in Mandatory Treatment'
46 See Knopp, Rosenberg, and Stevenson, *Report on the National Survey of Juvenile and Adult Sex-Offender Treatment Programs and Providers* (1986), 14.
47 Bradford, 'The Hormonal Treatment of Sexual Offenders'
48 Stordeur and Stille, *Ending Men's Violence against Their Partners*, 23–4. Stordeur and Stille cite: Deschner, *The Hitting Habit*; M. Faulk, 'Men Who Assault Their Wives,' *Medicine, Science, and the Law*, 14/3 (1974), 180–3, and 'Men Who Assault Their Wives,' in Roy, *Battered Women*; Lion, 'Clinical Aspects of Wifebattering,' in Roy, *Battered Women*; L. Schultz, 'The Wife Assaulter,' *Corrective Psychiatry and Journal of Social Therapy*, 6 (1960), 103–11; N. Shainess, 'Psychological Aspects of Wifebattering,' in

Roy, *Battered Women*; J. Snell, R. Rosenwald, and A. Robey, 'The Wifebeater's Wife: A Study of Family Interaction,' *Archives of General Psychiatry*, 11 (1964); and A. Symonds, 'Violence against Women: The Myth of Masochism,' *American Journal of Psychotherapy*, 33/2 (1979).

49 Knopp, *Retraining Adult Sex Offenders*, 26

50 Browning, *Stopping the Violence*, 1–2. While psychiatrists are not the only practitioners using intrapsychic treatments for male violence and other issues, their near omnipotence within the social service/medical communities has drawn several important criticisms. See Maeder, 'Wounded Healers,' and Burstow and Weitz, eds., *Shrink Resistant*.

51 Knopp, *Retraining Adult Sex Offenders*, 26

52 Bradford, 'Research on Sex Offenders'; Bradford's position was noted in this article.

53 Barbaree and Marshall, 'Treatment of the Sexual Offender,' 27–9, commenting on W.L. Marshall and S. Williams, 'A Behavioral Approach to the Modification of Rape,' *Quarterly Bulletin of the British Association for Behavioral Psychotherapy*, 4 (1975), 78. Marshall and Williams acknowledge that the measures they used may have fit better with the behavioural approach and slightly biased the results.

54 The program was described in Peters et al., 'Group Psychotherapy of the Sex Offender.' It was critiqued by J. Peters and H. Roether, 'Psychotherapy for Probationed Sex Offenders,' in Resnick and Wolfgang, eds., *Sexual Behavior*. The ten-year follow-up study was by J. Peters, 'A Ten-Year Follow-Up of Sex Offender Recidivism' (Unpublished manuscript, 1980). This evidence was cited in Barbaree and Marshall, 'Treatment of the Sexual Offender,' 22–9.

55 For more examples of intrapsychic treatment, see Barbaree and Marshall, 'Treatment of the Sexual Offender,' 22–9.

56 Knopp, *Retraining Adult Sex Offenders*, 26; Knopp was referring to sex offender programs.

57 See Bauer and Ritt, '"A Husband Is a Beating Animal"' and 'Wife-Abuse, Late Victorian English Feminists, and the Legacy of Frances Power Cobbes.'

58 Stanko, *Intimate Intrusions*, 3. For additional information on nineteenth-century feminist work against men's physical and sexual violence against women, Stanko cites: Kathleen Barry, *Female Sexual Slavery* (New York: Avon 1979), 14–38; Judith Walkowitz, *Prostitution and Victorian Society* (Cambridge: Cambridge University Press 1980); and Jeffrey Weeks, *Sex, Politics, and Society* (London: Longman 1981).
 While some first-wave feminists were struggling for better working

conditions, some for legislation to prevent wife-battering, and others for
improved work and education conditions for children, the efforts most
popularly remembered are those of the suffragettes in their struggle for
the vote. Since the mid-1970s there has been a veritable explosion of
women's history in a desperate attempt to compensate for the years of
silence. See, among others, Raeburn, *Militant Suffragettes*; Prentice and
Trofimenkoff, eds., *The Neglected Majority: Essays in Canadian Women's
History*, vols. 1 and 2; and Acton, Goldsmith, and Shepard, *Women at Work.*
59 Ralph Garofalo, of the Massachusetts Treatment Center, cited in Knopp,
   Retraining Adult Sex Offenders, 27
60 Evans, *Born for Liberty*, 282; and Robin Morgan, 'The Emergence of
   Women's Liberation,' in *Going Too Far*, 57–112. Morgan notes that the
   'Women's Liberation Movement surfaced with its first major militant
   demonstration on September 7, 1968, in Atlantic City, at the Miss
   America Pageant' (p. 64).
61 Martin, *Battered Wives*, 1–8; Schechter, *Women and Male Violence*, 11–183;
   and Guberman and Wolfe, eds., *No Safe Place*, 61–86
62 For more on the frequency and varieties of male violence against women,
   see above, chapter 1.
63 Morgan, ed., *Sisterhood Is Powerful*; Frankfort, *Vaginal Politics*; and
   Gordon, *Woman's Body, Woman's Right*
64 For a more detailed examination of how various social constructionist
   factors encourage male violence, see above, chapter 3.
65 H. Blumer, 'Social Problems as Collective Behavior,' *Social Problems*, 18
   (1971), 298–306; and M. Spector and J.I. Kitsuse, 'Social Problems: A
   Reformulation,' *Social Problems*, 21 (1973), 145–58, cited in Studer, 'Wife-
   Beating as a Social Problem: The Process of Definition'
66 Browning, *Stopping the Violence*, 1–2; and Knopp, *Retraining Adult Sex
   Offenders*, 27. Pressman, *Family Violence*, provides a thorough review of
   why women remain in assaultive relationships; cited in Browning,
   Stopping the Violence, 1–2.
67 E. Stark, A. Flitcraft, and W. Frazier, 'Medicine and Patriarchal Violence:
   The Social Construction of a "Private" Event,' *International Journal of Health
   Services*, 9/3 (1979), 461–93, cited in Browning, *Stopping the Violence*, 1–2
68 The material for this section on the differences between feminist and
   traditional therapies was synthesized from the following: Chesler, *Women
   and Madness*; Miriam Greenspan, 'An Introduction to Traditional Theory,'
   in *A New Approach to Women and Therapy*, 33–8; Brickman, 'Feminist, Non-
   sexist, and Traditional Models of Therapy'; Stanko, *Intimate Intrusions*
   (1985); Hutchinson and McDaniel, 'The Social Reconstruction of Sexual

Assault by Women Victims'; Collier, *Counselling Women*; and Bass and Davis, *The Courage to Heal*.

69 For information on the establishment of sexual assault crisis centres in North America, see: King and Webb, 'Rape Crisis Centres'; Renner and Keith, 'The Establishment of a Crisis Intervention Service for Victims of Sexual Assault'; and Gornick, Burt, and Pittman, 'Structure and Activities of Rape Crisis Centres in the Early 1980s.' For examples of feminist research on working with sexual assault victims, see above, chapter 2.

70 For an examination of the North American battered women's shelter movement, see Schechter, *Women and Male Violence*. For examples of feminist research on working with victims of physical violence by men, see above, chapter 2.

71 For more information on the often open hostility of the existing mental health system to the battered women's shelter movement, see Schechter, *Women and Male Violence*.

72 Securing adequate private and state money has been a constant struggle of the women's movement. Inadequate funding has restricted the ability of programs to meet the demand for service. Among others, see Martin, *Battered Wives*, 119–47, and MacLeod, *Battered But Not Beaten*, 49–68, 123–31.

73 Chapter 3 above reviews the issues in the feminist critique of the media's perpetuation of misogynist and hegemonic masculinity and femininity.

74 For more on the myths encouraging sexual assault and battering, see above, chapter 3.

75 For more information on the revision of sexual assault legislation in Canada, see: Ontario, Provincial Secretariat for Justice, *Information for the Victims of Sexual Assault* and *Helping the Victims of Sexual Assault*; Greenland, 'Dangerous Sexual Offender Legislation in Canada, 1948–1977'; Chappell, 'The Impact of Rape Legislation Reform'; Snider, 'Legal Reform and Social Control'; Gunn and Minch, *Sexual Assault*.

For a comparison of Canada with other countries see Greenland, 'Sex Law Reform in an International Perspective: England and Wales and Canada.'

For material on the United States see: Borgida, 'Legal Reform of Rape Laws'; Loh, 'Q: What Has Reform of Rape Legislation Wrought? A'; Myers and LaFree, 'Sexual Assault and Its Prosecution'; Galvin and Polk, 'Attrition in Case Processing'; Bienen, 'Rape Reform Legislation in the United States'; Dowdeswell, *Women on Rape*; and Estrich, *Real Rape*.

For material on changes to sexual harassment legislation, see above, chapter 1.

While many problems remain, significant changes have occurred in the police and court processing of battering cases. See, among others: Wasoff, 'Legal Protection from Wifebeating'; Burris and Jaffe, 'Wife Abuse as a Crime'; Jolin, 'Domestic Violence Legislation'; *Response* Staff, 'Responses to Wife Abuse in Four Western Countries,' *Response to the Victimization of Women and Children*, 8/2 (Spring 1985), 15–18; Crane et al., 'The Washington State Domestic Violence Act'; Hanmer and Stanko, 'Stripping Away the Rhetoric of Protection'; Ullrich, 'Equal But Not Equal'; Scott, 'Going Backwards'; Ursel and Farough, 'The Legal and Public Response to the New Wife Abuse Directive in Manitoba'; Fergusson et al., 'Factors Associated with Reports of Wife Assault in New Zealand'; and Dutton, 'The Criminal Justice Response to Wife Assault.'
76 Knopp, *Retraining Adult Sex Offenders*, 27

Chapter 5

1 Ralph Miliband, *The State in Capitalist Society* (London: Quartet 1980), 46
2 The physiological and intrapsychic treatment approaches have been discussed extensively; see chapter 4 above.
3 For some examples of family systems theory or practice, see: Taylor, 'Structured Conjoint Therapy for Spouse Abuse Cases'; Cook and Frantz-Cook, 'A Systematic Treatment Approach to Wife Battering'; Neidig, Friedman, and Collins, 'Domestic Conflict Containment'; Deschner, McNeil, and Moore, 'A Treatment Model for Batterers'; Weidman, 'Family Therapy with Violent Couples'; Deschner and McNeil, 'Results of Anger Control Training for Battering Couples'; and Harris, 'Counselling Violent Couples using Walker's Model.'
4 Stordeur and Stille, *Ending Men's Violence against Their Partners*, 25
5 Bograd, 'Family Systems Approaches to Wife Battering'
6 Ibid.
7 Stordeur and Stille, *Ending Men's Violence*, 25–6; and Rob Hall and Leo Ryan, 'Therapy with Men Who Are Violent to Their Spouses,' *Australian Journal of Family Therapy*, 5/4 (Oct 1984), 281–2
8 Stordeur and Stille, *Ending Men's Violence*, 25–6; Hall and Ryan, 'Therapy with Men Who Are Violent'; and Bograd, 'Family Systems Approaches.' Bograd does note that changes are occurring. Some systemic researchers have begun placing the responsibility for the violence solely with the man. As examples, she cites her 'Battered Women, Cultural Myths, and Clinical Interventions: A Feminist Analysis,' in New England Association for Women in Psychotherapy, eds., *Current Feminist Issues in Psycho-*

therapy (New York: Haworth 1982); Cook and Frantz-Cook, 'A Systemic Treatment Approach to Wife Battering'; and J. Geller, 'Conjoint Therapy: Staff Training and Treatment of the Abuser and the Abused,' in Roy, ed., *The Abusive Partner*.

9 For a review of the issues involved in our gender-based language, see Eakins and Eakins, *Sex Differences in Human Communication*.

10 Bograd, 'Family Systems Approaches,' paraphrasing D. Everstine and L. Everstine, *People in Crisis: Strategic Therapeutic Interventions* (New York: Brunner/Mazel 1983)

11 A. Rich, *On Lies, Secrets, and Silence* (New York: Norton 1979), quoted in Bograd, 'Family Systems Approaches,' 563

12 Bograd cites D. Saunders, 'Treatment and Value Issues in Helping Battered Women,' in A. Gurman, ed., *Questions and Answers in the Practice of Family Therapy* (New York: Brunner/Mazel 1981).

13 United States, Department of Justice, Law Enforcement Assistance Administration, *The Report from the Conference on Intervention Programs for Men Who Batter* (1979)

14 For more on the negative reaction to those adopting a family systems approach see McIntyre, 'Domestic Violence,' and Mathias, 'Lifting the Shade on Family Violence.'

15 U.S. Department of Justice, Law Enforcement Assistance, *Report on Men Who Batter* (1979)

16 Quoting Bograd, 'Family Systems Approaches,' who cited the APA Task Force, 'Report of the Task Force on Sex Bias and Sex Role Stereo-typing in Psychotherapeutic Practice,' *American Psychologist*, 30 (1975), 1169–75

17 Knopp, *Retraining Adult Sex Offenders*, 27; and Purdy and Nickle, 'Practice Principles for Working with Groups of Men Who Batter'

18 Don Long, 'Working with Men Who Batter,' in Scher, Stevens, Good, and Eichenfield, eds., *Handbook of Counselling and Psychotherapy with Men*, 308. Long cites Edward Gondolf and Diana Russell, 'The Case against Anger Control for Batterers' (Unpublished manuscript, 1987).

19 Barbara Hart, 'Accountability,' adapted from the keynote presentation, Baltimore Conference on Batterers; adapted by and quoted in RAVEN (Rape and Violence End Now), *The Ending Men's Violence National Referral Directory, Supplement*, inside front cover

20 Purdy and Nickle, 'Practice Principles.' The term 'cycle of violence' stems from Lenore Walker's research with battered women. Walker argued that violent men repeatedly proceed through three stages in the violence cycle: the escalation, the violent incident, and the honeymoon. Each man

has his own unique cycle cued by specific environmental, psychological, and physical factors. The length of time to complete the cycle also is specific to each offender. Some men may not be violent for several months, slowly escalating toward violence. Over time, the frequency and severity of the violence are likely to increase, unless the cycle is broken by the offender seeking help. See Walker, 'The Cycle Theory of Violence,' in *The Battered Woman*, 55–70.

21 Purdy and Nickle, 'Practice Principles'
22 Watts and Courtois, 'Trends in the Treatment of Men Who Commit Violence against Women,' 252
23 For example, see Purdy and Nickle, 'Practice Principles,' and Edleson, 'Working with Men Who Batter.'
24 Knopp, Rosenberg, and Stevenson, *Report on the National Survey of Juvenile and Adult Sex-Offender Treatment Programs and Providers* (1986), 14
25 Nicholas Groth, 'Juvenile and Adult Sex Offenders: Creating a Community Response' (A training lecture sponsored by the Tompkins County Sexual Abuse Task Force, Ithaca, NY, 16–17 June 1983); cited in Knopp, *Retraining Adult Sex Offenders*, 26
26 Long, 'Working with Men Who Batter'
27 Knopp, *Retraining Adult Sex Offenders*, 27
28 Ellerby, *Winnipeg Sexual Offender Clinic: Outpatient Assessment and Treatment Manual*, 20–3
29 Knopp, *Retraining Adult Sex Offenders*, 28
30 Ellerby, *Sexual Offender Assessment and Treatment Manual*, 20–3
31 A. Nicholas Groth, 'Treatment of the Sexual Offender in a Correctional Institution,' in Greer and Stuart, eds., *The Sexual Aggressor*, 160–76
32 Knopp, *Retraining Adult Sex Offenders*, 28
33 Gondolf, *Men Who Batter*, 123–58
34 Ibid.
35 Ibid.
36 Ellerby, *Sexual Offender Assessment and Treatment Manual*, 20–3
37 Ibid.
38 Ibid.; also Gondolf, *Men Who Batter*, 123–58
39 Groth, 'Treatment of the Sexual Offender.' Although Groth wrote this list in reference to sexual offenders, the same issues exist for batterers. Admittedly, our society's stigma against sexual perpetrators generally is stronger than against batterers. But at the level of the individual offender, there is no guarantee that this generalization would still hold.
40 This is a revision of the list provided by Stordeur and Stille, which was directed specifically at batterers (see *Ending Men's Violence*, 74).

41 This list is based on Ellerby, *Sexual Offender Assessment and Treatment Manual*, 2.

42 Finn, 'Men's Domestic Violence Treatment Groups,' 89

43 Knopp, Rosenberg, and Stevenson, *Report on the National Survey of Juvenile and Adult Sex-Offender Treatment Programs and Providers* (1986), 12

44 For a discussion on some of the issues involved with court-mandated clients, see, among others, Browning, *Stopping the Violence*, 23, and Groth, 'Treatment of the Sexual Offender.'

45 Groth, 'Treatment of the Sexual Offender'

46 Knopp, *Retraining Adult Sex Offenders*, 65

47 Groth, personal communication with F.H. Knopp, 31 August 1984, cited in Knopp, *Retraining Adult Sex Offenders*, 17

48 I. Dreiblatt, taped on-site interview by F.H. Knopp, 1 October 1981, cited in Knopp, *Retraining Adult Sex Offenders*, 17

49 Groth, 'Treatment of the Sexual Offender,' 161–2

50 Purdy and Nickle, 'Practice Principles'

51 Reilly and Gruszki, 'A Structured Didactic Model for Men for Controlling Family Violence.' For more on the issues related to the gender of the cofacilitators, see Stordeur and Stille, *Ending Men's Violence*, 166–8.

52 Gondolf, *Men Who Batter*, 96–102; Saunders, 'Helping Husbands Who Batter'; and Romero and Williams, 'Recidivism Among Convicted Sex Offenders'

53 Most of the framework for this section is from Ellerby, *Sexual Offender Assessment and Treatment Manual* (1987), 7–9. The process outlined by Ellerby parallels, with minor variations, the work of others who work with batterers or sexual offenders. For example, see: Stordeur and Stille, *Ending Men's Violence*, 126–7; Knopp, *Retraining Adult Sex Offenders*, 30; and Long, 'Working with Men Who Batter,' 308. Long cites Gondolf and Russell, 'The Case against Anger Control for Batterers,' and Wormith and Borzecki, *A Survey of Treatment Programs for Sexual Offenders in Canada*, 13.

54 Sonkin and Durphy, *Learning to Live without Violence*, 71–86

55 Ellerby, *Sexual Offender Assessment and Treatment Manual*, 7–9; and Long, 'Working with Men Who Batter,' 308

56 Stordeur and Stille, *Ending Men's Violence*, 77–8. For more on the intentions and motivations of men seeking counselling for their violence see Myers and Gilbert, 'Wife Beaters' Group through a Women's Center.'

57 Purdy and Nickle, 'Practice Principles,' 114; and Kaye, 'The Battle against Men Who Batter'

58 Bernard and Bernard, 'The Abusive Male Seeking Treatment'

59 Barbaree and Marshall, 'Treatment of the Sexual Offender,' 30–6; and Langevin and Lang, 'Psychological Treatment of Pedophiles'

60 Knopp, *Retraining Adult Sex Offenders*, 76
61 Purdy and Nickle, 'Practice Principles,' 113–14
62 Knopp, *Retraining Adult Sex Offenders*, 76–9
63 Ibid., 68–9
64 Carol Bohmer, 'Legal and Ethical Issues in Mandatory Treatment: The Patient's Rights versus Society's Rights,' in Greer and Stuart, *The Sexual Aggressor*, 3–21
65 Stordeur and Stille, *Ending Men's Violence*, 271–2; and Chantal Goyette and Jocelyne Leblanc, 'A Sample of Community Based Programs,' *Vis-à-Vis*, 6/2 (Summer 1988), 7
66 Stordeur and Stille, *Ending Men's Violence*, 100
67 For more on what is involved in working with batterers in crisis, see ibid., 100-10.
68 Ellerby, *Sexual Offender Assessment and Treatment Manual*, 7–9
69 Long, 'Working with Men Who Batter'
70 See Purdy and Nickle, 'Practice Principles,' 122. Purdy and Nickle's group was composed of 5 men under court order to attend, and 165 who came 'voluntarily.'

   It is acknowledged that these figures will not hold for all group situations, but they do provide some indication of the magnitude of the problem with dropouts.
71 For more on the use and effectiveness of control planning with violent men see: Ellerby, *Sexual Offender Assessment and Treatment Manual*, 7–9; Currie, *Treatment Groups for Violent Men*, 4–6; Sonkin and Durphy, *Learning to Live without Violence*, 33–7; Long, 'Working with Men Who Batter,' 308; Browning, *Canadian Programmes for Assaultive Men*, 38; and Reilly and Gruszki, 'A Structured Didactic Model.'
72 For more information on the use and effectiveness of non-violence plans for sexual or physical offenders, see: Sonkin and Durphy, *Learning To Live Without Violence*, 33–7; RAVEN, *Safety Planning: RAVEN Phase One Membership Guidebook*; U.S., Department of Justice, Law Enforcement Assistance Administration, *Report on Men Who Batter* (1979); Edleson, 'Working with Men Who Batter'; Purdy and Nickle, 'Practice Principles,' 119; Reilly and Gruszki, 'A Structured Didactic Model'; Stordeur and Stille, *Ending Men's Violence*, 191–2; and Frank Tracy, Henry Donnelly, Leonard Morgenbesser, and Donald Macdonald, 'Program Evaluation: Recidivism,' in Greer and Stuart, *The Sexual Aggressor*, 198–213.
73 Ellerby, *Sexual Offender Assessment and Treatment Manual*, 7–9
74 For more information on these clinical measures, see Stordeur and Stille, *Ending Men's Violence*, 137–8; and Ellerby, *Sexual Offender Assessment and Treatment Manual*, 8–10.

75 M. Zuckerman, 'Physiological Measures of Sexual Arousal in Humans,' in N.S. Greenfield and R.A. Steinbach, eds., *Handbook of Psychophysiology* (New York: Holt, Rinehart & Winston 1972), 709–40, cited in Ellerby, *Sexual Offender Assessment and Treatment Manual*, 10

76 W.L. Marshall, H.E. Barbaree, and D. Christophe, 'Sexual Offenders against Female Children: Sexual Preferences for Age of Victims and Types of Behaviour,' *Canadian Journal of Behavioural Science*, 18 (1986), 424–39, cited in Barbaree and Marshall, 'Treatment of the Sexual Offender,' 34; Knopp, Rosenberg, and Stevenson, *Report on the National Survey* (1986), 14; and C.M. Earls and W.L. Marshall, 'The Current State of Technology in the Laboratory Assessment of Sexual Arousal Patterns,' in Greer and Stuart, *The Sexual Aggressor*, 198–213

77 Barbaree and Marshall, 'Treatment of the Sexual Offender,' 5. Barbaree and Marshall cite G. Abel, M. Mittleman, and J. Becker, *Clinical Criminology: The Assessment and Treatment of Criminal Behaviour* (Toronto: M & M Graphics 1985); and R. Laws (1981), personal communication cited in Knopp, *Retraining Adult Sex Offenders*. Abel, Mittleman, and Becker estimate it to be less than 25 per cent of offenders seen in an outpatient setting while Laws reports that no more than 10 per cent of incarcerated offenders exhibit serious mental disorders.

78 Wormith and Borzecki note that in Canada client motivation rather than risk, which seems to be the greater criterion in the United States, is the more significant determinant of getting into a sexual offender group (see *A Survey of Treatment Programs for Sexual Offenders in Canada*, 11).

79 Goyette and Leblanc, 'Sample of Community Based Programs,' 7

80 Pirog-Good and Stets-Kealey, 'Male Batterers and Battering Prevention Programs,' 10

81 Long, 'Working with Men Who Batter,' 308

82 For an excellent review of the issues involved in working with a batterer in crisis, see Stordeur and Stille, *Ending Men's Violence*, 99–124.

83 Browning, *Canadian Programmes for Assaultive Men*, 53

84 For more on the issue of informed consent, see Ellerby, *Sexual Offender Assessment and Treatment Manual*, 5, and Bohmer, 'Legal and Ethical Issues in Mandatory Treatment.'

85 Reilly and Gruszki, 'Structured Didactic Model'

86 Stordeur and Stille, *Ending Men's Violence*, 240–1

87 For more on each of these ten points see Knopp, *Retraining Adult Sex Offenders*, 48–58, and Ellerby, *Sexual Offender Assessment and Treatment Manual*, 35–7. For more on the importance of the socialization material in the work of groups with offenders, see: Groth, 'Treatment of the Sexual

Offender,' in Greer and Stuart, *The Sexual Aggressor*, 160–76; Stordeur and Stille, *Ending Men's Violence*, 245–53; Saunders, 'Helping Husbands Who Batter'; Currie, *Treatment Groups for Violent Men*, 6–9; Reilly and Gruszki, 'Structured Didactic Model'; Long, 'Working with Men Who Batter'; and Purdy and Nickle, 'Practice Principles,' 120.

88 Browning, *Canadian Programmes for Assaultive Men*, 38; and Purdy and Nickle, 'Practice Principles,' 119–20

89 Groth, 'Treatment of the Sexual Offender'; Edleson, 'Working with Men Who Batter'; and Sonkin and Durphy, *Learning to Live without Violence*, 87–99

90 Ellerby, *Sexual Offender Assessment and Treatment Manual*, 43–50; and Edleson, 'Working with Men Who Batter'

91 Edleson, 'Working with Men Who Batter'

92 Purdy and Nickle, 'Practice Principles,' 119–20

93 Sonkin and Durphy, *Learning to Live without Violence*, 100–15; Reilly and Gruszki, 'Structured Didactic Model'; Edleson, 'Working with Men Who Batter'; and Stordeur and Stille, *Ending Men's Violence*, 224–5

94 Ellerby, *Sexual Offender Assessment and Treatment Manual*, 43–50. For more on the importance of communication skill training, see U.S., Department of Justice, Law Enforcement Assistance Administration, *Report on Men who Batter* (1979).

95 Saunders, 'Helping Husbands Who Batter'

96 Quoted in Stordeur and Stille, *Ending Men's Violence*, 227. For Meichenbaum's original work see his *Cognitive-Behavior Modification* and *Stress Inoculation Training*.

97 Davis, Eshelman, and McKay, *The Relaxation and Stress Reduction Workbook*, 100

98 Ellerby, *Sexual Offender Assessment and Treatment Manual*, 32–4

99 For more on the importance of cognitive restructuring to social constructionist groups, see: Edleson, 'Working with Men Who Batter'; Sonkin and Durphy, *Learning to Live without Violence*, 39–46; U.S., Department of Justice, Law Enforcement Assistance Administration, *Report on Men Who Batter* (1979); Barbaree and Marshall, 'Treatment of the Sexual Offender,' 33; Stordeur and Stille, *Ending Men's Violence*, 227–31; Browning, *Canadian Programmes for Assaultive Men*, 38; Saunders, 'Helping Husbands Who Batter'; Novaco, 'Stress Inoculation'; and Raymond Novaco, 'Anger and Coping with Stress,' in Y. Foreyt and D. Rathjen, eds., *Cognitive Behavior Therapy: Research and Application* (New York: Plenum 1978), 135–62.

100 Barbaree and Marshall, 'Treatment of the Sexual Offender,' 40–4

101 For more information on the use of aversion therapies, see Knopp, *Retraining Adult Sex Offenders*, 40–4; and Quinsey and Marshall, 'Procedures for Reducing Inappropriate Sexual Arousal: An Evaluation Review,' in Greer and Stuart, *The Sexual Aggressor*, 267–89.

102 Wormith and Borzecki, *Survey of Treatment Programs*, 20; and Bohmer, 'Legal and Ethical Issues in Mandatory Treatment'

103 Stordeur and Stille, *Ending Men's Violence*, 220–4; S.M. Levin, S.M. Barry, S. Gambaro, L. Wolfinsohn, and A. Smith, 'Variations of Covert Sensitization in the Treatment of Pedophilic Behaviour: A Case Study,' *Journal of Consulting and Clinical Psychology*, 5 (1977), 896–907, cited in Ellerby, *Winnipeg Sexual Offender Clinic: Outpatient Assessment and Treatment Manual*, 27; and Marshall, 'Procedures for Reducing Inappropriate Sexual Arousal: An Evaluation Review,' in Greer and Stuart, *The Sexual Aggressor*, 267–89

104 U.S., Department of Justice, Law Enforcement Assistance Administration, *Report on Men Who Batter*

105 Ellerby, *Sexual Offender Assessment and Treatment Manual*, 51–4

106 Groth, 'Treatment of the Sexual Offender'

107 C.G. Abel, 'Surveillance Groups' (Paper presented at the annual meeting of the ABTSA in Newport, Oregon, May 1987); Barbaree and Marshall, 'Treatment of the Sexual Offender,' 47–9

108 Sonkin, 'Therapists' Duty to Warn and Protect,' *Victims and Violence*, 1/1 (1986), 7–22; and Daniel Sonkin, 'The Assessment of Court-Mandated Batterers,' in Sonkin, ed., *Domestic Violence on Trial*, cited in Stordeur and Stille, *Ending Men's Violence*, 152–3

109 Stordeur and Stille, *Ending Men's Violence* (1989)

110 Groth, 'Treatment of the Sexual Offender,' 160–72. One study with incarcerated sex offenders has shown the importance of women's studies curricula in changing offenders' traditional gender beliefs. See Holly Devor, 'Teaching Women's Studies to Convicted Sex Offenders' (Burnaby, BC: Women's Studies Department, Simon Fraser University, unpublished report, 1987).

111 Saunders, 'Helping Husbands Who Batter'

112 For more on the use of relaxation therapies with sexual and physical offenders, see: Stordeur and Stille, *Ending Men's Violence*, 203–4, 231–3; U.S., Department of Justice, Law Enforcement Assistance Administration, *Report on Men Who Batter* (1979); Browning, *Canadian Programmes for Assaultive Men*, 38; Sonkin and Durphy, *Learning to Live without Violence*, 59–70; and Rosen and Fracher, 'Tension-Reduction Training in the Treatment of Compulsive Sex Offenders,' in Greer and Stuart, *The Sexual Aggressor*, 144–59.

113 Stordeur and Stille have an excellent section on the use of the man's most violent incident (*Ending Men's Violence*, 211–17).

114 Ibid.

115 Browning, *Canadian Programmes for Assaultive Men*, vii; and Kaye, 'Battle against Men Who Batter'

116 Wormith and Borzecki, *Survey of Treatment Programs for Sexual Offenders in Canada*, 5; and Canada, Working Group, Sex Offender Treatment Review, *The Management and Treatment of Sex Offenders: Report*, 38–9

117 Tom Kaczmarz, RAVEN, St Louis, MO; telephone interview with the author, 14 August 1990

118 See RAVEN, *The Ending Men's Violence National Referral Directory* (1987).

119 Tom Kaczmarz interview, 14 August 1990. Tom obtained the 307 figure from the National Domestic Violence Hotline.

120 Knopp, *Retraining Adult Sex Offenders* (1984), cited in Barbaree and Marshall, 'Treatment of the Sexual Offender,' 12

121 Knopp, Rosenberg, and Stevens, *Report on the Nationwide Survey of Juvenile and Adult Sex-Offender Treatment Programs and Providers*, 12

122 Pirog-Good and Stets-Kealey, 'Male Batterers and Battering Prevention Programs,' 9

123 Sonkin, Martin, and Walker, *The Male Batterer*, cited in Stordeur and Stille, *Ending Men's Violence*, 234. Sonkin and Martin were referring to the population of men who batter.

124 Wormith and Borzecki, *A Survey of Treatment Programs for Sexual Offenders*, 5

125 Kaye, 'The Battle against Men Who Batter'

126 Pirog-Good and Stets-Kealey, 'Male Batterers and Battering Prevention Programs'

127 This was concluded from Knopp's 1984 survey of 197 service programs for sexual offenders. See Knopp, *Retraining Adult Sex Offenders* (1984), cited in Barbaree and Marshall, 'Treatment of the Sexual Offender,' 12.

128 The Canadian Council on Social Development published a synopsis of its study in its newsletter; see Jurgen Dankwort, 'Programmes for Men Who Batter: A Snapshot,' *Vis-à-Vis: A National Newsletter on Family Violence*, 6/2 (Summer 1988). *Vis-à-Vis* noted that time and money did not permit them to conduct a detailed analysis, or to publish their results.

129 Pirog-Good and Stets-Keeley, 'Male Batterers and Battering Prevention Programs.' Pirog-Good and Stets-Kealey contacted 293 programs, and received a response from 59. They found that 98 of the 293 either no longer existed or had not provided services for batterers. Of the remaining 136 programs that had not responded, 20 per cent were randomly

selected and contacted by phone to determine their failure to respond. It was found that 78 per cent of the non-respondents do not currently provide services. The remaining 22 per cent did have programs but reported they did not respond because they had misplaced the survey, did not receive it, or had insufficient resources to respond. Pirog-Good and Stets-Kealey extrapolated from the 78 per cent of the non-respondents that they do not provide services for batterers and concluded that the total number of battering programs was approximately 89. Thus they had a 66 per cent response rate. They state that the 59 responses represent the largest number of respondents to such a survey to date.

130 Finn, 'Men's Domestic Violence Treatment Groups,' 89
131 Buckley, Miller, and Rolfe, 'A Windsor Model'
132 Bern and Bern, 'A Group Program for Men Who Commit Violence towards Their Wives'
133 Barbaree and Marshall, 'Treatment of the Sexual Offender,' 11–12
134 Pirog-Good and Stets-Kealey, 'Male Batterers and Battering Prevention Programs'
135 For more information on the cycle theory of violence see Walker, 'The Cycle Theory of Violence,' in Walker, *The Battered Woman*, 55–70. For a summary of Walker's cycle see above, this chapter, note 20.
136 Dankwort, 'Programs for Men Who Batter,' 1–3
137 Pirog-Good and Stets-Kealey, 'Male Batterers and Battering Prevention Programs,' 10. For more on the paucity of follow-up evaluations, see Finn, 'Men's Domestic Violence Treatment Groups.'
138 Wormith and Borzecki, *A Survey of Treatment Programs for Sexual Offenders*, 24
139 See, for example, Browning, *Canadian Programmes for Assaultive Men*, 45, and McEvoy, 'Men against Battering.'
140 Browning, *Canadian Programmes for Assaultive Men*, 53
141 Knopp, *Retraining Adult Sex Offenders*, 58–9
142 Dankwort, 'Programs for Men Who Batter,' 1–3; Pirog-Good and Stets-Kealey, 'Male Batterers and Battering Prevention Programs,' 10
143 Pirog-Good and Stets-Kealey, 'Male Batterers and Battering Prevention Programs,' 9; and Finn, 'Men's Domestic Violence Treatment Groups,' 90
144 Ibid.
145 Goyette and Leblanc, 'A Sample of Community Based Programs,' 7
146 Stordeur and Stille, *Ending Men's Violence*, 271–2
147 Pirog-Good and Stets-Kealey, 'Male Batterers and Battering Prevention Programs,' 9
148 Purdy and Nickle, 'Practice Principles,' 122

149 Pirog-Good and Stets-Kealey, 'Male Batterers and Battering Prevention Programs'
150 Ibid.
151 Robert Longo, 'Administering a Comprehensive Sexual Aggressive Treatment Program in a Maximum Security Setting,' in Greer and Stuart, *The Sexual Aggressor*, 177–97
152 The statement was made by Orville Pung, Minnesota's Commissioner of Corrections, quoted in M. Voss, 'Promising Results Seen in Minnesota Sex Offender Program,' *Des Moines Register*, 19 Sept 1983, and quoted in Knopp, *Retraining Adult Sex Offenders*, 22.
153 Edleson et al., 'Group Treatment for Men Who Batter.' Edleson et al. operationally defined physical abuse as 'the use by a man of his hands, feet, or other parts of his body to inflict physical damage or pain on his partner, including sexual abuse' (p. 20). Offender self-reports were the basis for the program evaluation. Reliability checks with the female partner were not carried out to protect 'confidentiality and fears that the women might be in danger of additional abuse if they supplied information that contradicted their partner's reports' (p. 20).
154 Purdy and Nickle, 'Practice Principles,' 120–2
155 Pirog-Good and Stets-Kealey, 'Male Batterers and Battering Prevention Programs,' 10–11
156 McEvoy, 'Men against Battering'
157 Barbaree and Marshall, 'Treatment of the Sexual Offender,' 26
158 W.E. Prendergast, Jr., *ROARE: Re-education of Attitudes (and) Repressed Emotions* (Avenel, NJ: Adult Diagnostic and Treatment Center Intensive Group Therapy Program 1978), cited in Barbaree and Marshall, 'Treatment of the Sexual Offender,' 25
159 M. Saylor, 'A Guided Self-Help Approach to Treatment of the Habitual Sexual Offender' (Paper presented at the 12th Cropwood Conference, Cambridge, England, 1979), cited in Barbaree and Marshall, 'Treatment of the Sexual Offender,' 26
160 For information on some of the issues involved in establishing a reputable evaluation program, see Tracy, Donnelly, Morgenbesser, and Macdonald, 'Program Evaluation: Recidivism Research Involving Sex Offenders,' in Greer and Stuart, *The Sexual Aggressor*, 198–213.
161 G.K. Sturup, 'Castration: The Total Treatment,' in Resnik and Wolfgang, eds., *Sexual Behaviour*, 361–82, cited in Barbaree and Marshall, 'Treatment of the Sexual Offender,' 9
162 T.C.N. Gibbens, K.L. Soothill, and C.K. Way, 'Sex Offenses against Young Girls: A Long-Term Record Study,' *Psychological Medicine*, 11 (1981),

351–7, cited in Barbaree and Marshall, 'Treatment of the Sexual Offender,' 9

163 Barbaree and Marshall, 'Treatment of the Sexual Offender,' 9

164 Ibid., 10

165 Ibid. The following is one example of a poor research design. Alan Rosenbaum reviewed a batterers' program that provides six sessions (1.5 hours per session). Six months after treatment, and every three months thereafter for two years, the men were contacted over the phone by a research assistant. It does not seem too cynical to conclude that, in such a context, it would be very easy for group members to lie or minimize the extent of their violence. See Rosenbaum, 'Group Treatment for Abusive Men.'

166 An example of this is Jerry Finn's review of North Carolina battering programs. He monitored the number of cases that returned to court on domestic abuse charges and used this to determine his success rate. Not surprisingly, this method resulted in an 85 per cent success rate. See Finn, 'Men's Domestic Violence Treatment Groups.'

   For more on the difficulty of relying on conviction reports, and their statistical loss of many offenders, see Menachem Amir, *Patterns in Forcible Rape* (New York: Harcourt, Brace, and World 1971), and Groth, Longo, and McFaddin, 'Undetected Recidivism among Rapists and Child Molesters,' cited in Romero and Williams, 'Recidivism among Convicted Sex Offenders.'

167 Barbaree and Marshall, 'Treatment of the Sexual Offender,' 8

168 Knopp, *Retraining Adult Sex Offenders*, 65

169 McEvoy, 'Men against Battering'

170 Barbaree and Marshall, 'Treatment of the Sexual Offender,' 9

171 Romero and Williams, in 'Recidivism among Convicted Sex Offenders,' for example, contend that five years is a minimum length of time for assessing recidivism among sexual offenders.

172 Rick Goodwin, 'Tales from the Front Lines,' *Vis-à-Vis*, 6/2 (Summer 1988), 5, 13

173 Pirog-Good and Stets-Kealey, 'Male Batterers and Battering Prevention Programs,' 10

174 Browning, *Canadian Programmes for Assaultive Men*, 50

175 Pirog-Good and Stets-Kealey, 'Male Batterers and Battering Prevention Programs,' 12; and Browning, *Canadian Programmes for Assaultive Men*, 50.

   While his research does not constitute a random sample of offender treatment programs, the present author contacted seven North American groups and found that, on average, it would take two weeks before an offender would be seen for an intake assessment and up to 16 weeks (four months) before he was admitted for group work. The contacts were with: Theresa Kennedy, Domestic Abuse Project, Minneapolis (2 and 12 weeks), 4 May 1990 telephone interview; Rob Gallup, director of Amend, Denver (0 and 4 weeks), 4 May 1990 telephone interview; Carol Saxby, Changing Ways, London (2 and 6 weeks), 4 May 1990 telephone interview; Arlene Thompson, Hiatus House, Windsor (2 and 10 weeks), 4 May 1990 telephone interview; Ron Schwartz, Evolve, Winnipeg (2 and 20 weeks), 7 May 1990 telephone interview; David Rice-Lampert, Community and Youth Corrections, Department of Justice, Province of Manitoba (0 and 36 weeks), 23 April 1990 telephone interview; and Romeo Beatch, NWT Family Counselling Service, Yellowknife (8 and 24 weeks), 15 May 1990 telephone interview.

    The long-waiting lists have significant effects. A voluntary client with low motivation is unlikely to return for treatment. While many clinicians argue there is merit in exposing all offenders – even those with low motivation – to the program material, the reality, as indicated by a Canadian survey of sex offender programs, is that programs are compelled to 'admit only those offenders showing motivation to change.' (Wormith and Borzecki, *A Survey of Treatment Programs for Sexual Offenders*, 9.)

176 McEvoy, 'Men against Battering'
177 For more on the ideological dilemmas the women's movement faces in working with men, see Schechter, *Women and Male Violence*, 258–67.
178 Telephone interview with Elaine Scott, director of the Family Violence Prevention Division, Health and Welfare Canada, November 1989
179 McEvoy, 'Men against Battering'
180 Chantal Goyette and Jocelyne Leblanc, 'Government Announces Family Violence Initiative,' *Vis-à-Vis*, 6/2 (Summer 1988), 6; Kaye, 'The Battle against Men Who Batter'; and 'Federal Government Announces New Family Violence Initiatives,' *Government of Canada News Release*, 7 June 1988
181 Canadian Press, 'Government's Commitment on Fighting Violence Questioned,' *Winnipeg Free Press*, 22 June 1989, 20
182 Browning, *Canadian Programmes for Assaultive Men*, vii
183 Ibid., 50
184 Chantal Goyette, Jocelyne LeBlanc, and Nahid Faghfoury, 'Exploring Alternatives to Sentencing in Wife Assault Cases,' *Vis-à-Vis*, 7/3 (Fall 1989), 10
185 Finn, 'Men's Domestic Violence Treatment Groups'
186 After significant lobbying by numerous grass-roots organizations, the state of Colorado passed a series of standards, which went into effect 1 April 1990, for the treatment of male physical offenders. See Colorado, State Committee on Domestic Violence, 'Colorado Standards for the

Treatment of Domestic Violence Perpetrators: April 1, 1990'; a copy of the report was provided to the author by Rob Gallup, director of Amend, Denver.

187 G.D. Robin, 'Forcible Rape: Institutionalized Sexism in the Criminal Justice System,' *Crime and Delinquency*, 23/2 (1977), 136–53, quoted in Galvin and Polk, 'Attrition in Case Processing'

188 Janet Bagnall, 'Rape Victims Find Judicial System Less Than Humane,' *Winnipeg Free Press*, 11 April 1990, 32

189 Canadian Press, 'Shirt Provoked Wife Beater, Judge Says,' *Winnipeg Free Press*, 15 July 1990, 6

190 Currie, *The Abusive Husband*, 7

191 Robert Freeman-Longo, taped on-site interview by F.K. Knopp, 17 October 1983, quoted in Knopp, *Retraining Adult Sex Offenders*, 15–16

192 A. Nicholas Groth, taped on-site interview by F.K. Knopp, and Knopp, 'Treatment of the Sexual Offender in a Correctional Institution,' in Greer and Stuart, *The Sexual Aggressor*, 160–76

193 Canadian Press, 'Wife-Beating N.S. Judge Suspended as MLAs Demand Review of Fitness for Bench,' *Winnipeg Free Press*, 22 June 1989, 16

194 Canada, Health and Welfare Canada, Family Violence Prevention Division, *Wife Battering and the Web of Hope*, 49; and David Rice-Lampert, Probation Officer, Community and Youth Corrections, Department of Justice, Province of Manitoba

195 Pirog-Good and Stets-Kealey, 'Male Batterers and Battering Prevention Programs,' 10–11

196 Goyette, LeBlanc, and Faghfoury, 'Exploring Alternatives to Sentencing in Wife Assault Cases,' 10

197 Brickman and Briere, 'Incidence of Rape and Sexual Assault in an Urban Canadian Population'

198 Bell, 'The Victim-Offender Relationship'

199 Bell, 'The Police Response to Domestic Violence'

200 In Canada, assault is now an offence, under sections 244 and 245 of the Criminal Code, and either the victim or the police can lay charges. See Kaye, 'The Battle against Men Who Batter,' and Ursel and Farough, 'The Legal and Public Response to the New Wife Abuse Directive in Manitoba.'

201 Sherman and Berk, 'The Specific Deterrent Effects of Arrest for Domestic Assault'

202 Chantal Goyette and Nahid Faghfoury, 'A Window on Family Violence in Canada: Results of *Vis-à-Vis* National Survey,' *Vis-à-Vis*, 7/3 (Fall 1989), 8–9

203 Russell, *Sexual Exploitation*, 101
204 For more on the 'hidden rapist,' see Watts and Courtois, 'Trends in the Treatment of Men Who Commit Violence against Women.'
205 McEvoy quoting Joan Gullen; see McEvoy, 'Men against Battering.'
206 Knopp, *Retraining Adult Sex Offenders*, xiii
207 Kaye, 'The Battle against Men Who Batter'
208 Hitchcock and Young, 'Prevention of Sexual Assault'; Brisken and Gary, 'Sexual Assault Programming for College Students'; and Roark, 'Preventing Violence on College Campuses'
209 Rowsey, Hall, and Coan, 'Rural Knowledge and Attitudes about Sexual Assault.'
    Three program examples include: Py Bateman, *Acquaintance Rape: Awareness and Prevention*, directed towards teenagers; Mark Stevens and Randy Bebhardt, *Rape Education for Men: Curriculum Guide* (the Ohio State University Rape Education and Prevention Program); and Mark Willmarth, *Not for Women Only!: A Rape Awareness Program for Men*.
210 Roark, 'Preventing Violence on College Campuses'
211 For more on the statistics, see above, chapter 1.
212 For more on the myths of sexual assault, see above, chapter 3.
213 For more on how men are socialized to be violent, see above, chapter 3.
214 For more on control planning, see this chapter, pp. 147–50 and 161–2.
215 Roark, 'Preventing Violence on College Campuses'
216 Drysdale, 'Claiming Their Rights'
217 Rick Goodwin, 'Tales from the Front Lines,' *Vis-à-Vis*, 6/2 (Summer 1988), 5, 13
218 McEvoy, 'Men against Battering'

Chapter 6

1 The concept of hegemonic masculinity, introduced above in chapter 3, involves examining the social and political forces within specific historic periods which afford greater social, political, and economic power to specific varieties of masculinity, while reducing the power of men who adopt other masculinities. Building upon this concept, Kenneth Clatterbaugh uses the term masculinist 'to apply to any point of view that offers an analysis of the social reality of [North] American men and offers an agenda for them' (Kenneth Clatterbaugh, 'Masculinist Perspectives,' *Changing Men*, 20 [Winter–Spring 1989], 4). Thus there can be conservative, gay, socialist, and other masculinists.
2 Ibid., 4–6
3 Ibid.

4 Klatch, *Women of the New Right*
5 Ibid., 120–1; and Ronald Toth, 'The Plain Truth about Abortion: Why So Little Understood?' *Plain Truth*, 50/4 (May 1985), 2–4, 42–3
6 Belsky and Steinberg, 'The Effects of Day Care.' While encouraging additional research, Belsky and Steinberg note that 'experience in high-quality center-based day care (1) has neither salutary nor deleterious effects upon the intellectual development of the child, (2) is not disruptive of the child's emotional bond with his[/her] mother, and (3) increases the degree to which the child interacts, both positively and negatively, with peers' (577).
7 Canadian statistics indicate that in 1986, 'compared with childless couples, families with one or two children were twice as likely to be poor, while families with three children or more were almost three times as likely to be poor.' See 'CCSD Joins in Call for an End to Child Poverty,' *Social Development Overview: Canadian Council of Social Development*, 6/2 (Winter 1989), 1.
8 Toth, 'The Plain Truth about Abortion,' 42–3
9 Rhonda Copelon and Kathryn Kolbert, 'Imperfect Justice,' *Ms.*, 18/1–2 (July–Aug 1989), 42
10 A 71 per cent figure was cited by Gloria Steinem, 'A Basic Human Right,' *Ms.*, 18/1–2 (July–Aug 1989), 39–41.
   Louis Harris pollsters state that 61 per cent of Americans support the original *Roe vs. Wade* decision, which gave American women the right to abortion. See 'The Facts of Life,' *Psychology Today*, 23/10 (Oct 1984), 10.
   A Gallup poll conducted in October 1988 revealed that 71.2 per cent of Canadians agree that 'abortion is a medical decision that should rest with the woman in consultation with her doctor.' Canadian Abortion Rights Action League (CARAL), 'Press Release: Vast Majority of Canadians Are Pro-choice.' *CARAL Press Release* (Toronto: CARAL Press, 19–20 Oct 1988).
11 Gloria Steinem, 'A Basic Human Right,' 40. The limits on *Roe vs. Wade* were further extended in 1977. Congressman Henry Hyde of Illinois introduced an amendment to the federal department of Health, Education and Welfare budget appropriation bill to slash state funding for abortions. After the amendment passed in 1978, Medicaid abortions dropped 96 per cent from 250,000 to 2,421. See Childbirth by Choice Trust, *Abortion in Law and History*, 11.
12 Steinem, 'A Basic Human Right,' 40
13 Copelon and Kolbert, 'Imperfect Justice,' 42
14 Ibid.
15 Peggy Simpson, 'The Political Arena,' *Ms.*, 18/1–2 (July-Aug 1989), 46

16 Steinem, 'A Basic Human Right,' 40–1
17 Simpson, 'The Political Arena,' 46; and Steinem, 'A Basic Human Right,' 40–1
18 Ibid. Approximately 82 per cent of American abortions are performed in free-standing clinics. Childbirth by Choice Trust, 'Facts on Abortion,' booklet (Toronto, Mar 1989), 3
19 Ann McDaniel, 'The Future of Abortion,' *Newsweek*, 17 July 1989, 14
20 Quoted in Eloise Salholz et al., 'Voting in Curbs and Confusion,' *Newsweek*, 17 July 1989, 18.
21 Kathryn Kolbert and Julie Mertus, 'Pro-Choice: Keeping the Pressure On,' *Ms.*, 1/4 (Jan–Feb 1991), 92
22 Ibid.; see also McDaniel, 'The Future of Abortion,' 14; Mary Suh, '*Webster* – One Year and Many Battles Later,' *Ms.*, July–Aug 1990, 87; and George Church, 'Five Political Hot Spots,' *Time*, 17 July 1989, 64.
23 Margaret Carlson and Steven Holmes, 'The Battle over Abortion,' *Time*, 134 (17 July 1989), 62–3
24 Salholz et al., 'Voting in Curbs,' 17
25 Rochelle Sharpe, 'She Died Because of a Law: Mother Denounces Parental Consent,' *Ms.*, 1/1 (July–Aug 1990), 80–1
26 Salholz et al., 'Voting in Curbs,' 19–20
27 Linda Greenhouse, 'Five Justices Uphold US Rule Curbing Abortion Advice: Clinic Aid at Issue,' *New York Times*, 24 May 1991, A1, A18; and Planned Parenthood Federation of America, *Title X*
28 Ibid.
29 Greenhouse, 'Five Justices Uphold US Rule,' and Nadine Brozan, 'Some Clinics Plan to Advise and Forgo Aid,' *New York Times*, 24 May 1991, A1, A18
30 Greenhouse, 'Five Justices Uphold US Rule,' and Philip Hilts, 'Clinics Seek to Overturn Rule on Abortion Advice,' *New York Times*, 25 May 1991, 9
31 Suh, '*Webster* – One Year and Many Battles Later,' 87
32 Childbirth by Choice Trust, *Abortion in Law and History*, 12–13; and Canada, Minister of Justice and Attorney General of Canada, *Justice Information: New Abortion Legislation Background Information* (Ottawa, 3 Nov 1989)
33 *Justice Information*
34 Donn Downey, 'Dodd Wins Bid to Have Abortion,' *Globe and Mail*, 12 July 1989, A1
35 Ibid.
36 D'Arcy Jewish, 'Abortion on Trial,' *Maclean's*, 102/31 (31 July 1989), 15
37 Jewish, 'Abortion on Trial,' 14–17; Bruce Wallace and Lisa Van Dusen, 'Abortion Agony,' *Maclean's*, 102/34 (21 Aug 1989), 12–14; and Alberto

Manguel, 'Chantale Daigle,' *Chatelaine*, 63/1 (Jan 1990), 38–41, 113–14
38 Men for Women's Choice, 'Five Reasons Why the Proposed Abortion Law Is No Compromise' (Toronto: Men for Women's Choice, mailing circular, Jan 1990), 1.
   In 1982, the Canadian physician labour force was 86 per cent male. See Woodward and Adams, 'Physician Resource Databank.'
39 Liberal Senator Stanley Haidasz, quoted in Geoffrey York, 'Senators Kill Abortion Bill with Tied Vote,' *Globe and Mail*, 1 Feb 1991, A1
40 Ibid.
41 Ron Schwartz, counsellor, Men's Program, Evolve, a Program of Klinic Community Health Centre, Winnipeg; telephone interview with the author, 5 June 1990
42 Clatterbaugh, 'Masculinist Perspectives,' 4
43 For more on the German National Socialist (Nazi) party's ideology and portrayal of masculinity and femininity, see, among others, Berthold Hinz, *Art in the Third Reich* (New York: Pantheon 1979), 110–76.
44 Goldberg, *The Inevitability of Patriarchy*, 194–5, cited in Clatterbaugh, 'Masculinist Perspectives,' 4–6
45 Goldberg, *The Inevitability of Patriarchy*, 194
46 Edward O. Wilson, *On Human Nature* (1979), cited in Clatterbaugh, 'Masculinist Perspectives,' 4–6
47 Crawford, *Thunder on the Right*
48 Ibid.
49 Barbara Ehrenreich, 'A Feminist's View of the New Man,' in Kimmel and Messner, eds., *Men's Lives*, 34–43
50 Interrante, 'Dancing along the Precipice: The Men's Movement in the 80's,' part I, *M.: Gentle Men for Gender Justice*, 9 (Summer–Fall 1982), 3–6, 20–1, part II, *M.: Gentle Men for Gender Justice*, 10 (Spring 1983), 3–6, 32; Lyttelton, 'Men's Liberation, Men against Sexism and Major Dividing Lines'; Lewis, 'Men's Liberation and the Men's Movement'
51 Ibid.
52 Ibid.
53 Ibid.
54 Clatterbaugh, 'Masculinist Perspectives,' 4; Jim Ptacek, 'Herb Goldberg and the Politics of "Free Men",' *M.: Gentle Men for Gender Justice*, 2 (Spring 1980), 10–11; and Robert Brannon, 'Are the "Free Men" a Faction of Our Movement?' *M.: Gentle Men for Gender Justice*, 7 (Winter 1981–2), 14–15, 30–2
55 Ibid.
56 Baumli, ed., *Men Freeing Men*

57 See, among others, Goldberg, *The Hazards of Being Male*.
58 Robert A. Sides, 'Sexual Anger with Women: Male Anger and Male Sexuality,' in Baumli, *Men Freeing Men*, 45
59 David Morrow, 'You Pay for Every Piece You Get,' in Baumli, *Men Freeing Men*, 49
60 Ibid.
61 Ibid.
62 See, for example, Goldberg, *The Hazards of Being Male*, *The New Male*, and *The New Male-Female Relationship*.
63 Sides, 'Women and Pornography,' in Baumli, *Men Freeing Men*, 53
64 Eugene Martin, 'Something about Pornography,' in Baumli, *Men Freeing Men*, 56–7
65 Baumli, 'A Reply to Eugene Martin's "Something about Pornography",' in *Men Freeing Men*, 57–9
66 Crean, *In the Name of the Fathers*, 7. For an excellent critique of the selective manner in which many men have become involved in parenting, see Segal, *Slow Motion*, 26–59.
67 See Baumli, *Men Freeing Men*, chapter 9, 'When Daddy Can't Be Daddy Anymore,' 163–202.
68 Crean, *In The Name of the Fathers*, 5–8
69 Ibid., 98–140
70 Ibid., 102
71 Ibid.
72 Ibid., 107
73 Ibid., 108
74 Ibid., 109–111
75 Ibid.; Crean was quoting Ron Sauvé of Fathers for Justice.
76 Ibid., 102
77 Suzanne Steinmetz, 'Battered Husbands: A Historical and Cross-Cultural Study,' in Baumli, *Men Freeing Men*, 207
78 *Transitions*, The Coalition of Free Men, 7/4 (July–Aug 1987)
79 Steinmetz, 'Violence and the Male Victim,' in Baumli, *Men Freeing Men*, 205–6. In the process of exploring the extent to which men are abused, another important point emerges from Steinmetz's statistics. When one combines the statistics on murder, rape, robbery, and aggravated assault, it is evident that men most need to fear other men.
80 Ptacek, 'Herb Goldberg and the Politics of "Free Men"'; and Brannon, 'Are the "Free Men" a Faction of Our Movement?'
81 The information on the Montreal massacre was gathered from a number of sources. See, among others: Canadian Press and Staff, 'Man in

Montreal Kills 14 Women,' *Globe and Mail*, 7 Dec 1989, A1–A2; Canadian Press, 'Terrified Students Describe Rampage by Man with Rifle,' *Globe and Mail*, 7 Dec 1989, A9; Emil Sher, 'Speaking about the Unspeakable,' *Globe and Mail*, 8 Dec 1989, A7; Victor Malarek, 'Killer's Note Blames Feminists,' *Globe and Mail*, 8 Dec 1989, A1–A2; Stevie Cameron, 'Violence against Women Assailed,' *Globe and Mail*, 8 Dec 1989, A1, A4; Brian Bergman et al., 'Sisterhood of Fear and Fury,' *Maclean's*, 102/51 (18 Dec 1989), 18–19; Barry Came et al., 'Montreal Massacre,' *Maclean's*, 102/51 (18 Dec 1989), 14–17; and Bruce Wallace et al., 'The Making of a Mass Killer: A Youth's Hidden Rage at Women, *Maclean's*, 102/15 (18 Dec 1989), 22.

82 Lynne Ainsworth, 'Male Students Mock Anti-Rape Campaign,' *Toronto Star*, 2 Nov 1989, A1, A36

83 Karen Barrett, 'Date Rape: A Campus Epidemic?' *Ms.*, Sept 1982, 50–1, 130

84 The Queen's Journal, 'Queen's Scandal Continues,' *Manitoban*, 77/17 (29 Nov 1989), 3

85 Dexter Guerrieri, 'Pornography and Silent Men,' *Changing Men*, 15 (Fall 1985), 9–10; and Kivel, 'The Fear of Men,' *Changing Men*, 17 (Winter 1986), 19

86 The Queen's Journal, 'Queen's Scandal Continues'

87 See, among others: Harrison, 'Warning'; Meinecke, 'Socialized to Die Younger?'; John Chapman, 'Increased Male Mortality and Male Roles in Industrial Societies,' *M.: Gentle Men for Gender Justice*, 7 (Winter 1981–2), 7–8; Skord and Schumacher, 'Masculinity as a Handicapping Condition'; Diagram Group, *Man's Body*; Grimm and Yarnold, 'Sex Typing and the Coronary-Prone Behavior Pattern'; Philip Korman, 'Hazards in the Workplace,' *Changing Men*, 16 (Summer 1986), 11–14, 43; and J. Cheyenne, 'Heart Failure,' *Changing Men*, 16 (Summer 1986), 25–6.

88 David Burns, *Feeling Good: The New Mood Therapy* (New York: New American Library 1981)

89 Llewellyn-Jones, *Everyman*, 102–24

90 Alex Comfort, ed., *The Joy of Sex: A Gourmet Guide to Lovemaking* (New York: Simon and Schuster 1972), back cover

91 Ibid., 248

92 See, among others: Greenberg, *The Birth of a Father*; Singer, Shechtman, and Singer, *Real Men Enjoy Their Kids*; Sandy Morgan, 'Walk a Mile in My Shoes: When Daddy Stays Home,' *Great Expectations*, 18/4 (July 1989), 26–9, 32; Lewis Rich-Shea, 'The Co-Parenting Father,' *Gentle Men for Gender Justice*, 12 (Spring–Summer 1984), 16–18; Hanson, 'Father/Child Relationships: Beyond "Kramer vs. Kramer"'; Ned O'Malia, 'Charlie's

Shower – Celebrating the Expectant Father,' *Ms.*, 10/8 (Feb 1982), 48–9;
Kyle Pruett, 'Do Dads Make Good Moms?' *Chatelaine*, July 1987, 40, 68–9;
George James, 'You've Come a Long Way, Dad: Father and the New-
born,' *Great Expectations*, 16/3 (July 1987), 49–50; and Ari Korpivaara,
'Play Groups for Dads,' *Ms.*, 10/8 (Feb 1982), 52–4.

93 Letty Cottin Pogrebin, 'Big Changes in Parenting: Are Men Discovering
the Joys of Parenthood?' *Ms.*, 10/8 (Feb 1982), 41–6; and Segal, *Slow
Motion*, 26–59. Joseph Pleck, an American sociologist, published *Working
Wives, Working Children* in 1985. He found that men with wives who
worked outside of the home did only 30 to 35 per cent of the family work.
Men whose wives did not work outside of the home did just 20 per cent.
Pleck was cited in Haynes, 'Who Is He.'

94 See, for example: Feigan Fasteau, *The Male Machine*; Dubbert, *A Man's
Place*; Stearns, *Be a Man! Males in Modern Society*; Nichols, *Men's Liber-
ation*; Gerzon, *A Choice of Heroes*; Garfinkel, *In a Man's World*; Druck and
Simmons, *The Secrets Men Keep*; and O'Neil, 'Male Sex Role Conflicts,
Sexism, and Masculinity.'

95 Clatterbaugh, 'Masculinist Perspectives'

96 Examples of Bly's work include: 'What Men Really Want,' *New Age*, May
1982; *A Little Book on the Human Shadow* (Memphis, TN: Raccoon Books
1986); *The Selected Poems* (New York: Harper and Row 1986); and *Iron
John: A Book about Men* (Reading, MA: Addison-Wesley 1990).

97 Christopher Burant, 'Of Wild Men and Warriors,' *Changing Men*, 19
(Spring–Summer 1988), 7–9, 46

98 See John Lee, *The Flying Boy: Healing the Wounded Man* (Austin, TX: New
Men's Press 1987), 101–12.

99 Burant, 'Of Wild Men and Warriors,' 46

100 Clatterbaugh, 'Masculinist Perspectives'

101 Jed Diamond, *Inside Out: Becoming My Own Man* (San Rafael, CA: Fifth
Wave Press 1983)

102 Clatterbaugh, 'Masculinist Perspectives,' 6

103 Walker in *The Battered Woman*, 19, states that there is a 50 per cent chance
that any woman living in America will be beaten. Diana Russell states
that, from her research, a woman in San Francisco has a 46 per cent
probability of becoming a victim of sexual assault or attempted sexual
assault at some point in her life. Russell considered the San Francisco
statistics to be fairly representative of other communities (see *Sexual
Exploitation*, 34–6).

104 Stordeur and Stille, *Ending Men's Violence against Their Partners*, 71–98;
and Virginia Coover, Ellen Deacon, Charles Esser, and Christopher

332 Notes to pages 230–2

Moore, *Resource Manual for a Living Revolution* (Philadelphia: New Society 1985)

105 Typifying the view of many black men, psychiatrists William Grier and Price Cobbs, in their 1968 bestseller *Black Rage* (New York: Basic Books 1968), wrote that 'whereas the white man regards his manhood as an ordained right, the black man is engaged in a never-ending struggle for its possession'; quoted in Shibley Hyde, *Half the Human Experience*, 133.

106 Lyttelton, 'Major Dividing Lines'

107 Brannon, 'Are the "Free Men" a Faction of Our Movement?'

108 For material on the racial dividing line, see: Tony Bell, 'Black Men in the White Men's Movement,' *Changing Men*, 17 (Winter 1986), 11–12, 44; Harry Brod, 'Unlearning Racism: Valuing Our Differences,' *Changing Men*, 17 (Winter 1986), 13; Icard, 'Black Gay Men and Conflicting Social Identities'; Staples, 'Masculinity and Race,' 169–83

For material on the sexual preference dividing line, see: Morin and Garfinkle, 'Male Homophobia' ; Bohn, 'Homophobic Violence'; and Herek, 'Beyond "Homophobia".'

For a useful integration of race, gender, class, and sexual preference issues, see Hoch, *White Hero, Black Beast*, and Segal, *Slow Motion*.

109 Also, being gay does not prevent one from being racist. See: Joseph Beam, 'No Cheek to Turn,' *Changing Men*, 17 (Winter 1986), 9–10; and Albert Luna, 'Gay Racism,' in Kimmel and Messner, *Men's Lives*, 440–7.

110 Staples, 'Masculinity and Race,' 169–83

111 Quoted in Evans, *Born for Liberty*, 282

112 For more on the debates within the political left about its relationship to feminism, see: Barrett, *Women's Oppression Today*; Godelier, 'The Origins of Male Domination'; Brenner and Ramas, 'Rethinking Women's Oppression'; Barrett, 'Rethinking Women's Oppression'; Weir and Wilson, 'The British Women's Movement'; Lewis, 'The Debates on Sex and Class'; and Tolson, *The Limits of Masculinity*.

Men on the left also have a history of homophobia. See Tom Kennedy, 'Homophobia and the Left,' in Snodgrass, ed., *A Book of Readings for Men against Sexism*, 166–9.

113 While many gay men have been very active in pro-feminist men's groups, their issues have not always been viewed as a major priority by the heterosexual majority. See Interrante, 'Dancing along the Precipice,' part II.

114 Gregory Tate, 'Say, Brother,' *Changing Men*, 17 (Winter 1986), 8; and Staples, 'Masculinity and Race,' pp. 169–83

115 Staples, 'Masculinity and Race,' pp. 169–83

116 Evans, *Born for Liberty*, 287–314
117 See, for example, Sidel, *Women and Children Last*, 49–76; and Gatlin, *American Women since 1945*, 24–48.
118 Young, *Gays under the Cuban Revolution*
119 John Stoltenberg, 'The Profeminist Men's Movement: New Connections, New Directions,' *Changing Men*, 20 (Winter–Spring 1989), 7–9
120 Lyttelton, 'Major Dividing Lines'
121 Adapted from Seattle Men against Rape and Louisiana Sissies in Struggle (LASIS), 'Men Stopping Rape,' *M.: Gentle Men for Gender Justice*, 13 (Fall 1984), 46. See also Lawrence Cohen, 'The Masks of Rape,' *Changing Men*, 20 (Winter–Spring 1989), 25–6; and Bateman and Mahoney, *Macho: Is That What I Really Want?*
122 Dexter Guerrieri, 'Pornography and Silent Men,' *Changing Men*, 15 (Fall 1985), 9–10. For an example of what was involved in the organization and implementation of one pro-feminist men's action against a porn theatre, see: Women against Porn, Men against Porn, 'Striking Back at the Porn Barons,' *M.: Gentle Men for Gender Justice*, 9 (Summer–Fall 1982), 14.
123 BrotherPeace, 'An International Day of Action to End Male Violence' (Cortland, NY 1989), advertising leaflet
124 Jon Cohen, 'BrotherPeace 1987,' *Changing Men*, 19 (Spring–Summer 1988), 44
125 Stein, 'An Overview of Men's Groups'; and Coté, Dare, and Muzychka, *Men Changing: A Resource Manual for Men's Consciousness Raising*
126 Interrante, 'Dancing along the Precipice,' part I. Another example of men's groups providing services for men who batter is New York City's Men's Coalition against Battering. See Edleson, 'Working with Men Who Batter,' 240.
127 For more information on the content of a pro-feminist, or social constructionist, treatment approach, see above, chapter 5.
128 Browning, *Stopping the Violence*, vii.
      The domestic violence programs for women and men at Klinic Community Health Centre in Winnipeg are examples of programs initiated prior to the provision of direct state funding. In the early 1980s, many members of Klinic's staff, concerned about the lack of services, struggled to create programs for battered women and male offenders. While the employees' salaries were paid by the provincial government, their work with domestic violence lacked official sponsorship. Counsellors were in the difficult position of having to squeeze these programs into an already overloaded service mandate. It was not until 1986, after

significant lobbying by Klinic staff and the local feminist community, that the provincial government agreed to fund the services separately and create the Evolve program as an identifiable program of Klinic providing counselling for domestic violence victims and offenders, and community education. (David Rice-Lampert, Probation Officer, Community and Youth Corrections, Department of Justice, Province of Manitoba; telephone interview with the author, 19 June 1990.)

129 See, for example, Men against Patriarchy, 'No More Silence about Violence: Men Oppose Militarism,' *M.: Gentle Men for Gender Justice*, 1 (Winter 1979–80), 3–4.

130 Robbie Mahood, general practitioner, Klinic Community Health Centre, Winnipeg; interview with the author, 5 June 1990

131 Men for Women's Choice, 'Five Reasons Why the Proposed Abortion Law Is No Compromise,' 1

132 Ibid.

133 Bill Dare, 'Consciousness Raising in Groups,' in Coté, Dare, and Muzychka, *Men Changing*, 45–53. For more on the similarities between men's and women's groups, see Shorr and Jason, 'A Comparison of Men's and Women's Consciousness-Raising Groups.'

134 Paul Kivel, 'The Fear of Men,' *Changing Men*, 17 (Winter 1986), 19

135 Ken Fisher, an Ottawa member of Partners in Change and the Ottawa Men's Forum; telephone interview with the author, February 1990

136 The estimate was Ken Fisher's and was cited in Nora Underwood, Laurie Gillies, and Dan Burke, 'Redefining Roles: "New Men" Are Striving to Change Stereotypes,' *Maclean's*, 14 Aug 1989, 46–7. See also Judy Steed, 'In Search of the New Man: Across the Country, Men Are Looking at Their Own Sexism,' *Globe and Mail*, 25 Feb 1989, D5.

137 Steed, 'In Search of the New Man'

138 Telephone interview with Ken Fisher, February 1990

139 Ibid.

140 Interrante, 'Dancing along the Precipice,' part I, 3–6, 20–1, and part II, 3–6, 32; and Lyttelton, 'Major Dividing Lines,' 33–4

141 The editorial collective, 'Thank You and Congratulations to the New National Men's Organization,' *M.: Gentle Men for Gender Justice*, 10 (Spring 1983), 20; and Jim Hanneken, NOMAS staffperson, 21 June 1990, telephone interview with the author.

142 Ibid. The name *M.: Gentle Men for Gender Justice* was changed to *Changing Men*. A more recent statement of principles is found in *Changing Men*, 18 (Summer–Fall 1987), 40, and 21 (Winter–Spring 1990), 44; and 'Statement of Principles,' in Kimmel and Messner, *Men's Lives*, 597–8. The orga-

nization's position on men's rights groups was clarified in *Changing Men*, 21 (Winter–Spring 1990), 43.

143 Hanneken, interview with the author
144 Michael Kimmel, 'NOCM Name Change,' *Brother*, 7/3 (Fall 1989), 4–5. NOMAS's address is 794 Penn Ave., Pittsburgh, 15221.
145 *Brother*, 7/3 (Fall 1989), 9
146 Eric Malmsten, of Metro Men against Violence, Toronto; telephone interview with the author, June 1990
147 See, among others, Pleck and Sawyer, eds., *Men and Masculinity*; David and Brannon, eds., *The Forty-Nine Percent Majority*; Snodgrass, ed., *A Book of Readings for Men against Sexism*; Cook et al., *The Men's Survival Resource Book*; Julty, *Men's Bodies, Men's Selves*; Pleck, *The Myth of Masculinity*; Reynaud, *Holy Virility*; Metcalf and Humphries, eds., *The Sexuality of Men*; Brod, ed., *The Making of Masculinities*; Kaufman, ed., *Beyond Patriarchy*; Kimmel and Messner, eds., *Men's Lives*; and Stoltenberg, *Refusing to Be a Man*.
148 *Integral: The Magazine for Changing Men* magazine is published in Toronto and is the major Canadian production. Its address is: P.O. Box 5579, Stn. A, Toronto, M5W 1N7. *Brother*'s address is c/o Ithaca Men's Network, P.O. Box 6711, Ithaca, NY, 14581-6711. *Changing Men*'s address is 306 N. Brooks St., Madison, WI, 53715, tel.: (608) 256-2565. Numerous individual groups or communities publish local newsletters.
149 See, for example, Nora Underwood, Laurie Gillies, and Dan Burke, 'Redefining Roles: "New Men" are Striving to Change Stereotypes,' *Maclean's*, 102/33 (14 Aug 1989), 46–7.
150 See, among others, RAVEN, *The Ending Men's Violence National Referral Directory*; Simoneau, *Répertoire de la condition masculine*; Ken Fisher for the Glebe New Men's Group, *Men's Groups: Towards a National Listing*; and NOCM/NOMAS, *Changing Male Roles*.
151 While more male singers are beginning to address issues central to pro-feminist men, Fred Small is one performer who has worked from this perspective for many years. See Michael Kimmel, 'Fred Small: From Legal Brief to Anti-Sexist Ballad,' *M.: Gentle Men for Gender Justice*, 13 (Fall 1984), 12–13.
152 Tom Mosmiller, Mike Bradley, and Michael Biernbaum, 'Are We the First? A Call for a Feminist Men's History,' *M.: Gentle Men for Gender Justice*, 4 (Fall–Winter 1980), 3–4, 21; Kimmel, 'Toward Men's Studies'; Brod, 'The New Men's Studies' and 'Themes and Theses of Men's Studies,' introduction to Brod, *The Making of Masculinities*, 1–17
153 Clatterbaugh, 'Masculinist Perspectives,' cites Snodgrass, *A Book of*

Readings for Men against Sexism, and Kaufman, ed., *Beyond Patriarchy*, as examples of the radical anti-sexist masculinism.

154 As an example of the liberal anti-sexist masculinism, Clatterbaugh cites Brod, *The Making of Masculinities*.

155 John Stoltenberg, 'On Gay Male Pornography and "Good Sex",' *M.: Gentle Men for Gender Justice*, 12 (Spring–Summer 1984), 11–13

156 Ibid. and 'You Can't Fight Homophobia and Protect the Pornographers at the Same Time,' *Changing Men*, 19 (Spring–Summer 1988), 11–13

157 Ken Fisher estimates, for example, that one-quarter of pro-feminist men are gay. See Underwood, Gillies, and Burke, 'Redefining Roles,' 47.

158 Interview with Ken Fisher, cited in Underwood, Gillies, and Burke, 'Redefining Roles,' 46–7

159 While much of it has yet to be implemented, several studies have indicated how best to identify homophobia and work toward its eradication. See, among others, Goldberg, 'Attitude Change among College Students toward Homosexuality'; Hansen, 'Measuring Prejudice against Homosexuality (Homosexism) among College Students'; Martin, 'Treatment of Homophobia; DeCrescenzo, 'Homophobia'; Messing, Schoenberg, and Stephens, 'Confronting Homophobia in Health Care Settings'; Plasek and Allard, 'Misconceptions of Homophobia'; Serdahely and Ziemba, 'Changing Homophobic Attitudes through College Sexuality Education'; Rabin, Keefe, and Burton, 'Enhancing Services for Sexual-Minority Clients'; and Lance, 'The Effects of Interaction with Gay Persons on Attitudes toward Homosexuality.'

160 Lyttelton, 'Major Dividing Lines,' 33–4

Chapter 7

1 The information pertaining to the potential role played by human service workers in business is from an unknown photocopied source. The citation was not provided. The original uncited source was modified to incorporate points relevant to sexual assault and offenders.

Appendix 2

1 Shorr and Jason, 'A Comparison of Men's and Women's Consciousness Raising Groups'

2 Bill Dare, 'Consciousness Raising Groups,' in Coté, Dare, and Muzychka, *Men Changing*, 45–53. The material for this appendix was drawn primarily from Dare's chapter. Another helpful resource for individuals starting

a pro-feminist men's group is Bob Brannon and Jim Creane, 'How to form a Men's Consciousness-Raising Group,' *M.: Gentle Men for Gender Justice*, 13 (Fall 1984), 35–7.

3 Appendix 1 lists some initial contact addresses.
4 For the section on feedback and constructive criticism, Dare, 'Consciousness Raising Groups,' 49–50, cites Peter Padbury's précis of Gracie Lyons, *Constructive Criticism* (San Francisco, IRT Press 1978).
5 Tony Krebs, *Facilitators Manual for Men's Consciousness and Support Groups* (Seattle: Metrocentre YMCA Seattle Men's Program's Unity 1982), cited in Dare, 'Consciousness Raising Groups,' 51–2

References

Books

Acton, Janice, Penny Goldsmith, and Bonnie Shepard. *Women at Work: 1850–1930*. Toronto: Canadian Women's Educational Press 1974

Armstrong, Louise. *The Home Front: Notes from the Family War Zone*. New York: McGraw-Hill 1983

Aronson, Elliot. *The Social Animal*. New York: W.H. Freeman 1976

– *Readings about the Social Animal*. New York: W.H. Freeman 1988

Averill, James. *Anger and Aggression: An Essay on Emotion*. New York: Springer-Verlag 1982

Barnhill, Lawrence (ed.). *Clinical Approaches to Family Violence: The Family Therapy Collection*. Rockville, MD: Aspen Publications 1982

Barrett, Michele. *Women's Oppression Today: Problems in Marxist Feminist Analysis*. London: Verso 1980

Bass, Ellen, and Laura Davis. *The Courage to Heal: A Guide for Women Survivors of Child Sexual Abuse*. New York: Harper & Row 1988

Bateman, Py. *Acquaintance Rape: Awareness and Prevention for Teenagers*. Seattle: Alternative to Fear 1982

Bateman, Py, and Bill Mahoney. *Macho: Is That What I Really Want?* Scarborough, NY: Youth Education Systems 1986

Baumli, Francis (ed.). *Men Freeing Men: Exploding the Myth of the Traditional Male*. Jersey City: New Atlantic Press 1985

Beneke, Timothy. *Men on Rape: What They Have to Say about Sexual Violence*. New York: St Martin's 1982

Berer, Marge. *Who Needs Depo-Provera?* London, ON: Community Rights Project 1984

Bérubé, Allan. *Coming Out under Fire: Gay Men and Women in World War II*. New York: Free Press 1990

Blackridge, Persimmon, and Sheila Gilhooly. *Still Sane*. Vancouver: Press Gang Publications 1985

Bly, Robert. *Iron John: A Book about Men*. Reading, MA: Addison-Wesley 1990

Brod, Harry (ed.). *The Making of Masculinities: The New Men's Studies*. Boston: Allen & Unwin 1987

Browne, Angela. *When Battered Women Kill*. New York: Free Press 1987

Browning, James. *Stopping the Violence: Canadian Programmes for Assaultive Men*. Ottawa: National Clearinghouse on Family Violence, Health and Welfare Canada 1984

Brownmiller, Susan. *Against Our Will: Men, Women, and Rape*. New York: Bantam Books 1975, 1980

Burstow, Bonnie, and Don Weitz (eds.). *Shrink Resistant: The Struggle against Psychiatry in Canada*. Vancouver: New Star Books 1988

Burstyn, Varda (ed.). *Women against Censorship*. Vancouver: Douglas & McIntyre 1985

Burt, Martha. 'Attitudes Supportive of Rape in American Culture.' *House Committee on Science and Technology. Subcommitte on Domestic and International Scientific Planning, Analysis, and Cooperation – Research into Violent Behavior: Sexual Assaults*. Hearing, 95th Congress, 2nd Session, 10–12 January 1978, 277–322. Washington, DC: US Government Printing Office

Cameron, Deborah, and Elizabeth Frazer. *The Lust to Kill: A Feminist Investigation of Sexual Murder*. New York: New York University Press 1987

Canada, Health and Welfare Canada, Family Violence Prevention Division. *Wife Battering and the Web of Hope: Progress, Dilemmas, and Visions of Prevention*. A discussion paper prepared by Linda MacLeod, May 1989

Canada, Working Group, Sex Offender Treatment Review. *The Management and Treatment of Sex Offenders: Report*. Ottawa: Minister of Supply and Services 1990

Chernin, Kim. *The Obsession*. New York: Harper and Row 1981

Chesler, Phyllis. *Women and Madness*. New York: Avon 1972

Childbirth by Choice Trust. *Abortion in Law and History: The Pro-Choice Perspective*. Toronto: Children by Choice Trust 1983

Clark, Lorenne, and Debra Lewis. *Rape: The Price of Coercive Sexuality*. Toronto: Women's Press 1977

Coakley, Jay J. *Sport in Society: Issues and Controversies*. St Louis: Times Mirror, Mosby College 1986

Collier, Helen. *Counselling Women: A Guide for Therapists*. New York: Free Press 1986

Collins, Anne. *The Big Evasion: Abortion, the Issue That Won't Go Away*. Toronto: Lester & Orpen Dennys 1985

Cooke, Christopher, Craig Wilkens, Jack Kennelly, Rob Scott, and Daven Henry (eds.). *The Men's Survival Resource Book: On Being a Man in Today's World*. Minneapolis: MSRB Press 1978

Cooper, Carey, and Marilyn Davidson. *High Pressure: Working Lives of Women Managers*. London: Fontana 1981

Coté, Pierre, Bill Dare, and Martha Muzychka. *Men Changing: A Resource Manual for Men's Consciousness Raising*. Sponsored by the Alternative Futures Institute. Ottawa: Carleton University Graphic Service 1984

Crawford, Allan. *Thunder on the Right: The New Right and the Politics of Resentment*. New York: Pantheon 1980

Crean, Susan. *In The Name of the Fathers: The Story behind Child Custody*. Toronto: Amanita Enterprises 1988

Currie, David. *The Abusive Husband: An Approach to Intervention*. Toronto: Clarke Institute of Psychiatry and Health and Welfare Canada 1988

– *Treatment Groups for Violent Men: A Practice Model*. Report on the Process and Outcome of Treatment with Violent Men in Groups. Toronto: Family Services Association, Feb 1982

David, Deborah, and Robert Brannon (eds.). *The Forty-Nine Percent Majority: The Male Sex Role*. Reading, MA: Addison-Wesley 1976

Davis, Martha, Elizabeth Eshelman, and Matthew McKay. *The Relaxation and Stress Reduction Workbook*. Oakland, CA: New Harbinger 1982

D'Emilio, John. *Sexual Politics, Sexual Communities: The Making of a Homosexual Minority in the United States, 1940–1970*. Chicago: University of Chicago Press 1983

Deschner, Jeanne. *The Hitting Habit: Anger Control for Battering Couples*. New York: Free Press 1984

Diagram Group. *Man's Body: An Owner's Manual*. Toronto: Bantam 1983

Dinkmeyer, Don, and Gary D. McKay. *Parent's Handbook: Systematic Training for Effective Parenting*. Circle Pines, MN: American Guidance Service 1982

Dobash, R. Emerson, and Russell Dobash. *Violence against Wives: A Case against the Patriarchy*. New York: Free Press 1979

Dowdeswell, Jane. *Women on Rape: Firsthand Feelings, Attitudes and Experiences from the Women Involved, Backed up by Facts*. Wellingsborough, UK: Thorsons Publishing Group 1986

Doyle, James. *The Male Experience*. Dubuque: Wm. C. Brown Co. 1984

Druck, Ken, and James Simmons. *The Secrets Men Keep: Breaking Their Silence Barrier*. Garden City, NY: Doubleday 1985

Dubbert, J. *A Man's Place: Masculinity in Transition*. Englewood Cliffs, NJ: Prentice Hall 1979

Dworkin, Andrea. *Pornography: Men Possessing Women*. New York: Putnam's 1980

Eakins, Barbara, and Gene Eakins. *Sex Differences in Human Communication*. Boston: Houghton Mifflin 1978

Easlea, Brian. *Fathering the Unthinkable: Masculinity, Scientists and the Nuclear Arms Race*. London: Pluto Press 1983

Ehrenreich, Barbara. *The Hearts of Men: American Dreams and the Flight from Commitment*. Garden City, NY: Anchor 1983

Ellerby, Lawrence. *Winnipeg Sexual Offender Clinic: Outpatient Assessment and Treatment Manual*. Winnipeg: Native Clan Organization 1987

Emmett, Steven Wiley (ed.). *Theory and Treatment of Anorexia Nervosa and Bulimia: Biomedical, Sociocultural, and Psychological Perspectives*. New York: Brunner/Mazel 1985

Estrich, Susan. *Real Rape: How the Legal System Victimizes Women Who Say No*. Cambridge, MA: Harvard University Press 1987

Evans, Sara. *Born for Liberty: A History of Women in America*. New York: Free Press 1989

Fausto-Sterling, Anne. *Myths of Gender: Biological Theories about Women and Men*. New York: Basic Books 1985

Feigen Fasteau, Marc. *The Male Machine*. New York: Dell 1975

Finkelhor, David, and Kersti Yllo. *License to Rape: Sexual Abuse of Wives*. New York: Free Press 1985

Fisher, Ken, for the Glebe New Men's Group. *Men's Groups: Towards a National Listing*. Ottawa: Glebe New Men's Group 1988

Fitzgerald, Maureen, Connie Guberman, and Margie Wolfe (eds.). *Still Ain't Satisfied: Canadian Feminism Today*. Toronto: Women's Press 1982

Ford, C. and F.A. Beach. *Patterns of Sexual Behavior*. New York: Harper 1951

Frankfort, Ellen. *Vaginal Politics*. New York: Bantam 1983

Garfinkel, Perry. *In a Man's World: Father, Son, Brother, Friend, and Other Roles Men Play*. New York: Mentor 1985

Gatlin, Rochelle. *American Women since 1945*. Jackson: University of Mississippi Press 1987

Gerzon, Mark. *A Choice of Heroes: The Changing Face of American Manhood*. Boston: Houghton Mifflin 1982

Gillespie, Cynthia. *Justifiable Homicide: Battered Women, Self-Defense, and the Law*. Columbus: Ohio State University Press 1989

Goldberg, Herb. *The Hazards of Being Male: Surviving the Myth of Masculine Privilege*. New York: Signet 1976

– *The New Male: From Macho to Sensitive But Still All Male*. New York: Signet 1979

– *The New Male-Female Relationship*. New York: Signet 1983

Goldberg, Steven. *The Inevitability of Patriarchy*. London: Temple Smith 1977

Gondolf, Edward. *Men Who Batter: An Integrated Approach for Stopping Wife Abuse*. Holmes Beach, FL: Learning Publications 1985

Gordon, Linda. *Woman's Body, Woman's Right: A Social History of Birth Control in America*. New York: Penguin 1977

Greenberg, Martin. *The Birth of a Father*. New York: Avon 1985

Greenspan, Miriam. *A New Approach to Women and Therapy*. New York: McGraw Hill 1983

Greer, Germaine. *Sex and Destiny: The Politics of Human Fertility*. London: Picador 1984

Greer, Joanne, and Irving Stuart (eds.). *The Sexual Aggressor: Current Perspectives on Treatment*. New York: Van Nostrand Reinhold 1983

Guberman, Connie, and Margie Wolfe (eds.). *No Safe Place: Violence against Women and Children*. Toronto: Women's Press 1985

Gunn, Rita, and Candice Minch. *Sexual Assault: The Dilemma of Disclosure, the Question of Conviction*. Winnipeg: University of Manitoba Press 1988

Hanmer, Jalna, and Mary Maynard (eds.). *Women, Violence and Social Control*. Atlantic Highlands, NJ: Humanities Press International 1987

Hoch, Paul. *White Hero, Black Beast: Racism, Sexism and the Mask of Masculinity*. London: Pluto Press 1979

Jaffe, Peter, David Wolfe, and Susan Kaye Wilson. *Children of Battered Women*. Newbury Park, CA: Sage 1990

Jehu, Derek, in association with Marjorie Gazan and Carole Klassen. *Beyond Sexual Abuse: Therapy with Women Who Were Childhood Victims*. Chichester, England: Wiley 1988

Julty, Sam. *Men's Bodies, Men's Selves*. New York: Dell 1979

Katz, Judy. *No Fairy Godmothers, No Magic Wands: The Healing Process after Rape*. Saratoga, CA: R & E Pub. 1984

Kaufman, Michael (ed.). *Beyond Patriarchy: Essays by Men on Pleasure, Power, and Change*. Toronto: Oxford University Press 1987

Kelner, Gary. *Homophobic Assault: A Study of Anti-Gay Violence*. Winnipeg: Gays for Equality 1983

Kendrick, Walter. *The Secret Museum: Pornography in Modern Culture*. New York: Penguin 1988

Kimmel, Michael, and Michael Messner (eds.). *Men's Lives*. New York: Macmillan 1989

Kinsman, Gary. *The Regulation of Desire: Sexuality in Canada*. Montreal: Black Rose 1987

Kitzinger, Sheila. *Women's Experience of Sex*. London: Dorlington- Kindersley 1983

Klatch, Rebecca. *Women of the New Right*. Philadelphia: Temple University Press 1987

Klinic Community Health Cenre. *Evolve: Men's Program Intake Form.* Winnipeg: Klinic, Inc. 1989

Knopp, Fay Honey. *Retraining Adult Sex Offenders: Methods and Models.* Syracuse, NY: Safer Society Press 1984

Knopp, Fay Honey, Jean Rosenberg, and William Stevenson. *Report on the Nation-wide Survey of Juvenile and Adult Sex-Offender Treatment Programs and Providers, 1986.* Prepared for the Prison Research Education/Action Project (PREAP), A Safer Society Program of the New York State Council of Churches. Syracuse, NY: Safer Society Press 1986

Lerner, Gerda. *The Creation of Patriarchy.* New York: Oxford University Press 1986

Llewellyn-Jones, Derek. *Everyman.* Oxford: Oxford University Press 1987

MacLeod, Linda. *Battered But Not Beaten: Preventing Wife Battering in Canada.* Prepared for the Canadian Advisory Council on the Status of Women. Ottawa/Hull: Supply and Services Canada, June 1987

McCombie, Sharon (ed.). *The Rape Crisis Intervention Handbook.* New York: Plenum 1980

McDonnell, Kathleen. *Not an Easy Choice: A Feminist Re-examines Abortion.* Toronto: Women's Press 1984

MacKinnon, Catherine. *Sexual Harassment of Working Women: A Case of Sex Discrimination.* New Haven: Yale University Press 1979

McLaren, Angus, and Arlene Tigar McLaren. *The Bedroom and the State: The Changing Practices of Contraception and Abortion in Canada, 1880–1980.* Toronto: McClelland and Stewart 1986

Martin, Del. *Battered Wives.* San Francisco: Volcano Press 1981

Medea, Andra, and Kathleen Thompson. *Against Rape.* New York: Farrar, Strauss & Giroux 1974

Meichenbaum, Donald. *Cognitive-Behavior Modification: An Integrative Approach.* New York: Plenum 1977

– *Stress Inoculation Training.* New York: Pergamon 1985

Mendelsohn, Robert. *Male Practice: How Doctors Manipulate Women.* Chicago: Contemporary Books 1981

Metcalf, Andy, and Martin Humphries (eds.). *The Sexuality of Men.* London: Pluto Press 1985

Mitzel, John. *Sports and the Macho Male.* Boston: Fag Rag Books 1976

Morgan, Robin. *Going Too Far: The Personal Chronicle of a Feminist.* New York: Vintage 1978

– (ed.). *Sisterhood Is Global: The International Women's Movement Anthology.* Garden City, NY: Anchor 1984

– (ed.). *Sisterhood Is Powerful: An Anthology of Writing from the Women's Liberation Movement.* New York: Vintage 1970

Morgentaler, Henry. *Abortion and Contraception*. Toronto: General 1982

Nemiroff, Greta Hofmann (ed.). *Women and Men: Interdisciplinary Readings on Gender*. Montreal: Fitzhenry & Whiteside 1987

Nichols, Jack. *Men's Liberation: A New Definition of Masculinity*. Markham, ON: Penguin 1980

NOCM/NOMAS. *Changing Male Roles: NOCM's Official Task Group Resource Manual*. Ithaca: NOCM 1988

Okun, Lewis. *Woman Abuse: Facts Replacing Myths*. Albany: State University of New York Press 1986

Ontario, Provincial Secretariat for Justice. *Information for the Victims of Sexual Assault*. Toronto: Province of Ontario 1979

– *Helping the Victims of Sexual Assault*. Toronto: Province of Ontario 1979

Ontario Medical Association. *Ontario Medical Review: Reports on Wife Assault*. Ottawa: Health and Welfare Canada 1988

Orbach, Susie. *Fat Is a Feminist Issue*. New York: Berkley 1979

Planned Parenthood Federation of America. *Title X: The Nation's Family Planning Program*. Washington: PPFA FS-E1, Rev. 12/90

Pleck, Joseph. *The Myth of Masculinity*. Cambridge, MA: MIT Press 1981

Pleck, Joseph, and Jack Sawyer (eds.). *Men and Masculinity*. Englewood Cliffs, NJ: Prentice-Hall, Spectrum 1974

Porteous, Trace, Rhona Loptson, and Nora Janitis. *Let's Talk about Sexual Assault*. Victoria: Victoria Women's Sexual Assault Centre 1984

Prentice, Alison, and Susan Mann Trofimenkoff (eds.). *The Neglected Majority: Essays in Canadian Women's History*, vols. 1 and 2. Toronto: McClelland and Stewart 1977, 1985

Pressman, B. *Family Violence: Origins and Treatment*. Guelph, ON: Office for Educational Practice, University of Guelph 1984

Prince Edward Island Advisory Council on the Status of Women. *Believe Her!: A Report on Sexual Assault and Sexual Abuse of Women and Children*. Prepared by Lyle Brehaut. Edited by Ruth Freeman. Mar 1989

Raeburn, Antonia. *Militant Suffragettes*. London: New English Library 1974

RAVEN. *The Ending Men's Violence National Referral Directory*, and *Supplement*. St Louis: St Louis Organization for Changing Men 1986

– *Safety Planning: RAVEN Phase One Membership Guidebook*. St Louis: St Louis Organization for Changing Men 1986

Resnick, H.L.P., and M.E. Wolfgang (eds.). *Sexual Behavior: Social, Clinical, and Legal Aspects*. Boston: Little, Brown 1972

Reynaud, Emmanuel. *Holy Virility: The Social Construction of Masculinity*. London: Pluto 1983

Rhodes, Dusty, and Sandra McNeill (eds.). *Women against Violence against Women*. London: Onlywomen Press 1985

Robbins, Joan Hammerman, and Rachael Josefowitz Siegel (eds.). *Women Changing Therapy: New Assessments, Values, and Strategies in Feminist Therapy.* New York: Haworth 1983

Roy, Maria (ed.). *The Abusive Partner: An Analysis of Domestic Battering.* New York: Van Nostrand Reinhold 1982

− (ed.). *Battered Women: A Psychosociological Study of Domesic Violence.* New York: Van Nostrand Reinhold 1977

Russell, Diana. *Rape in Marriage.* New York: Macmillan 1982

− *Sexual Exploitation: Rape, Child Sexual Abuse and Workplace Harassment.* Beverly Hills: Sage 1984

Russell, Diana, and Nicole Van de Ven (eds.). *Crimes against Women: Proceedings of the International Tribunal.* East Palo Alto, CA: Frog in the Well 1984

Sanford, Linda Tschirhart, and Mary Ellen Donovan. *Women and Self-Esteem: Understanding and Improving the Way We Think and Feel about Ourselves.* New York: Penguin 1988

Schechter, Susan. *Women and Male Violence: The Visions and Struggles of the Battered Women's Movement.* Boston: South End Press 1982

Scher, Murray, Mark Stevens, Glen Good, and Greg Eichenfield (eds.). *Handbook of Counselling and Psychotherapy with Men.* Newbury Park, CA: Sage 1987

Segal, Lynne. *Slow Motion: Changing Masculinities, Changing Men.* London: Virago 1990

Shibley Hyde, Janet. *Half the Human Experience: The Psychology of Women.* Lexington, MA: D.C. Heath 1980

Sidel, Ruth. *Women and Children Last: The Plight of Poor Women in America.* New York: Penguin 1987

Simoneau, Jean-Pierre. *Répertoire de la condition masculine.* Montreal: Les Editions Saint-Martin 1988

Singer, Wenda Goodhart, Stephen Shechtman, and Mark Singer. *Real Men Enjoy Their Kids: How to Spend Quality Time with the Children in Your Life.* Nashville: Abingdon 1983

Sivard, Ruth Leger. *World Military and Social Expenditures: 1986.* 11th edition. Washington, DC: World Priorities 1986

Smart, Carol, and Barry Smart (eds.). *Women, Sexuality, and Social Control.* London: Routledge & Kegan Paul 1978

Smith, Michael D. *Violence and Sports.* Toronto: Butterworths 1983

Smith, Susan. *Fear or Freedom: A Woman's Options in Social Survival and Physical Defense.* Racine, WI: Mother Courage Press 1986

Snodgrass, Jon (ed.). *A Book of Readings for Men against Sexism.* Albion, CA: Times Change Press 1977

Sonkin, Daniel (ed.). *Domestic Violence on Trial: Psychological and Legal Dimensions of Family Violence*. New York: Springer 1987

Sonkin, Daniel Jay, and Durphy, Michael. *Learning to Live without Violence: A Handbook for Men*. San Francisco: Volcano Press 1985

Sonkin, Daniel, Del Martin, and Lenore Walker. *The Male Batterer: A Treatment Approach*. New York: Springer 1985

Stanko, Elizabeth. *Intimate Intrusions: Women's Experience of Male Violence*. London: Routledge & Kegan Paul 1985

Stearns, Frederic. *Anger: Psychology, Physiology, Pathology*. Springfield: Charles C. Thomas 1972

Stearns, Peter. *Be a Man! Males in Modern Society*. New York: Holmes and Meier 1979

Stevens, Mark, and Randy Gebhardt. *Rape Education for Men: Curriculum Guide*. Columbus: Ohio State University Rape Education and Prevention Program 1984

Stoltenberg, John. *Refusing to Be a Man: Essays on Sex and Justice*. Portland, OR: Breitenbush Books 1989

Stordeur, Richard, and Richard Stille. *Ending Men's Violence against Their Partners: One Road to Peace*. Newbury Park, CA: Sage 1989

Straus, Murray, Richard Gelles, and Suzanne Steinmetz. *Behind Closed Doors: Violence in the American Family*. Garden City, NY: Doubleday 1980

Straus, Murray, and Gerald Hotaling (eds.). *The Social Causes of Husband-Wife Violence*. Minneapolis: University of Minnesota Press 1980

Thiessen, D.D. *The Evolution and Chemistry of Aggression*. Springfield: Charles C. Thomas 1976

Tolson, Andrew. *The Limits of Masculinity*. London: Tavistock 1977

Unger, Rhoda. *Female and Male: Psychological Perspectives*. New York: Harper & Row 1979

USA, Department of Justice, Law Enforcement Assistance Administration. *The Report from the Conference on Intervention Programs for Men Who Batter*. Washington: The Center for Women's Policy Studies 1979

Vadney, T.E. *The World since 1945*. Harmondsworth: Penguin 1987

Victoria Women's Sexual Assault Centre. *Working with Survivors of Sexual Assault*, ed. and produced by Trace Porteous, Alice Ages, Norrie Preston, Kathryn Rowe, and Sheila Benson. Victoria: Victoria Women's Sexual Assault Centre Publications Committee 1986

Walker, Lenore. *The Battered Woman*. New York: Harper Colophon 1979

Warshaw, Robin. *I Never Called It Rape: The Ms. Report on Recognizing, Fighting and Surviving Date and Acquaintance Rape*. New York: Harper & Row 1988

Williams, Juanita. *Psychology of Women: Behaviour in a Biosocial Context*. New York: W.W. Norton 1987

Willmarth, Mark. *Not for Women Only!: A Rape Awareness Program for Men*. Great Falls, MO: College of Great Falls 1985

Wormith, Stephen, and Mark Borzecki. *A Survey of Treatment Programs for Sexual Offenders in Canada*. Ottawa: Solicitor General of Canada Report No. 1985-35, 1985

Young, Allen. *Gays under the Cuban Revolution*. San Francisco: Grey Fox 1982

Zilbergeld, Bernie. *Male Sexuality: A Guide to Sexual Fulfillment*. Toronto: Bantam 1981

Articles in Periodicals

Anderson, Wayne, and Barbara Bauer. 'Law Enforcement Officers: The Consequences of Exposure to Violence.' Special Issue: *Counselling and Violence. Journal of Counselling and Development*, 65/7 (Mar 1987), 381–4

Arkin, William, and Lynne Dobrofsky. 'Military Socialization and Masculinity.' *Journal of Social Issues*, 34/1 (1978), 151–68

Balswick, J. 'The Inexpressive Male: Functional Conflict and Role Theory as Contrasting Explanations.' *Family Coordinator*, 28 (1979), 331–6

Balswick, J., and C. Peek. 'The Inexpressive Male: A Tragedy of American Society.' *Family Coordinator*, 20 (1971), 363–8

Bandy, Carole, Dale R. Buchanan, and Cynthia Pinto. 'Police Performance in Resolving Family Disputes: What Makes the Difference?' *Psychological Reports*, 58/3 (June 1986), 743–56

Barbaree, Howard, and William Marshall. 'Treatment of the Sexual Offender.' Chapter prepared for R.M. Wettstein (ed.), *Treatment of the Mentally Disordered Offender*. New York: Guilford Press, submitted Sept 1987

Barnard, George W., Hernan Vera, Maria I. Vera, and Gustave Newman. 'Till Death Do Us Part: A Study of Spouse Murder.' *Bulletin of the American Academy of Psychiatry and the Law*, 10/4 (1982), 271–80

Barrett, Michele. 'Rethinking Women's Oppression: A Reply to Brenner and Ramas.' *New Left Review*, 146 (July–Aug 1984), 123–8

Bauer, Carol, and Lawrence Ritt. '"A Husband Is a Beating Animal": Frances Power Cobbes Confronts the Wife-Abuse Problem in Victorian England.' *International Journal of Women's Studies*, 6/2 (Mar–Apr 1983), 99–118

– 'Wife-Abuse, Late Victorian English Feminists, and the Legacy of Frances Power Cobbes.' *International Journal of Women's Studies*, 6/3 (May–June 1983), 195–207

Baxter, Richard L., Cynthia de Reimer, Ann Landini, Larry Leslie, et al. 'A Content Analysis of Music Videos.' *Journal of Broadcasting and Electronic Media*, 29/3 (Summer 1985), 333–40

Becker, Judith V., Linda J. Skinner, Gene G. Abel, Roz Axelrod, and Eileen C. Treacy. 'Depressive Symptoms Associated with Sexual Assault.' *Journal of Sex and Marital Therapy*, 10/3 (1984), 185–92

– 'Sexual Problems of Sexual Assault Survivors.' *Women and Health*, 9/4 (Winter 1984), 5–20

Becker, Judith V., Linda J. Skinner, Gene G. Abel, Julia Howell, and Kathy Bruce. 'The Effects of Sexual Assault on Rape and Attempted Rape Victims.' *Victimology*, 7/1–4 (1982), 106–13

Bell, Daniel J. 'The Police Response to Domestic Violence: A Replication Study.' *Police Studies*, 7/3 (Fall 1984), 136–44

– 'Domestic Violence: Victimization, Police Intervention, and Disposition.' *Journal of Criminal Justice*, 13/6 (1985), 525–34

– 'The Victim-Offender Relationship: A Determinant Factor in Police Domestic Dispute Dispositions.' *Marriage and Family Review*, 12/1–2 (1987), 87–102

Belsky, Jay, and Laurence Steinberg. 'The Effects of Day Care: A Critical Review.' *Annual Progress in Child Psychiatry and Child Development*, 1979, 576–611

Berk, Richard A., Sarah F. Berk, Phyllis J. Newton, and Donileen Loseke. 'Cops on Call: Summoning the Police to the Scene of Spousal Violence.' *Law and Society Review*, 18/3 (1984), 479–98

Berkowitz, L. 'Some Thoughts on Anti and Prosocial Influences of Media Events: A Cognitive-Neoassociation Analysis.' *Psychological Bulletin*, 95 (1984), 410–27

Berlin, Fred, and Carl Meinecke. 'Treatment of Sex Offenders with Antiandrogenic Medication: Conceptualization, Review of Treatment Modalities, and Preliminary Findings.' *American Journal of Psychiatry*, 138/5 (May 1981), 601–7

Bern, Elliot H., and Linda Lyon Bern. 'A Group Program for Men Who Commit Violence towards Their Wives.' *Social Work with Groups*, 7/1 (Spring 1984), 63–77

Bernard, J.L., and M.L. Bernard. 'The Abusive Male Seeking Treatment: Jekyll and Hyde.' *Family Relations Journal of Applied Family and Child Studies*, 33/4 (Oct 1984), 543–7

Bidwell, Lee, and Priscilla White. 'The Family Context of Marital Rape.' *Journal of Family Violence*, 1/3 (Sept 1986), 277–87

Bienen, Leigh. 'Rape Reform Legislation in the United States: A Look at Some Practical Effects.' *Victimology*, 8/1–2 (1983), 139–51

Blume, Sheila. 'Alcohol Problems in Women.' *New York State Journal of Medicine*, 82/8 (July 1982), 1222–4

Bogal-Allbritten, Rosemarie B., and William L. Allbritten. 'The Hidden Victims: Courtship Violence among College Students.' *Journal of College Student Personnel*, 26/3 (May 1985), 201–4

Bograd, Michele. 'Family Systems Approaches to Wife Battering: A Feminist Critique.' *American Journal of Orthopsychiatry*, 54/4 (1984), 558–68

Bohn, Ted R. 'Homophobic Violence: Implications for Social Work Practice.' *Journal of Social Work and Human Sexuality*, 2/2–3 (Winter–Spring 1983–4), 91–112

Borgida, Eugene. 'Legal Reform of Rape Laws.' *Applied Social Psychology Annual*, 2 (1981), 211–41

Bowen, Gary L., and Andrea J. Sedlak. 'Toward a Domestic Violence Surveillance System: Issues and Prospects.' *Response to the Victimization of Women and Children*, 8/3 (Summer 1985), 2–7

Bowker, Lee H. 'Marital Rape: A Distinct Syndrome.' *Social Casework*, 64/6 (June 1983), 347–52

Bradford, John. 'Research on Sex Offenders.' *Psychiatric Clinics of North America*, 6/4 (Dec 1983), 715–31

– 'The Hormonal Treatment of Sexual Offenders.' *Bulletin of the American Academy of Psychiatry and the Law*, 11/2 (1983), 159–69

Brenner, Johanna, and Maria Ramas. 'Rethinking Women's Oppression.' *New Left Review*, 144 (Mar–Apr 1984), 33–71

Brickman, Julie. 'Feminist, Nonsexist, and Traditional Models of Therapy: Implications for Working with Incest.' *Women and Therapy*, 3/1 (Spring 1984), 49–67

Brickman, Julie, and John Briere. 'Incidence of Rape and Sexual Assault in an Urban Canadian Population.' *International Journal of Women's Studies*, 7/3 (1984), 195–206

Briere, John, and Neil Malamuth. 'Self-Reported Likelihood of Sexually Aggressive Behavior: Attitudinal versus Sexual Explanations.' *Journal of Research in Personality*, 17 (1983), 315–23

Briere, John, Neil Malamuth, and James Check. 'Sexuality and Rape Supportive Beliefs.' *International Journal of Women's Studies*, 8/4 (Sept–Oct 1985), 398–403

Briskin, Karen, and Gary Juneau. 'Sexual Assault Programming for College Students.' *Journal of Counselling and Development*, 65/4 (Dec 1986), 207–8

Bristow, Ann. 'State v. Marks: An Analysis of Expert Testimony on Rape Trauma Syndrome.' *Victimology*, 9/2 (1984), 273–81

Brod, Harry 'The New Men's Studies: From Feminist Theory to Gender Scholarship.' *Hypatia*, 2/1 (Winter 1987), 179–96

Brown, Stephen. 'Police Responses to Wife Beating: Neglect of a Crime of Violence.' *Journal of Criminal Justice*, 12/3 (1984), 277–88

Bryson, Lois. 'Sport and the Oppression of Women.' *Australia and New Zealand Journal of Sociology*, 19/3 (Nov 1983), 413–26

Buchanan, Dale, and Patricia Perry. 'Attitudes of Police Recruits towards Domestic Disturbances: An Evaluation of Family Crisis Intervention Training.' *Journal of Criminal Justice*, 13/6 (1985), 561–72

Buckley, Lola Beth, Donna Miller, and Thomas Rolfe. 'A Windsor Model.' *Social Work with Groups*, 6/3–4 (Fall–Winter 1983), 189–95

Bunting, Alyce, and Joy Reeves. 'Perceived Male Sex Orientation and Beliefs about Rape.' *Deviant Behavior*, 4/3–4 (Apr 1983), 281–95

Burgess, Ann Wolbert, Carol Hartman, Robert Ressler, John Douglas, and Arlene McCormack. 'Sexual Homicide: A Motivational Model.' *Journal of Interpersonal Violence*, 1/3 (Sept 1986), 251–72

Burgess, Ann Wolbert, and Lynda Lytle Holmstrom. 'The Rape Victim in the Emergency Ward.' *American Journal of Nursing*, 73/10 (July–Dec 1973), 1741–5
- 'Rape Trauma Syndrome.' *American Journal of Psychiatry*, 131/9 (Sept 1974), 981–6

Burris, Carole, and Peter Jaffe. 'Wife Abuse as a Crime: The Impact of Police Laying Charges.' *Canadian Journal of Criminology*, 25/3 (July 1983), 309–18

Burstyn, Varda. 'Porn Again: Feeling the Heat of Censorship.' *Fuse*, 45 (Spring 1987), 11–18

Burt, Martha. 'Cultural Myths and Supports for Rape.' *Journal of Personality and Social Psychology*, 38/2 (1980), 217–30

Burt, Pauline. 'A Study of Women Who Both Were Raped and Avoided Rape.' *Journal of Social Issues*, 37/4 (1981), 123–37

Buzawa, Eva. 'Police Officer Response to Domestic Violence Legislation in Michigan.' *Journal of Police Science and Administration*, 10/4 (Dec 1982), 415–24

Byers, Sandra, and Paula Wilson. 'Accuracy of Women's Expectations Regarding Men's Responses to Refusals of Sexual Advances in Dating Situations.' *International Journal of Women's Studies*, 8/4 (Oct 1985), 376–87

Cammaert, Lorna. 'How Widespread Is Sexual Harassment on Campus?' *International Journal of Women's Studies*, 8/4 (Sept–Oct 1985), 388–97

Chandler, Susan, and Martha Torney. 'The Decisions and the Processing of Rape Victims through the Criminal Justice System.' *California Sociologist*, 4/2 (Summer 1981), 155–69

Chappell, Duncan. 'The Impact of Rape Legislation Reform: Some Comparative Trends.' *International Journal of Women's Studies*, 7/1 (Jan–Feb 1984), 70–80

Check, James, and Neil Malamuth. 'An Empirical Assessment of Some

Feminist Hypotheses about Rape.' *International Journal of Women's Studies*, 8/4 (Sept–Oct 1985), 414–23

Cobb, Nancy, Judith Stevens-Long, and Steven Goldstein. 'The Influence of Televised Models on Toy Preference in Children.' *Sex Roles*, 8/10 (Oct 1982), 1075–80

Cohen, Lawrence, and Susan Roth. 'The Psychological Aftermath of Rape: Long-Term Effects and Individual Differences in Recovery.' *Journal of Social and Clinical Psychology*, 5/4 (1987), 525–34

Collins, E.G.C., and T.B. Blodgett. 'Sexual Harassment – Some See It – Some Won't.' *Harvard Business Review*, 59/2 (1981), 76–95

Comstock, George. 'Sexual Effects of Movie and TV Violence.' *Medical Aspects of Human Sexuality*, 20/7 (July 1986), 96–101

Connell, Bob. 'The Concept of "Role" and What to Do with It.' *Australian and New Zealand Journal of Sociology*, 15/3 (Nov 1979), 7–17

Cook, David, and Anne Frantz-Cook. 'A Systemic Treatment Approach to Wife Battering.' *Journal of Marital and Family Therapy*, 10/1 (Jan 1984), 83–93

Costin, Frank. 'Beliefs about Rape and Women's Social Roles.' *Archives of Sexual Behavior*, 14/4 (Aug 1985), 319–25

Crane, Susan, Peggy Pahl, James Young, Judith Shenk, et al. 'The Washington State Domestic Violence Act: An Evaluation Project.' *Response to the Victimization of Women and Children*, 8/3 (Summer 1985), 13–16

DeCrescenzo, Teresa. 'Homophobia: A Study of the Attitudes of Mental Health Professionals toward Homosexuality.' *Journal of Social Work and Human Sexuality*, 2/2–3 (Winter–Spring 1983), 115–36

Demaré, Dano, John Briere, and Hilary Lips. 'Violent Pornography and Self-Reported Likelihood of Sexual Aggression.' *Journal of Research in Personality*, 22/2 (1988), 140–53

Deschner, Jeanne, and John McNeil. 'Results of Anger Control Training for Battering Couples.' *Journal of Family Violence*, 1/2 (1986), 111–20

Deschner, Jeanne, John McNeil, and Marcia Moore. 'A Treatment Model for Batterers.' *Social Casework*, 67/1 (Jan 1986), 55–60

DiVasto, Peter. 'Measuring the Aftermath of Rape.' *Journal of Psychosocial Nursing and Mental Health Services*, 23/2 (Feb 1985), 33–5

Dobash, R. Emerson, and Russell Dobash. 'The Nature and Antecedents of Violent Events.' *British Journal of Criminology*, 24/3 (July 1984), 269–88

– 'Wives: The "Appropriate" Victims of Marital Violence.' *Victimology*, 2/3–4 (1978), 426–42

Dolon, Ronald, James Hendricks, and Steven Meagher. 'Police Practices and Attitudes toward Domestic Violence.' *Journal of Police Science and Administration*, 14/3 (Sept 1986), 187–92

Donnerstein, Edward. 'Pornography and Violence against Women.' *Annals of the New York Academy of Sciences*, 347 (1980), 227–88

Donnerstein, Edward, and Daniel Linz. 'The Question of Pornography.' *Psychology Today*, 20/12 (Dec 1986), 56–9

Drysdale, Carla. 'Claiming Their Rights.' *Office Equipment and Methods*, 34/5 (June 1988), 46, 48–9

Dunning, E.G., J.A. Maguire, P.J. Murphy, and J.M. Williams. 'The Social Roots of Football Hooligan Violence.' *Leisure Studies*, 1/2 (May 1982), 139–56

Durkin, Kevin. 'Television and Sex-Role Acquisition: 1. Content.' *British Journal of Social Psychology*, 24/2 (June 1985), 101–13

Dutton, Donald. 'Interventions into the Problem of Wife Assault: Therapeutic, Policy, and Research Implications.' *Canadian Journal of Behavioural Science*, 16/4 (Oct 1984), 281–97

– 'Wife Assaulter's Explanations for Assault: The Neutralization of Self-Punishment.' *Canadian Journal of Behavioural Science*, 18/4 (Oct 1986), 381–90

– 'The Criminal Justice Response to Wife Assault.' *Law and Human Behaviour*, 11/3 (Sept 1987), 189–206

Eberle, Patricia. 'Alcohol Abusers and Non-Users: A Discriminant Analysis of Differences between Two Subgroups of Batterers.' *Journal of Health and Social Behavior*, 23/3 (Sept 1982), 260–71

Edleson, Jeffrey. 'Working with Men Who Batter.' *Social Work*, 29/3 (May–June 1984), 237–42

Edleson, Jeffrey, and Mary Brygger. 'Gender Differences in Reporting of Battering Incidences.' *Family Relations Journal of Applied Family and Child Studies*, 35/3 (July 1986), 377–82

Edleson, Jeffrey, David Miller, Gene Stone, and Dennis Chapman. 'Group Treatment for Men Who Batter.' *Social Work Research and Abstracts*, 21/3 (Fall 1985), 18–21

Eisenstock, Barbara. 'Sex-Role Differences in Children's Identification with Counterstereotypical Televised Portrayals.' *Sex Roles*, 10/5–6 (Mar 1984), 417–30

Eron, Leonard, and L. Rowell Huesmann. 'Television as a Source of Maltreatment of Children.' *School Psychology Review*, 16/2 (1987), 195–202

Eron, Leonard, Rowell Huesmann, Patrick Brice, Paulette Fischer, and Rebecca Mermelstein. 'Age Trends in the Development of Aggression, Sex Typing, and Related Television Habits.' *Developmental Psychology*, 19/1 (Jan 1983), 71–7

Fergusson, David, John Horwood, Kathryn Kershaw, and Frederick Shannon. 'Factors Associated with Reports of Wife Assault in New Zealand.' *Journal of Marriage and the Family*, 48/2 (May 1986), 407–12

Finn, Jerry. 'The Stresses and Coping Behavior of Battered Women.' *Social Casework*, 66/6 (June 1985), 341–9
– 'Men's Domestic Violence Treatment Groups: A Statewide Survey.' *Social Work with Groups*, 8/3 (Fall 1985), 81–94
Fischer, Gloria. 'College Student Attitudes toward Forcible Date Rape: Changes after Taking a Human Sexuality Course.' *Journal of Sex Education and Therapy*, 12/1 (Spring–Summer 1986), 42–6
Fitch, Frances, and Andre Papantonio. 'Men Who Batter: Some Pertinent Characterisitcs.' *Journal of Nervous and Mental Diseases*, 171/3 (Mar 1983), 190–2
Frank, Ellen, and Barbara Stewart. 'Treating Depression in Victims of Rape.' *Clinical Psychologist*, 36/4 (Summer 1983), 95–8
Frazier, Patricia, and Eugene Borgida. 'Rape Trauma Syndrome Evidence in Court.' *American Psychologist*, 40/9 (Sept 1985), 984–93
Freedman, Jonathan. 'Effects of Television Violence on Aggressiveness.' *Psychological Bulletin*, 96/2 (Sept 1984), 227–46
Friedrich-Cofer, Lynette, and Aletha Huston. 'Television Violence and Aggression: The Debate Continues.' *Psychological Bulletin*, 100/3 (Nov 1986), 364–71
Frieze, Irene. 'Investigating the Causes and Consequences of Marital Rape.' *Signs*, 8/3 (Spring 1983), 532–53
Galvin, Jim, and Kenneth Polk. 'Attrition in Case Processing: Is Rape Unique?' *Journal of Research in Crime and Delinquency*, 20/1 (Jan 1983), 126–54
Gilmartin-Zena, Pat. 'Rape Impact: Immediately and Two Months Later.' *Deviant Behavior*, 6/4 (1985), 347–61
Girelli, Steven, Patricia Resick, Susan Marhoefer-Dvorak, and Catherine Hutter. 'Subjective Distress and Violence during Rape: Their Effects on Long-Term Fear.' *Violence and Victims*, 1/1 (Spring 1986), 35–46
Godelier, Maurice. 'The Origins of Male Domination.' *New Left Review*, 127 (May–June 1981), 3–17
Goldberg, Raymond. 'Attitude Change among College Students toward Homosexuality.' *Journal of American College Health*, 30/6 (June 1982), 260–8
Goldstein, Diane, and Alan Rosenbaum. 'An Evaluation of the Self-Esteem of Maritally Violent Men.' *Family Relations*, 35 (July 1985), 425–8
Goodman, Amy. 'The Case against Depo-Provera.' *Multinational Monitor*, Feb–Mar 1985, 4–21
Gornick, Janet, Martha Burt, and Karen Pittman. 'Structure and Activities of Rape Crisis Centers in the Early 1980s.' *Crime and Delinquency*, 31/2 (Apr 1985), 247–68

Gray, Susan. 'Exposure to Pornography and Aggression toward Women: The Case of the Angry Male.' *Social Problems*, 29/4 (Apr 1982), 387–98

Greenland, Cyril. 'Sex Law Reform in an International Perspective: England and Wales and Canada.' *Bulletin of the American Academy of Psychiatry and the Law*, 11/4 (1983), 309–30

– 'Dangerous Sexual Offender Legislation in Canada, 1948–1977: An Experiment That Failed.' *Canadian Journal of Criminology*, 26/1 (Jan 1984), 1–12

Grimm, Laurence, and Paul Yarnold. 'Sex Typing and the Coronary-Prone Behavior Pattern.' *Sex Roles*, 12/1–2 (Jan 1985), 171–8

Groth, Nicholas, Robert Longo, and J. Bradley McFaddin. 'Undetected Recidivism among Rapists and Child Molesters.' *Crime and Delinquency*, 28/3 (July 1982), 450–8

Gunter, Barrie. 'Do Aggressive People Prefer Violent Television?' *Bulletin of the British Psychological Society*, 36 (May 1983), 166–8

Gunter, Barrie and Adrian Furnham. 'Personality and the Perception of TV Violence,' *Personality and Individual Differences*, 4/3 (1983), 315–21

– 'Perceptions of Television Violence: Effects of Programme Genre and Type of Violence on Viewers' Judgement of Violent Portrayals.' *British Journal of Social Psychology*, 23/2 (June 1984), 155–64

Gutman, Jonathan. 'The Impact of Advertising at the Time of Comsumption.' *Journal of Advertising Research*, 22/4 (Aug–Sept 1982), 35–40

Hanmer, Jalna, and Elizabeth Stanko. 'Stripping away the Rhetoric of Protection: Violence to Women, Law and the State in Britain and the USA.' *International Journal of the Sociology of Law*, 13/4 (Nov 1985), 357–74

Hanneke, Christine, and Nancy Shields. 'Marital Rape: Implications for the Helping Professions.' *Social Casework*, 66/8 (Oct 1985), 451–8

Hanneke, Christine, Nancy Shields, and George McCall. 'Assessing the Prevalence of Marital Rape.' *Journal of Interpersonal Violence*, 1/3 (Sept 1986), 350–62

Hansen, Gary. 'Measuring Prejudice against Homosexuality (Homosexism) among College Students: A New Scale.' *The Journal of Social Psychiatry*, 117 (1982), 233–6

Hanson, Shirley. 'Father/Child Relationships: Beyond "Kramer vs. Kramer".' *Marriage and Family Review*, 9/3–4 (Winter 1985/6), 135–50

Hantover, Jeffrey. 'The Boy Scouts and the Validation of Masculinity.' *Journal of Social Issues*, 34/1 (1978), 184–95

Harris, Jane. 'Counselling Violent Couples using Walker's Model.' *Psychotherapy*, 23/4 (Winter 1986), 613–21

Harrison, James. 'Warning: The Male Sex Role May be Dangerous to Your Health.' *Journal of Social Issues*, 34/1 (1978), 65–86

Haynes, David. 'Who Is He: New, Revised, or Updated? Fathers in the '80s.' *Today's Parent*, 4/4 (July 1987), 20–5

Heim, Nikolaus. 'Sexual Behavior of Castrated Sex Offenders.' *Archives of Sexual Behavior*, 10/1 (1981), 11–19

Herek, Gregory. 'Beyond "Homophobia": A Social Psychological Perspective on Attitudes toward Lesbians and Gay Men.' *Journal of Homosexuality*, 10/1–2 (Fall 1984), 1–21

Hitchcock, Ruth, and Dixie Young. 'Prevention of Sexual Assault: A Curriculum for Elementary School Counsellors.' *Elementary School Guidance and Counselling*, 20/3 (Feb 1986), 201–7

Hoffman, Pat. 'Psychological Abuse of Women by Spouses and Live-in Lovers.' *Women and Therapy*, 3/1 (Spring 1984), 37–47

Homant, Robert, and Daniel Kennedy. 'Police Perceptions of Spouse Abuse: A Comparison of Male and Female Officers.' *Journal of Criminal Justice*, 13/1 (1985), 29–47

Hucker, S., R. Langevin, R. Dickey, L. Handy, J. Chambers, and S. Wright. 'Cerebral Damage and Dysfunction in Sexually Aggressive Men.' *Annals of Sex Research*, 1/1 (1988), 33–78

Huesmann, L. Rowell, Kirsti Lagerspetz, and Leonard Eron. 'Intervening Variables in the TV Violence-Aggression Relation: Evidence from Two Countries.' *Developmental Psychology*, 20/5 (Sept 1984), 746–75

Hutchinson, Chris Huntley, and Susan McDaniel. 'The Social Reconstruction of Sexual Assault by Women Victims: A Comparison of Therapeutic Experiences.' *Canadian Journal of Community Mental Health*, 5/2 (Fall 1986), 17–36

Icard, Larry. 'Black Gay Men and Conflicting Social Identities: Sexual Orientation versus Racial Identity.' *Journal of Social Work and Human Sexuality*, 4/1–2 (Fall–Winter 1985–6), 83–93

Jensen, Inger, and Barbara Gutek. 'Attributions and Assignment of Responsibility in Sexual Harassment.' *Journal of Social Issues*, 38/4 (Winter 1982), 121–36

Jolin, Annette. 'Domestic Violence Legislation: An Impact Assessment.' *Journal of Police Science and Administration*, 11/4 (Dec 1983), 451–6

Jouriles, Ernest, and Daniel O'Leary. 'Interspousal Reliability of Reports of Marital Violence.' *Journal of Consulting and Clinical Psychology*, 53/3 (June 1985), 419–21

Kalmuss, Debra, and Judith Seltzer. 'Continuity of Marital Behavior in Remarriage: The Case of Spouse Abuse.' *Journal of Marriage and the Family*, 48/1 (Feb 1986), 113–20

Kanin, Eugene. 'Date Rapists: Differential Sexual Socialization and Relative Deprivation.' *Archives of Sexual Behavior*, 14/3 (June 1985), 218–32

Kaye, Marcia. 'The Battle against Men Who Batter.' *Canadian Living*, 15/8 (Aug 1989), 45–6, 48, 50, 52–3

Kilpatrick, Dean. 'Rape Victims: Detection, Assessment and Treatment.' *Clinical Psychologist*, 36/4 (Summer 1983), 92–5

Kilpatrick, Dean, et al. 'Mental Health Correlates of Criminal Victimization: A Random Community Survey.' *Journal of Consulting and Clinical Psychology*, 53/6 (Dec 1985), 866–73

Kimmel, Michael. 'Toward Men's Studies.' *American Behavioral Scientist*, 29/5 (May–June 1986), 517–29

King, Elizabeth, and Carol Webb. 'Rape Crisis Centres: Progress and Problems.' *Journal of Social Issues*, 37/4 (1981), 93–104

Kohn, Alfie. 'Make Love, Not War: We Keep Hearing We Are an Aggressive, Warlike Species, Scientists Keep Telling Us We Have a Choice.' *Psychology Today*, 22/6 (June 1988), 35–8

Kuhl, Anna. 'Community Responses to Battered Women.' *Victimology*, 7/1–4 (1982), 49–59

Lance, Larry. 'The Effects of Interaction with Gay Persons on Attitudes toward Homosexuality.' *Human Relations*, 40/6 (June 1987), 329–36

Langevin, R., and R.A. Lang. 'Psychological Treatment of Pedophiles.' *Behavioral Sciences and the Law*, 3 (1985), 403–19

Lauderdale, Helen. 'The Admissibility of Expert Testimony on Rape Trauma Syndrome.' *Journal of Criminal Law and Criminology*, 75/4 (Winter 1984), 1366–1416

Lenox, Michelle, and Linda Gannon. 'Psychological Consequences of Rape and Variables Influencing Recovery: A Review.' *Women and Therapy*, 2/1 (Spring 1983), 37–49

Leonard, Kenneth, Evelyn Bromet, David Parkinson, Nancy Day, and Christopher Ryan. 'Patterns of Alcoholism Use and Physically Aggressive Behavior in Men.' *Journal of Studies on Alcohol*, 46/4 (July 1985), 279–82

Leonard, Kenneth, and Stuart Taylor. 'Exposure to Pornography, Permissive and Nonpermissive Cues, and Male Aggression toward Females.' *Motivation and Emotion*, 7/3 (Sept 1983), 291–9

Lewis, Jane. 'The Debates on Sex and Class.' *New Left Review*, 149 (Jan–Feb 1985), 108–20

Lewis, Robert. 'Men's Liberation and the Men's Movement: Implications for Counsellors.' *Personnel and Guidance Journal*, 60/4 (Dec 1981), 256–9

Liebert, Robert. 'Effects of Television on Children and Adolescents.' *Journal of Development and Behavioral Pediatrics*, 7/1 (Feb 1986), 43–8

Linz, Daniel, Edward Donnerstein, and Steven Penrod. 'The Effects of Multiple Exposures to Filmed Violence against Women.' *Journal of Communication*, 34/3 (Summer 1984), 130–47

Lipton, Mark. 'Masculinity in Management: Type A Behavior and the Corporation.' *Organizational Development Journal*, 3/1 (Spring 1985), 6–9

Loeb, Roger. 'A Program of Community Education for Dealing with Spouse Abuse.' *Journal of Community Psychology*, 11/3 (July 1983), 241–52

Loh, Wallace. 'Q: What Has Reform of Rape Legislation Wrought? A: Truth in Criminal Labelling.' *Journal of Social Issues*, 37/4 (Fall 1981), 28–51

Longo, Robert. 'Sexual Learning and Experience among Adolescent Sexual Offenders.' *International Journal of Offender Therapy and Comparative Criminology*, 26/3 (1982), 235–41

Lopatz, Helen, and Barrie Thorne. 'On the Term "Sex Roles".' *Signs*, 3 (1978), 718–21

Loye, David, Roderick Gorney, and Gary Steele. 'An Experimental Field Study.' *Journal of Communication*, 27/3 (Summer 1977), 206–16

Lyttelton, Ned. 'Men's Liberation, Men against Sexism and Major Dividing Lines.' *Resources for Feminist Research*, 12/4 (Dec–Jan 1983–4), 33–4. Reprinted in Greta Hoffmann Nemiroff (ed.), *Women and Men: Interdisciplinary Readings on Gender*, 472–7. Montreal: Fitzhenry & Whiteside 1987

McEvoy, Maureen. 'Men against Battering.' *Goodwin's*, Fall 1984, 20, 22–4

McGregor, James. 'Risk of STD in Female Victims of Sexual Assault.' *Medical Aspects of Human Sexuality*, 19/8 (Aug 1985), 30–42

McIntyre, Deborah. 'Domestic Violence: A Case of the Disappearing Victim.' *Australian Journal of Family Therapy*, 5/4 (Oct 1984), 249–58

Maeder, Thomas. 'Wounded Healers.' *The Atlantic Monthly*, 263/1 (Jan 1989), 37–47

Mahoney, E.R., Michael Shively, and Marsh Traw. 'Sexual Coercion and Assault: Male Socialization and Female Risk.' *Sexual Coercion and Assault*, 1/1 (Jan 1986), 2–8

Makepeace, James M. 'Life Events Stress and Courtship Violence.' *Family Relations*, 32/1 (Jan 1983), 101–9

Malamuth, Neil, and Joseph Ceniti. 'Repeated Exposure to Violent and Nonviolent Pornography: Likelihood of Raping Ratings and Laboratory Aggression against Women.' *Aggressive Behavior*, 12/2 (1986), 129–37

Malamuth, Neil, and James Check. 'The Effects of Aggressive Pornography on Beliefs in Rape Myths: Individual Differences.' *Journal of Research in Personality*, 19/3 (1985), 299–320

Martin, Clyde. 'Treatment of Homophobia.' *Corrective and Social Psychiatry and Journal of Behavior Technology: Methods and Therapy*, 29/3 (1983), 70–3

Martin, Patricia, Dianna DiNitto, Sharon Maxwell, and Diane Norton. 'Controversies Surrounding the Rape Kit Exam in the 1980s: Issues and Alternatives.' *Crime and Deliquency*, 31/2 (Apr 1985), 223–46

Mathews, William. 'Violence in College Couples.' *College Student Journal*, 18/2 (Summer 1984), 150–8

Mathias, Barbara. 'Lifting the Shade on Family Violence.' *Family Therapy Networker*, 10/3 (May–June 1986), 20–9

Mattern, Kimberly, and Byron Lindholm. 'Effects of Maternal Commentary in Reducing Aggression Impact of Televised Violence on Preschool Children.' *Journal of Genetic Psychology*, 146/1 (Mar 1985), 133–4

Mayerson, Suzin, and Dalmas Taylor. 'The Effects of Rape Myth Pornography on Women's Attitudes and the Mediating Role of Sex Role Stereotyping.' *Sex Roles*, 17/5–6 (Spring 1987), 321–38

Meinecke, Christine. 'Socialized to Die Younger? Hypermasculinity and Men's Health.' *Personnel and Guidance Journal*, 60/4 (Dec 1981), 241–5

Messing, Alice, Robert Schoenberg, and Roger Stephens. 'Confronting Homophobia in Health Care Settings: Guidelines for Social Work Practice.' *Journal of Social Work and Human Sexuality*, 2/2–3 (Winter–Spring 1983–4), 65–74

Miller, Kimball, and Elaine Miller. 'Self-Reported Incidence of Physical Violence in College Students.' *Journal of American College Health*, 32/2 (Oct 1983), 63–5

Miller, William, Ann Williams, and Mark Bernstein. 'The Effects of Rape on Marital and Sexual Adjustment.' *American Journal of Family Therapy*, 10/1 (Spring 1982), 51–8

Modlin, Herbert. 'Traumatic Neurosis and Other Injuries.' *Psychiatric Clinics of North America*, 6/4 (Dec 1983), 661–82

Morin, Stephen, and Ellen Garfinkle. 'Male Homophobia.' *Journal of Social Issues*, 34/1 (1978), 29–47

Moschis, George, and Roy Moore. 'A Longitudinal Study of Television Advertising Effects.' *Journal of Consumer Research*, 9/3 (Dec 1982), 279–86

Muehlenhard, Charlene, Debra Friedman, and Celeste Thomas. 'Is Date Rape Justifiable? The Effects of Dating Activity, Who Initiated, Who Paid, and Men's Attitudes toward Women.' *Psychology of Women Quarterly*, 9/3 (Sept 1985), 297–309

Muehlenhard, Charlene, and Melaney Linton. 'Date Rape and Sexual Aggression in Dating Situations: Incidence and Risk Factors.' *Journal of Counselling Psychology*, 34/2 (Apr 1987), 186–96

Myers, Martha, and Gary LaFree. 'Sexual Assault and Its Prosecution: A Comparison with Other Crimes.' *Journal of Criminal Law and Criminology*, 73/3 (Fall 1982), 1282–1305

Neidig, Peter, Dale Friedman, and Barbara Collins. 'Domestic Conflict Containment: A Spouse Abuse Treatment Program.' *Social Casework*, 66/4 (Apr 1985), 195–204

– 'Attitudinal Characteristics of Males Who Have Engaged in Spouse Abuse.' *Journal of Family Violence*, 1/3 (Sept 1986), 223–33

Novaco, Raymond. 'Stress Inoculation: A Cognitive Therapy for Anger and Its Application to a Case of Depression.' *Journal of Consulting and Clinical Psychology*, 45/4 (1977), 600–8

O'Keefe, Nona, Karen Brockopp, and Esther Chew. 'Teen Dating Violence.' *Social Work*, 31/6 (Nov–Dec 1986), 465–8

O'Neil, James. 'Male Sex Role Conflicts, Sexism, and Masculinity: Psychological Implication for Men, Women, and the Counselling Psychologist.' *The Counselling Psychologist*, 9/2 (1981), 61–80

Oppenlander, Nan. 'Coping or Copping Out: Police Service Delivery in Domestic Disputes.' *Criminology: An Interdisciplinary Journal*, 20/3–4 (Nov 1982), 449–65

Palys, T.S. 'Testing the Common Wisdom: The Social Content of Video Pornography.' *Canadian Psychology*, 27/1 (Jan 1986), 22–35

Pelton, Charles. 'Family Protection Team.' *Conciliation Courts Review*, 21/1 (June 1983), 87–94

Peltoniemi, Teuvo. 'Family Violence: Police House Calls in Helsinki, Finland in 1977.' *Victimology*, 5/2–4 (1980), 213–24

Peters, J., J. Pedigo, V. Stag, and J. McKenna. 'Group Psychotherapy of the Sex Offender.' *Federal Probation*, 32 (1968), 41–6

Phillips, David. 'The Impact of Mass Media Violence in US Homicides.' *American Sociological Review*, 48/4 (Aug 1983), 560–8

Pierce, Chester. 'Television and Violence: Social Psychiatric Perspectives.' *American Journal of Social Psychiatry*, 4/3 (Summer 1984), 41–4

Pirog-Good, Maureen, and Jan Stets-Kealey. 'Male Batterers and Battering Prevention Programs: A National Survey.' *Response to the Victimization of Women and Children*, 8/3 (Summer 1985), 8–12

Plasek, John Wayne, and Janicemarie Allard. 'Misconceptions of Homophobia.' *Journal of Homosexuality*, 10/1–2 (Fall 1984), 23–37

Plenge, H. 'Die Behandlung erhelich ruckfalliger Sexualdelinquenten, vornehmlich der Homosexuellen, unter Berucksichtigung der Kastration.' *Monatsschr. Kriminol. Strafrechtsreform*, 44 (1961), 15–41

Ponzetti, James, Rodney Cate, and James Koval. 'Violence between Couples: Profiling the Male Abuser.' *Personnel and Guidance Journal*, 61/4 (Dec 1982), 222–4

Popiel, Debra, and Edwin Susskind. 'The Impact of Rape: Social Support as a Moderator of Stress.' *American Journal of Community Psychology*, 13/6 (Dec 1985), 645–76

Potts, Richard, Aletha Huston, and John Wright. 'The Effects of Television Form and Violent Content on Boys' Attention and Social Behavior.' *Journal of Experimental Child Psychology*, 41/1 (Feb 1986), 1–17

Powell, Gary. 'Effects of Sex Role Identity and Sex on Definitions of Sexual Harassment.' *Sex Roles,* 14/1–2 (Jan 1986), 9–19

Purdy, Frances, and Norm Nickle. 'Practice Principles for Working with Groups of Men Who Batter.' *Social Work with Groups,* 4/3-4 (Fall–Winter 1981), 111–22

Rabin, Jack, Kathleen Keefe, and Michael Burton. 'Enhancing Services for Sexual-Minority Clients: A Community Mental Health Approach.' *Social Work,* 31/4 (July–Aug 1986), 294–8

Rak, Diana, and Linda McMullen. 'Sex Role Stereotyping in Television Commercials: A Verbal Response Mode and Content Analysis.' *Canadian Journal of Behavioural Science,* 19/1 (Jan 1987), 25–39

Raum, Bernard. 'Rape Trauma Syndrome as Circumstantial Evidence of Rape.' *Journal of Psychiatry and Law,* 11/2 (Summer 1983), 203–13

Reilly, Patrick, and Roger Gruszski. 'A Structured Didactic Model for Men for Controlling Family Violence.' *International Journal of Offender Therapy and Comparative Criminology,* 28/3 (Dec 1984), 223–34

Renner, Edward, and Ann Keith. 'The Establishment of a Crisis Intervention Service for Victims of Sexual Assault.' *Canadian Journal of Community Mental Health,* 4/1 (Spring 1985), 113–23

Renner, Edward, and Carol Wackett. 'Sexual Assault: Social and Stranger Rape.' *Canadian Journal of Community Mental Health,* 6/1 (Spring 1987), 49–56

Renner, Edward, Carol Wackett, and Shelley Ganderton. 'The "Social" Nature of Sexual Assault.' *Canadian Psychology,* 29/2 (Apr 1988), 163–73

Resick, Patricia, Lois Veronen, and Karen Calhoun. 'Assessment of Fear Reactions in Sexual Assault Victims: A Factor Analytic Study of the Veronen-Kilpatrick Modified Fear Survey.' *Behavioral Assessment,* 8/3 (Summer 1986), 271–83

Ressler, Robert, Ann Burgess, John Douglas, Carol Hartman, and Ralph D'Agostino. 'Sexual Killers and Their Victims: Identifying Patterns through Crime Scene Analysis.' *Journal of Interpersonal Violence,* 1/3 (Sept 1986), 288–308

Ressler, Robert, Ann Burgess, Carol Hartman, John Douglas, and Arlene McCormack. 'Murderers Who Rape and Mutilate.' *Journal of Interpersonal Violence,* 1/3 (Sept 1986), 273–87

Riger, Stephanie, and Margaret Gordon. 'The Fear of Rape: A Study in Social Control.' *Journal of Social Issues,* 37/4 (1981), 71–92

Roark, Mary. 'Preventing Violence on College Campuses.' *Journal of Counselling and Development,* 65/7 (Mar 1987), 367–71

Romero, Joseph, and Linda Williams. 'Recidivism among Convicted Sex Offenders: A 10-Year Followup Study.' *Federal Probation,* 49/1 (Mar 1985), 58–64

Romero, Mary. 'A Comparison between Strategies used on Prisoners of War and Battered Women.' *Sex Roles*, 13/9–10 (Nov 1985), 537–47

Roscoe, Bruce, and Nancy Benaske. 'Courtship Violence Experienced by Abused Wives: Similarities in Patterns of Abuse.' *Family Relations Journal of Applied Family and Child Studies*, 34/3 (July 1985), 419–24

Roscoe, Bruce, and Tammy Kelsey. 'Dating Violence among High School Students.' *Psychology: A Quarterly Journal of Human Behavior*, 23/1 (1986), 53–9

Rosenbaum, Alan. 'Group Treatment for Abusive Men: Process and Outcome.' *Psychotherapy*, 23/4 (Winter 1986), 607–12

Rowsey, Jeanette, Orman Hall, and Eileen Coan. 'Rural Knowledge and Attitudes about Sexual Assault: The Impact of a Rape Awareness Campaign.' *Journal of Rural Community Psychology*, 5/2 (Fall 1984), 33–44

Rozee-Koker, Patricia, and Glenda Polk. 'The Social Psychology of Group Rape.' *Sexual Coercion and Assault*, 1/2 (Mar–Apr 1986), 57–65

Rubinstein, Eli. 'Televised Violence: Approaches to Prevention and Control.' *Prevention in Human Services*, 2/1–2 (Fall–Winter 1982), 7–18

– 'Television and Behavior: Research Conclusions of the 1982 NIMH Report and Their Policy Implications.' *American Psychologist*, 38/7 (July 1983), 820–5

Ruch, Libby, Susan Meyers Chandler, and Richard Harter. 'Life Change and Rape Impact.' *Journal of Health and Social Behavior*, 21/3 (Sept 1980), 248–60

Ruch, Libby, and Michael Hennessy. 'Sexual Assault: Victims and Attack Dimensions.' *Victimology*, 7/1–4 (1982), 94–105

Santiago, Jose, Fred McCall-Perez, Michele Gorcey, and Allan Beigel. 'Long-Term Psychological Effects of Rape in 35 Rape Victims.' *American Journal of Psychiatry*, 142/11 (Nov 1985), 1338–40

Saunders, Daniel. 'Helping Husbands Who Batter.' *Social Casework*, 65/6 (June 1984), 347–53

– 'When Battered Women Use Violence: Husband Abuse or Self-Defense?' *Violence and Victims*, 1/1 (Spring 1986), 47–60

Scheppele, Kim, and Pauline Bart. 'Through Women's Eyes: Defining Danger in the Wake of Sexual Assault.' *Journal of Social Issues*, 39/2 (Summer 1983), 63–81

Schipper, Henry. 'Filthy Lucre: A Tour of America's Most Profitable Frontier.' *Mother Jones*, 5/3 (Apr 1980), 30–3, 60–2

Schrink, Jeffrey, Eric Poole, and Robert Regoli. 'Sexual Myths and Ridicule: A Content Analysis of Rape Jokes.' *Psychology: A Quarterly Journal of Human Behavior*, 19/1 (1982), 1–6

Schwartz, Lori, and William Markham. 'Sex Stereotyping in Children's Toy Advertisements.' *Sex Roles*, 12/2 (Jan 1985), 157–70

Scott, Jocelynne. 'Going Backwards: Law Reform and Women Bashing.' *Women's Studies International Forum*, 9/1 (1986), 49–55

Serdahely, William, and Georgia Ziemba. 'Changing Homophobic Attitudes through College Sexuality Education.' *Journal of Homosexuality*, 10/1–2 (Fall 1984), 109–16

Sharma, Anu, and Harold Cheatham. 'A Women's Center Support Group for Sexual Assault Victims.' *Journal of Counselling and Development*, 64/8 (Apr 1986), 525–7

Sherman, Barry, and Joseph Dominick. 'Violence and Sex in Music Videos: TV and Rock 'n' Roll.' *Journal of Communication*, 36/1 (Winter 1986), 79–93

Sherman, Carl. 'The Stuff That Men Are Made Of.' *Men's Health*, 4/3 (Fall 1989), 71–3

Sherman, Lawrence, and Richard Berk. 'The Specific Deterrent Effects of Arrest for Domestic Assault.' *American Sociological Review*, 49/2 (Apr 1984), 261–72

Shields, Nancy, and Christine Hanneke. 'Attribution Processes in Violent Relationships: Perceptions of Violent Husbands and Their Wives.' *Journal of Applied Social Psychology*, 13/6 (Nov–Dec 1983), 515–27

Shorr, Susan, and Leonard Jason. 'A Comparison of Men's and Women's Consciousness Raising Groups.' *Group* 6/4 (Winter 1982), 51–5

Shotland, R. Lance. 'A Preliminary Model of Some Causes of Date Rape.' *Academic Psychology Bulletin*, 7/2 (Summer 1985), 187–200

Shotland, R. Lance, and Lynne Goodstein. 'Just Because She Doesn't Want to Doesn't Mean It's Rape: An Experimentally Based Causal Model of the Perception of Rape in a Dating Situation.' *Social Psychology Quarterly*, 46/3 (Sept 1983), 220–32

Shotland, R. Lance, and Charles Stebbins. 'Bystander Response to Rape: Can a Victim Attract Help?' *Journal of Applied Social Psychology*, 10/6 (1980), 510–27

Sigelman, Carol, Carol Berry, and Katherine Wiles. 'Violence in College Students' Dating Relationships.' *Journal of Applied Social Psychology*, 14/6 (Nov–Dec 1984), 530–48

Silbert, Mimi. 'Prostitution and Sexual Assault: Summary of Results.' *International Journal of Biosocial Research*, 3/2 (1982), 69–71

Skord, Kenneth, and Brockman Schumacher. 'Masculinity as a Handicapping Condition.' *Rehabilitation Literature*, 43/9–10 (Sept–Oct 1982), 284–9

Snider, Laureen. 'Legal Reform and Social Control: The Dangers of Abolishing Rape.' *International Journal of the Sociology of Law*, 13 (1985), 337–56

Staples, Robert. 'Masculinity and Race: The Dual Dilemma of Black Men.' *Journal of Social Issues*, 34/1 (1978), 169–83

Stein, Peter, and Steven Hoffman. 'Sports and Male Role Strain.' *Journal of Social Issues*, 34/1 (1978), 136–50

Stein, Terry. 'An Overview of Men's Groups.' *Social Work with Groups*, 6/3–4 (Fall–Winter 1983), 149–61

Stewart, Barbara, Carol Hughes, Ellen Frank, Barbara Anderson, et al. 'The Aftermath of Rape: Profiles of Immediate and Delayed Treatment Seekers.' *Journal of Nervous and Mental Disease*, 175/2 (Feb 1987), 90–4

Studer, Marlena. 'Wife Beating as a Social Problem: The Process of Definition.' *International Journal of Women's Studies*, 7/5 (Nov– Dec 1984), 412–22

Summers, Gertrude, and Nina Feldman. 'Blaming the Victim versus Blaming the Perpetrator: An Attributional Analysis of Spouse Abuse.' *Journal of Social and Clinical Psychology*, 2/4 (1984), 339–47

Sutherland, Richard. 'Olympic Ideals Seem to Be Fading Further Away.' *Current Therapy*, 2/3 (Apr 1989), 12–13, 15–16, 24

Sutherland, Sandra, and Donald Scherl. 'Patterns of Response among Victims of Rape.' *American Journal of Orthopsychiatry*, 40/3 (Apr 1970), 503–11

Taylor, John. 'Structured Conjoint Therapy for Spouse Abuse Cases.' *Social Casework*, 65/1 (Jan 1984), 11–18

Turner, Sandra, and Flora Colao. 'Alcoholism and Sexual Assault: A Treatment Approach for Women Exploring Both Issues.' *Alcoholism Treatment Quarterly*, 2/1 (Spring 1985), 91–103

Turner, Susan, and Constance Shapiro. 'Battered Women: Mourning the Death of a Relationship.' *Social Work*, 31/5 (Sept-Oct 1986), 372–6

Ullrich, Vivienne. 'Equal But Not Equal: A Feminist Perspective on Family Law.' *Women's Studies International Forum*, 9/1 (1986), 41–8

Ursel, Jane, and Dawn Farough. 'The Legal and Public Response to the New Wife Abuse Directive in Manitoba.' *Canadian Journal of Criminology*, 28/2 (Apr 1986), 171–83

Waaland, Pam, and Stuart Keeley. 'Police Decision Making in Wife Abuse: The Impact of Legal and Extralegal Factors.' *Law and Human Behavior*, 9/4 (Dec 1985), 355–66

Walker, Gillian, Lynda Erikson, and Lorette Woolsey. 'Sexual Harassment: Ethical Research and Clinical Implications in the Academic Setting.' *International Journal of Women's Studies*, 8/4 (Sept–Oct 1985), 424–33

Wasoff, Frances. 'Legal Protection from Wifebeating: The Process of Domestic Assaults by Scottish Prosecutors and Criminal Courts.' *International Journal of the Sociology of Law*, 10/2 (May 1982), 187–204

Watts, Deborah, and Christine Courtois. 'Trends in the Treatment of Men Who Commit Violence against Women.' *Personnel and Guidance Journal*, 60/4 (Dec 1981), 245–9

Weidman, Arthur. 'Family Therapy with Violent Couples.' *Social Casework*, 67/4 (Apr 1986), 211–18

Weir, Angela, and Elizabeth Wilson. 'The British Women's Movement.' *New Left Review*, 148 (Nov–Dec 1984), 74–103

Wetzel, Laura, and Mary Ross. 'Psychological and Social Ramifications of Battering: Observations Leading to a Counselling Methodology for Victims of Domestic Violence.' *Personnel and Guidance Journal*, 61/7 (Mar 1983), 423–8

White, Barbara, and Donald Mosher. 'Experimental Validation of a Model for Predicting the Reporting of Rape.' *Sexual Coercion and Assault*, 1/2 (1986), 43–55

Williams, Tannis, Merle Zabrack, and Lesley Joy. 'The Portrayal of Aggression on North American Television.' *Journal of Applied Social Psychology*, 12/5 (Sep–Oct 1982), 360–80

Wilson, Margo, and Martin Daly. 'Competitiveness, Risk Taking and Violence: The Young Male Syndrome.' *Ethology and Sociobiology*, 6/1 (1985), 59–73

Woodward, Christel, and Orvill Adams. 'Physician Resource Databank: Numbers, Distribution and Activities of Canada's Physicians.' *Canadian Medical Association Journal*, 132 (15 May 1985), 1175–88

Wooley, Marilyn, and Mary Ann Vigilanti. 'Psychological Separation and the Sexual Abuse Victim.' *Psychotherapy*, 21/3 (Fall 1984), 347–52

Worden, Robert, and Alissa Pollitz. 'Police Arrests in Domestic Disturbances: A Further Look.' *Law and Society Review*, 18/1 (1984), 105–19

Wright, Rogers. 'Of Slithy Toves, Rape-Trauma Syndrome, Burn-out, etc.' *Psychotherapy in Private Practice*, 3/1 (Spring 1985), 99-108

Yassen, Janet, and Lois Glass. 'Sexual Assault Survivor Groups: A Feminist Practice Perspective.' *Social Work*, 29/3 (May–June 1984), 252–7

Zacker, J., and M. Bard. 'Further Reading on Assaultiveness and Alcohol Use in Interpersonal Disputes.' *American Journal of Community Psychology*, 5/4 (1977), 373–83

Zillmann, Dolf, and Jennings Bryant. 'Pornography, Sexual Callousness, and the Trivialization of Rape.' *Journal of Communication*, 32/4 (Fall 1982), 10–21

Interviews

Beatch, Romeo. Executive Director, North West Territories Family Counselling Service, Yellowknife. Telephone interview with author, 15 May 1990

Ferguson, Tara. Account Executive, MuchMusic Inc. Telephone interview with author, 23 April 1990

Fisher, Ken. An Ottawa member of Partners in Change and the Ottawa Men's Forum. Telephone interview with author, February 1990

Gallup, Rob. Director of AMEND, Denver. Telephone interview with author, 4 May 1990

Jamieson, James. Lt. Col., Canadian Armed Forces, Ottawa. Telephone interview with author, 23 April 1990

Kaczmarz, Tom, RAVEN, St Louis. Telephone interview with author, 14 August 1990

Kennedy, Theresa. Domestic Abuse Project, Minneapolis. Telephone interview with author, 4 May 1990

Mahood, Robbie. General Practitioner, Klinic Community Health Centre, Winnipeg. In-person interview with author, 5 June 1990

Parrington, Lorraine. Counsellor, Sexual Assault Crisis Programme, Klinic Community Health Centre. In-person interview with author, 12 April 1990

Rice-Lampert, David. Probation Officer, Community and Youth Corrections, Department of Justice, Province of Manitoba. Telephone interviews with author, 23 April and 14 June 1990

Saxby, Carol. Changing Ways, London, Ont. Telephone interview with author, 4 May 1990

Schwartz, Ron. Counsellor at Evolve, Winnipeg. Telephone interview with author, 7 May 1990

Scott, Elaine. Director of the Family Violence Prevention Division, Health and Welfare Canada. Telephone interview with author, November 1989

Thompson, Arlene. Hiatus House, Windsor. Telephone interview with author, 4 May 1990

Films

Not a Love Story: A Film about Pornography. National Film Board of Canada, Studio D, 1981

Dyer, Gwynne. *War: Anybody's Son Will Do*. National Film Board of Canada, 1983

Index

368 Index

Berlin, Fred, 116

biofeedback. *See* social constructionist treatment programs: use of
relaxation techniques

biological conservatives, 193, 201–3.
See also conservative masculinists;
moral conservatives

biological determinism, 201–2; and
men's rights advocates, 206. *See
also* physiological explanations of
male violence

biological nature and militarism, 76

biosocial explanations, 114–19. *See
also* physiological explanations of
male violence

biosocial researchers, 49–50, 114. *See
also* physiological explanations of
male violence

biosocial treatments of male violence, 112–19. *See also* physiological explanations of male violence

birth control: counselling and censorship, 93; men and, 272

bisexuality, 272

Blackmun, Harry A., 196–8

blaming the victim, 32, 36, 40–1;
counteracting, 257; through the
use of family systems approaches,
128–33; by judges, 181; by men's
rights advocates, 206; by moral
conservatives, 194, 202; by offenders, 143–4, 148; by police, 184;
rather than society, 133; and sexual assault myths, 98–9; television
industry avoiding responsibility,
69; perpetuated by traditional
victim treatment, 122–4

Bleier, Ruth, 48

Bly, Robert, 227–8

Bograd, Michele, 128–32

Bowker, Lee, 22–3

Boy Scouts, 55, 78–80, 291n.51

'boys' club, 232

Bradford, John, 116–17, 119

brain structures: animal studies of,
49; and male violence, 49, 112–14.
See also physiological explanations of male violence; physiological treatments of male violence

Brandow, Ron, 262

breadwinner role, 203–4, 223–4

breaking the silence on male violence, 249; necessity of, 251; pro-
feminist men on, 235; role of
women in, 4

Brief Anger Aggression Questionnaire, 151

Briere, John, 100

British Columbia Federation of
Labour, Women's Rights Committee, 27

Brother, 335n.148

BrotherPeace, 238, 243–4

Browning, James, 172, 179

Bryson, Lois, 106

buddy system, 72

bulimia, 41

Bundy, Ted, 17

Burt, Martha, 100

Bush, George, 203; and abortion,
195

Buss Durkee Hostility Inventory,
151

Cadogan, David, 262

Calgary Men's Network, 262

Cameron, Deborah, 17

Canada: Bill C-43, 199–200 (*see also*
Men for Women's Choice); Health
and Welfare, Family Violence

men and sexual harassment, 29;
among offenders, 11. *See also*
dividing lines
Clatterbaugh, Kenneth, 193; on
conservative masculinists, 201–2
client as expert, feminist recognition
of, 123
clients' rights movement, 118
Coalition of Free Men, 205
Cobb, Nancy, 64–5
Cobbe, Frances Power, 120
cognition, role of: biological conservatives ignoring the, 202; in
human behaviour, 48
cognitive filtering and restructuring
of social reality, 160. *See also* self-
talk
cognitive restructuring. *See* self-talk
Cold War, 56
college students. *See* university
students
Colorado, State Committee on
Domestic Violence, 323n.186
combat duty, 73. *See also* military
commercials, children's viewing of,
64–5, 294n.77. *See also* media
communication skills: encouraged
by liberal critics of traditional
masculinity, 224; using the media
to improve, 185; men needing to
learn, 82; need for, 189; non-violent, 235; not encouraged by male
activities, 107; and offenders, 10,
137, 154, 157–8; in prisons, 140; in
schools, 186; needed in sexual
relationships, 221–2. *See also*
social constructionist treatment
programs
communication styles and family
systems approaches, 128–30

communism and masculinity, 56.
See also socialist organizations
community groups, mobilizing, 257
competition in sport, 80, 104–7
concentration camp survivors, 37
confidentiality: with offenders,
144–6, 153; in pro-feminist men's
groups, 265
conflict resolution skills: children
and, 80, 224; and the military, 76;
need for, 189; and offenders, 136,
168; initiating programs for, 254
Conflict Tactics Scale, 151
conformity: and male peer groups,
85–7; in sport, 102–4
Connecticut Correctional Institute,
Sex Offender Program, 175, 181
Connell, Robert, 58
consciousness-raising, among
women, 121
conservatism, social, and MSRI theory, 58
conservative masculinists, 192–203;
differences from pro-feminist
men, 234; manipulating misogynist values among men, 233; and
the pornography debate, 92–3. *See
also* biological conservatives;
moral conservatives
constructive criticism, giving and
receiving, 268–71. *See also* communication skills
continuum of male violence against
women, 4–5
contraception, limitation on availability of, 30, 282n.99
control plans for non-violence, 188;
creation and use of, 137, 147–50,
161–2, 166–7, 224, 315n.71,
315n.72; and men's health, 220

confronting, 255, 257; by culture and ethnicity, 54; and familial traditions, 54; minimized by liberal feminists, 232–3; importance of linking, 247; view of men's rights advocates on, 207; non-hegemonic men's critique of, 231, 234, 246–7, 332n.108; splitting the men's movement, 204; perpetuated by sport, 106–7; pro-feminist men and, 246–8; by race, xv, 38, 53, 204, 211, 231, 291n.44, 332n.108; by religion, xv, 211; by sex, xv; by sexual preference, xv, 53, 211, 231, 291n.44, 332n.108

Divorced Dads Incorporated, 205

Dobash, R., 110

Dobash, R. Emerson, 110

Dodd, Barbara, 198–9

Domestic Abuse Project (DAP), 239

domination in a pro-feminist men's group by individual members, 270–1

Dominick, Joseph, 68

Donnerstein, Edward, 94

double standards, 98

dowry-burning, 18

Dreiblatt, I., 141

drug and/or alcohol use or abuse: conflicts over, 24; explanation of the term, 279n.75; in the military, 73; moral conservative explanation of, 194; and offenders, 119, 142, 150, 152, 154, 158, 166; and peer group pressure, 84; relation to male violence, 9, 52, 128, 181–2; social service workers excusing male violence, 184; and victims of male violence, 40–1, 122

Dufresne, Martin, 262

Dunlop-Addley, Joseph, 262

Dutton, Donald, 52, 178

Dyer, Gwynne, 70, 77

dysfunctional family, 130

Early Sexual Experience Self-Report Questionnaire, 151

eating disorders among victims, 41–2

Eberle, Patricia, 9

Edleson, Jeffrey, 174

education system, using the: for teaching assertiveness and communication skills, 186; for improving awareness about male violence, 186–9, 254–5; for initiating sexuality courses, 255

effective communication. See communication skills

effeminacy, 55, 291n.47

Ehrenreich, Barbara, 88

Ellerby, Lawrence, 165

Elliot, Frank, 49, 112

emotional abuse. See violence, emotional

emotional effects of male violence, xvi, 3, 13, 31; anger, 32; depression, 32–3; disinterest in/or fear of interpersonal, emotional, or sexual contact, 33–4; increased fear and anxiety, 34–5; memory loss, numbness, or disassociative behaviours, 35–6; diminished self-esteem and self-confidence, and increased self-blame and deference, 36–7; suicidal or homicidal thoughts and actions, 37–9; damaged or destroyed trust, 39–41

England, Victorian, 120

Environics Research, 241

hospitals: observations at, 43; victims using emergency wards, 186
Hostility toward Women Scale, 151
housework: conflicts over, 24; men doing, 272, 331n.93
human service workers and how to intervene, 256
humour, use and importance of, 258
hypermasculinity, 55; and the military, 71

impotence, 221
impulse control, offenders and, 119, 134–5
incest survivors and eating disorders, 41. See also victims
industrialization, effects on masculinity, 55
Inside Out, 228
Integral: The Magazine for Changing Men, 335n.148
intellectualizing in a group, 270
intergenerational transmission of violence, 59, 62–3, 292n.64
interpersonal communication skills. *See* communication skills
Interrante, Joe, 204
intrapsychic explanations of male violence: definition, xvi, 46, 51–3; feminist opposition to, 122; limits of, 189; affecting offender sentencing, 181; pro-feminist men's critique of, 239; psychologists using, 119
intrapsychic treatments of male violence, 109, 119–20; feminist critique of, 128; problems with, 132–3
Island Men, 262

Jack the Ripper, 17

jealousy, conflicts over, 24
jobs, conflicts over, 24
Johns Hopkins Hospital, 116
Johnson, A.G., 25
jokes, sexist, 14, 87, 104, 216, 218, 253; and the Queen's University anti-rape campaign, 215; effects of, 218
The Joy of Sex, 222
judging in a pro-feminist men's group, 271
judicial system. *See* criminal justice system
Jung, Carl: New Age men and, 227
juvenile delinquency, moral conservative explanations of, 194

Kaufman, Michael, 262
Kennedy, Robert, 103
Kingston, Ontario, 214, 243
Kingston Men's Forum, 262
Klinic Community Health Centre, 262, 333n.128
Kodak advertisement, 223
Koss, Mary P., 21

language: and family systems interventions, 129–30; as gender-based, 129, 312n.9; pro-feminist men's critique of, 240
lawyers: communication with therapists, 146; doubting victims, 35
learned helplessness, 14, 287n.78. *See also* cycle of violence; Walker, Lenore
learning theories, 37
Leonard, Kenneth, 9
Lépine, Marc, 212–14, 216
lesbians, persecution of, 30
Lever, Bev, 177

xvii, 3, 13, 38, 128–33, 143–4, 229; and offenders, 4, 17, 116–19; in pornography, 92; as the primary treatment concern, 131; psychological and institutional brutality, 30; public demand for an end to, 178, 249; relegated as a women's issue, 190; results in no set response among women, 31, 35; as socially created, 53–4, 107–8; limits on society's role, 108; some potential solutions for, 251–9; terminology, 129–30, 178; women initiating violence, 35; treatment of symptoms rather than the problem, 33; types and frequency of, 730. *See also* academia; battering; children; drug/alcohol use or abuse; emotional effects of male violence; family; intergenerational transmission of violence; male responsibility for male violence; male silence about male violence; media; military; physical effects of male violence; physiological explanations of male violence; intrapsychic explanations of male violence; pornography; social contructionist treatment programs; sport; state response

males, university: and rape myth acceptance, 100; pornography consumption rates among, 300n.155

Manitoba Men's Network, 262

marital rape, 21–4, 38, 40; definitions of, 278n.66; effects of, 34, 43, 287n.79; influenced by the Hale doctrine, 112. *See also* sexual assault

marriage: men's rights advocates' views on, 207; and 1950s hegemonic masculinity, 203–4

Marshall, William, 114–15, 119, 151, 171

Martin, Del, 22

Martin, Eugene, 208

Marxists. *See* non-hegemonic masculinists; socialist organizations

masculine essence: view of New Age men, 226; view of pro-feminist men, 234

masculinist, definition, 192–3, 325n.1

masculinities: corporate profits from traditional varieties of, 251; biological conservative view on, 201–3; as a fluid construct, 57; and the military, 69–77, 88, 297n.108; influenced by MSRI theory, 54–61; and national security, 74–5, 297n.1–05; in the nineteenth century, 55, 291n.52; limited, on television, 64, 293n.71; threatened by speaking out, 218; and unemployment, 56. *See also* sex-role identity theory; socialization, male

masculinity, hegemonic. *See* hegemonic masculinity

McCarthy, Senator Joseph, 56

McDonald's restaurants, 91

media, xvi, 250; and corporate support, 65–7; and date rape, 21; encouraging male violence, 63–9, 87, 240; and images of fathers, 222–3; feminist critique of, 125; focusing on women who kill in self-defence, 38–9, 286n.52; men's rights advocates view of men in,

recidivism, 119–20; levels of violence, 63; and mental illness, 52, 99, 119–20, 150–2; monitoring of, 165–6; and motivation, 116, 141–6, 152, 314n.56; New Age men's view of, 227–9; learning paraphrasing, 157–8; parenting skills, 158–9; peer support in treatment, 167–8, 170; police influence on recidivism, 9–10, 17, 184; and pornography, 154; presenting issues of, 139, 142–3, 314n.56; pro-feminist men providing treatment for, 238–9; recidivism, 9–10, 165, 174, 184; use of relaxation techniques, 137, 150; research needed, 175–6, 257; as a response among men, 192; and responsibility for the violence, 9, 112, 134–7, 143, 150, 152, 230; self-esteem of, 10; self-reports of, 10, 174, 321n.153; and self-talk, 156–7, 159; and stereotaxic surgery, 112–14; suicide lethality of, 142, 146–7, 152, 166; therapists contacting support networks of, 144, 165; therapists excusing offender violence, 122; under-reporting, 9; using multiple forms of violence, 12; and victim empathy, 10, 137, 150–1, 154, 159, 166, 218; views on aggression, 137; violent response to women's independence, 201; violence increasing over time, 166; violent incidents, 148–50; willingness to listen to other men, 245. *See also* battering; children: assessing an offender's view of; drug and/or alcohol use or abuse: and offenders; intrapsychic treatments of male violence against women; physiological treatments of male violence against women; marital rape; myths; sexual offenders; sexual assault; social constructionist treatment programs; violence, emotional; weapons

Olympic Games, 55; purpose of revival, 105–6
Ontario Supreme Court and abortion, 198–9
Ottawa-Carleton Family Services Centre, 179
Ottawa-Hull Men's Forum against Sexism, 262
Owens, Jesse, 106

Paige, Satchel, 106
Palys, Ted, 96
Pangborn, Ken, 210
Papantonio, Andre, 9
paraphrasing, teaching offenders, 157–8
parental consent laws, 197
parenting, 272; and the escalation toward violence, 224; and promotion of hegemonic masculinity, 82, 84; liberal critics of traditional masculinity views on, 222–4; male involvement in, 208–9, 222–4, 255; men's rights advocates' views on, 208–9; teaching offenders, 158–9
Partners in Change, 243
paternalism, 217
paternity leaves, 209; initiating, 255
patriarchy: men's rights advocates' protection of, 205, 210; needing to be addressed, 190; origins of, 53, 290n.42

welfare state, dismantling the, 250
West Germany, and castrated sex
  offenders, 115
Whig-Standard, and the Queen's University anti-rape campaign, 215
white male supremacy, 201
White Ribbon Campaign, 262
wildman, 227–8
Wilson, Edward, 202
Wilson, E.O., 46–7
Windsor, Ontario, 171
women: and abortion, 194–200;
  biological conservative view on,
  201–5; blamed by New Age men,
  228; breaking the silence on male
  violence, 120–6; deference to men,
  36–7; devalued by men, 84–5; fear
  among, 3, 16, 20, 34–5; financial
  dependence on men, 10; questionable improvement in opportunities for, xv; learning their history,
  255; instigating violence, 35; listening to their stories, 4, 13, 121,
  130, 249; and the judicial system,
  125, 183, 310n.75; assessing an
  offender's view of, 150–1; as military wives, 73–4; moral conservative view on, 194, 200–1; and
  murder, 210; objectified by men,
  85, 218; pathologized by traditional victim therapy, 122; their perception of men affected by
  violence, 33; viewed as property,
  99, 217; restricted by historic legal
  and moral codes, xv, 110–12;
  reporting to police, 25; safety of,
  189, 256; as second-class citizens,
  123; and self-defence courses, 236;
  self-esteem upon leaving an abusive relationship, 16; services for,

122–5; in shelters, 287n.80; surgical mutilation of, 30, 282n.96; in
  the Third World, 17–18, 281nn.95
  and 96; war against, 190. *See also*
  abortion; emotional effects of
  male violence; feminism; feminists; military; physical effects of
  male violence; women's movement; victims of male violence
Women in Trades Questionnaire, 27
women's movement: breaking the
  silence on men's violence, xvi,
  109, 120–6; as a catalyst for social
  change, xv, 4, 120–6, 190–1, 251;
  critique of male socialization and
  violence, 99–100, 302n.1–66; global repercussions of, 274n.2; dilemma over work with offenders,
  177; under neo-conservative
  attack, 203; 1970s revival of, 200,
  274n.2; and the revision of offender treatment, 125–6; opposing
  pornography, 92; critique of traditional victim therapy, 122–5;
  valuing 'women's work,' 123;
  victories of, threatened, xv, 251.
  See also feminism; feminists;
  women
Woolsey, Lorette, 29
working mothers, moral conservative objections to, 194
World War I: and masculinity, 58,
  297n.108; and U.S. recruits, 55–6,
  292n.53
World War II and pornography, 88

Yllo, Kersti, 23
Yorkshire Ripper, 17

Zukerman, M., 151